Jack Kerouac King of the Beats

A Portrait

Barry Miles

Henry Holt and Company
New York

Henry Holt and Company, Inc.
Publishers since 1866
115 West 18th Street
New York, New York 10011

Henry Holt® is a registered trademark
of Henry Holt and Company, Inc.

Library of Congress Cataloging-in-Publication Data
Miles, Barry, 1943–
Jack Kerouac, king of the Beats : a portrait / Barry Miles.
p.   cm.
Includes bibliographical references and index.
ISBN 0-8050-6043-X (alk. paper)
1. Kerouac, Jack, 1922–1969.   2. Authors, American—20th century—
Biography.   3. Beat generation—Biography.   I. Title.
PS3521.E735Z778   1998
813'.54—dc21   98-35289
[B]   CIP

Henry Holt books are available for special promotions and
premiums. For details contact: Director, Special Markets.

First American Edition 1998

Printed in the United States of America
All first editions are printed on acid-free paper.∞

1   3   5   7   9   10   8   6   4   2

Contents

K397 Mi

Preface

In the long hot summer of 1959, I was sixteen, living with my parents in the countryside outside a small market town in the Cotswolds. I had just left grammar school and was waiting to begin my first term at art college. My adolescent thoughts were taken up with artists in garrets living the Bohemian life. The trouble was that all the artists I had heard of had lived the Bohemian life at least half a century before and were all long dead. However, I had seen a documentary on television about something called the Beat Generation in San Francisco and it seemed to be a modern-day equivalent. I had been given the address of City Lights Bookshop in San Francisco as a place that sold Beat Generation literature and I wrote asking for a catalogue.

When it arrived it was a small postcard listing a dozen titles. I had only vaguely heard of the Beats, and had never heard of any of the authors on the list, but simply by reading the titles of the books I knew I had hit pay dirt. My literature class at grammar school stopped at Siegfried Sassoon's *Memoirs of a Fox-Hunting Man*. I had discovered the work of Gide, Sartre, Camus, James Joyce and Samuel Beckett in my local library, but nothing had prepared me for books with titles like *Second April*, *Pictures of a Gone World*, and *Gasoline*. After finding out the exchange rate, I decided that I could afford to spend $2.00. I ordered a copy of *On the Road*, because it sounded just like the sort of thing I wanted. The Signet paperback edition was then 50¢. I also ordered a copy of Allen Ginsberg's *Howl*, because it seemed like a brilliant title for a book even though I had never heard of Ginsberg and, at 75¢, it cost more. The rest went on poetry broadsides: Bob Kaufman's *Abomunist Manifesto* and Gregory Corso's *Bomb*. Getting the American currency took some time as it had to be ordered by the post office, but eventually I acquired two dollar bills and mailed them off.

Jack Kerouac

I can still remember the package arriving, hand-addressed, and with the City Lights Books logo on the address label. *On the Road* proved to be the book I had been searching for. The cover showed a drawing of a perfectly ordinary-looking guy in a pair of chinos and a striped Breton T-shirt, with short hair and a kerchief round his neck. He was surrounded, like in a cinema advertisement, by a tableau of small scenes from the book: the shadow of a trumpet player, a couple embracing, a Black girl in a bikini dancing in a smoky nightclub, a beatnik hunched over a bottle on a café table attended by two 'chicks', and, on the horizon, a 1940s American car accelerating up a hill. It was fantastically romantic. The cover line said it all: 'This is the bible of the "Beat Generation" . . . that tells all about today's wild youth and their frenetic search for Experience and Sensation.' The back-cover copy was even better: 'Wild drives across America – buying cars, wrecking cars, stealing cars, dumping cars, picking up girls, making love, all-night drinking bouts, jazz joints, wild parties, hot spots . . . This is the odyssey of the Beat Generation, the frenetic young men and their women restlessly racing from New York to San Francisco, from Mexico to New Orleans in a frantic search – for Kicks and Truth.' I burnt through *On the Road* in one sitting, feeling suddenly trapped in the sleepy little Cotswold town and longing for the endless American highways. This was what I wanted: to be a Beat, to follow in the footsteps of Jack Kerouac.

Together with a friend from school, I set out to hitchhike around Britain, heading first for Cornwall. Our first lift was with a vicar in a three-wheeled bubble car which almost immediately broke down, leaving us at the roadside, still within sight of the parish church. It was hardly Route 66, but, as I later found out, even in Kerouac's day Route 66 had been sidelined by the new superhighways and Kerouac himself was forced to take the bus. My schoolfriend and I hitched along the coast, living off bread and cheese, drinking cheap red wine from the bottle, spending the nights in barns, hitting the road early. I had my copy of *On the Road* in my pocket. It wasn't the same as crossing the American continent, but I saw my first palm trees, growing in Cornwall, and explored the mysterious empty wastes of Romney Marsh. We finished up at the Partisan Coffee House in Soho where a bearded man wearing sunglasses at night-time strummed a guitar and people sat around playing chess and drinking coffee from glass cups. It was pretty good.

If Kerouac did nothing more than inspire thousands of kids to get out on the road to explore the world and themselves, then he would still have his place in history. Certain books have that catalytic quality: George Du Maurier's *Trilby* sent thousands of young men and women to Paris to be artists. It gave the English language a new metaphor for a villain – 'Svengali' – and Trilby, the book's heroine, became so popular that a hat was named after her. Michael Arlen's *The Green Hat* did the same thing, on a smaller scale, for the jazz age in London, encouraging all manner of frivolous aristocrats to forsake the hunt in favour of smoking cigarettes, driving fast cars and drinking highballs in Mayfair. JD Salinger's *The Catcher in the Rye* exemplified teenage angst in small-town America, and the search for real experience in a world of 'phoneys'.

Kerouac went one better: he was the 'King of the Beats'. His was the worship of pure physical energy, of movement, exuberance, of the vitality, joy and spontaneity of youth, tinged with just a touch of sentimentality. In a much-quoted passage from *On the Road* he wrote:

> The only people for me are the mad ones, the ones who are mad to live, mad to talk, mad to be saved, desirous of everything at the same time, the ones who never yawn or say a commonplace thing but burn, burn, burn like fabulous yellow Roman candles exploding like spiders across the stars and in the middle you see the blue centerlight pop and everybody goes 'Awww!'.

What was it that made him into a late-twentieth-century icon? In the sixties his friend Allen Ginsberg was the godfather of the counterculture, preaching the expansion of consciousness, spirituality and anti-war political activism. Another friend, William Burroughs, was the hero of the underground-press revolutionaries, plotting to overthrow the control mechanisms of the state. Their books sold by the thousand while in America, though not in Britain, all but two of Jack's books were out of print, forgotten and neglected. Jack was not a sixties hero. In the nineties, his fans would be puzzled to find that this was the case. In the sixties he was still alive, a living, stumbling contradiction of the sixties ethic.

During the early period of the counterculture, underground youth movement, Jack was perceived by the hippies, if they thought of him at all, as a right-wing, anti-hippie, anti-communist, pro-Vietnam war, alcoholic redneck, though towards the end of the decade these perceptions began to change as hippies left the cities for the land and country communes. Whatever their attitudes towards him as a man, it was nevertheless Kerouac's groundwork that paved the way for so-called youth culture. As William Burroughs wrote: 'Writers are, in a way, very powerful indeed. They write the script for the reality film.'[1]

In the seventies, Kerouac's image began to change, largely through the efforts of Allen Ginsberg, who tirelessly promoted his cause. In 1973 the first ground-breaking biography appeared, by Ann Charters, and his books gradually drifted back into print. With Kerouac himself safely out of the way, it was easier for him to become the spiritual father of the hippies. In 1979 Barry Gifford and Lee Lawrence published *Jack's Book: An Oral Biography of Jack Kerouac*, followed the next year by Dennis McNally's *Desolation Angel*. In 1983, the standard work on Kerouac, Gerald Nicosia's meticulously researched *Memory Babe*, was published by Grove. From then on the trickle of secondary material became a flood.

As I write this, all of his books are available. One of his letters to Neal Cassady is on sale for $3,500 from a New York rare-book dealer, an inscribed first edition of *On the Road* sells for $4,500, and the paperback edition is published by Penguin Twentieth Century Classics with a scholarly introduction and bibliography. Actor Johnny Depp is said to have paid John Sampas, the controller of Kerouac's estate, $50,000 for a collection of Kerouac memorabilia including his raincoat, hat and suitcase. The estate was paid $20,000 by Volvo to quote Jack's words in print and TV advertising: on the television screen a cool middle-aged couple drive through unspoilt mountain scenery while the husband recites from *On the Road* in the passenger seat.

In 1995, Roman Coppola completed the screenplay of *On the Road* which his father, Francis Ford Coppola, was intending to direct. Five thousand actors showed up at the open audition for the part of Kerouac. Ann Charters and Lawrence Ferlinghetti were hired as consultants. In San Francisco, the Hotel Bohème opened in North Beach, inspired by the Beat Generation. In Chicago a restaurant called Kerouac Jack's[2] opened: upmarket Italian-American seafood, brick walls and secondhand furniture. Instead of the usual Muzak, the restrooms featured tapes of Jack reading from his work. In 1991, an episode[3] of NBC-TV's popular American television series *Quantum Leap* had the time-travelling hero, Sam Beckett, appear in Big Sur in the summer of 1958 where he enlisted Jack Kerouac (played by Michael Bryan) to help save a young woman from a biker gang.

Burroughs and Ginsberg were quickly discovered by the more literate end of rock 'n' roll, and appreciation of Kerouac followed just a little later. Jack gets a name-check in two of Van Morrison's songs: 'On Hyndford Street' on the *Hymns to the Silence* album (1991), and in 'Cleaning Windows' on the *Beautiful Vision* album (1982). In 1986, ex-Police guitarist Andy Summers released 'Search for Kerouac', which was followed the next year by 'Hey, Jack Kerouac' by 10,000 Maniacs, and The Go-Betweens' 'The House That Jack Kerouac Built'. Earlier, Aztec Two-Step recorded 'The Persecution and Restoration of Dean Moriarty' (1972), Tom Waits did 'Jack and Neal' (1977), and King Crimson recorded 'Neal and Jack and Me' (1982). There are literally dozens of other rock and punk records relating to Kerouac, one of the best being Willie Alexander's 1977 single 'Kerouac'. In March 1997, Rykodisc released an entire CD of tributes called *Kerouac – Kicks Joy Darkness* with tracks by artists like Lydia Lunch, Michael Stipe, Steven Tyler, Joe Strummer, Juliana Hatfield, John Cale, Johnny Depp and Come, Patti Smith, Warren Zevon, Jeff Buckley and Eric Andersen. They all performed numbers using texts by Kerouac as lyrics. Some simply read them, others performed music with them – only Patti Smith had the temerity to improvise on Kerouac's words. The rock and roll community had finally discovered Jack, albeit some years after the influence of Burroughs and Ginsberg.

Writer and chronicler of popular culture Jon Savage has written:

> It is in the nature of icons that they are never static; that, like standard texts, they are redefined by each successive generation or microgeneration. Much of this is to do with the complex set of circumstances that turn a human being into an icon – a state that holds within itself something of the godlike, or at least the symbolic. This is different from either fame (earned) or celebrity (unearned notoriety): it has to do both with achievement – capturing the national or global imagination through a cultural product – and the way in which individual characteristics and/or life stories tap into the reservoir of archetypes.[4]

Private life has now become public life and virtually anyone seems likely to have their lifestyle, opinions and personal life studied by curiosity seekers in the way once reserved for rock musicians, movie stars and members of royal families. Writers were early candidates for such attention – Lord Byron was one of the first – and the exploits of the Lost Generation, Dylan Thomas and others have filled many gossip columns. Kerouac was an unprepared victim of the publicity machine. His sudden fame in the late fifties filled any bar he was in with well-wishers, groupies and hangers-on, all anxious to boast they bought him a drink or had sex with him, or both. However, with the onset of the sixties and a new set of cultural values, Kerouac sank into obscurity, only to emerge phoenix-like in the nineties.

The hippies of the sixties did not need him, his ideas had already been absorbed and they already had everything that he stood for as an icon: sexual freedom, drugs, the open road. He was seen as a redneck throwback, and his pro-Vietnam-war stance put him beyond the pale as an Eisenhower-era anachronism. However, the young people of the late eighties and nineties came of age in the long, dark ice age of Ronald Reagan and Margaret Thatcher, an era of anti-drug hysteria and the rise of the religious right. This new generation, many of them born in the sixties, had to start all over again rediscovering archetypes and icons that they could use. The late fifties – Kerouac's period of fame – and the early sixties – the birth of The Beatles, The Rolling Stones and Dylan – fused into one. Today's youth sees them all as from the same period: Kerouac and Beatlemania. They are only six years apart and it all happened a long time before this generation was even born.

In fact the Beat Generation was never really tied to a particular time-frame: many of its more recent adherents are still around. William Burroughs died at 83 in 1997 but rarely moved out of Kansas during the last five years of his life. Allen Ginsberg was more accessible, hanging out with the likes of Paul McCartney, Philip Glass, Johnny Depp, Beck and Patti Smith until his death, also in 1997. If Kerouac was still alive he would no doubt be a red-faced, jowly old curmudgeon, but in removing himself from the scene and dying relatively young he has the image advantage over the other Beats.

Due to the fact that he withdrew from the public eye, his image remains frozen in the fifties: the handsome face, the strong cheekbones, the furrowed brow, straight nose and once again glamorous swept-back quiffed hairstyle. In his youth he had the French good-looks of an Alain Delon or Charles Boyer combined with the all-American naivety and air of bemused innocence given to many of the Hollywood screen good-guys like Gregory Peck or Robert Mitchum. Critic David Widgery has remarked upon the resemblance between Kerouac and the young Ronald Reagan in his lumberjack shirt advertising cigarettes. Kerouac has become a cultural icon along with the young Marlon Brando, the young Elvis and James Dean.

Kerouac has done a John Lennon. It is always a good career move to die young. In Lennon's case no one can criticise or even seriously challenge the accepted image of John as the Prince of Peace and leading avant-garde exponent, as the critic Albert Goldman found when his carefully researched biography was dismissed as bad-mouthing the dead. In fact the Kerouac cult has much in common with the John Lennon cult, even though they are a decade apart with Kerouac very much a pre-sixties figure and Lennon the epitome of the sixties. Both were perceived by the public as leader of their group, both died young but already well past their peak of creativity, and both became the subjects of mythomania, a canvas upon which youth acts out its own desires and fantasies with little regard for the facts of their heroes' actual lives.

If Kerouac's writing career is seen in terms of popular culture, it would probably be more accurate to draw a parallel with Elvis than with John Lennon, and have Jack's later books such as *Vanity of Duluoz*, *Satori in Paris* and *Pic* represent his 'Fat Elvis' period. He even became obese and florid like Elvis, but no one saw him in those late days except a few fellow drinkers in suburban towns. His image remained that of the good-looking hipster on the jacket of *On the Road*.

It could be said that Allen Ginsberg was so convinced of the genius of his friends that he almost single-handedly dragged the Beat Generation into existence. It is amazing that all three roommates of the East 115th apartment in 1945 – Jack Kerouac, William Burroughs and Allen Ginsberg – should become well-known writers. It was largely due to Ginsberg's tireless efforts that any of them got published in the first place, and through the long dark years, when no one else believed in their genius, Ginsberg was ever supportive. Kerouac in particular was nurtured in the rich glow of his admiration.

There has been a mistaken tendency to create a special category for Kerouac to protect him from conventional literary criticism. To do so only isolates him from the general reader and removes him from academic scholarship. Some fans hail him as the greatest writer of all time and will brook no criticism of his life or work, but to proclaim Jack and his work inviolate does his long-term reputation no good at all. Ultimately it is posterity that will decide which books are good and which are not, a process that has already begun: *On the Road* is regarded as his greatest work, closely followed by *The Subterraneans*, whereas *The Town and The City* and *Desolation Angels* are often dismissed as minor, and virtually everyone agrees that *Pic* is a disaster.

One of the greatest limitations of his work was that he only wrote about himself, which was only of interest if he had done something of interest. Many fans were disappointed when they met him because they thought *he* was the hero of *On the Road*, that he was Dean Moriarty (Neal Cassady). Not so. He was the guy who followed Neal around and wrote it all down. 'A true writer should be an observer and not go around *being* observed. Observing – that's the duty and oath of a writer,' Jack told Al Aronowitz in the *New York Post*. This of course links Kerouac directly to Christopher Isherwood, and the deservedly famous paragraph from the opening page of *Goodbye to Berlin*: 'I am a camera with its shutter open, quite passive, recording, not thinking. Recording the man shaving at the window opposite and the woman in the kimono washing her hair. Some day, all of this will have to be developed, carefully printed, fixed.' Kerouac, however, was not so keen on the 'develop, print and fix' side of the deal.

Though he longed for critical acceptance, Kerouac resolutely and somewhat petulantly remained in a hermetic little literary corner of his own making, plotting a map of his own consciousness, writing his slightly fictionalised journals, or 'picaresque narratives' as he called them: 'The novel's dead. I broke loose from all that and wrote picaresque narratives. That's what my books are.'[5]

But it is not really that simple. With the exception of *The Town and the City*, which is constructed in traditional novel form, his work is located in an uneasy limbo between fiction and memoir. It satisfies few of the definitions of fiction: he attempts no heroic or adult themes. There is no story. That is to say there is no plot or denouement. As the characters are all real people, there is no novelistic character development and he created no great fictional characters. Because his only concern is himself, his characters have no life when he is not there to observe them. When they leave the room they simply no longer exist. His time-frame is more or less arbitrary, just a book-length chunk of his life, though it is sometimes framed by travel: usually by him leaving home to have an adventure, having it, then returning home to his mother.

As memoirs, his books are also unsatisfactory because the names of his friends and associates have been changed. The location of the action in *The Subterraneans* was moved from the Lower East Side of New York to North Beach, San Francisco, and there are traditional fictional elements in some of the books: *Doctor Sax*, for instance, contains a lot of fantasy material and probably qualifies more as a novel than memoir. Even more difficult to position is *Visions of*

Gerard, a sentimental description of the life of his elder brother
Gerard, who died at the age of nine when Jack was four years old.
The book contains long passages of dialogue and many detailed
descriptions of Jack's feelings which a four-year-old could not
possibly remember. The book is therefore, in a sense, fictional from
beginning to end, though it was based upon stories – highly
exaggerated and coloured by time – told him by his mother. The
book might be best seen as a memoir by his mother, with Jack acting
as her ghostwriter.

Kerouac is important for the quality of his actual prose, which is
often splendid, and also for his great vision of America. He tackled
the impossible: to encompass the country's vast size, in all its detail
and complexity, and set it down in its physical beauty and grandeur.
Its parking lots and saloons, its good ol' boys and bartenders, the
highways, the American Saturday night, the wail of train whistles,
the crunch of car doors, the universality of the sounds of the
American night, the vibrant optimism and energy which is the
signature of America.

The majority of readers find the books about the members of the
Beat Generation the most interesting, and the so-called 'Lowell
Novels' less so. The adventures of Neal Cassady, Gary Snyder, Allen
Ginsberg and William Burroughs are more attention-grabbing than
details of who won which race at a Lowell High School track event
or the scores of sand-lot baseball games in 1937. Though we must
always remember the words of Jacques Barzun, Jack's professor at
Columbia, who famously wrote that whoever would understand
America had better first understand baseball.

Perhaps it does not matter how Jack's writing is classified as long
as one is aware that 'the great rememberer' did not feel obliged to
stick to the facts – or, for that matter, to check them – because he
was writing a story. He disliked fiction, but saw nothing wrong in
making a real story more interesting. It would be a mistake to base
a biography on the books, because they describe only one aspect of
his life, and are fictionalised portraits of just a few of his friends.
They also account for only a small portion of his life, most of which
was spent living with his mother in the suburbs, and, of course, they
never address his shabby treatment of his daughter or his friends.

There are superb portraits of Neal Cassady and Gary Snyder in
Jack's books but he never captures Allen Ginsberg and his proposed
William Burroughs book was never written. The picture of Gregory
Corso in *The Subterraneans* is one-dimensional, as is his description

of Lucien Carr. Ultimately none of this matters because *Jack* was the subject of his books, and his books were a chronicle of his life. To a certain extent he was a victim of what his fellow countryman TS Eliot called 'Fatal American introspectiveness', which he was unable to escape from. He created the 'Duluoz Legend', a multi-volume autobiography, and died firmly believing that he was the greatest writer since Shakespeare.

In using his own life as the subject for his work, Kerouac was, of course, not alone: Henry Miller, for example, used his own adventures as the subject for his books, but he also wrote travel books (his guide to Greece remains one of the best), literary criticism, essays, a biography of DH Lawrence, and was generally a man of letters. Anaïs Nin may be famous for her volumes of journals, but she also wrote many novels, short stories, essays and literary studies. Writers from Marcel Proust to Louis-Ferdinand Celine, Laurie Lee to Thomas Wolfe, used their own experience as the basis for their fiction, but revised and rewrote extensively until the books had a life of their own, independent of their author.

This brings us to another problem with Kerouac: namely that without knowing who the characters are – Ginsberg, Burroughs, Corso, Snyder, Holmes, etc. – some of the books, such as *Desolation Angels* or *Vanity of Duluoz*, lose much of their interest. Only when the central character is strong enough to hold up in fiction do his books work. It did not matter that when *On the Road* was first published the cast of characters was unknown to its readers: the book worked because Cassady was such a powerful character.

These days, it would be hard to approach Kerouac's books without some knowledge of the cast because the story of the Beat Generation has become well known; there have been dozens of books and anthologies devoted to it and I have on my shelves more than thirty books about Kerouac alone. Since a fresh reading is now impossible, one must look for an informed one, and, in this sense, the biographies and scholarly essays have become an essential part of his oeuvre.

In this book, I try to do two things. First, I examine Kerouac as an icon, to find what it was that caused this shy, nervous, troubled young man, who could not even drive a car, to become a cultural icon, the epitome of fifties cool, a dashing romantic figure in conformist America. I also examine the myth that Kerouac himself perpetuated: that the books tell the true honest story of his life. I try to separate the work from the man, even though the work is informed by the life, because I see significant differences between the two. I see Kerouac not as a novelist, not as a diarist nor chronicler – though there are elements of all of these things in his work – but as a storyteller. The tales have their basis in fact, but are filtered through Jack's imagination and are told from his very personal viewpoint.

Kerouac is brilliant at word portraits of ordinary people and their environment. He captured the romance and promise of America, the rootlessness and mobility of Americans roaming across their vast land. He was writing in the golden age of the railroads, when the great steam locomotives roared across the country, the lonesome wail of their whistles as much a part of a small town as its architecture. In fact, steam and smoke play a big part in Kerouac's descriptions, particularly in *The Town and the City*, as signifiers of human activity and action. He caught the details: the hobos' campfire under a bridge; the busted settee on the porch; the exhausted waitress; the luncheonette with the thirties chrome trim stained and dirty, mirrors cracked at the corners, the top of the stools rubbed down to the bare metal by countless fat-assed, dungaree-clad truck drivers, gas station attendants, warehousemen and cops.

Jack experienced life. He was driven by personal demons; he anguished over his relationship with his mother; he was self-destructive and hurt those around him, alienating many friends by his incautious remarks, his rudeness and callous behaviour. But as Burroughs said in his obituary: 'Kerouac was a writer. That is to say he *wrote*. Many people who call themselves writers and have their names on books are not writers and they do not write. The difference being a bull fighter who fights a bull is different from a bullshitter who makes passes with no bull there. The writer has been *there* or he can't write about it.'[6] Jack had been there.

Kerouac was important for three reasons. He chronicled the activities of the Beat Generation, recording the anecdotes and incidents for posterity, describing the participants and their loves and hates and squabbles and endless travels.

More significant in terms of his overall impact on American literature, he was the first to crystallise the experience of crossing the immense continent. *On the Road* is a 'road book': like a 'road movie', it is a very American book filled with wonder at the vastness of the land and wide-eyed with enthusiasm at the endless possibilities and opportunities it offers. More than Wolfe or the other writers before him, Kerouac resolved the American experience and condensed it into fast-moving prose. This is Kerouac as storyteller:

captivating, brisk, energetic, attention-grabbing. It is a remarkable achievement.

Finally there was Kerouac's impact on society, in particular upon so-called youth culture. This impact stemmed from his openness and his rejection of the American consumer culture of the forties, when the USA boasted of having the world's highest standard of living. Though he hated them, and they knew little of his work, the hippies were nonetheless Kerouac's spiritual heirs. He showed that the conspicuous consumerism, the giant cars, split-level homes and suburban conformism of the fifties were not the way to happiness. In the fifties he once again uttered Walt Whitman's message: 'Strong and content I travel the open road'.[7] He proposed an alternative to soulless American conformity, and towards the end of the sixties, when tens of thousands of hippies deserted the cities in favour of hippie communes and the simplicity of country life, they began to rediscover his work and often took *The Dharma Bums* as one of their inspirational texts.

His books acquired a life of their own, separate from the man who had by now become embittered and resentful. And, in the eighties, another new generation took up his work and remade him in the image they wanted: their Kerouac was handsome, wore khakis in GAP advertisements, and once again preached personal freedom in an age of conformism. Jack was back.

JACK KEROUAC
KING OF THE BEATS

1 Lowell

Jack's father was born Joseph Alcide Leon Kirouack on 5 August 1889 in Saint Hubert, a village on a lake in the foothills of the Notre Dame Mountains in the county of Rivière-du-Loup,[1] Quebec. The nearest big town was Rivière-du-Loup itself, about 45 miles to the west, on the southern shore of the great Saint Lawrence River. The Kirouacks were potato farmers, eking out a living in an inhospitable land of bitter winters, black flies and mosquitoes. It was a brutally hard life: five months of cold and snow, then back-breaking work digging potatoes out of the black earth. Kerouac described it, though he never went there: 'The winds bring plague dust from all the way to Baffin and Hudson and where roads end and the Iroquois Arctic begins, the utterly hopeless place to which the French came when they came to the New World ...'[2] One wonders what grim humour caused the settlers to name a nearby village Saint-Louis-du-Ha! Ha! Jack's ancestors were among the earliest generations of French settlers to clear the forests and farm the banks of the Saint Lawrence.

Jack claimed French aristocratic blood, and in the publisher's questionnaire for *Lonesome Traveller*, he wrote, 'My people go back to Breton France, first North American ancestor Baron Alexander Louis Lebris de Kérouac of Cornwall, Brittany, 1750 or so, was granted land along the Rivière du Loup after victory of Wolfe over Montcalm; his descendants married Indians (Mohawk and Caughnawaga) and became potato farmers.' Kerouac is a Breton name: there is a hamlet called Kérouac near Rosporden, halfway between Quimper and Quimperlé in West Finistère, off the Côte de Cournaille, and other hamlets nearby have similar names. Scholars have been unable to substantiate Kerouac's aristocratic claim, but instead traced his family to a bourgeois French merchant, Maurice-Louis-Alexander Le Brice de Kerouack, who married in Saint Ignace,

Quebec in 1732 and died in 1736. His three sons married French-Canadian women, not Indians; Jack got his Indian blood from his mother. His name reveals his ancestry:

Jack was christened 'Jean Louis Kirouac (Keroack), son of Leo Kérouack and Gabrielle L'Evesque.' On his birth certificate he was called Jean-Louis Lebris de Kerouac, Louis being Gabrielle's father's christian name, and Jean the maiden name of her mother Josephine. In this way his maternal family names were perpetuated for another generation. Jack was fascinated by his surname and told many conflicting stories of its origin. Late in his life he visited Paris and Brittany with the ostensible purpose of examining French genealogical records, but by then he was a complete alcoholic, the trip turned into a pathetic comedy of errors and he was unable to achieve his aim.

> My family is 5,000 years old. People bug me, they say what the hell kind of a name is Kerouac anyway? It's easy. Just a real old Irish name – Keltic. 'Ker' means house in Keltic. 'Ouac' means 'on the moor'. But my family travelled far. They started in Ireland, travelled to Wales, then Cornwall, then Brittany, where they learned the old French, then 400 years ago to Canada. One of the Iroquois nations is named Kerouac.[3]

He gave another derivation to Ted Berrigan in an interview for *Paris Review*, telling him that 'ker' meant 'water' and 'ouac' was 'the language of' in Gaelic, the name being a derivation of the Irish 'Kerwick.' Jack never revealed the source of his etymology. The Celtic languages divide into two principal dialects: the northern Goidelic (Irish, Scottish Gaelic and Manx) and the southern Brythonic, which includes Welsh, Breton and Cornish. All the standard references show that as a noun, in Old Celtic and Gaelic, 'ker' or 'kerre', 'car' or 'carr', and the Breton 'karr', usually meant a wagon or chariot (thus the modern 'car'). But 'car' or 'cer' in Cornish, the Welsh 'câr' and the Breton 'kîr', or 'kér' are related to the French 'cher' or 'chéri' – 'dear', 'beloved' – which seems more likely. I could find nothing remotely resembling 'ouac' in any of the Celtic language lexicons, but Norman French has the word 'oac'h', also spelt 'ozac'h' and 'ozec'h', meaning husband or head of the household, which seems a possible origin: Ker-ouac = Beloved husband.

In 1971, *Athanor* magazine published a wonderful drunken poetic history of his family:

In ancient times, in a land which was known as Brittany by the Gauls, but even before the Gauls discovered it, . . . there were in Ireland the Kerouacs . . . One of them was known as Isolde the Fair, and she was kidnapped by the Cornishman and taken to Cornwall where Tristan fell in love with her. But to prove his love he had to kill the Modoch, who was the great monster of Ireland. He killed the Modoch . . . but, in some way or another, the Kernouacks went to Cornwall a thousand years before Christ.

In the southwest country of England inhabited by the Celts, the name of the language is Kernouac. And we had a castle there with moats and I was a young knight and, on early mornings in spring when the robins sing in the mist, I had to strap on my headdress and meet the great monsters of Brittany. And then something happened with the Cornish rebellion and they said, 'Let's get the hell out of here and cross the channel into Brittany France.' They went there and their name was no longer Kernouack, it was Kerouac.

Then one of my fathers, François Louis Alexander Lebris de Kerouac, says, 'I think I'll go to Canada with Montcalm and defeat Wolfe for the valley of the St Lawrence.' But Wolfe defeated the goddam French. All the defeated French officers, and he was a Baron from Brittany, got 100 miles along Rivière de Loup, Wolfe River.

Meanwhile this guy François, the Breton baron, meets a beautiful young Iroquois squaw, says, 'O brother, what a nice little squaw princess.' Goes north with her hunting and trapping. Has six or seven sons. Some of them go hunting and trapping north, some of them go down. Finally, their grandsons settle, filter down into New England. I'm mostly eighty percent French and twenty percent Iroquois. And way back, like I told you, Cornish and Irish.

Kerouac was extremely proud of his Celtic heritage, and he did retain many 'Celtish' characteristics, several of which can be identified in his writing. The Celtish civilisation sprang from the Iron Age, and their use of manufactured tools enabled them to clear forests, develop agriculture and become formidable adversaries in war, as the Greeks and Romans were to find. Unlike the great Mediterranean civilisations, the Celts did not develop the art of writing until the fifth century AD, very late in their history, and even then it was not central to their civilisation. Their past was recorded orally, by word of mouth, which is why we have no written records of them except by Greek and Roman writers. Whereas the Greeks and Romans pooled their individual experiences by writing them down and rendering them communal property, the Celts were unable to accumulate knowledge in great quantity. All their traditions and history were transmitted orally.

This led to the development of advanced oral techniques: the embodiment of history and legend in long epic poems and sagas which could be committed to memory and which were recited before the chief and his followers in the great hall. (It took twenty years for a student to commit the complete canon to memory.) Throughout history, among illiterate peoples the training of memory was always cultivated to a degree unheard of by book readers. The Romans were very impressed by the eloquence of the Gauls and wealthy families always employed them as tutors for their sons. In Jack Kerouac's case, he was dubbed 'memory babe' by his friends for his prodigious feats of memory, which served him well in re-creating events and describing locations sometimes many years after the event.

Because the whole of their moral philosophy was embodied in their poetry and obtainable no other way, the Celts came to regard all knowledge as a spiritual possession and its acquisition was seen as spiritual or 'inspired'. 'Inspiration' was highly valued, as it was with Kerouac. His belief in spontaneous prose – that the only correct way to tell a story is straight off, without interfering with the original inspiration, as if telling it to a crowd of buddies in a bar – showed that traces of the epic oral tradition lived on in Kerouac 1,500 years after his people learnt to write. Like them he held words to be sacred. He told Ted Berrigan:

> Did you ever hear a guy telling a long wild tale to a bunch of men in a bar and all are listening and smiling, did you ever hear that guy stop to revise himself, go back to a previous sentence to improve it, to defray its rhythmic thought impact . . . if he pauses to blow his nose, isn't he planning his next sentence? And when he lets that sentence loose, isn't it once and for all the way he wanted to say it? Doesn't he depart the thought of that sentence and, as Shakespeare says, 'forever holds his tongue' on the subject, since he's passed over it like a part of the river flows over a rock once and for all and never returns and can never flow any other way in time?[4]

And so the same Celtic tradition that informed the work of Yeats, Joyce, Dylan Thomas and Samuel Beckett can be seen to reach

Kerouac through a different historical and geographical route. The result is a common intensity of vision, vivid storytelling and the drawing of material from diverse, surreal and unlikely sources to give richly textured, fast-paced writing.

Shortly after the birth of Jack's father, Leo, in 1889, the Kirouacs moved to Nashua, New Hampshire, in the United States, where the Nashua River meets the Merrimack. There Leo's father, Jean-Baptist, started a lumber business. He did well enough to send Leo to a private school in Rhode Island, though his younger sons went to parochial school and his daughter went to the nuns. After his schooling, Leo Kéroack, as he styled himself, began work for a French language weekly called *L'Impartial*. He learnt how to set type and write news reports. The owner, Louis Biron, bought out a bankrupt French newspaper, *L'Etoile*, in Lowell, Massachusetts, a dozen miles to the south-east of Nashua, further down the Merrimack. Biron sent Leo to work on *L'Etoile* as a general-purpose reporter, translator, writer, advertisement salesman and typesetter. Leo moved in with relatives but, typically, when it was time to look for a wife, Leo returned to his own tightknit community in Nashua. There he met Gabrielle Ange L'Evesque, a 'neat French Canadian' girl, born in St-Pacôme, in Kamouraska county, about 75 miles upriver from Rivière-du-Loup towards Quebec. She was of Norman stock but her grandmother was half-Iroquois, the source of Kerouac's high cheekbones and presumably what he called 'our semi-Iroquois French-Canadian accent'.[5]

Gabrielle's parents had moved to Nashua where her father first became a mill worker then a tavern keeper. Her mother died when she was very young, and she was orphaned at the age of fourteen by the death of her father in 1909. In the years before she met Leo, she spent her life working as an assistant in a shoe shop. All of this history was included unchanged by Kerouac in *The Town and the City*, except that Nashua became Lacoshua. Gabrielle and Leo married on 25 October 1915 and went to live in Lowell, where Leo continued to work for *L'Etoile*.

Lowell was a textile town named after industrialist Francis Cabot Lowell, who utilised the power of the Merrimack River by constructing the Pawtucket Dam and cutting a canal. Eventually there were six miles of canals and a 'mile of mills' producing cloth and shoes and making fortunes for their owners in Boston but doing little for the inhabitants of Lowell except bring them to an early death, their lungs clogged with lint. It was a grimy working-class town of red-brick industrial buildings with tall, billowing smoke stacks, wooden-frame houses and low, wooden apartment buildings. The mills were worked by Greeks, Irish, Poles and French Canadians, each with their own tightknit community, united by language and a common culture. It was 'a town rooted in earth in ancient pulse of life and work and death, that makes its people townspeople and not city people', as Kerouac described it in *The Town and the City*. It was not a large town, about 80,000 people, living on either side of the Merrimack, clustered around the manufacturing centre.

The French Canadians lived in 'Little Canada', Pawtucketville, across the Moody Street bridge from the small downtown area. It was a community unto itself, with its own churches, schools, shops, newspapers and social facilities. The cultural connections were much more with Quebec and Montreal than with nearby Boston, and for many of the older members of the community there was little to indicate that they were not still living in Canada. French Canadians, unlike most other immigrant groups, did not arrive in America through Ellis Island. There was no enforced border between the USA and Canada until the twenties, and the contacts and frequent comings and goings of family members between the large French-Canadian communities, in Vermont, New Hampshire, Massachusetts and Maine, and Quebec proper maintained a genuine sense of community.

Leo and Gabrielle's first child, Francis Gerard, was born in 1916, followed two years later by Caroline, known as Ti Nin (Petite Nin), and finally, on 12 March 1922, came Ti Jean. Jack was born in the ground-floor apartment of 9 Lupine Road, a free-standing, three-storey wooden clapboard house in the French-speaking Centralville quarter. It was on a dirt street of identical houses all with a front porch built right up to the sidewalk and a back porch overlooking a small yard. He did not remember the house. In 1925 the family moved two blocks to 35 Burnaby Street and the following year to 34 Beaulieu Street, a little closer to the river, following the path of aspirational immigrants throughout the country, moving to bigger houses and better neighbourhoods. The Beaulieu Street house was a square, boxlike, two-storey structure with a covered front door reached by four steps to the side as the house was built too close to the street for a proper stoop.

Jack never lived anywhere in Lowell for more than four years. This rootlessness extended from his childhood into his adult life when he moved his mother, with all her furniture and pots and pans, from one city to another: Northport, New York State; Orlando, Florida; Rocky Mount, Carolina; Berkeley, California. It was as Joyce

Johnson wrote: 'as if home could be pitched like a tent'. This is part of Kerouac's appeal to his fellow Americans: he articulates the rootlessness of families moving from town to town, of children who grow up all across the country with no real sense of place, of the upwardly (or downwardly) mobile family, moving house every few years into higher or lower income-bracket neighbourhoods.

Leo did well in Lowell. He left *L'Etoile* to set up his own print shop, Spotlight Print, where, in addition to handbills and other such work, he published his own little newspaper, the *Spotlight*, which featured his own reviews of local theatrical productions. He was a well-known figure in the town though not necessarily well-liked: muscular, short, stocky, overweight, loud, verbose, opinionated, bigoted, leaving a trail of cigar smoke behind him as he stamped from place to place. He was a sporting man who followed the horses and managed a few semi-pro wrestlers and boxers, promoting the occasional fight. He was a classic small-town personality. A big fish in a small pond.

Leo, though no doubt a believer, had little time for the Church or priests even though he shared many of their prejudices. Jack's mother, however, went to church and lit a candle every day, as did most of the women in the neighbourhood. The Catholic Church had an enormous power over the French-speaking community and played an important role in keeping the mill workers servile and acquiescent. The Church sided with the mill owners against the union organisers, telling the parishioners that man was born to work and the more hours they worked, the less hours they would have to sin. Before World War II, American and Canadian urban Catholic communities were so involved with Church life that real-estate ads listed homes and apartments by parish name: 'Holy Redeemer, 2 bed,' or 'Resurrection, cottage'.[6] To the Church hierarchy, the parish was sacred space and Catholics were encouraged to buy property because in that way they were linked physically to a parish. Specially blessed statues of the Virgin Mary were circulated from one household to another, staying a few weeks in each, and members of the congregation had their house blessed by a visiting priest once a year. It was not until the civil-rights movement of the sixties that the Church began to change its philosophy and feel that its concerns were universal rather than parochial. Up until World War II it remained resolutely opposed to Blacks or Jews moving into neighbourhoods under its control.

There were no Blacks to speak of in Lowell, so Jack was not

exposed to racial hatred, but he grew up as an unthinking anti-Semite. In his interview for *Paris Review*, Kerouac boasted to Ted Berrigan that on one occasion in the 1940s, his father and mother were walking arm in arm through the old Jewish neighbourhood of the Lower East Side in New York: 'And here comes a whole bunch of rabbis walking arm in arm ... teedah – teedah – teedah ... and they wouldn't part for this Christian man and his wife. So my father went POOM! and he knocked a rabbi right in the gutter. Then he took my mother and walked on through. Now if you don't like that, Berrigan, that's the history of my family.'

Kerouac's correspondence contains numerous diatribes against the Jews who run the publishing industry, and his friendship with Allen Ginsberg was often marred by anti-Semitic remarks. Jack's father referred to Allen as 'the cockroach' and after Leo Kerouac's death Jack's mother refused to allow Allen into the house – something Jack went along with. Even when Ann Charters visited Jack, late in his life, to work on his bibliography, she overheard Jack and his mother talking in French, wondering if she was Jewish. Eventually Jack asked her what her name was before she married. He was embarrassed when he realised that she had overheard their conversation.

During the 1930s, when anti-Semitism in the United States was on the rise, Charles E Coughlin, a young Roman Catholic priest, was its most prominent spokesman. He is now seen as the father of 'hate radio'.[7] Every Sunday afternoon he broadcast a sermon from the pulpit of a small church in Royal Oak, Michigan which was listened to by Catholics gathered around their radio sets across the nation. He received an average of 80,000 letters a week, more than the President, and in 1933 a national poll voted him the 'most useful citizen of the United States'. His message was simple: Jewish bankers – referred to by the euphemism 'international bankers' – ruled the world and were to blame for the Depression and the rise of communism. Jewish interests were leading America into the war. In 1936 the Vatican tried to curb his activities but his bishop supported him and it was not until 1940 that he was taken off the air. He continued to publish his right-wing journal, *Social Justice*, until 1942 when the Federal Government stepped in and threatened to charge him with sedition. This then was the received 'wisdom' of American Catholics at that time and, though Coughlan probably did not number many French speakers among his listeners, they received more or less the same message from their own pulpits.

Jack was also given a massive dose of Catholic guilt about sex.

American Catholicism is Jansenist, despite the fact that Jansenius was denounced as a heretic, and it preaches an extreme puritanism. Jack was taught that the body was evil, that to even touch his sex organ in the bath was sinful, and to get an erection almost guaranteed going straight to hell. Jack told dreadful stories about the nuns at parochial school who made him ashamed of his body.

Years later, Jack told Allen Ginsberg about an incident which occurred when he was twelve years old. He was standing in the bathtub and his mother was bathing him – she still did this, even at this age – when Jack got an erection. His mother was outraged and the event became the subject of a recurring dream throughout his life. His mother was fiercely anti-sex, as taught by her church. It would have been inconceivable for Jack to bring a partner back to his mother's house, even when he was in his thirties, because sex was forbidden unless the partners were married. Even to mention the subject beneath her roof was taboo. As a child, Jack used to masturbate into handkerchiefs which he would then furtively wash out so that his mother did not find any evidence of his 'sin'. Even so, she had her suspicions, and often demanded to know why his handkerchiefs were damp.

This attitude to sex and the body was something which Jack later had to consciously battle against in order to achieve honesty in his writing. It sounds as if he regarded this honesty as sufficiently sinful to require confession, as his priest, Father Morissette, revealed: 'Lowell certainly was not ready for Kerouac. In the Victorian, puritanical, Jansenistic city – such as it still is in many ways – his books are anathema, though his books are not shocking by today's standards. In his time and upbringing, the very thought of kissing was deemed a sin, and he really believed he was committing a sin by using sexy language. He begged forgiveness, but he felt he had to "sin" sometimes to be strong and arresting.'[8]

Jack's Jansenist Catholic upbringing served to inculcate the usual double standard: good girls and bad girls, madonnas and whores. Jack saw nothing wrong in going with prostitutes, and in fact lost his virginity to one. Before alcoholism dampened his spirits, he had an adventurous sex life among the Bohemian women of the Beat Generation, but when he married, he became a Victorian patriarch, treating his second and third wives with a callous brutality which would these days probably have landed him in court. These were the attitudes of his childhood peers, ingrained, unthinking, unreconstructed. It was an attitude best summed up by a few lines in *Maggie Cassidy*, where he has his friend George Apostolos (called Gus

Rigopoulos in the book) advise him how to treat Maggie: 'Screw her then leave her take it from an old seadog – women are no good . . . Kick 'em in the pants, put 'em in their place.' It was an attitude that would uncomfortably resemble Jack's own in later life. The young Ti Jean absorbed the old peasant values: the hearth, food on the table, the Church, kith, kin and kinder. He later saw himself as a *felaheen*, a peasant, an outsider to industrial society, upholding the old values.

Lowell was a town of small, localised ethnic neighbourhoods, of wooden clapboard houses which creaked as they expanded in the sweltering summers, and settled under the snow in the harsh winters – though not so harsh as those of the Saint Lawrence Seaway. Jack huddled up to the potbellied kitchen stove in winter, and lay belly down, his head against the cool linoleum, reading the Sunday comics in the heat of summer. Seasonal change in New England is very dramatic and the passage of time is fixed in the memory by long, hot, lazy summers and the slush and snow of winter.

Viewed from the end of the century, it requires a considerable effort to imagine how life must have been in pre-war small-town America, but Kerouac does a superb job in capturing the atmosphere in *The Town and the City* and *Doctor Sax*. Many of the immigrant communities had recently arrived: houses and apartments were filled with grandparents who spoke only Greek, Polish, French or whatever. There was a sense of rootlessness, of not being a part of mainstream American culture and yet being cut off, forgotten, by their own. This was doubly so for the French Canadians, who, despite the familial connections to Quebec, in most cases had to look back centuries to find a connection with France herself.

French culture was preserved in the language, the Church and family life. Jack's family spoke a local dialect of French called *joual* which would have drawn a near blank in Paris. Jack always called his mother Memere, and was himself known as Ti Jean. Traces of Breton cuisine also seem to have survived down the centuries in the Kerouac clan. In *The Town and the City* Kerouac provides enormous Proustian catalogues of food, most of which are common to all Americans, but in one scene the mother offers her sons three Breton staples: pancakes, sardines and beans. Galettes or crêpes are Brittany's most famous dish and originated there (crêpes are also eaten by Jack's family in *Doctor Sax*).The mother also says she has some Maine sardines, sardines being Brittany's most important contribution to the picnic tables of the world. They are a major industry and even have a museum devoted to them at Concarneau. Finally, she has recently baked some beans, which, if they were broad beans – fèves – would definitely have been a Breton dish.⁹ Similarly, Jack's family eat beans on several occasions in *Doctor Sax*: 'lard in my beans, brown, just a little hot – and with all that good hot ham that falls apart when you put your fork in it.' Brittany has several sorts of pork lard, and its use is a tradition which the Kerouac family seem to have perpetuated in their migrations.

Pork is the predominant meat in Brittany and baked combinations of pork and vegetables are the staple diet. Pork chops frequently appear in Kerouac's books, as well as a porkball stew, described by Jack's sister, Nin, in *Doctor Sax*: 'the balls of soft meat, the potatoes, the carrots, the good fat juice . . .' Kerouac writes extensively about food, not with the exquisite gourmand eye of Proust, but with the lip-smacking enthusiasm of a hungry truck driver facing a huge American steak. In a 1957 interview, he said, 'Don't assert yourself and nothing happens to you. The only thing that matters is food and drink. And I write to celebrate that.'¹⁰ As one final footnote, in *The Town and the City* the Martin family sometimes drink wine, as Jack's own family presumably did. Jack's favourite tipple was not beer but wine, albeit the sweet wine of hoboes, but nonetheless the national drink of France.

When Jack was in his infancy, life in Burnaby Street, and then in Beaulieu Street, was overshadowed by the protracted illness of his elder brother Gerard. For two long years the little boy suffered painfully from rheumatic fever, spending much of the time at home in bed. He died in 1926 aged nine, when Jack was only four. Though in adulthood Jack only had one dim memory of his brother – that of Gerard slapping him across the face – Gerard was to become a dominant figure in his life. Gerard was a frail sickly child who was only rarely able to attend school. By all accounts, he was an exceptional boy: kind, gentle, loving, and deeply religious. He took it upon himself to give his younger brother a religious education and would take Jack to the grotto on Pawtucket Street outside the Franco-American orphanage, where the twelve stations of the Cross were displayed in a series of illuminated glass cases like giant lanterns, each one containing a painted tableau. There he explained the meaning of each one to the toddler who would have been much too little to understand. In *Visions of Gerard*, Jack retells the story of Gerard's sad life, based on the exaggerated accounts recounted to him over the years by his mother, who idealised and sanctified her favourite son.

Perhaps because his own small frame hurt so much, Gerard was sensitive about cruelty to animals. Kerouac describes an instance of him saving a mouse from a trap, only for it to be eaten by the family cat who was then sternly rebuked. Gerard fed the birds, kept a rabbit, and taught little Jack to love animals. Together they would lie on the floor and watch kittens sip milk from their saucer. His mother's religiosity combined with the teaching of the nuns at school had made Gerard a very devout child and he coped with his illness by submerging himself in the teachings of the Church, praying and shedding tears over Christ's suffering on the cross, desperately yearning for heaven to escape his painful body. Jack spent as much time as possible playing at his brother's bedside, and became jealous when Gerard's friends came to visit. To Jack, Gerard was his special friend, his wise, saintly older brother. It must have been a harrowing experience for the entire family to see a child dying in agony, but particularly so for four-year-old Jack, who learnt about suffering and death before he could even read.

In *Visions of Gerard*, Kerouac writes that, on the last day Gerard ever attended school, he nodded off to sleep at his desk. He awoke and told the nuns that he had seen a vision of the Virgin Mary who came to take him away to heaven in a little wagon pulled by two snow-white lambs. On his death bed, these same nuns came to write down his last saintly words in their notebooks. Whether this was true or not, Gerard was constantly held up by his mother as a model of perfection, a child saint, an impossible role model of goodness for Jack to follow. Jack records his jealousy that Gerard always got his breakfast before him, and his anger that Gerard was the one everybody fussed over. 'There's no doubt in my heart that my mother loves Gerard more than she loves me.'[11] It was difficult for a four-year-old to understand that the older boy got special treatment because he was ill.

On hearing of Gerard's death, Jack ran joyfully to inform his father, glad that Gerard would no longer suffer, thinking his father would share his feelings. He had probably overheard grown-ups say that death would put an end to his suffering, would be the most merciful course of events. He was severely reprimanded, but perhaps, unconsciously, he was pleased that he was now the centre of attention, that he would now be his mother's favourite son. A Freudian viewpoint suggests he would have harboured unconscious feelings of hatred towards Gerard, and would probably even have wished him dead. This is a common element in the relationship between siblings, even when they are very fond of each other. However, the fulfilment of this unconscious wish gave the four-year-old a terrible unresolved guilt for the rest of his life.

With Gerard's death Jack was suddenly the centre of Gabrielle's life. She worried over his health and fed him special foods. She bathed and mollycoddled him. On an unconscious level he probably blamed himself for Gerard's death, but now revelled in the attention that it brought him. He had vied, usually unsuccessfully, with his brother for his mother's attention; now he had it all. Gerard's death affected Jack profoundly: he was beset with worries, he saw swarms of white dots before his eyes, he saw religious statues move their eyes, he was scared of shadows and would not sleep alone. For years after Gerard's death, Jack slept tucked up safely between his mother and his sister Nin. For the first few sorrow-filled months after Gerard died, Jack would sit motionless in the parlour, in a daze, doing nothing. He grew increasingly pale and thin. But then, as the horrendous events passed into memory, he began to play again, though now he played alone and with more introspection – his older sister Nin had her own girlfriends. He played the old family Victrola and acted out movie scenarios to the music, some of which he developed into long serial sagas, to be 'continued next week'. In one of them the plot led to the hero being left tied up with rope, so Jack tied himself up and rolled around on the grass where the local children, coming home from school, saw him and laughed and thought he was crazy.

In 1927, Leo's finances took a turn for the worse, probably caused more by his gambling debts than by the Depression. Shortly after Gerard's death he moved his family to an apartment at 320 Hildreth Street, in Centralville. His intention may also have been to get his family away from the many painful reminders of little Gerard and his suffering. Jack was now old enough to go to school, which enabled Gabrielle to go to work. She returned to her profession as a skiver, cutting the leather at a shoe factory.

Still confused and unsettled by the tragedy of his brother's death, five-year-old Jack's small, circumscribed world now expanded. He was sent to the Saint Louis de France Parochial School, in Centralville, to be taught by the same nuns who had regarded brother Gerard as a saint-who-had-walked-among-them. Jack was a poor substitute and they soon let him know it with regular beatings. At Saint Louis de France Jack was taught to pray to Sainte Thérèse of Lisieux, known as Sainte Thérèse of the Infant Jesus, a child saint, the consumptive daughter of a Brittany watchmaker. Her diary, *The Story of a Soul*, was a turn-of-the-century bestseller. She had become a nun at fifteen and kept a diary while dying of tuberculosis. In her diary she told how she would 'spend her heaven doing good upon earth' and promised a 'shower of roses' for those who prayed for her after her death. The nuns even showed the children a film made about a statue of Sainte Thérèse that supposedly moved its head. The cheap portraits of her sold by the Catholic Church show her surrounded by lambs and roses, the origin of all the lambs and roses in Kerouac's prose (and, by extension, all the lamby love in Allen Ginsberg's letters). Sainte Thérèse's family name was Martin, the name Kerouac used for the central family of *The Town and the City*. Even late in his life, whenever he was feeling particularly down, Jack would offer up a prayer to little Sainte Thérèse and claim to get relief.

At parochial school, morning lessons were in English, a language Jack had not previously spoken. They switched to French after luncheon, when they pledged allegiance to *la race Canadienne Française*. Morning prayers were in English but the biblical stories, catechism and history of the Church were all taught in French, preserving the division between the French Catholic community and mainstream American culture, and consolidating the hold that the Church had over its flock. One of Jack's earliest memories was learning to say 'door' instead of 'porte'.

Jack had trouble with the English language and still spoke it poorly at the age of eleven. His command was described as 'halting' even when he was eighteen. All his life, Jack had the greatest respect for words, perhaps partly because English was his second language. As a teenager he had to listen very attentively in order to understand it, and in doing so he heard the deep rhythms and scansion and learnt to love it.

This love of Shakespeare's tongue was something that he later shared with Lucien Carr, his friend from Columbia days. Carr says they were both: 'overawed by the beauty, the versatility and strength and the majesty of the English language. When he wasn't writing silly shit – as he got to doing – when he was seriously dealing with the language, Jack was a true genius. He probably knew far more about the language than I did, and he was capable of deciphering the most arcane poetry. He had a real feel for it.'[12] To Jack, words were sacred in a way they might not have been to a natural English speaker. Allen Ginsberg said that he never really understood Shakespeare until Jack read it aloud to him.

Leo's finances continued to deteriorate, not because his printing plant was not making money, but because he was gambling most of it away on the horses. In 1929 the family was forced to move further down the street to 240 Hildreth, moving again the next year to 66

West Street, in Centralville. This was a two-storey, freestanding, A-frame clapboard house with a front porch running its whole width. Jack lived there from the age of seven until he was ten. Considering the huge number of moves and houses and apartment buildings he lived in, it is remarkable that he retained such a sense of place in his writing about Lowell. The houses, however, were very similar, all wooden, cheaply built, on small plots of land or in low, wooden tenement blocks, and they were mostly within walking distance of each other. Because of the frequent moves, he extended his affection for the place out from the hearth to include the whole town.

Jack was transferred to Saint Joseph's Parochial School where he became one of their best students. Despite the emphasis on religion, Jack was always satisfied with his early education and in 1960 wrote: 'Parochial schools gave me a good early education that made it possible for me to begin writing stories and even one novel at the age of eleven.'[13] These he wrote out in nickel notebooks, a habit he kept throughout his life, never going anywhere without a small notebook tucked in the pocket of his checked work shirt.

Jack was just the right age to catch the end of vaudeville. His father printed the programmes for the Keith Theatre, which was on the Keith-Albee vaudeville circuit. He was able to see both WC Fields and the Marx Brothers live. Jack was seven when talking pictures took over from the old silent movies and made the Marx Brothers and WC Fields into international stars. Jack and Nin were given free entry instead of having to pay the eleven cents children's admission because of Leo's connection with the theatre. They spent much of their spare time absorbing the early offerings of Hollywood.

Jack's literary career began with comic books when, at the age of eight, he began to draw his own comic strips. The first crudely drawn effort was called *Kuku and Koko at the Earth's Core*. These soon became highly developed sagas, including one called *The Eighth Sea*. Next, he wrote his own magazines, in imitation of *Liberty* magazine, and kept his own extensive horseracing newspapers going by documenting the results of the races conducted in his bedroom using ball bearings and marbles. In 1959 he told Walter Gutman that he first started writing when he was three years old, but that his sister threw away all his childhood writings one day when she cleaned out the attic. This sounds apocryphal as it is unlikely that he could read or write at that tender age, and if he could he would certainly have told us.

The family moved once more, to 16 Phebe Avenue, another

two-storey wooden house with a covered porch, this time down near the Moody Street Bridge in Pawtucketville where they were to settle from 1933 until 1935. From this time until his college days, one of the biggest influences on his imagination was *The Shadow*, the most popular of all the pulp magazines. The pulps were literally made from wood-pulp paper, the cheapest available. They were printed in vast quantities and only cost a dime. They were large format, with usually 128 pages between lurid colour covers. They consisted of a novel of anything up to 60,000 words, supported by a number of shorter stories. There were usually about 250 titles on the news-stand at any given time, most of them quarterlies, but among the hundreds of characters and thousands of stories there was one character who stood out from the rest, whose thrilling exploits captured the public's imagination: Lamont Cranston, known to the underworld as The Shadow. With his slouch hat concealing his features, his swirling black cloak and his secret identity, he was a forerunner of Batman and the superheroes. Armed with twin 45s, and commanding a complex web of secret agents, he battled an ever-growing array of supervillains: The Creeper, Mox, The Blur, The Green Terror, The Condor, The Hand, The Python and The Gray Fist.

He was cloaked entirely in black, that being except for his head, on which there was a dark slouch hat. The headpiece was quite effective as the cloak, for both hid his face, but neither concealed his hands.

Encased in thin black gloves, those fists were thrusting toward the open doorway and from each projected a huge automatic, guns that the strange invader had whipped suddenly from hidden holsters.

Unseen lips produced a peal of sudden mirth – a strange, shuddering mockery, like a whisper that had come to life. The tone, sinister in its threat, was a challenge to foemen . . . The rival blondes were getting their first impression of the formidable warrior who was known as THE SHADOW![14]

His battle against crime spawned dozens of imitators. Walter Brown Gibson, author of *The Shadow*, was born in 1897. In the twenties he was a reporter on the *Philadelphia Ledger*, where he learnt to tell a story. He taught himself sleight of hand and card tricks, and wrote books about conjuring and several about Houdini, the great escape artist. When he was 33, the publishers Street and Smith offered him the job of writing for their new quarterly, *The*

Shadow magazine. The Shadow had begun as a mysterious voice, advertising the new issues of *Detective Story* magazine on Street and Smith's Thursday-evening radio mystery show, and introduced that evening's drama with a knowing peal of laughter. The voice caught on with the public and in 1931 Street and Smith started *The Shadow* magazine to protect their copyright. Gibson wrote 75,000 words for the first issue, which sold out virtually overnight. The same happened with the second issue, and Street and Smith made it a monthly. Gibson soon found himself delivering two 60,000-word novels each month. In his first year he wrote 28 full-length Shadow stories, a staggering 1,680,000 words at $750 a story.

It would be interesting to know if Kerouac knew anything about Gibson since he used the same method of spontaneous prose, though in Gibson's case he was simply working to a very tight deadline. Gibson had three typewriters set up and composed in one single draft, moving on to the second typewriter when the first began to 'get tired' and then to the third. His fingers would swell and bleed.

> To meet *The Shadow* schedule I had to hit 5,000 words or more per day. I geared for that pace and found that instead of being worn out by 5,000 words I was just reaching my peak. I made 10,000 words my goal and found I could reach it. Some stories I wrote in four days each, starting early Monday morning, finishing late Thursday night ... By living, thinking, even dreaming the story in one continued process, ideas came faster and faster.[15]

Altogether he wrote 282 Shadow novels, averaging one 60,000-word novel every other week from 1931 until July 1946.

The famous WOR radio show featuring The Shadow used the magazine as its source of characters, but Gibson himself was not involved. Over a swelling organ playing Omphale's *Spinning Wheel* the mysterious voice intoned, 'The weed of crime bears bitter fruit! Who knows what evil lurks in the hearts of men? THE SHADOW KNOWS!' A line that Kerouac loved to quote. The show was made even more compelling by the fact that, from 1937 to 1939, The Shadow was played by Orson Welles, whose distinctive modulated tones fixed the character for ever in the listener's memory.

Jack probably began to read *The Shadow* when he was about eleven, shortly after the magazine was launched. The Shadow appears in a number of his books, and many of his characteristics are appropriated by him, in the best postmodernist tradition, for the main character in *Doctor Sax*, the volume of the Duluoz Legend that covers this period of his childhood: 'Doctor Sax was like The Shadow when I was young, I saw him leap over the last bush on the sandbank one night, cape-a-flying . . .'

Drawings by Kerouac of Doctor Sax – a sinister dark profile half-hidden by hat and cloak – are copies of the Edd Cartier black and white drawings used to illustrate *The Shadow*. In *Doctor Sax*, Jack described how, as a child, he would haunt the backyards of Phebe Avenue and Sarah Avenue after sunset, disguised as The Black Thief in an old slouch hat, and his sister's rubber beach cape, 'red and black like Mephistopheles', stealing his friends' toys and leaving them frightening notes.

Some of his descriptions have the same flavour as Gibson's, such as this from *Doctor Sax* which is similar to Gibson's original above: 'Doctor Sax swept into the salon, his cape flowing and looping, his slouch hat half concealing a secret, malevolent leer . . .'

Jack appears to have been the all-American boy: he ate prodigious numbers of hamburgers, drank ice-cream sundaes, played baseball on a sand lot with local kids, and was passionate about sports. However, it is at Phebe Avenue that we first begin to see signs of the obsession with his mother, and of hers with him, which was to dominate his adult life. In *Doctor Sax* he writes that one night, aged twelve, he refused to sleep alone and spent the whole night sleeping with his mother and sister. His sister found the bed too cramped for three and transferred herself to Jack's bed in the middle of the night. He reports how he lay huddled against his mother's great warm back with his eyes open, watching the shadows from the trees outside on the wall and at the screen, and feeling that nothing could harm him. Feeling that the night could take him only if it took his mother with him, and she wasn't afraid of shadows on the window shade.

Luckily after that, and by unconscious arrangement, in a flu epidemic my mother and I were semiquarantined in bed for a week where (mostly it rained) I lay reading 'The Shadow Magazine,' or feebly listening to the radio downstairs in my bathrobe, or blissfully sleeping with one leg thrown over my mother in the night time – so secure did I become that death vanished into fantasies of life. The last few days were blissful contemplations of the Heaven in the ceiling. When we were well again, and got up, and joined the world again, I had conquered death and stored up new life.

A particular incident enforced another connection between sex and death in his mind when his dog, called Beauty in *Doctor Sax*, was run over by a car:

I heard the news of its death at precisely that moment in my life when I was lying in bed finding out that my tool had sensations in the tip – they yelled it up to me thru the transom, 'Ton chien est mort!' (Your dog is dead!) and they brought it home dying ... Beauty dies the night I discover sex, they wonder why I'm mad.

In 1935, as Leo's fortunes declined still further, the Kerouacs moved round the corner to 35 Sarah Avenue. It was a short street of only six houses, very similar to the one they had just left but at a lower rent. These nondescript wooden houses that he occupied during his adolescence are written about with a particular poignancy in his Lowell books. The memories are universal: of his mother's sheets stiff with frost on the line, or of digging paths through the drifting crystalline snow, cutting a deep trench to make a high ice wall on either side; or standing side by side with his mother, peering through the rain-washed front windows as a heavy storm turned the dirt street to a sea of mud.

This same year, in order to bring in extra money, Leo began managing the bowling lanes at the Pawtucketville Social Club on Moody Street, where his loudmouth style enabled him to keep order and become a popular figure among the regulars. Then, in 1936, came the great flood. The Merrimack burst its banks after heavy rain falling on frozen ground was unable to soak away. A great head of water roared downstream carrying a tremendous debris of roofs, sheds, fences. In Centralville the flood water reached thirteen feet above street level and thousands of telephone poles from a creosoting factory upstream battered and smashed their way through the flooded streets, causing enormous damage. Jack was fourteen years old at the time and his long description of the river in flood in *Doctor Sax*, clearly based on personal experience, is masterful. The Kerouacs' house on Sarah Avenue was safe enough, but Leo's printing plant on Bridge Street was damaged. Though it was not fully inundated, he was not insured, and his finances were so precarious that it took only this small setback to put him out of business. At the Social Club he took to drinking heavily. He was a bad drunk and became maudlin and weepy and would often have to be carried home by his friends.

Through his schoolfriend Scotty Beaulieu (Scotty Boldieu in *Doctor Sax*), fourteen-year-old Jack made new friends: Roland Salvas, GJ Apostolos, and Vinny Bergerac. They would meet in Vinny's parents' front parlour and play cards or wrestle and lark about. Jack soon became the leader of this little group; he would sing the loudest, shout the most, and would sometimes bring along scripts and get them to act out short plays for any members of Vinny's family who happened to walk into the room. The core of the group was Jack, GJ and Scotty; Scotty described them as The Three Musketeers. Jack's mother disapproved, thinking that her Jackie should be friends with a better class of boy. But, no matter how boisterous he became in private with his chums, out in public he became once more a shy and introspective child. These two sides of his personality were never integrated. Throughout his life he would veer hazardously from one to the other.

The next year, Jack's sister Caroline married Charlie Morissette, a man much older than she. Her mother tried to prevent her, but just as soon as she turned eighteen, on 30 May 1937, they were wed, leaving Jack the only child in the nest. Jack himself was growing up, developing muscles. He began to excel on the track at school and it looked as if he was all set to become an athlete, one of America's thick-necked heroes, glorified by parents and the media, worshipped by cheerleaders and younger boys.

He began to take an active interest in girls and, on New Year's Eve, he danced with the girl who was to become the subject of his book *Maggie Cassidy*. Her name was Mary Carney, and she lived down by the railroad tracks. Mary was a tall, slender girl, known to her friends as 'Stretch'. She was a resolutely small-town girl with no interest in travel or in any of the attractions of the big city. Her only desire in life was to settle down in Lowell and have a family. They began to see a lot of each other and she began to talk of getting engaged. She let him kiss her – for hours at a time until their mouths were numb – but nothing else was permitted. Jack's overheated imagination was easily able to contemplate how it would be, living with Mary, surrounded by their large Catholic family, but even then he realised that if he married and moved away from home he would have to give up his mother's cooking. He shied away from marriage.

He remembered it all in later life: Saturday night in America, hanging out in Page's drugstore after class with Mary, two-timing her with another girl, all the memories of adolescence. Jack's friend Phil Chaput dated Mary after Jack. Chaput said, 'she used to say he was shy. That's why I think he made up a lot of what went on between him and Mary in that book.' It is possible that he exaggerated and intensified his teenage feelings in *Maggie Cassidy* to the same extent that he rhapsodised over Lowell in the book, seeing beyond the grimy mills and canals to create a mythic town where factory chimneys pierced the sky. Jack's Lowell had ancient trees growing on the rocky north side, the earth beneath them scattered with lost Indian arrowheads. The pebble banks of the Merrimack were full of hidden beads dropped by barefoot Indians. This is the Lowell of *Doctor Sax*, his great paean to childhood and adolescence and the Lowell of lonely nights, longing for Mary, listening to the distant whistles of the great steam locomotives and dreaming of what would happen in his life.

Jack knew early on that he wanted to be a writer and even went to consult a priest about it. Father Armand 'Spike' Morissette was 'on duty' that night at the rectory of Saint Jean Baptiste when the teenage Jack presented himself. Morissette has published his reconstruction of their conversation:

Jack: 'Everybody is laughing at me.'
Father Morissette: 'Why?'
'Because I want to be a writer.'
'I'm not laughing.'
'You're not?'
'No, I think it's wonderful.'
'Well, I'll be a writer. I'll write a lot of books.'
'More power to you. It's possible. Writers are people like us.
But let me warn you, you're in for a lot of disappointments.'
'I don't mind.'
'Then congratulations. I'll be helping you, if I can. Writers can
be very important. They can influence countless people.'

Father Morissette told Jack that he would have to go to New York City if he really wanted to be a writer. Knowing that Jack was poor, he suggested that he apply for a scholarship of some kind to get to college there. In this way, events were set in motion which resulted in the boy from the small New England town being given a football scholarship to Horace Mann School in New York, going from there to Columbia University, and achieving his childhood ambition, though not without years of frustration and disappointment.

2 Columbia University

Jack arrived at Horace Mann in the autumn of 1939. He and his mother walked in the grounds, inspecting the athletics field and the flower gardens and imagining his future success in New York. Memere loved it: she wanted to live in New York, be near the city, go to shows. She imagined Jack graduating, going to Columbia and becoming a successful insurance-company executive. The Horace Mann School for Boys, one of two experimental high schools operated by Columbia University's Teachers' College as a college for the training of teachers, was at Riverside Avenue and 252nd Street in the rural Riverdale section of the Bronx. It was a solid, ivy-covered, grey granite structure, built on a bluff, surrounded by rock formations and ravines leading down to the river, with a tremendous view east out over the vast green expanse of Van Cortland Park, more than a thousand acres of parkland, golf courses and lakeside, originally the hunting ground of the Mohican Indians.

Horace Mann was a prep school for Columbia College, expensive, exclusive and described by Jack as 96% Jewish. Jack, who grew up with the children of Polish and Greek immigrants, now had to deal with another group. Had it been the Lower East Side of Manhattan, he would probably have felt more at home, but these were the children of wealthy families and at first he felt out of his depth. Many of the students would arrive each morning in chauffeur-driven limousines, bringing delicious packed lunches with them, prepared by the family cook. Seventeen-year-old Jack, one of the few scholarship boys, had to ride the rattling subway all the way from his step-grandmother's house in Brooklyn, up through Manhattan to the Bronx to 242nd Street and Broadway, a journey of about twenty miles. At first he did not mind because he was seeing all the strange new characters of New York, but the excitement soon wore off and the long journey began to pall. The trip took over two hours, which meant that the only time he had to study was on the train.

Jack was at Horace Mann as a ringer, one of ten or twelve good football players recruited to the school each year in order to give the team some credibility. They were given free tuition but not expected to attain the same academic standards as the regular fee-paying students. Jack soon justified his selection. Horace Mann won their second game 27-0 after Jack knocked a potential touchdown runner from Saint John's Prep School unconscious with a head-first tackle. The incident left a bad taste in Jack's mouth and he felt guilty for hurting the Saint John's player for no good reason. But it was the last game of the season that made 'the name of Kerouac law in the dormitories', as one newspaper put it. For three years running Horace Mann had been unable to score against Tome, a Maryland team with an unbroken run of victories. Jack played brilliantly, making the headlines in the sports sections of the *New York Times*, the *Herald Tribune* and the Lowell papers. One headline told the story: 'Horace Mann Vanquishes Tome 6-0 on Kerouac's 70 Yard Runback in First Play.' Jack's touchdown was the only score in the game.

Though a shy boy, Jack soon made friends, at first with his fellow team-members, then with the other new boys. Despite the class differences, the other students were friendly and welcoming and Jack soon entered a world of fine wines, napkin rings and servants. He began hanging out with the sons of Wall Street financiers and bankers, one of whom, Pete Gordon, showed him around New York, introduced him to Dixieland jazz, and sometimes took him home for weekends. That year Jack invited Pete and another friend, Bob Olsted, back to Lowell for Thanksgiving.

Jack became part of a wise-cracking, fast-talking crowd consisting of Burt Stollmack, Morty Maxwell, Dick Sheresky and Eddy Gilbert, all of whom enlivened classes with their brilliant wit, or so they believed. Eddy Gilbert became a good friend and Jack would often stay the weekend at his parents' mansion in Flushing. Eddy would pay Jack two dollars a paper to do his English essays for him, but it didn't do him any good. Gilbert says: 'I was a whiz at mathematics – so he did my English themes, I did his math – but I kept on getting 70 minus in English – he kept on almost flunking math.'[1] The problem was, of course, that the teachers knew what they were doing.

Back in Lowell for Christmas, Mary Carney asked Jack to do to her what he did to 'them girls in New York'. Jack had been boasting about his sexual exploits in Manhattan. But the idea had been drummed into him that, if he wanted to marry Mary, then it was better to wait. 'Aw, Maggie, I can't do that to you!' he says in *Maggie Cassidy*, 'thinking it too sinful bigcity to do it to her'.

Jack made two lasting friendships at Horace Mann: Henri Cru and Seymour Wyse. It was Seymour Wyse who was to introduce him to modern jazz. Seymour was born in London, in West Hampstead, in 1923 (not in Liverpool as Jack wrote) and went to the Charterhouse School. In March 1939, when Hitler's tanks rolled into Austria, his father sent Seymour, his mother and younger brother to New York because he thought they would be safer in the United States. Seymour's father went on to serve in the Eighth Army in the invasion of Italy.

Seymour was a big jazz fan and had met Duke Ellington on the *Ile de France* on the crossing to New York. It was at an Ellington concert in New York that Seymour met Donald Wolf, a fellow jazz fan who was attending Horace Mann. Wolf spoke highly of the school so Seymour's mother, who had no knowledge of American schools, sent Seymour there. It was through Donald Wolf that he was introduced to Jack Kerouac. Wyse and Wolf are thought to be Dick and Jay in *The Town and the City*.

Seymour introduced Jack to the Apollo, the Savoy Ballroom, Kelly's Stable and the Golden Gate, where Jack first heard and met members of the Count Basie Band. One of his favourite players was Roy Eldridge, who, though known primarily as a high-note man, is generally acknowledged as the bridge between swing and bebop trumpet. Jack and Seymour would travel all over town to hear Eldridge play, and his tight, exciting, easily accessible style made a good introduction to bebop for the teenagers.

Jack learnt fast. Jazz became a lifelong love and was to exert a considerable influence upon his writing. He was introduced to it at a crucial period in its history: the point of transition between the big bands, with their tight arrangements and powerful rhythm sections, and the small experimental groups where the emphasis was on improvisation. After experiencing the incredible Swing Machine that was the Count Basie Orchestra, Jack was no longer interested in the Dixieland style, introduced to him only months before by Pete Gordon. Basie's driving rhythm section, powered by Jo Jones on drums, Walter Page on bass, Freddie Green's chugging guitar and, of course, the Count's own piano, quickly transported Jack into a different world, a journey through time punctuated by 'blats' from the horn section and featuring incredible solos from Buck Clayton on trumpet and Lester Young's slurring, urban tenor explorations.

Jack was entranced and was immediately moved to write about his experiences. His first article, 'Count Basie's Band Best in Land: Group Famous for Solid Swing', written under the guidance of Seymour Wyse and Donald Wolf and based upon an interview with Basie himself, appeared in the *Horace Mann Record* for February 1940. 'Basie's swing arrangements are not blaring,' he wrote, 'but they contain more drive, more power, and more thrill than the loudest of corn artists can acquire by blowing their horns apart.' It was followed the next month by 'Glen Miller Skipped School to Play Trombone, Now is Nation's Most Popular Dance Band'. For this piece he managed to get an interview with Miller, visiting him backstage at the Paramount. Jack was surprised when Miller swore, using the word 'shit' just as an ordinary person might.

Kerouac's keenest appreciation of jazz was to remain centred on the music from this transitional period. Though he later claimed to 'have every record Charlie Parker ever made', he consistently misspelt Parker's name (for some reason he also misspelt Sonny Stitt and Brew Moore's names) and it is clear that it was Lester Young who remained his greatest love. Jack's recognition of 'the Prez' was prescient: early in 1940, when Young was still with the Count Basie Orchestra, Jack prophesied that Young would popularise the tenor saxophone as a solo instrument (though Coleman Hawkins might have demurred that he had already made it popular). However, it was not until 1942 that Lester recorded his first date as a bandleader (a trio with Nat King Cole) and December 1943 when he recorded the famous Lester Young Quartet sessions with Slam Stewart on bass. (Stewart gets a mention in *On the Road*.)

It is hard to establish when Jack first heard Charlie Parker. It's unlikely to have been during Bird's first brief sojourn in New York with guitarist Biddy Fleet and Banjo Burnie in 1939, when Parker is said to have invented bebop while playing 'Cherokee'. Parker played at the Savoy Ballroom in Harlem with the Jay McShann Big Band to great acclaim, and jammed at Clark Monroe's Uptown House, but Jack most likely first saw Bird a little later in the 1942 to 1945 period when he played tenor for Earl Hines. He may even have witnessed the legendary Charlie Parker-Dizzy Gillespie partnership which began with the Billy Eckstine Band in 1944 and flourished in their own unit, playing 52nd Street in 1945. Parker was an important influence in the development of Kerouac's 'spontaneous bop prosody' which came later.

Jack and Seymour Wyse shared their interest in jazz with another Horace Mann student, Albert Avakian, whose brother George had recently graduated from Horace Mann and was running a Greenwich Village jazz club called Nicks, as well as reviewing and producing records. George had just produced a series of Chicago-style jazz albums (albums got their name from a collection of 12″ 78 rpm discs housed literally in an album like a photograph album) and sent Horace Mann a set for their record library. Jack and Albert reviewed the records and interviewed George for a piece in the *Record*. Jack was already translating his experiences into words.

Jack graduated from Horace Mann in June 1940 but, since he could not afford to buy the requisite formal white suit, he instead listened to the ceremony from the lawn near the gym, lying on the grass, glancing through Walt Whitman, as the speeches mingled with the birdsong in the clear blue sky and another chapter of his life came to an end.

Back in Lowell for the summer, Jack was supposed to be studying the two courses he had failed at Horace Mann: chemistry and French. It was a matter of some embarrassment for Jack to find that the French-Canadian *Joual* that he used at home was so far removed from the correct usage of French that he flunked the course. He never did make up the credits. This was an important summer for Jack. On the one hand, it was his last innocent spell as an adolescent, hanging out with GJ and Sammy, drinking beer, telling stories and whooping it up on the streets of Pawtucketville after dark. It was also important to his love life. He had to decide what his intentions were towards Mary Carney.

While Jack was having a tortured chaste love affair with Mary he was at the same time sleeping with a much more worldly girl called Peggy Coffey. It was a dichotomy typical in his life: Mary essentially represented Memere – stability and traditional Lowell family values; Peggy wanted to be a jazz singer, to get out of Lowell and see the world. She was an experienced young woman whom his friends thought much better suited to him than Mary. Jack was torn between the two. Later, he was able to use this experience in his book *Maggie Cassidy*.

There was a further, important new dimension to life in Lowell: his friendship with Sebastian Sampas. Sampas had literally shown up at his parents' house at Gershom Avenue one day and called his name from the street. It had been several years since Jack had seen him but apparently Sebastian had heard that he and Jack had similar interests in literature and philosophy and decided to look him up. Sebastian was involved with a literary round table: a group of idealistic young men, mostly with literary pretensions, who called themselves The Young Prometheans and whose avowed aim was the betterment of mankind. The idea appealed greatly to Jack and he was soon included as a member.

A reading circle or discussion group is perhaps more common to French culture than Anglo-American literary society: Stephane Malarme had his Thursday Night group and, as a youth, André Breton had a group of friends who called themselves The Sophists, whose meetings were strictly barred to non-members. Discussion groups (groups of friends with mutual interests, of which the Beat Generation is a good example) are often the forerunners of café circles or literary movements.

The Young Prometheans – Jack Kerouac, Sebastian Sampas, Cornelius 'Connie' Murphy, Ed Tully, John 'Ian' MacDonald, Jim O'Dea and George Constantinides – met to discuss literature, progressive politics and philosophy. They were 'based on the Brotherhood of Man, and on the mass energies of several participants'.[2] At this time Kerouac saw himself as left wing, and got many of his ideas from the radical *PM* newspaper, but he was sceptical about the Moscow-led American Communist Party. In March 1943 he told Sebastian Sampas in a letter, 'I am a Leftist . . . I couldn't be otherwise. I may not be a Party-liner . . . they haven't done any good and most of them are a trifle too intolerant . . . and unless the Party improves here, I'll never join it. It too must suffer "change".'[3]

Sammy, as Sebastian was known, was by all accounts a rather effeminate young man who affected a cigarette holder, occasionally wore an overcoat as a cape, and was given to sobbing uncontrollably at the realisation that all beauty ultimately decays. He sometimes sang romantic songs to Jack and was known to jump on tables to publicly declaim Shelley or Lord Byron. Allen Ginsberg later described Sebastian and Jack as having a romantic attachment but doubted if sex was involved. Ginsberg says, 'I think he thought of Sampas as being homosexually in love with him, he had a sort of crush on him, and Jack was in love with Sebastian.'[4]

Naturally, Jack's parents disliked Sebastian intensely, feeling that he was a pernicious influence. In fact his influence was entirely commendable. He was better read than Jack and introduced him to two authors who would change his life: one was William Saroyan, whom Jack always loved and admired, and the other was Thomas Wolfe, who was to become the major literary influence upon Jack's writing and thought, inspiring him to explore America, to go on the road.

In September 1940, Jack went on to Columbia College and no longer had to make the long commute from Brooklyn. He was first given a room in Hartley Hall, but it had cockroaches and he would have had to share with another student. He was able to use his influence as a scholarship footballer to get himself a single room in Livingstone Hall, which was normally reserved for graduate students. At first Jack was a proper Joe College: the strong, handsome football player sitting at his desk in his sports jacket, the classical station, WQXR, playing on the radio as he filled the room with fragrant tobacco smoke from his newly purchased pipe and frowned studiously over his books, sometimes glancing at the view of the Columbia quad from his window.

He hung out with his fellow football jocks and, as usual, he went along with the crowd, doing what they did. This led him to take part in something he regretted for the rest of his life. One evening, he and two or three other football players went down to Greenwich Village 'fag-baiting'. Their selected victim was walking along the street carrying a violin, a clear indication to them that he was gay. They hounded him into an alley and broke the violin over his head while the terrified musician kept crying, 'I'm not a fairy! I'm not a fairy!' Jack's friend Lucien Carr later told how it preyed upon Jack's mind: 'It never left him. He used to get drunk and say, "We never should have hit that man with his violin." '

Lou Little, the Columbia coach, made him a wingback, and Jack was determined to make a good impression. He practised hard and played well but broke his leg in the third game of the year when he was tackled by two men as he caught a punt in a game against Saint Benedict's. He heard something crack as he twisted himself free but the trainer thought it was only a sprain. For a week Jack limped through football practice and was accused by coach Lou Little of faking injury. Finally, an X-ray revealed a hairline crack and his leg was set in a huge plaster cast. He was out of the team for the season.

While waiting for his bones to heal, he spent his time sitting in the Lion's Den, a restaurant in the basement of John Jay Hall, which in those days was the student-union building. The Lion's Den was done out as a German beer hall with thick, dark wooden beams and a fireplace, what Kerouac called a 'mahogany type restaurant'. There was a row of booths at the back where students sometimes went for serious discussions with their professors over a glass or two of wine. The waiters were all students. It was more expensive than the regular cafeteria where Jack had washed dishes to pay for his board. Jack sat right in front of the fireplace, eating big steaks and hot-fudge sundaes, reading Thomas Wolfe and William Saroyan, his crutches by his side, and watched the boys and girls dance. He ran up an enormous bill, charged to his football scholarship, the nonpayment of which later caused him to be 'unwelcome on campus'.[5]

Jack explored New York City: examining the antiquities of the Metropolitan Museum of Art, engaging in political discussions with the orators in Union Square, wandering around Greenwich Village and going to movies on Times Square. He even watched the 1941 Easter Parade on Fifth Avenue with his friend GJ, who was visiting from Lowell. Most of all, he had great thoughts of becoming a writer. He read voraciously and stayed up all night talking excitedly with his college friends. One of his new aquaintances at Columbia was William F Buckley Jr, who was later to have his own television talk show. Jack always retained a tremendous admiration for Buckley and was later to share his right-wing sentiments.

On 6 March 1941, Jack hitchhiked to Lowell for the weekend and saw Sebastian, who was home from Emerson College, Boston, where he was studying dramatic art. Jack brought with him a one-act play, written two days before at 3 a.m., which they discussed over banana splits at Marion's drugstore. One week later, Jack sat chatting to his friend Howie Marton at Marton's father's Manhattan apartment, smoking 50¢ cigars in the study until 5 a.m. when they strolled in Central Park to see the sun rising over the skyline of the East Side. For Jack it was a period of wide-eyed exploration and wonderment. He was absorbing experience and information like a sponge.

In April Jack wrote to Sebastian: 'George [Apostolos] came over that weekend and we possessed the bodies of a few women.'[6] Jack had lost his virginity to a prostitute on Times Square in December 1939,[7] and seems to have used prostitutes rather than girlfriends for sex during his first few years in New York. Certainly, in September 1940 he had taken George and Scotty to visit a prostitute named Lucille at the New American Hotel and they all three had sex with her.[8] However, when he was out on the town by himself, he often headed up to Harlem, where he had developed a taste for the Black prostitutes who hung around the jazz clubs.

During the summer of 1941, Jack once more returned to Lowell, where he continued to visit Mary and occasionally hitchhiked to Boston with Sebastian Sampas. At summer's end, he helped his mother pack for the move to West Haven, Connecticut, where Leo had found a job as a Linotype operator. His father had rented an apartment, sight unseen, which was so bad that Gabrielle refused to take it, so the furniture was put in storage and they stayed in a hotel until something habitable came up. For $40 a month they took a seaside cottage three and a half miles from the town centre but conveniently near the trolleycar line. It was a three-bedroom house with an attic at 5 Bradley Point in the Seabluff area, a row of cottages used mostly as summer rents with a parlour window looking straight out over the ocean.

In the middle of September, back at college, Jack quarrelled with his coach, Lou Little, who refused to start him in Columbia's first football game of the season. Jack dropped out of school in disgust. Jack wrote:

> I was back in the fall of '41 for the season – I was a sophomore now and going to be on the varsity – and I don't know. I was getting very poetic by this time, and I'd get very black and broody and everything. I packed my suitcase and walked right out in front of Lou Little. He said, 'Where are you going?' I said, 'Oh, this suitcase is empty. I'm going to my grandmother's house to get some clothes.' And I walked out with a full suitcase. Then I went to Virginia to become a big poet.[9]

Lou Little told Jack to be back by eight. Jack took the subway down to Brooklyn with all his gear, said goodbye to his Uncle Nick, telling him that he was going back to Baker Field, and walked down the hot September streets of Brooklyn hearing Franklin Delano Roosevelt's 'I hate war' speech coming out of every barbershop. He took the subway to the Eighth Avenue Greyhound bus station and bought a ticket to the South, where he intended to begin his career as a writer: 'That was the most important decision in my life so far,' he wrote in *Vanity of Duluoz*. 'What I was doing was telling everybody to go jump in the big fat ocean of their own folly. I was also telling myself to go jump in the big fat ocean of my own folly. What a bath! It was delightful. I was washed clean.'

Jack took a bus to Washington DC and rented a room in a cheap hotel. He wrote to Sebastian: 'I don't know what I've done – afraid to go home, too proud and too sick to go back to the football team, driven and weary with no place to go ... I was lonely, sick, and cried.'[10] He told Sampas that he wanted to write a novel, a play, a book of short stories, a radio script and 'at least one deathless line'.

Summoning up his courage, he returned home to face the anger of his father and to reveal his plans for a career in literature to his family. Inevitably, he quarrelled with his father, who thought that he was mad to quit Columbia and said so vociferously. Jack had always told his friends that he was going to Columbia for an education and that the football playing was simply a means to an end. In fact, he had sometimes expressed embarrassment at playing football, feeling that this crude physical side of himself was at odds with the artistic, sensitive writer he believed himself to be.

There was no need for him to drop out of Columbia: a way could have been found to continue his scholarship without him being on the team. But Jack used his paranoia about Lou Little to fuel his own self-destructive tendency and acted against his own best interests. It was a pattern which was to repeat itself throughout his life. Later, Jack's friend Lucien Carr said that Jack was ambivalent about Columbia. As usual he was split in two: one half was resentful because his pride in himself as a great football player had been hurt; 'the other was guilt, that he got into this thing with Lou Little, and bounced out, and quit ... he thought Lou Little had done him wrong.'[11]

At the end of September Jack left by train for Hartford, Connecticut, where he had somehow found a job pumping gas. There he spent his time reading Thomas Wolfe's *Of Time and the River*, William Saroyan, Dos Passos and William James. Meanwhile, the ever restless Kerouac family was on the move again. After Thanksgiving they left West Haven and returned to Lowell, where they rented a place to live at 74 Gershom Avenue, in Pawtucketville, just over the Moody Street Bridge from Downtown.

The bombing of Pearl Harbour occurred on 7 December 1941 and, to his friends' surprise, Jack, who had shown little interest in the war up until then, decided to enlist in the Navy. While waiting to receive his papers, he worked for a short time as a sports reporter on the *Lowell Sun*, who were pleased to have the well-known local footballer on the staff. Sometimes it was Jack's father who proudly set his words in type, which helped ease some of the tension between father and son.

While Jack waited for his Navy papers he made a few trips: in April to Washington DC to visit a friend and, shortly after that, to Arlington, Virginia, where he worked for a month and a half as a labourer on the construction site of the Pentagon, before being fired because the field boss could never find him – Jack sometimes spent whole days walking through the villages and lanes of Virginia, returning only to punch the time clock. After that, he continued south, amazed by the sheer size of America and accumulating impressions that he was later to use in *The Town and the City*. As he travelled, he considered his future and, swallowing his pride, he turned and headed back to Lowell. Here he wrote to Lou Little, asking if he could return to Columbia. Arrangements were discussed, but Jack had failed chemistry in his freshman year at Columbia and lost his scholarship. He needed $400 to pay his way at Columbia until his scholarship was reinstated.

One night in the bars of Lowell, Jack met a merchant mariner called George Murray and, in the course of an all-night talk, Murray told him that seamen were paid between $1,500 and $2,000 for making the five-month return trip to Russia. That kind of money would solve his financial problems so a few days later Jack went to Boston, took out his seaman's papers, applied for a passport, and joined the National Maritime Union. Each morning he hitchhiked down from Lowell and spent the day waiting around the Union Hall for a ship that needed crew. Financial considerations were not his only motivation: like most young men of his age there was a genuine altruism in his desire to serve his country. He wrote to an ex-girlfriend, Norma Blickfelt:

> I wish to take part in this war, not because I want to kill anyone, but for a reason directly opposed to killing – the Brotherhood. To be with my American brothers . . . for their danger to be my danger . . . I want to return to college with a feeling that I am a brother of the earth, to know that I am not snug and smug in my little universe. And I want to write and write and write about the Merchant Marine . . .[12]

He was hired as a scullion on the SS *Dorchester* and on 18 July 1942 they sailed from Boston harbour, taking a thousand construction workers to Greenland. Jack took with him a little black bag containing *The Outline of History* by HG Wells, *Death in Venice* by Thomas Mann, a collection of classical literature, and copies of *The Shadow* magazine. He was hoping that the voyage would provide enough material for a book, though some of his experiences would prove to be unsuitable. According to Charles Jarvis's book, *Visions of Kerouac*, it was on the Dorchester that Jack had his first full-fledged homosexual experience.

Jarvis was a friend of his from Lowell and, in the mid-sixties, he and his friend James Curtis took Jack around to visit an English friend who, along with his wife and mother-in-law, were fans of Jack's writing. The older woman politely led the conversation by saying, 'Well, you certainly have travelled, Mr Kerouac. Your books are marvellous testimonials of that.'

Jarvis wrote that Jack played along with the role, bowed his head and adopted what he thought was an English accent: 'Yes, madame,' he said, 'I have gone hither and yon, I have sailed the bounding main. I got buggered once when I was a handsome lad sailing as a scullion on the high seas.' In Jarvis's eyes this was not said for effect, but was Kerouac abandoning a pose, dropping a pretence, and telling the truth as he experienced it. Jarvis and Curtis snickered and then laughed out loud. Jack glared at them and resumed: 'Yeah, that's right,' he told the mother-in-law. 'I was corn-holed by a nasty, lecherous fatso cook who deflowered me.'

The young Englishman joined in the laughter, but his mother-in-law behaved with decorum. 'Oh you poor boy. How dreadful,' she commiserated.

'Oh, it was dreadful all right,' said Kerouac. 'Yes, my dear, it was dreadful.'

(Energised by his reminiscences, Jack then proceeded to entertain his hosts with long narratives of life on the road, raucous songs and sudden bursts of dancing.)

The North Atlantic was a dangerous place to be in the summer of 1942. In *Vanity of Duluoz* Jack describes how German U-boats made two unsuccessful attacks on the *Dorchester*. Jack was at work in the galley, frying bacon for a thousand men, two strips each, when he heard two loud explosions outside as the *Dorchester* dropped depth charges on the German subs. It was against this background of fear and constant danger that Jack wrote to Sebastian from Collieries, near Sydney on the north coast of Nova Scotia, that he got drunk and 'conversed biologically with a woman thrice' to the sad sound of factory whistles from the coal mines and the detriment of his wallet.[13] On its next voyage, without Jack, the SS *Dorchester* was torpedoed by a U-boat and hundreds of men drowned in the icy water, including many of Jack's friends from the kitchen galley.

In late October Jack sailed into New York harbour to find Sebastian Sampas waiting for him on the pier and, when he got to Lowell, Jack found that Lou Little had made arrangements for him to return to Columbia. Jack wrote:

Lou Little had a telegram there saying, 'You can come back on the team if you want.' I went back, worked out for a week, and the Army game came up. My great enemy, Henry Mazur, was making long runs for Army. He was the guy in 'The Town and the City' who pushed me out of the shower when I was a little kid. You see, we played together at Lowell High. He was a senior and I was a freshman. I was going to get him in that game. But Lou Little didn't put me in so I, pooh, I quit.

But the reason I quit was deeper than that. I was just sitting in my room and it was snowing, and it was time to go to scrimmage, time to go out in the snow and the mud and bang yourself around. And then, suddenly, on the radio it started – Beethoven. I said, 'I'm going to be an artist. I'm not going to be a football player. That's the night I didn't go to scrimmage. And I never went back to football, see?[14]

That was how Jack saw it in 1959. However, in 1942, writing to Sebastian Sampas in late November, Jack said that Columbia seemed tame in comparison to the momentous events of the war and that he thought he would go back to the Merchant Marine for the duration of the war as an ordinary seaman rather than wait for an officer's uniform in the Navy proper. He wrote, 'I hear of American and Russian victories, and I insist on celebrating. In other words, I am more interested in the pith of our great times than in dissecting "Romeo and Juliet" . . .' But, for a few weeks more, he remained in his university dorm.

Another friend of Jack's from Horace Mann had also just returned to the city from a spell in the Merchant Marine. Henri Cru was a tall, jolly Frenchman with impeccable manners, whose family had emigrated to the USA in 1906, though he was himself born in Williamstown, Massachusetts. He attended Horace Mann Lower School then spent three years at a boarding school in Verneille, near Paris, before returning to Horace Mann. Henri Cru wrote: 'Jack approached me in a most friendly fashion and tried to talk to me in French. I had been born into a French family and Canadian French is hilarious to a Frenchman, but he was a real good kid and we became good friends.'

On 14 July 1942, Henri Cru obtained his seaman's papers and that afternoon he shipped out from Norfolk, Virginia on the *Santa Anna*, a Grace Line freighter, as an assistant electrician. His trip took him to New Zealand and Australia, then back to Los Angeles, where Grace Line fired him and paid his train fare back to New York. Shortly after his return in October, he met Edith Parker in the West End Bar.

Edie Parker was a wealthy young woman from Grosse Pointe, Michigan, who first arrived in New York to complete High School in the fall of 1941, having persuaded her mother (her parents were divorced) that Grosse Pointe High School did not have the facilities for the artistic career she planned for herself. She lived with her grandparents at the Fairmount apartment block at 438 West 116th Street, overlooking the garden of Columbia president Nicholas Murray Butler. Edie did not like the racially mixed high school she was attending and soon began to skip school in favour of the West End Bar which was just up the street.

The West End Bar was on Broadway at 113th right across the street from the Columbia campus. It was a combination of bar and cafeteria, divided in two by a partition. To the left of the revolving door were the steam tables heaped with inexpensive food: mashed potatoes and corned beef, knockwurst and cabbage, which you took to a booth to eat. The tables were run by a Danish chef called Otto who had a hatred of college boys, and a particular hatred of anyone who gave their order twice, in case he hadn't heard it the first time. Despite his nasty temper he could be relied upon for a free bowl of soup in an emergency. To the right was the bar, its white-tiled floor sprinkled with sawdust, and, across from the bar, a row of booths. Of the two bartenders, Bill and Johnny, the students preferred Bill, a well-built, fair-haired man in his early thirties, who arrived each day on his motorcycle, which he kept parked outside. Bill enjoyed talking with the students, always remembering to give them their fourth drink free. Johnny, on the other hand, was an Irish Catholic, a right-wing ex-miner who drank whiskey on duty and thought all students were communists. His arguments usually ended with the line: 'After the war, I warn you, you bastards, you'll be hanged.' Despite this the bar was a favourite with more radical students, but it was also patronised by local people, regulars who saw the students come and go. There was a blonde hooker in her fifties who dropped in for a couple of hours each night to play the jukebox, and a woman dressed entirely in black who sat at the same place at the bar every evening, staring into space, saying nothing.[15] It was here that Jack was to meet Lucien Carr, it was here that Lucien Carr, and Allen Ginsberg sat drinking Pernod, imagining it was absinthe; it was here that Lucien Carr and David Kammerer set off for their ill-fated drink on the banks of the Hudson which was to end in Kammerer's death. The West End was the New York stage set for the early days of the Beat Generation as much as any of the apartments and dorms.

Edie and her sister used to spend their summers at their grandparents' large summer house in the coastal resort of Asbury Park, New Jersey. Edie had a number of boyfriends and admirers there and decided that her grandparents' house, closed up for the winter, would be perfect for a Halloween party. She was caught and shipped off back to Grosse Pointe in disgrace. From November 1941 until September 1942, she did war work in Detroit. Then, having atoned for her sin, she was permitted to return to Manhattan. Edie's grandfather had died and her grandmother welcomed the idea of Edie once more living in her apartment at the Fairmount. A few weeks later, in October 1942, she met Henri Cru.

Henri told literary critic Dave Moore[16] that he and Edie spent the night drinking and talking in the company of a young man whom Henri took to be her boyfriend. When it was time for the West End to close, Henri politely said goodnight and how happy he was to have met her. To which she replied, 'Aren't you going to take me home?' When Henri suggested that her boyfriend might object, she revealed that the other man was her brother.[17] They went to Henri's apartment and immediately went to bed.

Edie has always maintained that they met in the elevator of the Fairmount as Henri's mother lived in the same building as her grandmother and the two older women were good friends. However they got together, it was a fortuitous connection because it was through Edie that the key members of the Beat Generation were to meet. Edie was a lot of fun to be with, always the life of the party, and Henri was very attracted to her. He told Moore that she was a good sport, 'wore a lot of sweaters, was built like a brick chicken house and had legs that looked quite long because she wore high heels most of the time.'[18] Another time he wrote, 'Edith Parker had a body as hard as an Olympic gymnast and the best figure and the sexiest pair of legs I've ever seen in my 27 trips round the world.'[19]

Though Edie had something of a reputation for her sexual liaisons, she was not promiscuous; most of the time she was faithful to one man at a time. However, Henri was somewhat taken aback when, shortly after they got together, she introduced Henri to someone as her fiancé. When he demurred, she explained that, since they had been intimate, she automatically assumed they were engaged. The relationship does seem to have been intense. Edie's sister noted in her diary for 27 December 1942, when Henri and Edie met her train: 'by the way, he's right in there, hot damn.'

Henri had decided to make the Merchant Marine his career and he found that, if he wanted to get a ship, he would have to take the next hiring that came up at the Union Shipping Hall as his sixty days ashore were almost up. Concerned for Edie's well-being, he decided to ask his buddy Jack to keep an eye on her while he was away. A few days into January 1943, he took her to Jack's fifth-floor dormitory at Columbia and then all three went to lunch. Edie says:

Henri Cru and I were rather involved and he wanted to make an impression on me and he said he had a very wonderful genius friend and he would like me to meet him, so he arranged for us to have a luncheon. We went to the New York Delicatessen and Jack joined us and I immediately ate six sauerkraut hot dogs and from that time on Jack said he was madly in love with me.[20]

Edie, growing up among yachts and servants, had apparently not encountered hot dogs before.

Jack seems to have wasted no time: the next day Edie received a love letter from him, delivered by hand, which read: 'Go to the deepest part of the forest, and there you will find a rock. Look under the rock and there you'll find my heart.'[21] With Henri away, Edie quickly took up with Jack. Edie's grandmother much preferred Henri to Jack, who was quite unsophisticated in comparison, and thought Edie had behaved disgracefully towards Henri. Fortunately, Edie's grandmother was rather deaf, and did not hear Jack and Edie when they crept into the apartment to make love on her red velvet couch. Henri appears to have sailed away knowing nothing about it. Edie was clearly still very attached to Henri, and in her correspondence over the next few months she suggested bringing him to Grosse Pointe and told various friends how much she missed him, 'especially at night'. When asked at the end of February if she was engaged to Henri, she replied, 'Yes and no.'

Though very attracted to each other sexually, things were not yet serious between Jack and Edie when, a couple of weeks after they got together, Jack finally quit Columbia and returned to Lowell. What Edie didn't know when he left was that either Jack or Henri Cru had made her pregnant. With them both away, and neither of them committed to her in any formal way, Edie confessed to her grandmother and endured a painful lonely abortion in late January 1943.

After graduating Horace Mann, Seymour Wyse had gone on to study accountancy at New York University while Jack went to Columbia. They saw very little of each other during this period but, when Jack was in the Merchant Marine, he invited Seymour to stay with him at his parents' house in Lowell for a couple of weeks over Christmas 1942. Wyse told David Moore:[22]

We had a lot of fun up there. It was very strange, because we were both interested in baseball at the time, and individually we had invented a game which we pooled together and actually made into one game which we tried to patent – a card game – it was quite a good game. We didn't patent it, but we played it, and that's what we were doing in Lowell most of the time.[23]

Jack remembered the game and used it to while away the time when he was fire watching in the Cascades in 1956. Jack describes the game in tedious detail in section 10 of *Desolation Angels*, while acknowledging that Seymour Wyse (Lionel) was its co-inventor when he came to stay in Lowell for Christmas 'and the pipes froze'. Wyse recalled Jack's parents: 'I remember his father – he was not somebody I liked. His mother was, well, she was a very dominating woman. Jack was very much under her influence but, so far as her communication with anybody outside of Jack, I don't think there was any. So, although I knew them in so far as I stayed there and they were very hospitable, there was no relationship between myself and them at all.' Wyse met Sebastian Sampas while he was there – 'He was a nice man' – and presumably some of the other Prometheans. Early in 1943, Wyse joined the Canadian Air Force and was stationed at Lachine, near Montreal, but whenever he came to Manhattan on leave he and Jack would get together.

In Lowell Jack continued to work on the novel he had begun about the Merchant Marine, *The Sea is My Brother*, writing neatly by hand in a notebook. The characters include three brothers: Big Slim, Peter and Wesley Martin. Peter Martin was the name he later used for the character closest to himself in *The Town and the City*. The final manuscript has not yet surfaced. Edie said that she had it in her attic in Grosse Point, Michigan, left there by Kerouac when he lived there with her in 1945. One of the few descriptions of it comes from Allen Ginsberg, who read it when he first got to know Jack:

'He had been reading a lot of Thomas Mann and Thomas Wolfe, and it was like heavy Germanic symbolic prose. As I remember, there wasn't much naturalistic plot. There was a lot of great prose poetry about the surface of the ocean, the space of the stars at night and the bow of the ship lifting and falling under the stars, and the romance of being a sailor, and hidden mysterious angels under the waves, and great whales mooning in the north, something like that. Something Gnostic and pretty . . . sort of mystical heavy prosed work.'

Jack had shown the first draft of the book to his old professor, Raymond Weaver, at Columbia. Though Jack was no longer enrolled at the college, Weaver was interested and saw him privately. He read the book sympathetically and gave Jack a list of books to read that he thought might help him, including works on the Egyptian Gnostics and Plotinus, and Herman Melville's *Pierre*. There were very few Gnostic texts available at the time, but presumably Jack read the *Pistis Sophia*. He probably found some of the heretical practices interesting, too, such as the Phibionites' idea that grinding down evil and sin required at least 365 successive sexual unions with 365 different women. Jack's exposure to Gnosticism is significant because it prefigures his later interest in Buddhism. Gnosticism shares the Buddhist view that the world is an illusion. This would be his first encounter with the sense of emptiness common to all the Gnostic teachings.

In March 1943, Jack's application to join the Navy came through but he failed the medical examination in Boston which would have made him a pilot in the Naval Air Force V-12 programme. Instead he was sent for basic training to the naval training station in Newport, Rhode Island. Jack survived the discipline and drill for about three weeks before he snapped: 'I was in the navy, but I was discharged after two months. Schizoid personality. They gave me a rifle and they sent me marching out on the drill field, right turn, left turn, and I said, "Aw. I don't want to do this," and I went to the library and started to read . . .'[24]

Jack had taken particular exception to the rule which forbade him to smoke before breakfast. One morning he stood on parade with a cigarette hanging between his lips. The commanding officer inspecting the troops smacked it out of his mouth and Jack hauled back and punched him. It was after this that he laid down his rifle and repaired to the library, where the military police arrested him and took him by ambulance to the base sickbay for observation and psychological testing. He was asked about his emotional life, his girlfriends and one-night stands. The psychiatrist was particularly interested when Jack told him that he was more closely attached to his male friends, spiritually and emotionally, than to his various women. Jack was said to suffer from 'extreme preoccupation' and, when asked if he was the centre of attention in any group, Jack naturally said yes. The doctor looked for 'unreal ideas' in his makeup and asked if he had any 'bizarre hallucinations or behaviour'. Jack listed his quitting Officer's Training at Columbia University as pretty bizarre. He explained to the doctor that he dedicated his actions to experience in order to write about them, 'sacrificing myself on the altar of Art'.[25]

Jack was not surprised to be diagnosed as suffering from schizophrenia, or 'dementia praecox' as it was then called, but was insulted when, on asking for a typewriter in order to finish his novel, *The Sea is My Brother* – which they had studied closely – the doctors humoured him, saying: 'The poor boy, now he's under the "bizarre delusion" that he's a writer.' Jack did recognise that he had a psychological problem and described it to his friend George Apostolos in Lowell:

> One of the reasons for my being in hospital, besides dementia praecox, is a complex condition of my mind, split up, as it were, in two parts, one normal, the other schizoid. My schizoid side is the Raskolnikov-Dedalus-George Webber-Duluoz side, the bent and brooding figure sneering at the world of mediocrities, complacent ignorance, and bigotry exercised by ersatz Ben Franklins; the introverted, scholarly side; the alien side. My normal counterpart, the one you're familiar with, is the half-back-whoremaster-alemate-scullion-jitterbug-jazz-critic side, the side in me which recommends a broad, rugged America; which requires the nourishment of gutsy, redblooded associates . . .[26]

He associated Sebastian and the Prometheans with the former, and his Moody Street drinking buddies with the latter, a personality split which widened in later life when he chose the latter half of his personality, to the exclusion of his intellectual, academic and Beat Generation friends.

While in the base hospital Leo visited him and delivered a diatribe against the 'Marxist Communist Jews' who were trying to drag America into the war, and told Jack that he was doing the right thing. This marked a significant difference between Jack and his father. Leo had the conservatism often encountered in first-generation immigrants and many of Leo's attitudes were essentially still French Canadian. One should not forget that Quebec was a collaborationist state during the war: it supported Vichy France and condemned General de Gaulle to death in absentia. But these were not Jack's views; he was a patriotic American. It was Naval discipline that he was objecting to.

When it looked like Jack might be found sane, he staged a final exhibition of his insanity. One Saturday morning, just as a group of visiting top brass were inspecting the troops, Jack ran stark-naked across the parade ground yelling 'Geronimo!'. It had the required effect and shortly afterwards he was diagnosed as having a schizoid personality. In May 1943, Jack was given an honourable discharge for having an 'indifferent character.' His courage and desire to serve his country was not in question. It was still his intention to join the Merchant Marine and brave the German submarines waiting in the cold waters of the North Atlantic.

3 The Beat Generation

In March 1943, following her abortion, Edie took a job as a driver in the Port of Embarkation, in Brooklyn, where she worked until June. In April she left her grandmother's apartment and moved in with her friend Joan Vollmer, who lived at apartment 28 at 420 West 119th Street, in the short block between Morningside Park and Columbia University. Joan was married to Paul Adams, an ex-Columbia-student who was away fighting for his country. Joan was what Herbert Huncke called a 'college widow'; there were many of them at Columbia, living in large apartments with their boyfriend or husband away in the armed forces. Joan was a very intelligent woman with a quirky sense of humour. She was well-read, with a sardonic, curious mind. In other circumstances she might have been an intellectual. She was studying journalism and took virtually every daily newspaper. She enjoyed reading in the bath, particularly Proust and the newspapers, and spent so long in the tub that, if you wanted to talk, you had to sit on the edge of the bath to do it while she flipped through the papers. She was attractive, with a wide face and high, intelligent forehead. Her sense of humour worked well with Edie's and they had a fine time together.

Edie had several boyfriends after Jack returned to Lowell, and broke off with Henri Cru when he returned from a convoy taking military supplies to Liverpool. Cru took the rejection very badly and later claimed that he did not speak to Edie again for forty years. However, when Jack returned to New York after his Navy debacle and looked up Edie, they found that the old magic was still there. Jack was soon dividing his time between 119th Street and Ozone Park, Queens, where his parents now lived.

With both their children gone, Leo and Gabrielle had decided to move to New York where jobs were easy to find in the burgeoning wartime weapons industries, and where Gabrielle would be closer to her 'Jacky'. In March 1943, they packed up the furniture for the umpteenth time, including the $5 piano and Jack's writing desk, and took an apartment above a drugstore at 133-01 Crossbay Blvd, in Ozone Park near the Aqueduct Race Track and Idlewild – later John F Kennedy – Airport. It was a low, two-storey corner building, brick on the ground floor with wooden siding on the floor above, looking rather like the kind of building you would see in Lowell. Here Jack's parents returned to their old professions: Leo's skill as a Linotype operator enabled him to quickly find a job, and Gabrielle made shoes for the Army in Brooklyn. They went to Broadway shows and ate dinner in Manhattan restaurants. It was a second honeymoon for them, everything that Gabrielle had always wanted, and they were happier than they had been in many years.

Jack and Edie were also a happy couple. Jack may have been the smart one, but Edie had better taste and showed him the way around a menu and made subtle suggestions on how he could improve his wardrobe. They did the normal things a young couple might do, including spending the July 4th weekend at Edie's grandmother's place in Asbury Park, where both got badly sunburnt on the beach.[1]

In August, Joan's lease came to an end and she gave up her apartment. She moved to 421 West 118th Street, apartment 62, and this time the lease was signed by Joan, Edie and Jack – an unusual commitment for him, particularly as he was about to ship out with the Merchant Marine. Despite an evidently happy life, Jack's mind was set on shipping out once more, possibly to prove that he was not a coward. To try to prevent him from exposing himself to the danger of the North Atlantic U-boats, Edie told him what happened to her the last time he went away and explained about her abortion. Jack was furious, he raged and yelled, but there was little he could do after the fact. Edie later said that he seemed much more interested in perpetuating his name than in actually having a child and bringing it up.

A few weeks after the move to 118th Street, in September[2] 1943, Jack left on the SS *George Weems*, with a hold full of bombs bound for Liverpool. He was gone for two months. One of the books he had with him on the voyage was John Galsworthy's *Forsyte Saga*, which combines three novels – *The Man of Property*, *In Chancery* and *To Let* – to make one continuous story of three generations of Forsytes. Kerouac later wrote[3] that it was the *Forsyte Saga* that gave him an 'idea about saga, or legends, novels connecting into one grand tale', something he later developed into what he called the Duluoz Legend. (The name Duluoz, which he was already using at this time, appears to be a fusion of the Greek name Daoulas, which was common in Lowell, and Stephen Dedalus, the autobiographical hero of James Joyce's *Portrait of the Artist as a Young Man*.)

Jack had told Edie and Joan to go out to his parents' place in Ozone Park while he was away in Liverpool and get his record collection, which they did. Leo and Gabrielle were astonished to be confronted by these two sassy females, neither of whom Jack had ever mentioned, but they allowed them to carry away his precious bop records. Despite her penchant for having a good time, Edie did her share of war work and, while Jack was away, she spent three months working at Todd's Shipyard in Hoboken, taking the ferry across the Hudson each day.

It was raining when Jack returned early in October and he was soaking when he rang on the bell. Edie opened the door in her shorts and gasped, 'I never thought I'd see you again!' Joan came to the door to see who it was, saw the look in their eyes, and began laughing: 'Edie's gonna get screwed tonight!'

Jack and Edie picked up right where they left off and apparently discussed marriage. Edie informed her sister they were to be wed and, a week later, on 27 October, they took the train to Grosse Pointe to spend a week with her parents. Edie also met Jack's parents and they occasionally had dinner together, but the relationship was strained. They also made several visits to Lowell, but Edie found the small mill town provincial and dull. That Christmas, Jack took a job delivering telephone books in order to get enough money to buy his mother a present and Edie worked at Best and Co. He and Edie were supposed to spend Christmas Day with his parents, but she backed out at the last moment and he went alone. Edie told her mother, 'I feel strange with his parents.'[4]

Jack was pinning his hopes on a job at 20th Century Fox, writing synopses of film scripts. He saw this as a way into writing for Hollywood. January was spent working at the National Music Association, living at home except when he and Edie had a specific date to see each other. Jack appears to have insisted that if they married they would have to live with his parents in Queens, a situation that Edie had moved to New York specifically to escape. Edie complained to her mother: 'I keep after Jack to get married because it's so horrible alone, but he just won't because of all this mix-up between me and him staying with his family has us both horribly upset.' She told her mother that Jack's solution to the problem was to get married secretly and live together. It could mean that Jack's parents were objecting to them living 'in sin', though it is hard to see how this would solve the problem unless Jack's parents were let in on the secret.

When Jack was away at sea, Edie had resumed her interest in men, particularly the V-12 cadets she met at the West End. Knowing Jack as well as she did, she had realised it was pointless to wait for him: he might not come back or, when he did return, he might no longer be interested in her. One of the new friends she made was Lucien Carr, who was to become an important player in the Beat Generation saga. As is usual with Edie, there is some dispute over where she met Lucien. It was probably at a drawing class at Columbia, where she was studying painting with George Grosz, whose drawings of pre-war Berlin paralleled Isherwood's *Berlin Stories*. She became aware of Lucien watching her from across the studio and invited him back to 118th Street. She was attracted by his dashing good-looks: green slanted eyes, longish blond hair falling over his face, and also by his arrogant sarcastic manner. Though still a precocious teenager, Lucien Carr was worldly-wise and came from a similarly wealthy, sophisticated background to her own. They became good friends, and Lucien felt very much at home in the apartment, stopping by to take a shower or make himself a snack between classes.

When Jack returned, Edie, in her ebullient way, told Jack all about her life while he was away at sea, including many stories about Lucien. It was not long before they met. Edie and Jack walked into the West End, and Edie pointed him out, sitting in a booth with friends. Jack had been suspicious of this new rival and his first response was 'Looks to me like a mischievous little prick'. He could see why she was attracted to him. He was attracted to Lucien himself. He later described him as an absolute physical and spiritual male beauty with 'complete intelligence, language pouring out of him, Shakespeare reborn almost, golden hair with a halo around it'.[5]

The three of them began spending time together. Edie and Lucien invited Jack to attend George Grosz's life-drawing class at Columbia, but the sight of a naked brunette looking him right in the eye was too much for him and he had to run back to the apartment and take a shower. Towards the end of March, Lucien took up with a new girlfriend, Céline Young, a student at Barnard, who often accompanied them, as did Joan. They were a young college crowd and, though Jack was slightly older, it was as if he had never left Columbia. Lucien thought that Jack and Edie made a great couple and described Edie as a 'strong, wiry little bitch but, man, she really was the best woman that Jack ever got involved with, bar none. They were *perfect*, they were really perfect . . . Jack couldn't be led, he was recalcitrant, and he was a pig, but he was everything in a man that she ever thought could exist'.[6]

Jack and Lucien got on well. Lucien's approach to life was similar to that of the Dadaists: accept nothing, trust no one and ridicule everything. Jack liked Lucien's utter disregard for convention and was impressed by his sophistication and arrogance: Lucien once famously threw a dish of veal parmesan over his shoulder saying, 'This is crap,' and calmly sipped his wine as the waiter ran to clear the mess. He and Jack began to drink together at the West End and Lucien continued to use Edie's apartment as a refuge. In *Vanity of Duluoz*, Jack tells numerous stories about hi-jinks together, which Lucien later confirmed in an interview. One time when they were both drunk – which was frequently – Lucien put Jack in an empty barrel and rolled him along the sidewalks of Upper Broadway. Another time, again drunk, they went out in a downpour and sat in a puddle where they sang at the top of their voices and poured black ink over each other's head.

Lucien also once made an unorthodox entry into the apartment: 'Lucien came in through the fire escape ... there were gunshots down in the alley – Pow! Pow! and it was raining and my wife says, here comes Lucien. And here comes this blond guy through the fire escape, all wet. I said, "What's all this about, what the hell is this?" He says, "They're chasing me." '[7] The story as Jack told it in *The Town and the City* was a classic Carr escapade. Lucien Carr had been involved in a bar fight and the police were after him: 'I got shot at with a shotgun. I used to go across the roof where you could stand on a tile ... to go in through a back window.'[8] All the drinking and late nights of course meant that Lucien's studies suffered and once Jack wrote Lucien's English paper for him, which was overdue. Jack described Piccadilly Circus and his trip to Liverpool as a Merchant Marine. Lucien got an A.

As he often did with the characters in his books, Jack exaggerated Lucien Carr's background. When Jack first took Lucien to Lowell to meet his parents, the two of them, accompanied by Jack's father, went across the street to have a beer. When Lucien pulled out his money, Leo stopped him, saying, 'No, I can buy a millionaire's son a beer!' Clearly Jack had overstated Lucien's family background. Lucien's father had walked out on his family when Lucien was two years old, in order to become a sheep herder in Wyoming and work as a bank guard when the weather got too rough. Lucien was still very young when his father died and never knew him. Jack was correct, however, in thinking that Lucien came from a prominent

Saint Louis family. Benjamin Gratz, Lucien's maternal grandfather, had been a successful businessman in Saint Louis, dealing in jute and hemp fibres and in manufacturing bags. This had enabled Lucien's mother, Marion, to give him a middle-class upbringing with private schools, foreign travel, hotels and restaurants. His mother's sister was married to a Rockefeller and lived in Greenwich, Connecticut. But the millionaire aristocratic background that Jack wrote into existence for Lucien was only loosely based on fact, like the fictional trust fund he invented for William Burroughs which dogged Burroughs for the rest of his life.

Lucien had a problem, a *bête noire*. Ever since he was ten years old in Saint Louis he had been hounded by David Kammerer, a tall redheaded homosexual, fourteen years older than he. Kammerer had fixated on Lucien because he had had a previous relationship with a boy in Paris who looked just like him. They met when Lucien joined a Cub Scout Pack of which Kammerer was the leader. Kammerer was from the same social background: his father was a partner in Von Schrenk and Kammerer, a firm of consulting engineers in Saint Louis. Young Carr would often visit Kammerer at home. Kammerer was a well-built man, over six feet tall and working at this time as a physical education instructor at Washington University, Saint Louis. Lucien liked Kammerer as a friend and was flattered by his attention, which made him feel important. When Lucien was fourteen, Kammerer, then twenty-eight, took him on a tour of Mexico, acting as his guide and mentor, and it was there that he made his first homosexual advances towards him. Lucien was confused: abandoned by his own father, who was in any case now dead, Kammerer had become a father figure to him whose views and opinions he respected. To have him fawning and love-sick placed Lucien in a very confusing situation, putting him in a position of power over the older man. It was then, at the age of fourteen, that Lucien began to drink heavily, most likely as the result of the stress of the situation.

Lucien moved away from Saint Louis, to the Phillips-Andover Academy, in Andover, Massachusetts, but Kammerer followed. He was ordered out of town by an alert headmaster but Kammerer simply moved to the suburbs of the town and was still able to exert his influence over Lucien from there. Not long afterwards, Lucien was expelled from Andover for going out after hours.

When he was sixteen, Lucien's mother found more than fifty love letters from Kammerer in his room, and was determined to separate them, this time by sending Lucien to Bowdoin College in Brunswick, Maine, and from there to the summer school of the University of

Chicago. But all the time Kammerer followed like a tame dog, taking jobs as a janitor, or dish washing, utterly controlled by his obsession. It was in Chicago that they met up with Kammerer's friend William Burroughs – also originally from Saint Louis. Kammerer was not a typical stalker; he and Lucien were actually friends, and Kammerer was able to keep himself under control, but his constant presence and continual demands were driving the boy crazy. It was in Chicago that Kammerer persuaded him to go on some kind of spree, the end result of which was that Lucien attempted suicide. He sealed the windows, put a pillow in the gas oven, and lay with his head inside and the gas turned on. Fortunately, Kammerer came to visit – for some reason on horseback with a society girlfriend at his side. He smelt the gas, kicked the door in, and dragged Lucien out into the hallway, where he recovered. Lucien was sent to a psychiatrist but, with Kammerer always around, no one could help him. Lucien tried once more to escape his attention, this time by arranging a transfer from the University of Chicago to Columbia, but Kammerer, as usual, followed him, taking a job as a janitor in Greenwich Village.

And so, for Jack, the next character to appear onstage was David Kammerer. Jack walked into the West End Bar one night and saw Lucien sitting in a booth with a large man with a big red beard. Jack went over and Lucien said, 'Jack, doesn't this guy look just like Swinburne?' Jack agreed and Lucien introduced them, describing Kammerer as 'the guy that's been following me all over the country'. Kammerer gradually insinuated himself into the group, despite the considerable disparity in ages, getting to know Joan and Edie and their other college friends. Kerouac once described Kammerer's speech pattern to Neal Cassady, saying that his voice became quieter and quieter until finally you couldn't hear him any more, but that when he spoke to Lucien his voice remained on the same level, as if he was not interested in speaking to anyone else. This suggests that Kammerer was actually a very weak character, lacking the confidence to speak to anyone except Lucien, whom he knew would listen.

Next to enter Jack's life was Allen Ginsberg, who was to become his greatest advocate and supporter, and without whom Jack might never have been published at all. Allen had just arrived at Columbia and was four crucial years younger than he. He was born in 1926 in Newark, New Jersey, and grew up in Paterson, New Jersey, where his father was a schoolteacher. He had developed an enormous tolerance for anti-social behaviour from looking after his mother, Naomi, who was schizophrenic, later to be the subject of Ginsberg's great poem *Kaddish*. Naomi Ginsberg came to the United States as a young girl from Russia. Shortly after her marriage to Louis Ginsberg she began to exhibit symptoms of schizophrenia, but it was only after the birth of her two children that her condition became acute. Allen grew up in a troubled household: Naomi would hear voices, thought people were plotting against her, and would prowl around the house naked making it difficult for Louis to ever have friends or neighbours to visit. When she got too confused and became a danger to herself, Naomi would go to hospital, first a private nursing home, then later the big state mental hospitals of New Jersey and New York. Allen would often have to stay home from school to attend to her, and became adept at dealing with madness and eccentricity. As an adult, Allen often did not notice behaviour which most people would find strange, and he was able to deal with deranged and confused people with compassion and calm.

Allen's father, Louis, was a poet in the lyric verse tradition and had published several collections of poetry. He had a regular column of terrible puns in the local newspaper and was a well-liked member of the community. Allen grew up in a left-wing household: his father was a socialist and his mother a member of the Communist Party. Allen had a keen interest in politics and it was his intention to become a labour lawyer in order to help the working class, in the footsteps of his brother, Eugene, who was exactly five years older and already studying to become a lawyer. By the time Allen arrived at Columbia, he was having second thoughts about his choice of career. He was a dreamy, thoughtful child, often musing on the mysteries of existence: 'I would go into some kind of swoon, thinking how mysterious the universe was and how lonely I was.' He was already aware that he was homosexual, though he was still a virgin, and keeping this dark secret also set him apart from his friends and family. It was inevitable that at Columbia he should be attracted to the more sensitive, artistic set, rather than the other students in the pre-law classes.

A few days before Christmas 1943, Allen was walking down the long corridor on the seventh floor of the Union Theological Seminary to his room when he heard beautiful music. Most of the transoms above the doors were dark, as students had already gone home for the holidays, but one was lit up, a room where a new boy had recently moved in. Intrigued, Allen knocked on the door. It was answered by 'the most angelic-looking kid I ever saw'. The new boy was Lucien Carr, transferred to Columbia from the University of Chicago. They quickly became friends.

Lucien was two years older than Allen and introduced him to a Bohemian world that Allen described simply as 'wonderland'. Lucien took him on his first visit to Greenwich Village, where he introduced him to David Kammerer, then living at 48 Morton Street, off Seventh Avenue, where he worked as a janitor. On their first visit to Kammerer, Allen noticed 'Lu-Dave' written on the wall above the bed, and wondered about it. Allen had told no one about his homosexual feelings, and now here he was, walking around the Village 'where all the fairies lived' with a beautiful friend. One of the first entries in Ginsberg's 1943 notebook is a transcription of a little song that Lucien liked to sing: 'Violate me/in violent times/the vilest way that you know./Ruin me/ravage me/on me no mercy bestow.'

Lucien naturally told Allen all about the seaman athlete he had met, who also wrote books. He gave Allen Jack's address. Allen was anxious to meet a real writer and, early in January 1944, when he returned to Columbia after the holiday break, he went over to visit. Jack was sitting, dressed in a white T-shirt and chino pants, waiting for Edie to serve him his breakfast when Allen arrived. Allen said: 'I was a little scared of him, he was a big strong intelligent-looking football player merchant seaman and I was kind of a ninety-pound weakling New Jersey Jewish intellectual freshman at Columbia.'

Jack said: 'In walks Ginsberg, sixteen years old, a freshman, with his ears sticking out at the time. The first thing he said to me was "Discretion is the better part of valour".'

Allen: 'He looked at me and said, "Aw, where's my eggs?" But we talked and we discovered we both realised we were both on earth only temporarily. So there was a kind of understanding of the flowerness of the moment, a phrase of the day that we used.'

Jack suggested that they take a walk, and they wandered around the Columbia campus in the frosty winter air, towards 122nd Street where Allen had lived at the Union Theological Seminary. Allen and Lucien were both assigned rooms there because the Columbia dorms were all full of V-12 wartime cadets. Lucien had moved out to the Warren Hall Residency Club, a small student hotel on West 115th Street, and Allen had followed suit to be near him. As they passed the Theological Seminary, Allen told Jack that when he left the seventh floor for the last time he turned round and bowed to the room and said 'Goodbye', bowed to the door, bowed to the hall, and said 'Goodbye' to each step as he went down, conscious that he was leaving for ever, and that a part of his life was already over. Allen: We immediately got into a soul conversation about how our souls behaved in the face of change. Jack immediately recognised that as a characteristic ritual acknowledgement of mortal knowledge and said 'Gee, you know, that's the way I think a lot too. I have thoughts like that all the time.' And he told me how, when he was in Lowell, Massachusetts, he used to stand in the back yards at night when everybody was eating supper and realise that everyone was a ghost eating ghost food. Or sometimes that he was a ghost, watching the living people. I think that determined his descriptions of me later on in all of his books where he sees me as off in a dark corner brooding, which is an image he constantly has of me tapping my foot or holding my chin half in the darkness, half in the shadow, brooding. A sort of a caricature of the melancholy poet. I think it was that conversation that determined our affection and trust.[10]

It was also a conversation which pointed in the direction of 'The New Vision', an early form of what might be called the philosophy of the Beat Generation.

In March 1944, Jack received the news that Sebastian Sampas had died in hospital in Algiers, North Africa, after being wounded in action during the Allied landing at Anzio. In late 1943, the Allied campaign to liberate Italy from the Germans was at a stalemate along the Gustav Line, a natural stronghold of mountainous terrain stretching across the country just north of Naples. The commander of the American Fifth Army, General Mark Clark, ordered amphibious assaults on the beachheads at Anzio and Nettuno, north of the Gustav Line, to clear the road to Rome. On 22 January 1944, 40,000 Allied troops of the American Fifth Army, Sixth Corps and the British First Infantry Division were landed.

After initial success, the Allies were pinned down on the beachhead by a vastly superior German force. The Allies held the beachhead but the cost was high: Allied forces suffered nearly 28,000 casualties, Sebastian among them. Finally, with long-awaited reinforcements, the Allies broke out in late May and ultimately marched victoriously into Rome in June 1944.[11]

Jack was devastated. He wrote a tearful letter to his dead friend, half in French, half English, in which he seems almost mad with grief. Sebastian had been his closest friend, his confidant both in emotional and intellectual matters. Part of the dualism of Jack's nature was that he always needed someone in that confidant role, an intellectual stimulus, to balance the good-ol'-boy barfly side of him. Allen Ginsberg appeared in his life at just the right time to fill this role, and in many ways Allen was more suitable than Sebastian, prepared to devote limitless energy to promoting Jack and his work, and able to see beyond his anti-Semitism, his callousness, and rudeness when it arose.

Jack told Al Aronowitz in 1959: 'I always had a friend like Allen. In Lowell I had a friend called Sebastian who was just like him – you know, always a weird, poetic Latin type. Latin – well I mean dark, dark mysterious. Allen is the sweetest man in the world.'

He also spoke of the latest addition to the group, a mysterious friend of Lucien and David Kammerer's from Saint Louis called William Seward Burroughs: 'We had a gang of friends from Saint Louis, a clique of rich guys, decadent, intellectual types – from Harvard. We started forming a circle around Burroughs and the rest of them . . . Burroughs was Old Bull Lee in *On the Road*.'

Edie Parker wrote: 'Bill was a mentor but he was much more than that. He was a teacher of all we yearned to know. He taught us restaurants, psychology, European Flavours of life, and many underground fascinating tales. We adored him and hung on every word he spoke.'[12]

Jack wrote: 'So, Burroughs went around and found everybody else . . . actually there was none of them who was really bad, except maybe Phil White. He used to kill storekeepers, but we didn't find out about that until later when he was arrested.'[13]

David Kammerer was responsible for introducing William Burroughs to Jack, though they were bound to meet because Lucien already knew him from Chicago, where Burroughs had been attending Count Korzybsky's course in General Semantics. Kammerer and Burroughs showed up at Jack's door on a warm day in late spring. It was the middle of the afternoon. Jack and Edie had just had sex and she was sleeping. Jack was coming out of the shower with a towel round him when they rang the doorbell. Bill was tall and thin, a black hat on his head, but dressed for summer in seersucker trousers. Jack brought them in and made them at home on the couch. They talked. Bill's reason for visiting was to inquire about the Merchant Marine, saying he was interested in shipping out, but it was obvious that he really just wanted to meet Jack, whom he had heard so much about from both Lucien and David Kammerer. Bill explained that he was working as a bartender in the Village and sometimes served summonses to make a little extra money.

Bill was thirty years old with pale-blue eyes and fine wispy hair, always flattened by his habitual wearing of a hat – he still adopted the pre-war dress code of his youth. He had a flat mid-Western accent with clipped Harvard-educated tones. Bill was named after his grandfather, who had invented the adding machine and was the founder of the giant Burroughs Corporation. Unfortunately, the family had unloaded their shares during the Depression and he received no income from that source. They were still a wealthy family by Saint Louis standards, though not as wealthy as some. Bill and his brother, Mortimer, grew up in a household with a butler, maid, nanny and yardman, and his aunts chugged around town in steam cars.

Bill was sent to the Los Alamos Ranch School, in New Mexico, for his sinus trouble. There he was forced to ride 'a stubborn, spiteful, recalcitrant horse' and take part in outdoor activities. Bill was pleased to hear that during the war the school was sequestered by the government for the Manhattan project and it was there, in Bill's old classroom, that the atomic bomb was invented. 'It seemed so right, somehow,' he commented later.[14] At Los Alamos he had developed a crush on a fellow pupil and realised that he was gay. He also wrote his first stories there, in the manner of the crime thrillers and westerns of the day, though such intellectual activity as writing was discouraged by the headmaster.

At Harvard he shared a cottage with his friend Kells Elvins, and together they wrote a spoof on the sinking of the *Titanic*, which they called 'Twilight's Last Gleaming'. Bill used it later, virtually unchanged, in his book *Nova Express*. After Harvard he went to study medicine in Vienna, where it was not necessary to have studied pre-med, but the growing Austrian support for the Nazis made him return to the USA. Before leaving, he married a Jewish woman, Ilsa Klapper, who ran something of a literary salon in Vienna but whose attempts to find refuge outside the country had so far failed. As a result of her marriage she was granted American citizenship and escaped persecution and possibly death. Bill made no demands upon her, nor she upon him, and they lived their own lives. They saw each other throughout the war, usually to have lunch, and when the war ended she returned to Europe.

Back in the States, Burroughs drifted to New York, where he began psychoanalysis to try to gain some control over his life, going first to the Freudian Doctor Herbert Wiggers. Bill had a series of unhappy love affairs, and went as far as to cut off his little finger at the first joint in order to prove his love for one of his lovers. This earned him some time in the Payne-Whitney psychiatric hospital, where he was transferred by his parents after Doctor Wiggers had shanghaied him into Bellevue.

Jail or mental hospital or both seemed to be a prerequisite for the founder members of the Beat Generation: Ginsberg was to spend time in the Columbia Psychiatric Institute; Gregory Corso, who came on the scene a little later, spent time in Bellevue and in jail; Lucien went to jail for two years; Joan Vollmer was briefly in Bellevue for amphetamine psychosis; Neal Cassady was to spend two years in jail in California; Herbert Huncke was in and out of jail most of his life; and Jack was thrown out of the Navy as psychotic.

When America finally entered the war, Bill tried to do his bit, but none of the armed forces had a position suitable for his special skills. His mother pulled a few strings and he almost finished up in the fledgling CIA, but his old Harvard housemaster was on the selection committee and remembered Burroughs all too well as the man who kept a ferret and a gun in his room and did not join any of the clubs.

He worked for nine months as an exterminator in Chicago, a job that he very much enjoyed and was the longest period of regular employment he ever had. It was here that he lived in Mrs Murphy's rooming house, which was to occur in his later writing. When his friends Lucien Carr and David Kammerer arrived in town, the one following the other, they all spent time together. When Lucien transferred to Columbia, Kammerer went, too, and Bill decided to follow them.

Jack divided his time almost equally between his parents in Ozone Park and Edie at West 118th Street. By all accounts, this period with Edie was one of the happiest times of his life. Jack had an attractive, fun-loving girlfriend and a number of close male friends who were interested in his every word. People were always dropping by and the apartment became a sort of literary salon. Jack himself was writing furiously. Edie: 'Every night, no matter how late we were up and out, I went to sleep with a typewriter in my ear. He wasn't ready for marriage. He wanted to be a writer.'[15] We do not know for sure what he was writing, but it was probably early drafts of *Galloway*, the novel retitled early in 1946 as *The Town and the City*. (As early as September 1943, in a letter to Edie, Jack referred to Lowell as Galloway, presumably in reference to some piece of writing about it.[16])

Jack called Edie 'Bird Note', a pun on the shape of her nose, which was very thin and aquiline and shaped like a bird's beak, and also a reference to Charlie 'Yardbird' Parker and his ebullient stream of notes. They went to the jazz clubs in Harlem, though this was mainly when Seymour Wyse was around, and they spent a huge amount of time at the West End with Lucien, David Kammerer and Allen Ginsberg. Burroughs was around sporadically and was not yet fully integrated into the scene. Joan Vollmer had been seeing various young men, mostly Columbia students, and was pregnant, supposedly by her husband, Paul Adams, who was away in the armed forces. In April she returned to her parents in Albany, New York, to have the child. (There has been speculation in some of the Beat Generation books that Joan's child was by someone other than Paul Adams. Herbert Huncke, in an interview, said that the child behaved very much like her mother but did look much more like her father, Paul Adams, whom Huncke had met.[17] On the other hand, Joan's best friend, Edie Parker, states categorically that Julie was not Paul Adams's daughter. She was more likely to know the true identity of the father, but never told.[18])

In those pre-women's-liberation days, women were expected to fit in around their men and be forever at their beck and call. Jack could do virtually anything he wanted. He got up when he liked and sometimes spent all night talking and drinking with friends and didn't come home at all. Edie: 'As for standing by our men, that was the only way we knew how to go. We were a different breed than women are today.'[19] In many ways their life was very innocent at this point: they drank but there were no drugs on the scene yet, not even marijuana. Sexually, however, they were quite active. Wartime had shaken some of the American Puritan morality and Joan, Edie and Céline were all sleeping with their men, something which became more unusual a decade later, even in Greenwich Village, as the sterile fifties cast a stranglehold over America. Edie: 'As far as I'm concerned we were very moral . . . it's amazing that they think we had these great big sex orgies. We would sit around and read books and talk about them.'[20] This doesn't quite gell with the note in Allen Ginsberg's journal for the period about 'playing strip poker with Joan and Céline', unless they waited until Edie went out. When GJ came to visit Jack from Lowell, one of Edie's girlfriends answered the door to him naked, while Jack wore only a towel wrapped round himself. It was only a prank but GJ was suitably shocked. Life with Edie was so different from life with Leo and Gabrielle that Jack wrote in his journal that he must have a split personality because when he got home to Ozone Park he could not remember a thing about his life at 118th Street.[21]

After the surprise visit of Edie and Joan Vollmer to Ozone Park the previous summer, Jack's parents were concerned that he was mixed up with a fast crowd. Jack's sister Nin to wrote him in July[22] asking what was going on between Edith and him, saying that their parents seemed awfully worried. She asked if he was living with Edie: 'If so I'm terribly disappointed in you. In behaving thus, you're not being my own sweet brother who was fine, dignified and on his way up to a bright future. That kind of living is for other people, Jack dear, but not for us.' She lectured him on family pride and told him that Gabrielle and Leo had brought them up to have high moral standards and it was their duty to see that they kept them through life. Like her parents, she could not understand why Jack had to live in the city at all and thought that he should be at home in Ozone Park, looking after his folks.

Jack was not out on the town with Edie every night. Most of the time he, Lucien and Allen Ginsberg were deeply immersed in discussions about what they called 'The New Vision' or 'Supreme Reality'. This was based upon William Butler Yeats's *A Vision*, which concerns itself with the unity of all beings and proposes a hermetic system in which all people's character traits are cast into 28 separate categories based on the phases of the moon, ranging from flat objective to intense subjective. Using the same system, it also places civilisations in that same order. It is a beautiful piece of prose writing which affected both Kerouac's and Ginsberg's style quite considerably.

In May, Jack once more tried to get a ship in New Orleans, hoping for a Caribbean or South American run, but to no avail. He returned dejectedly to New York, but in June his attempts at a job as a script synopsis writer finally paid off and he started work at Columbia Pictures in Rockefeller Center. He had his own office and secretary and felt that things were happening for him at last.

For Lucien, Kammerer's obsessive behaviour was once more becoming a major problem and he realised that he would again have to leave town in the hope that Kammerer would not follow him. The incident which forced this decision was when Kammerer appeared at Edie and Jack's apartment looking for him and, finding no one at home, tried to hang their newly acquired kitten, Kitkat, in an act of vengeance because Lucien spent so much time there. Fortunately, Burroughs turned up in time to save its life. (Lucien was there most of the time with Céline, who had become a close friend of Edie's. She and Edie worked together on Staten Island and often spent weekends at Céline's mother's house on Long Island.)

To get away from Kammerer, Lucien decided to take a supply ship to Europe, and Jack immediately said he'd join him. Jack's good job at Columbia Pictures had only lasted a few weeks and he was at a loose end once more. They excitedly formulated a plan to jump ship as soon as they reached France and walk to Paris to be there for the Liberation. They would pretend to be French: Jack would do the talking and Lucien would be his mute brother.

Lucien had seaman's papers from a summer vacation job, but his only actual experience was in New York Harbour on a rusty oil tanker, and in Bayonne and Staten Island transporting aircraft fuel. They found a ship but as they approached the gangplank a sailor warned them that the chief mate was a 'fascist'. Finding no one on board, they helped themselves to roast beef and milk from the ship's galley. At that moment, the chief mate arrived on the scene and appeared to confirm the departing sailor's opinion. When they asked if they could make the trial run to Albany – the ship's first port of call – before signing on for France, he tossed them ignominiously off the ship.

It did seem that the Merchant Marine was the only way for Jack to earn the kind of money he needed to marry Edie – if he was indeed serious about this – and he continued his efforts to get a ship. By mid-July he was signed up and living on board, taking his share of watch duties while the boat was loaded ready for departure. The boat was in dry dock, so he was not receiving any pay, and whenever he could get time off he returned to Edie's or to Ozone Park. As it happened, subsequent events ensured that Jack missed the voyage.

The night of 14 August 1944 was hot and humid. When the West End Bar closed at 3 a.m., Lucien Carr left with David Kammerer and, taking a bottle with them, they went to sit on the grassy bank below Riverside Park at 115th Street at Riverside Drive, overlooking the Hudson River where there was a slight breeze. Kammerer began his usual demands, insisting that Lucien let him give him a blow job. Lucien was completely drunk and, when Kammerer lunged at him, he was no match for the heavier, stronger man. In the course of the struggle Lucien managed to get out his boy-scout pocket knife and open the blade. He stabbed Kammerer twice rapidly in the chest and then panicked when Kammerer keeled over unconscious. He rolled Kammerer's body to the water's edge and then used the laces from Kammerer's shoes to tie his hands and feet. He took off Kammerer's shirt and tore it into strips, which he used to tie up the body. He then fastened Kammerer's belt round his arms.

Working in frantic drunken haste, he heard some passers-by and, unsure whether anyone had seen him or not, he gathered as many rocks and stones as he could quickly find and shoved them into the pockets of Kammerer's khaki trousers and down the legs. Then he pushed the weighted body into the muddy river.[23] At first it would not sink, so Lucien stripped off his clothing, carefully laid it on the river bank, then waded into the water until he was able to give the body a shove out into the swift-flowing water, where the current took it.

At first Lucien toyed with the idea of running away and joining the Merchant Marine but immediately had second thoughts. Unsure what to do, he hailed a cab on Riverside Drive and went to ask Bill Burroughs for his advice. When Bill let him in, Lucien told him, 'I just killed the old man.'

'So this is how it ends,' Burroughs thought.[24]

Ever one for a dramatic gesture, Lucien threw a bloodstained packet of Lucky Strike on the table and said, 'Have the last cigarette.' Bill immediately broke them up and disposed of them down the lavatory.[25] 'I'll get the hot seat,' Lucien said. 'Don't be absurd,' said Burroughs, 'a good lawyer will get you off on self defence.' He advised him to tell his mother and then do everything and say everything that the family lawyer told him. Lucien left him at dawn and headed over to West 118th Street to see Jack.

At dawn, Lucien woke Jack with the words, 'I just got rid of the old man.' Edie did not understand and Jack quickly shooed her into the kitchen to fix them all breakfast. Lucien explained what had happened and asked Jack to come with him for a walk. Lucien still had the murder weapon, which Jack helped him to dispose of, covering him while he dropped it down a drain. For some reason he also had Kammerer's glasses. These they buried in Morningside Park, at the end of the block, with Jack pretending to piss against a tree to distract passers-by while Lucien dug a hole and buried them. Together they wandered around Harlem. Lucien borrowed money from his psychiatrist, without telling him what had happened, and then he and Jack went to midtown to see a movie and look around the Museum of Modern Art. In the course of these perambulations, Lucien finally screwed up the courage to turn himself in. He went to see his aunt, who immediately contacted the family lawyers.

On Monday afternoon, 14 August, Lucien, accompanied by his lawyer, appeared at the office of District Attorney Frank S Horan and nervously told his story to Jacob Grumet, the Assistant DA in charge of the Homicide Bureau. Grumet was disbelieving at first as there was no corpse and no one had reported Kammerer missing. He thought that he maybe had a crank on his hands. He did, however, hold Lucien without charge while he investigated. The West Side Detective Bureau and Homicide Squad both assigned men to the case, but there was no body at 115th Street. Lucien remained in Horan's office and spent most of the night reading WB Yeats's *A Vision* and the poetry of Arthur Rimbaud, while the police began to feel they were victims of an elaborate hoax.

Lucien offered to show them where he had buried the glasses and took them to the spot where he and Jack had disposed of the evidence. This made them more inclined to believe him but it was not until 2.30 that afternoon that they were convinced, when coast guards reported a body floating in the Hudson off 108th Street. By the time marine police and the coast guard towed the body ashore to the West 79th Street float, Lucien, his lawyer Vincent J Malone, and his interrogators were on hand. All but one of the rocks had fallen from Kammerer's clothing, permitting the corpse to float. Lucien identified the body and was then taken to the Elizabeth Street Police Station and booked on a charge of homicide.

After interrogating him further and getting the full story, including how he went first to see Burroughs and then spent the day with Jack, the police went to 118th Street and arrested Jack as a material witness. Both he and Edie were taken to the precinct house but Edie was released when they realised she was not involved. Jack was told that if Lucien was charged with murder then he would very likely be charged as a material witness or accessory for helping dispose of Kammerer's glasses and the murder weapon.

On 17 August the papers reported that Lucien 'listened lackadaisically to the proceedings' and 'showed little interest' as he was arraigned before magistrate Anna M Kross in Homicide Court. He held Yeats's *A Vision* in his hand and had a brown-paper parcel of clean laundry with him, given to him by his mother.[26] After the hearing, Lucien was taken to The Tombs, where he was held in solitary confinement. In among his clothing was another book: *The Third Morality* by Henry Fitzgerald Heard. The *New York Herald Tribune* reported that 'Carr rocked his questioners in the district attorney's office with liberal use of polysyllable words and deep philosophical observations. Whenever there was a pause in interrogation he picked up *A Vision* and resumed reading.'[27]

On the same day, a miserable John Kerouac (as he was charged) appeared in court before Judge John J Sullivan in General Sessions, held as a material witness. The court was told that Jack had helped

Lucien bury Kammerer's glasses. 'I only watched him bury the glasses, and Carr said he was going to give himself up,' Jack interjected.[28]

'You came very close to becoming an accessory after the fact,' the prosecutor replied. When his bail was set at $5,000, Jack whistled. He seemed very concerned at the amount and asked the judge to reduce it to a point that his parents might be able to meet and told the court that he and his fiancée had had blood tests taken and planned to be married that day. He was told that when he had council he could apply to have his bail lowered and Judge Sullivan assured him, 'They'll take very good care of you in the new city prison.' In fact, when Leo Kerouac heard about it, he exploded in anger: 'No Kerouac was ever involved in murder before!' and refused to help Jack at all. So in the Bronx jail he remained.

William Burroughs was also arrested as a material witness, but was released the next day on a $2,500 bail bond after his father, Mortimer, flew into town and paid it. Bill then returned with him to Saint Louis, promising to be back in New York a week later to be present at Lucien's arraignment.[29] Bill explained to the police that he did not tell them about the crime because he understood that Lucien was about to surrender to the authorities. In fact, Lucien did not give himself up until the next day.

On 24 August, a Manhattan Grand Jury returned a second-degree murder indictment against Lucien and the original homicide charge against him was dismissed.[30] While Jack was in jail, Allen wrote to him to report that he and Edie had visited Kammerer's old apartment on Morton Street and looked at his room. They found that all the pencilled graffiti on the walls had been covered over with white paint by the landlord, including the emblem where plaster had fallen away which read 'Lu-Dave'. It was as if Kammerer had never existed.

It is often thought that Jack and Edie's wedding was a marriage of convenience to get Jack out of jail but, as far back as October 1943, Edie had told her parents she was getting married. She and Jack had already taken the required blood tests before Lucien appeared at their apartment to announce his disposal of Kammerer. In fact there is evidence to suggest that 22 August had already been fixed as their wedding day. Certainly this is what Jack told the court and this would also explain the blood tests. Marriage now became imperative since Edie's mother would not advance her the money to pay his bail bond unless they were wed. So on 22 August 1944 Jack was released from the Bronx prison for one hour and taken by a detective to the Municipal Building where he and Edie were married. Céline Young was the maid of honour and two detectives acted as the witnesses, one of whom bought them several rounds of drinks afterwards before escorting Jack back to jail.

On 30 August, Jack was released on bail of $2,500 after General Sessions Judge John J Sullivan reduced his bond from $5,000.[31] A few days later, Jack and Edie travelled to her mother's home in Grosse Pointe, Michigan. Edie: 'We asked my mother for $100 to go back to Grosse Pointe and on the way we sat in the baggage car because it was so crowded on the trains. He sat on the casket of a soldier with a flag on it. He lived there with the dog, two cats, my mother, my sister and I, and every single day of his life there he would go into the bathroom and read Shakespeare and the Bible and we never could get in.'[32]

From the moment the chauffeur-driven limousine collected them at the station, Jack once more felt a terrible sense of social inferiority in Edie's luxurious surroundings which, coupled with his own pride and sense of superiority as a writer, made for difficult relations with the Grosse Pointe set. He dressed even more sloppily than usual, always had a few days' growth of beard upon his face, and sullenly announced that he was 'an artist' if any of Edie's friends dared to inquire what he did for a living. Jack was also painfully aware that, while his own mother had spent most of her life as a skiver in a shoe factory, Edie's mother owned the Ground Gripper Shoes Corporation. Jack had previously enjoyed himself in Grosse Pointe, but this time he had arrived at a social disadvantage, fresh from jail and in debt to Edie's mother.

Unintentionally fuelling Jack's inferiority complex, Mrs Parker called their neighbour, Dick Fruehauf, and arranged an easy job for Jack as a ball-bearings inspector at the Fruehauf Trailer Company in Detroit. Edie, for her part, worked as a riveter at Chrysler, doing her bit for the war effort. Working enabled Jack to pay Mrs Parker back the money she had loaned Edie to get him out of jail, but the way he had obtained the job did not help him feel at home among Edie's sports-car and yacht-owning friends.

Several of Edie's girlfriends, including one called Jane Beebe, saw him as a rather romantic figure and took him to their beds. Edie retaliated, first with Ewart Smith, whom she returned to in the summer of 1945, and Dick Sahlin, who was her boyfriend on and off from 1945 until 1948. Life was not all that bad: there were parties, picnics and Jack found a local redneck bar called The Rustic Cabin which suited his tastes. One time Edie's father, Walter – who was divorced from her mother, Charlotte – took them across Lake Saint Clair on his yacht and Jack sent his mother a postcard from Canada.

Not everyone was happy to see Jack and Edie marry. Her ex-fiancé for one. Almost forty years later, Henri Cru wrote to Edie: 'I was on a ship when you married Jack and was I surprised when I returned . . . my best friend had married my fiancée.'[33] The person most upset by this new development was Gabrielle. She was distraught at her Jack leaving home and tried her best to make him feel guilty. 'I'm still not able to realise you have left me for good,' she wrote, adding, 'It seems so strange not to have you around New York. Oh well, and after moving way out here too. Just to enjoy all this with you.'[34] She need not have worried for, within a month, Jack and Edie had parted and the prodigal son was soon back in the city, dividing his time between Manhattan and Ozone Park.

While Jack was away in Michigan, the wheels of the law were still slowly turning for Lucien. On 15 September 1944, wearing a light-brown suit, his hair plastered down with cream, and shifting nervously from one foot to another, Lucien appeared before Judge George L Donnellan in General Sessions Court. He gave the judge his most 'honourable' look and pleaded guilty of manslaughter in the first degree. Lucien's council, Kenneth M Spence, told the court how Kammerer had 'hounded' Carr from city to city for the last five years and said that 'the older man exercised a strong influence over the boy'. Assistant District Attorney Jacob Grumet told the court that Carr was 'emotionally unstable as a result of the improper advances' that Kammerer was alleged to have made and was, in addition, intoxicated when he pulled his boy-scout knife and stabbed Kammerer. The Judge set 6 October as the date for sentencing.[35] The usual term for manslaughter was five to twenty years but the sentence depended very much on an 'autobiography' that the probation officer had Lucien write, which was to be submitted to Judge Donellon.

Lucien remained detached, withdrawn and superior, which was the only way he knew how to deal with the situation, though clearly the events had had a sobering effect on him. On 21 September he wrote to Allen from The Tombs saying that he missed music more than anything else: 'Oh, to have my Brahms Sextet to teach me the meaning of tortured introspection.'

Céline Young wrote to Jack in Grosse Pointe a few days before the Judge was due to pass sentence, expressing her concern:

Had Lucien felt less pride in having Dave dog his footsteps he might have gotten rid of Kammerer before this and in a socially acceptable manner. The chief criticism of Lucien, and his probation officer observed this too, is that Lucien's values are all intellectual ones . . . If he persists in the idea that he has done a messianic service by ridding the world of Dave, he is becoming too presumptuous a judge. When he loses that pride in doing away with Dave, then I hope he is let out immediately. I know he is very remorseful at times . . . Mrs Carr has pictured (Dave) to me as a veritable Iago, who at every turn in Lucien's life has appeared and dissuaded him from the proper course, as she puts it, 'purely for love of evil' . . . His influence on Lucien, this past year at least, was definitely to be destroyed at all costs.[36]

Céline told Jack that she had not written to Lucien because they had been getting on badly and she had tried to call off their relationship before. Now that he was in jail and she was back at school, this seemed like a good time to try again. Jack, in his self-centred way, read this as an invitation to take Lucien's place.

Judge Donnellan sentenced Lucien to an indeterminate term in the Elmira Reformatory. He said, 'It is my opinion that this boy might not have been convicted of anything had he gone to trial [for second-degree murder]. Even if he had been convicted, I doubt if it would have been anything but manslaughter in the second degree.' The Assistant District Attorney Jacob Grumet had previously told the court that because the knife used in the killing had not been recovered by the police and there was no eyewitness, a second-degree murder conviction could not be obtained.

The Judge agreed but said, 'I feel this boy deserves some punishment, but in an institution where he will be under good medical care, not in a prison where he will be constantly associated with hardened criminals.' The court was told that Lucien had been drinking since he was fourteen and had frequently drunk to excess. He was described as unstable and having a split personality but that he could be 'turned into a useful citizen' under the supervision of psychiatrists and educators. By giving Lucien an indeterminate term, it meant that Lucien's release was entirely dependent upon his behaviour and rehabilitation. He was warned that, though he might be released within eighteen months if his behaviour warranted it, he would be shifted to Sing Sing to serve a possible fifteen-year sentence if he did not comply with reformatory regulations. Lucien was taken from City Prison on 9 October and eventually served two years at Elmira Reformatory.[37]

Lucien appears to have handled prison well and learnt to adapt to its restrictions. Allen Ginsberg wrote to his brother, Eugene Brooks:

I got a long letter from Carr, who is somewhat sobered up from a decadent philosophic nihilism that used to be his attitude: he is reflective, more guilt, I suppose, and beginning to transvalue his attitudes and surrender to mores. After a long discussion of *Jude the Obscure*, Tolstoi, and Spinoza, he concludes, 'As for prison life, I can't say I enjoy the discipline of steel bars, however it is a negative discipline and one can learn much under duress esp in a society where one's confreres are all in the same boat. Amazingly strong animal – man.'[38]

When Jack arrived back in New York from Grosse Pointe, he signed on the SS *Robert Treat Paine*, and went to stay with Allen in his small room at the Warren Hall Residential Club while waiting to ship out. He told his mother that he was going to the South Pacific and he might not be back until spring. Jack had always been attracted to Céline Young and, with Lucien out of the picture and Edie in Grosse Pointe, Jack had arrived back in New York expecting to have a big affair with her. Céline was beautiful. She had a French mother and spoke better French than he did. She flirted with him and they spent a night necking, but Céline was already seeing Hal Chase and Jack was rebuffed. He attempted to get Allen to act on his behalf and one night at the West End he asked him, 'Ginsberg, why don't you actively help me [seduce Céline]. Remember the joys of altruism!' Allen noted the conversation in his journal but Jack, who often read Allen's journals, later annotated it as 'inaccurate!'. In *Vanity of Duluoz* he describes 'trying to make her' as 'the rattiest thing of all my life' because he still regarded her as Lucien Carr's property. Scorned, he concludes, 'That woman was a menace anyway.'

One night at the West End with Allen and Céline, she made eyes at two sailors and a fight developed. Jack and the sailors went outside and Jack landed some good punches before having his head banged on the stone sidewalk. The bartender broke it up and the three of them went to Jack's tiny room on the sixth floor of Warren Hall. He wept with his head in Céline's lap all night. But that was as close as he got to intimacy with her, unless we believe what he wrote earlier, in November 1950, in *Visions of Cody*: 'I actually did that exact thing in 1944 . . . and was embedding my beautiful prick in the beautiful soft, wet between-legs slam of Cecily Wayne and coming with a bulging head.' *Vanity of Duluoz* is often inaccurate but in this instance it sounds the more accurate of the two.

The SS *Robert Treat Paine* left New York on 18 October. Because of the acute shortage of seamen, the union had allowed Jack to sign on as an acting able bodied seaman despite his lack of knowledge of ship operations. The bosun, however, soon noticed and began taunting him, calling him 'Pretty Boy', 'Baby Face' and 'Handsome'. Jack was no match for the burly bosun and, fearing that he would be raped on the high seas, Jack jumped ship in Norfolk, Virginia, their first port of call. Jack was always ashamed of the fact that as the result of this incident the Maritime Union blacklisted him for a year during wartime.

Back in New York, Jack once more stayed with Ginsberg until a vacant room became available in the building. It was during one of their all-night conversations, lying on the bed as dawn approached, that Ginsberg confessed for the first time to anyone that he was gay. He knew that Jack would not reject his confession, even if he wasn't interested in him sexually. Allen told him that he loved him and Jack let out a long groan, not of anger but of dismay at all the complications to which this was surely going to lead. Allen remained a virgin and did not have sex with Jack until about six months later.

Aside from Allen and Céline, Jack had told no one that he was back in the city because he was intending to hide himself away and write. Allen borrowed books from the Columbia library for him, and Jack's reading continued in the direction first suggested by Burroughs and Lucien Carr: WB Yeats, Aldous Huxley, Nietzsche, Arthur Rimbaud and Lautréamont. These last two seem to have been the main influence on him, particularly *Les Chants de Maldoror* by the self-styled Comte de Lautréamont, who died penniless in Paris in 1850 at the age of 24. A perfect role model for an aspiring writer.

Ensconced in his small garret-like room, lit only by flickering candlelight, Jack solemnly tied a piece of string around his arm as a tourniquet, cut himself, and wrote out a quotation from Nietzsche in his own blood: 'Art is the highest task and the proper metaphysical activity of this life.' Just to be sure he did not forget, he used a few remaining drops of blood to inscribe 'BLOOD' on a small calling card which he then carefully labelled THE BLOOD OF THE POET and tacked on the wall as a constant reminder to himself of his high-minded vocation. Other quotations, using more conventional implements, joined his bloody gallery, including a line from Rimbaud: 'When shall we go, over there by the shores and mountains, to salute the birth of new work, the new wisdom, the flight of tyrants, and of demons, the end of superstition, to adore . . . the first ones?' Kerouac: 'I had a ritual once of lighting a candle and writing by its light and blowing it out when I was done for the night . . . also kneeling and praying before starting – I got that from a French movie about George Frederick Handel.'[39] Finally, in order not to detract from the purity of his art, he burnt each day's work lest it be seen as anything other than the highest artistic expression with no conceivable practical or material use.

He worked hard, with no distractions except to see Ginsberg twice a week to get drunk and exchange his library books. Together they had long conversations about 'The New Vision' and introduced the word 'sacramental' into their speech as a description of their writing. An entry from Jack's journal for 16 November 1944 shows the state of mind that Jack was in at the time:

> Art so far has rationalised my errantry, my essential Prodigal Son behaviour. It has also been the victim of an ego craving fame and superiority. I have been using art as a societal step-ladder – which proves that my renunciation of society is yet incomplete. Self-Ultimacy I saw as the new vision – but I cravenly turned it to a use in a novel designed to gain me, the man of the world, respect, idolatry, sexual success, and every other thing that goes with it. Au revoir à l'art, then.[40]

Clearly not all of Jack's work was destroyed at the end of each day for we know that in November Ginsberg read two pieces by Jack: a short story called *God's Daughter* and a fragment from a work in progress called *I Bid You Love Me*.

Burroughs returned from Saint Louis in December and was appalled at the candles and dripping blood: 'My God, Jack, stop this nonsense and let's go out and have a drink.' Bill took Jack out to dinner and a movie. Appropriately they saw Jean Cocteau's first film, *The Blood of the Poet* (1930). Afterwards, according to *Vanity of Duluoz*, back at Bill's Riverside Drive apartment Bill offered him a hit of morphine as an antidote to all that romanticism. (This could not have happened as Burroughs did not get introduced to morphine until at least six months later. The book was written late in Jack's life when his legendary memory was clouded by alcohol.)

And so began what Jack called in *Vanity of Duluoz* 'a year of low, evil decadence'. Allen Ginsberg and he continued to evolve their concept of a New Vision and Self Ultimacy in art, which prefigured their later philosophy of the Beat Generation. Kerouac and William Burroughs began collaborating on a novel. The three main Beat Generation writers were now at work.

4 The 115th Street Commune

Towards the end of 1944 Seymour Wyse arrived back in town after his eighteen months in the Canadian Air Force and went to work at Greenwich Records, a jazz record shop on Greenwich Avenue at Seventh Avenue in Greenwich Village across from what was then the National Maritime Union building. It was owned by record producer Jerry Newman, who also owned the Esoteric record label. Allen Ginsberg: 'Jerry Newman was very central to the development of a lot of the literary articulations later on. He and Seymour Wyse taught Kerouac his early bop and jazz approach.'

Jerry Newman reportedly drank a lot and used to mix wormwood with his Pernod to make an approximation of absinthe. Allen Ginsberg: 'It was a combination that Kerouac and I had read about in Rimbaud's life, and Jerry Newman was the only guy that we knew who could get us drunk on wormwood, so it was like a big literary experience.'

In addition to his huge record collection, Jerry Newman had an enormous collection of tapes, not just of live jazz but dirty songs, jokes and radio clips. One that they all particularly enjoyed was a tape they called 'The Drunken Newscaster', in which an inebriated BBC announcer read the news and by a slip of the tongue said, 'Princess Margaret spent the weekend inside her parents at Balmoral Castle.'[1] Jack and Allen would often walk down to Greenwich Records and Seymour would play them the latest sides by Charlie Parker or Lester Young. Ginsberg:

Wyse and Kerouac used to riff together verbally and sing along with a lot of the records that Wyse played in the store. And according to Kerouac all that experience of the exhalation of breath, spirit, in bop music, was the determinant influence on his poetry style and prose, particularly in pieces like 'Brakeman on the Railroad', which is pretty early and in long passages of *Visions of Cody* and *Old Angel Midnight*. That was all determined by about 1944. His ear was determined by then. It wasn't yet reflected in *The Town and the City* – he didn't really parallel the long breath, variable noted line that was described as like a bird flight of Charlie Parker until he started his spontaneous writing style with *On the Road*.

Edie came to town in mid-December to try a reunion with Jack. She remembered how Jack and Seymour would walk on opposite sidewalks, scat singing and riffing with each other, late at night on the way home from a club. It was something that Jack continued to do always. David Amram has recalled how Jack riffed to his French horn in 1959, fifteen years later.

Seymour Wyse's brother was an editor on *Downbeat* magazine, so they always knew who would be playing where after hours. Jack and Edie, often with Joan Vollmer in tow, spent a lot of time together in the clubs in Harlem and through Jerry Newman they got to know many of the musicians. Once, Lester Young took Edie and Jack to Minton's Playhouse and turned Jack on to pot for the first time.[2] One permanent souvenir of Jack's involvement with early bebop is a Dizzy Gillespie track named after him. At a recording session by Dizzy, Jerry Newman taped a track based on the chord changes of 'Exactly Like You' and gave it the title 'Kerouac' in order not to pay publishing royalties. Gillespie didn't know Jack, but liked the sound of his name.

A few days after Bill Burroughs returned to the city from Saint Louis, Jack and Allen decided to pay him a formal visit. Burroughs was living on Riverside Drive at 60th Street in a small but rather grand apartment lent to him by a Harvard friend. Though Bill had been on the periphery of the scene during the spring and early summer of the previous year, they had usually seen the older man only with Lucien or David Kammerer and felt that they didn't really know him. They had already been influenced by his library, again mostly via Lucien, and thought that it was time to know him better. So it was a conscious decision on their part when they arranged to visit in order to 'investigate the state of Burroughs's soul'.

Allen Ginsberg:

Jack and I already had an understanding about the nature of our soul; it was a definite apprehension of our own mortality, in Jack's case somewhat in terms of Thomas Wolfe. It was a soul understanding that Jack and I had that everybody had to be tender towards each other because you were only in your own one place very briefly, in a sense ghosts because so transient, everybody lost in a dream world of their own making. Really a kind of farewell dream. We talked about that a lot and that really was the basis of the Beat Generation, the poignant kewpee-doll dearness of personages vanishing in time.

Jack and Allen were not suggesting that these thoughts were in any way unique. They assumed that any sensitive person would have an awareness of impending death and think somehow along these lines. However, these were not ideas to be found in most of the literature of that time. Allen Ginsberg said: 'Without the realisation of the mortal turn, most people's descriptions of things lack the emotional weight of realisation that what they're seeing is a vision in a dream; insubstantial as a dew drop in a bubble.'

Bill received them with great courtesy and with a certain formality. Lucien had already introduced them to several of Bill's favourite authors: Rimbaud, Lautréamont and Yeats – it was Bill's copy of WB Yeats's *A Vision* that Lucien had with him in court – but now Bill gave them the full benefit of his wide reading and experience. Burroughs lent them *Journey to the End of the Night* by LF Celine, a book which had an enormous impact on Jack. Celine was writing autobiographical prose which looked as if it was written as a stream of consciousness, particularly when he used his ellipsis (. . .) instead of conventional punctuation. (In fact Celine wrote a thousand words for every hundred that finished up in the final draft of his books, but it looked speedily written to Jack.) In addition, Celine used demotic French, French as it was literally spoken, rather than the language of the French Academy, and the realisation that this was possible came as another breakthrough for Jack.

Bill spoke at length about Count Korzybski's *Science and Sanity*, and the theory of general semantics. Allen and Lucien had already received his lecture but Jack had not. To be brief: Korzybski believed that most unhappiness sprang from people attempting to apply 'either/or' Aristotelian logic to situations where it is not applicable.[3] He thought that this orientation distorted reality and gave the example of a chair. Aristotelian logic assumes that something is either a chair or it is not, whereas there are many kinds of chairs, from armchairs to dentist's chairs, thrones to cinema seats, kitchen chairs to deck chairs; it all depends how you define the word 'chair'.

Korzybski proposed that there was no such thing as 'chairishness'. There is only chair one, chair two, chair three, etcetera. This he called 'indexing'. By extension he suggested that a neurotic might hate all mothers, a situation caused by a traumatic experience in his childhood. The neurotic thinks that all mothers are alike because they are called by the same word. If he learnt to index them – mother one, mother two, mother three – he would then see that all mothers were not identical to his own and some of his problem would be cured. In addition, his own mother is also no longer the same mother he had as a child, so Korzybski proposed mother 1910, mother 1911, and so on. Once he understood this, the neurotic's hatred was supposed to diminish considerably.

Bill lent them a pile of books: Cocteau, Blake, Kafka, Joyce and Celine. He discussed Vico's circular theory of history and showed them a volume of illustrations of the Mayan Codices. He explained how the Mayan priests used the calendar as a control system and how their language worked. As they left, their brains reeling with information, Bill presented Allen with an old, red, clothbound edition of Hart Crane's poems – Allen had not heard of him – and gave Jack a copy of Oswald Spengler's *The Decline of the West*, translated by Charles Francis Atkinson, a book which was to have a profound effect upon him.[4] 'Edify your mind, my boy,' said Bill, inscribing it to Jack.

Spengler was not new to Jack – he and Allen had read the introduction the previous summer – but, with Bill's recommendation, Jack read the book with greater attention. Allen Ginsberg:

> Spengler was really important because it influenced Jack's prose style. There is a passage in *Visions of Cody* in which he dedicates the book partially to Atkinson, for his ability to translate Spengler's great German Wagnerian prose, to translate his long sentences, for his comprehension of the concept of the *fallaheen* which becomes, in *Visions of Cody* and in *On the Road*, this great sentence, this aphorism 'the earth is an Indian thing'.

It was from Spengler that Jack received what would now be called an eco-consciousness: the idea that the earth was being plundered, that natural resources were being squandered. It gave him a sympathetic understanding of Third World cultures, of the people left out of so-called civilisation. It was on his first visit to Mexico, when he saw peasants tilling the earth, that he first understood what

Spengler was saying. He muses in *Desolation Angels* about the purpose of his job as a fire watcher, which was to make sure that the great forests of pine did not burn down, because the forest service intended sections to be logged and made into paper towels and toilet tissues. He became a great advocate of the simple life, holding the belief that the basics of food and shelter were sufficient, and he never did fully succumb to American consumerism.

Edie's reunion with Jack had lasted until Christmas but no longer, and she returned to Grosse Pointe in time for the New Year. A few days later, Jack was contacted by Edie's father to say that she had been seriously hurt in a car crash. She was with a group of friends when they ran into a tree. Several of them were killed and she was thrown through the windscreen and required 52 stitches. Jack quickly took the train to Grosse Pointe but, when he arrived, he saw a wreath hanging on the door, assumed that Edie was dead, and fainted away into the snow heaped by the door. In his French Catholic community a wreath could only mean death, though a Christmas holly wreath is such a common American tradition that it is surprising he had not encountered it before. When he regained consciousness, he found that Edie was alive and recovering. Jack stayed for about a week, then borrowed $100 from Mrs Parker to take himself to New Orleans where he was sure he could find a boat that would hire him. But the Maritime Union blacklist had reached Louisiana and Jack was unable to find a ship. A disgusted Mrs Parker wrote to Edie's sister: 'Jack went back this week. What a bad apple he is.'[5]

Jack returned to New York and wrote to Edie, again asking her to join him. She arrived in the city in late March but moved in with her grandmother. The reason for this was twofold: she was seeing Ewart Smith, known as 'Smitty' as well as Jack, and did not want to declare herself one way or the other. She dated both of them and on one occasion they all three dined together. During the meal Jack graciously offered to divorce Edie so that Smitty could marry her. It was all very civilised. The other reason was that her grandfather had died and left her $500 which she intended to use to move in with her old flatmate Joan Vollmer as soon as the estate money came through. This way she would regain her freedom.

Joan's daughter Julie was born in late June and, in early September 1944, Joan, accompanied by her baby, had returned to the city. She signed a lease under her married name of Mrs Paul Adams on apartment 35, 419 West 115th Street, between Amsterdam Avenue and Morningside Heights, adjoining the Columbia dormitories of

Hartley Hall and Livingstone Hall. She had six large rooms for $150 a month and planned to take in flatmates to share the rent. She began a light-hearted affair with John Kingsland, a seventeen-year-old Columbia student with an infectious sense of humour and worldly-wise attitude. He lived on campus in a small attic room at the top of Hastings Hall. He had been a regular visitor at Jack and Edie's apartment and had narrowly avoided being picked up by the police when they came looking for Jack as a material witness to the Kammerer killing.

Allen Ginsberg was also on the move: he gave up his room at Warren Hall – with Lucien no longer living there it had lost its main attraction – and moved to Livingstone Hall, next door to the apartment building where Joan lived.

For the three months beginning in December 1944, ever since Burroughs's salutary dousing of the candles, Jack and Bill spent a great deal of time with each other. This was the period of their only literary collaboration: a novel based upon the Lucien Carr-David Kammerer affair called *And the Hippos Were Boiled in Their Tanks*, a Burroughs title taken from the last line of a news broadcast, the provenance of which is disputed. It has been variously attributed to a report of a fire in the Saint Louis Zoo or the effects of bombing on a European zoo. Kerouac claimed, 'Burroughs and I were sitting in a bar one night and we heard a newscaster saying, ". . . and so the Egyptians attacked blah blah . . . and meanwhile there was a great fire in the zoo in London and the fire raced across the fields and the hippos were boiled in their tanks! Goodnight, everyone!" That's Bill, he noticed that. Because he notices them kind of things.'[6] Burroughs, however, disputed this and said that the fire was in a travelling circus.

The book was written in the hard-boiled style of James Cain and Dashiell Hammett, and Bill and Jack wrote alternate chapters. Apart from poems, jointly written with Allen Ginsberg, Lew Welch and Albert Saijo, this was Jack's only literary collaboration. Burroughs, however, found collaboration stimulating: his first text had been jointly written with Kells Elvins and he later wrote a number of books with Brion Gysin, once again alternating passages or chapters. Whose idea the collaboration was is hard to decide but it is most likely to have been Kerouac's as Burroughs had not yet identified himself as a writer. A note among Ginsberg's papers from this period reports a conversation with Bill:

Ginsberg: 'I heard you wrote a novel.'
Burroughs: 'It wasn't a novel. It's only twenty pages long. I

finished that and decided that I had said everything I have to say. I haven't written a word since.'

Burroughs was referring to the 1938 collaboration with Kells Elvins: 'Twilight's Last Gleamings'. In fact, during the period in 1940 when Bill was in Bellevue and the Payne Whitney Clinic, Bill's dream records and interview notes show that he was at least interested in writing and even had fantasies of becoming a great writer.

Jack did not find the collaboration very productive: when he presented his work for Burroughs's approval, Bill would only grunt or mutter a noncommittal 'It's alright' or 'Good'. However, by March of 1945, their novel was in the hands of an agent and being read by Simon and Schuster. They both appear to have had great expectations of its success. Jack described it as a 'portrait of the "lost" segment of our generation, hard-boiled, honest, and sensationally real'.[7] He was already thinking generationally. The rigour of their work schedule had amazed their friends. Duncan Purcell, a friend of Edie and Joan's and frequent visitor to the old 118th Street apartment, wrote to Edie: 'I suppose [Burroughs] should be commended for keeping Kerouac at work for a longer period than ever before in history.'

It was during this time that Jack and Allen, impressed by Joan's intelligence and thinking it might be amusing to do a little match making, had taken Bill Burroughs over to visit her. Ginsberg: 'Jack and I decided that Joan and Bill would make a great couple. They were a match for each other, equally tuned and equally witty and funny and intelligent, equally well-read, equally refined.'[8]

Jack and Allen were unaware that Bill was gay, but they were correct in thinking that Bill and Joan would get on well together and it was the beginning of the only serious relationship Burroughs ever had with a woman. Burroughs: 'We had all these, in retrospect, very deep conversations about very fundamental things. Her intuition was absolutely amazing.'

Psychoanalysis was extremely popular in New York in the late forties, and Bill Burroughs was being analysed by Doctor Federn, a Viennese member of the original Freud seminar who had been analysed by Freud himself. This was a subject that interested Jack very much for he was well aware that he had psychological problems. On 16 March 1945, Jack went to visit Burroughs and, in the course of a long conversation on this subject, Burroughs told him that he would never ever be able to get free from his mother unless he made a proper break of it instead of always running home every time he encountered a small problem in his life. Bill told him, 'Well, Jack, the trouble with you is that you're just tied to your mother's apron strings.' Burroughs saw that Jack was going in circles around his mother and that as he got older the circle would get smaller and smaller. This chilling prophecy disturbed Jack greatly and, after leaving Bill's place, he went immediately to Allen's room in Livingstone Hall to discuss it with him. He recognised that he was very closely tied to his mother and that he had internalised many of her ideas but had never thought of her as the source of his problems before.

Jack had recently been talking to a psychoanalyst who attributed his troubles to the death of his brother Gerard – but the death of his brother and his fixation on his mother were of course related. In fact, two days before the talk with Bill, he wrote a letter to his sister, Nin, in which he observed that his life appeared to operate in cycles: he jumped from his wife, Edie, to the Merchant Marine, returned back home to Memere, went back to Edie, back to sea, back home.

Jack told Nin:

> He says I don't want to be successful, that something destructive in me, in my subconscious mind, works against all that, which explains why I never finish important projects or why I don't stick to jobs or to anything for that matter. And what is most fantastic, that the reason I have this subconscious will to failure, a sort of death-wish, stems from something I did before I was five years old and which stamped upon me a neurotic and horrible feeling of *guilt*. Now all I remember about Gerard, for instance, is his slapping me on the face, despite all the stories Mom and Pop tell me of his kindness to me. The psychoanalyst figured that I hated Gerard and he hated me – as little brothers are very likely to do, since children that age are primitive and aggressive – and that I wished he were dead, *and he died*. So I felt that I had killed him, and ever since, mortified beyond repair, warped in my personality and will, I have been subconsciously punishing myself and failing at everything.[9]

Jack regarded his success on the football field and his freshman year at Columbia as occurring only because he was being directed by elders. It was not until he went off on his own that he was able to exercise his destructive will against himself, dropping out of

Columbia, getting thrown out of the Navy, destroying his marriage to Edie. Jack told his sister that, if the book that he and Burroughs had recently completed was published, he would use the money to get psychoanalysed.

A Freudian perspective is helpful in trying to understand Jack's problems and the self-destructive masochism which blighted his life. A combination of factors not only led him to replace Gerard as his mother's favourite, but to supplant his father also. With the aid of the Church and sympathetic friends, Gabrielle was able to express her grief more easily than Leo, who held his feelings back. Unable to share their grief, they grew apart from each other and Leo began drinking heavily. Distanced from her husband, Jack became not only the replacement for the favourite son but the 'man of the house' – a position abandoned, at least temporarily, by Leo.

As I said before, Gerard's death had a profound effect on four-year-old Jack, who was beset with fears. He was too frightened to remain in his own room and slept instead with his mother and sister. We do not know the sleeping arrangements at the Kerouac household, but it appears that they retained the traditional peasant system of the father sleeping alone and the children sleeping with the mother until they were old enough for their own rooms. Gerard's death returned both Jack and his sister to Gabrielle's bed. For Jack this represents what psychoanalysts would call Oedipal triumph in fantasy. We do not know the specific causes or events, but the death of the brother opened the way to the mother and led to a situation where Jack was unable to resolve his infantile Oedipus complex, resulting in a lifelong fixation upon his mother. This attachment, which in Freudian terms becomes a neurotic masochism, meant that he was unable to ever have a satisfactory, fulfilling relationship with a woman because he was never able to get beyond his initial childhood fixation on the mother.

It also produced unconscious guilt about his suppressed incestuous feelings towards his mother, which resulted in the self-destructive behaviour which was ultimately to end his life. Freud has described how this type of masochist acts in a self-destructive manner in order to be chastised by 'the great parental power of Destiny. In order to provoke punishment from this last representative of the parents, the masochist must do what is inexpedient, must act against his own interests, must ruin the prospects which open out to him in the real world and must, perhaps, destroy his own real existence.'[10] This self-destructive tendency dominated Jack's life, causing him – and others – endless pain.

According to Freud the incomplete repression of the Oedipus complex results in a weak superego, that part of the being which controls social behaviour, responsibility, ethics and morality – the internalised parental authority made your own. Jack's perverse attachment to his mother would therefore explain his later selfish behaviour towards his friends: his refusal to help Neal Cassady when he went to jail; his selfish exploitation of the hospitality of both Burroughs and Ginsberg; his jealousy and cruelty toward John Clellon Holmes; his unthinking exploitation of Aileen Lee, using her as the subject for *The Subterraneans*; and his intention to go against Lucien Carr's wishes and write a book about the death of David Kammerer. It can also be seen as the neurotic cause of his icy-hearted rejection of his own daughter in favour of his mother, which is otherwise almost impossible to comprehend.

Jack spent his life trying to blot out unconscious scenarios – memories or fantasies – of events that he did not want to have in his consciousness. Like Oedipus, who blinded himself when he realised that Jocasta was his mother, Jack went on blinders, drinking himself into a state of oblivion. There is no way of ever knowing if Memere abused him for her own sexual needs when he was little, but she did propose sex many years later when he was in his thirties. Whatever happened, it is certain that she had a psychic hold over him which stunted his normal growth and development and that this was something that she actively participated in. As Jack wrote in his 1957 poem 'Lucien Midnight': '. . . I'm/my mother's son and my mother/is the universe . . .'[11]

There is no way of proving any psychological speculation and it is only useful if it explains previously inexplicable events. However, there is enough evidence in Kerouac's own published dreams to indicate mother fixation and unconscious incest guilt: 'Night . . . My mother and I are arm in arm on the floor, I'm crying afraid to die, she's blissful and has one leg in pink sexually out between me and I'm thinking "Even on the verge of death women think of love and snaky affection" . . . Woman? Who's dreaming this?'[12]

His mother did everything in her power to discourage all of Jack's girlfriends, not just his first two wives. She wrote them hate letters, warning them to stay away from her son, and denigrated them in any way that she could. She had a resolute hold over Jack that he consciously went along with. Anna Freud wrote: 'It is extremely unlikely that a child will outgrow his or her Oedipal fantasies in situations where father or mother, either consciously or unconsciously, elevates the child to a substitute sexual partner or commits real acts of seduction with him.'[13] This was the case with Memere. She was his partner in life, the only woman he ever went on the road with, his closest friend, effectively his wife.

Jack's actual wife, Edie, was in the city at her grandmother's apartment for two months, seeing both Smitty and Jack, driving her grandmother mad with her indecision. She stayed on and off at Joan's apartment on 115th Street with Jack, usually for about a week at a time, but never properly moved in. In April she flew down to Norfolk, Virginia, in search of Smitty, but was unable to find him. Towards the end of May, she and her grandmother moved to the summer house in North Asbury Park, New Jersey, for the entire season. She seems to have chosen Smitty as the best bet, and remained estranged from Jack, not answering his letters, until late September when she returned to the city. The relationship with Smitty came to an end sometime during the summer, so she returned to New York unencumbered.

In the course of his investigations of the 8th Avenue lowlife, Bill Burroughs met the man who would provide the name for the Beat Generation: Herbert Huncke. He was described by Jack in *The Town and the City*: 'A small, dark, Arabic-looking man with an oval face and huge blue eyes that were lidded wearily always, with the huge lids of a mask. He moved about with the noiseless glide of an Arab, his expression always weary, indifferent, yet somehow astonished too, aware of everything. He had the look of a man who is sincerely miserable in the world.' Huncke was a Times Square hustler, a thief and a junkie. He came from a well-to-do family in Chicago, but his relations with his parents went downhill after a gentleman friend sent him flowers. He left home and after travelling around the country several times he washed up in New York City towards the end of 1939. He naturally gravitated to Times Square and 42nd Street.

Huncke had been introduced to drugs in Chicago but in New York he developed a considerable habit, which he financed by working as a male prostitute and petty thief. He moved in the seedy underworld of pimps and pushers, thieves and fences of stolen goods, hookers and junkies. Huncke had no morality at all, not even the loyalty found among thieves. He would steal from anyone, however poor. The cops on Times Square were so disgusted by him that they nicknamed him 'The Creep' and, from time to time, banned him altogether from the neighbourhood.

One of his acquaintances was a would-be hoodlum called Bob Brandenberg who worked as a soda-jerk in a drugstore near the

Columbia campus. Bill Burroughs often frequented the soda fountain and struck up an acquaintance with Brandenberg. Together they would discuss the life of crime, which on Brandenberg's side was largely imaginary, and which for Burroughs was a detached scientific investigation, similar to his field studies in anthropology at Harvard. One day Bill leant across the counter and asked Brandenberg if he could shift a machine gun and some morphine syrettes, the results of a heist by a friend of his. Brandenberg said he could and took him to his home on Henry Street beneath the Manhattan Bridge on the Lower East Side.

Burroughs later described the place as looking like a chop-suey joint. It was a railroad apartment with a bathtub in the kitchen, each room leading to the next. The living room was lit by a red bulb and had red lacquered tables, a black L-shaped couch and a large, coloured wheel painted on the ceiling in garish reds, yellows and pinks. The windows were draped to make perpetual night-time. Bob lived with Vickie Russell, a stunning, slim, six-foot-tall prostitute with shoulder-length mahogany hair. Like Edie, she was from a wealthy family in Grosse Pointe, Michigan, but she had walked off the bus from Detroit at the 50th Street bus terminal, straight into the arms of a pimp called Knuckles who somehow talked her into coming back to his place. He held her prisoner until she cooperated and then he broke her in with a couple of other 42nd Street whores. But she was too intelligent to remain under his control: she got herself a switchblade, wore a knuckleduster under her glove, and set up on her own.

Bob and Vickie's two flatmates were Herbert Huncke and Bozo, a fat, failed vaudeville performer with tattooed arms and hands who worked as an attendant at a Turkish baths and was what Quentin Crisp calls an effeminate homosexual. People came and went all night at the apartment, clomping up the metal stairs to stash a crudely jemmied coin box from a pay toilet or to hide a gun. The men used to enjoy watching Vickie take a perfumed bubble bath in the kitchen, her hair piled on top of her head, and a favourite occupation was to take speedballs and lie on the floor watching the coloured ceiling wheel until it spun round in their heads.

When Bill Burroughs arrived with Bob, he handed his snap-brim fedora, gloves and overcoat to Bozo, who, upon seeing a man of education and taste, murmured apologies about the state of the place. Huncke was immediately paranoid, thinking that Bill was a cop, but soon changed his attitude when he found that Bill was trying to unload morphine syrettes. Huncke and his friend, fellow junkie

Phil 'The Sailor' White, had been sitting around waiting for Bob to get home in order to borrow enough money from him to cash a morphine script.

Bill retained some of the syrettes in order to experiment with morphine himself. Needless to say, he soon wanted more and quickly went from the position of the man with drugs to sell, to wanting to buy them himself. His main collaborator on the drug investigations was Allen Ginsberg, who joined Bill in his experiments with the original syrettes, though he was never addicted – taking care never to use with any regularity so that a dependence pattern was not built up. On one visit to Riverside Drive, Ginsberg made notes on the procedure for taking morphine as well as a catalogue of Burroughs's library.

Shortly after this, Bill moved to a cheap furnished room above Riordan's Bar at 58th Street and 9th Avenue, near Columbus Circle, which in those days was a seedy neighbourhood at the edge of Hell's Kitchen. Bill had not been careful with his morphine experiment and had developed a $30-a-day habit, two caps three times a day.[14] He spent much of his time sitting in his black, soup-stained suit, staring at the ill-fitting window, which was caulked with rolled newspaper, watching the steam leak from the radiator. Jack often visited him there and he and Bill would sometimes sit and talk with Bill's old landlady, who had escaped from the Nazis to America, and she would tell them all about Europe in the thirties. It was while he was living above Riordan's Bar that Bill occasionally helped Phil 'The Sailor' White to roll drunks on the subway ('I was making the hole with the sailor . . .').

In his quest to experience the depths, Bill began a systematic investigation of the local lowlife, exploring all the bars between 60th and Times Square. It was Times Square that attracted him the most and, by the late summer, unless they were in the West End, Bill, Jack and Allen were to be found at the Angle Bar, on the east side of 8th Avenue at 43rd Street, which became their central meeting place. The Angle Bar was L-shaped – hence its name[15] – wrapping itself around the jeweller's on the corner with an entrance on to 43rd Street. This meant it was possible to walk in and slip out of the other entrance if you were being followed – a not unfamiliar occurrence for many of its clientele.

It was frequented by male hustlers from 42nd Street, car thieves, second-storey men, burglars trying to unload hot goods, dealers pushing grass, junkies looking to score, undercover narcs keeping tabs on everybody, unsuccessful cowboys from the rodeo at the new

Madison Square Garden up the avenue at 50th Street, and young
kids who arrived in town and didn't make it any further than the bus
terminal one block down the avenue. Burroughs, Kerouac and
Ginsberg sat in the booths, joined in the fall by Edie or Joan and
other friends, gradually getting to know the regulars, absorbing the
images and information for later use in their writing.

Even allowing for Burroughs's role as a teacher, it may seem
curious that the Beat Generation should have chosen Times Square
rather than Greenwich Village as their hangout, but this was wartime
and Times Square was the nation's vibrant, exciting nerve centre.
The legitimate theatres had all been forced into the side-streets by the
movie palaces and the sky above Manhattan was lit by crisscrossed
spotlights as Hollywood's latest offerings were premiered. It was an
area of enormous hotels, fashionable restaurants filled with famous
people, a wall of light and colour that was open 24 hours a day.
Heavy traffic thundered down the avenues and Broadway, cabs
honked and policemen blew their whistles, the latest news was spelt
out in giant moving letters by white light bulbs that raced around the
facade of the Times Building like a tickertape. The wide sidewalks
were packed with people: millionaire playboys and derelicts,
gum-chewing office boys and honeymooning couples. Gangsters and
racketeers with bodyguards eyed beautiful highly paid chorus girls
and dime-a-dance hostesses, the young stars of stage and screen
pushed past the ageing stars of burlesque. Pickpockets, male hustlers,
prostitutes, beggars, cops twirling night-sticks, boxers and panhan-
dlers thronged past the taxi dance halls, chop-suey places, cut-rate
haberdasheries, movie 'grind' houses showing continuous double-
feature programmes or burlesque shows, sideshows and penny
arcades.

There were fruit-juice stands, lunch counters, theatre-ticket agents,
cigar stores, newsagents. On the south side of the street was a Horn
and Hardart automat that was open all night and where a plate of
baked beans cost 20¢, and there was an all-night Bickfords in the
middle of the block on the north side with tables where hustlers and
junkies could sit with a cup of coffee for hours talking without being
bothered, watching the passing show. The Apollo Theater, next
door, showed foreign movies, and it was here that Jack and the
others saw Peter Lorre in *M*[16], Jean-Louis Barrault's mime in
Children of Paradise[17], Jean Cocteau's *The Blood of the Poet* and
Fritz Lang's *Metropolis*. Here Jack saw the great Jean Gabin series,
Port of Shadows[18] *La Bête Humaine*[19], *Pépé le Moko*[20], and *La Belle
Équipe*[21], which influenced him enormously. Allen Ginsberg:

'Hairy-wristed masculine Jean Gabin who was like a man's man, but a real man's man with tenderness and sensitivity like a Frenchman. It appealed to Kerouac's nature as distinct from the overly macho American with no delicacy.' Gabin's appeal to Jack was also to do with his own self-image, as explained by Ginsberg: 'He thought he was hairy. His notion of himself was hairy: black hairy genitals, dumb Kannuk thickness. He thought girls didn't like him because he was too thick – coarse. His body image was of coarseness, thickness and black unappetising hairiness.'[22] But here was Gabin, the sensitive hairy Frenchman, a perfect role model.

The day that Bill had warned Jack that he was tied to his mother's apron strings, 16 March, was significant for Allen Ginsberg, too. After discussing his problems with Bill, Jack had gone to see Allen and ask his opinion. They stayed up late, talking in Allen's room at Livingstone Hall. Allen's roommate, William Lancaster, retired to bed, but the door between their two rooms was open. Eventually they retired, sleeping chastely, Allen in pyjamas and Jack in his underwear. The next morning they were rudely awoken by the assistant dean. Allen had been having problems with his cleaning lady, an old Irish lady whom he suspected of being anti-Semitic. It was some time since she had cleaned his windows and, to illustrate this fact, Allen had graffitied the grime with the slogan 'Butler has no balls', a reference to Dean Butler, the head of Columbia. He also added an eye-catching 'Fuck the Jews', illustrated with the skull and crossbones icon he was to use throughout his life.

The graffiti had the desired effect of catching her eye but, rather than clean the window, the offended lady reported it. At 8 a.m., the assistant dean of student-faculty relationships, Dean Furman, came charging in and demanded that Allen wipe the offensive remarks from his window. Jack took one look, recognised Furman, who had been one of his coaches working with Lou Little, jumped out of bed, ran to William Lancaster's room, which was now unoccupied as William was already up and out, jumped into the still warm bed and pulled the covers up over his head. Later that day, Allen appeared before Assistant Dean McKnight, who told him that Kerouac was 'a lout and unwelcome on campus', charged Allen $2.35 for an overnight visitor, and suspended him from Columbia until such time as a psychiatrist determined that he was of fit mind to attend such an institution.

No longer permitted to stay at Livingstone Hall, Allen immediately transferred his few belongings to Joan's apartment on 115th Street.

The legendary commune was beginning to take shape. Jack was still living at his parents' house in Ozone Park, but he frequently came into the city to see Allen, Bill and his other friends. He and Allen were very close and spent a great deal of time together. They enjoyed walking, and explored the city, from Harlem to the downtown financial section. One favourite walk was across the wooden footway of the Brooklyn Bridge.

It was on one of these walks, in late summer, that he and Allen had sex for the first time, masturbating each other among the trucks at the end of Christopher Street, under the elevated West Side Highway – an area which twenty years later would become the centre of the New York gay scene. The incident probably meant little to Jack, whose main sexual attraction was to women, but to Allen it was the fulfilment of a long campaign. Allen wrote to Jack: 'You were right, I suppose, in keeping your distance. I was too intent on self-fulfilment, and rather crude about it, with all my harlequinade and conscious manipulation of your pity.'[23]

The summer came and the group dispersed: Céline Young stayed in New York, working at the *New York World-Telegram* before going to her parents' place in Pelham, New York, but her boyfriend, Hal Chase, returned to Denver, Colorado. Edie Parker Kerouac remained in North Asbury Park, not answering Jack's letters. Joan and Julie went to Loudonville, near Albany, to stay with her parents in the country. Bill Burroughs returned to Clayton, the wealthy suburb of Saint Louis where his parents lived, where he presumably kicked his habit. Allen Ginsberg decided to get seaman's papers and went for training at the US Maritime Service Training Centre at Sheepshead Bay in Brooklyn, where he wore a crisp white uniform, scrubbed the decks, learnt to handle a rifle and took watch on board ship. Whenever he had leave he would stay at 115th Street or return to his parents in Paterson, New Jersey, but he was effectively off the scene for three and a half months beginning 1 August. Jack spent part of the summer working as a busboy in a Jewish resort hotel in the Catskills, before leaving because they didn't leave him big enough tips.[24] Then in late August he managed to get his old script-reading job at Columbia Pictures back again and was back to making $50 to $60 a week.

With Allen away in Brooklyn, Jack's social life revolved around Hal Chase, the 'hero of the sunny west', a brilliant anthropology student at Columbia who was having an affair with both Céline Young and Bill Burroughs. Bill had returned to New York in mid-August and moved into a $4.50-a-night hotel on Park Avenue.

He and Jack had a reunion on 'Surrender Night' and, together with Jack Fitzgerald, Jack's old friend from Columbia, and his girlfriend Eileen, they joined in the celebrations in Times Square.

After Eileen and Jack went home, Jack and Bill stayed on, trying to pick up women. Bill wore a Panama hat, and something about his appearance seemed to put them off. Jack got the impression that, as Bill stared out over the sea of heads, he was seeing a 'sea of poppies, as far as the eye can reach.'[25] Bill returned to his hotel and Jack went to stay with Jack Fitzgerald and Eileen. He wrote to Allen: 'I went to Eileen's and layed her while Jack slumbered beside us.' Eileen was one of a number of girls that Jack had his eye on that summer.

Jack rarely instigated anything. He preferred the role of observer, going along with the action, taking notes. Sometimes this had its dangers, such as when Bill took him to a homosexual orgy. Jack was so filled with remorse that he cancelled an appointment to see Bill the next day. Allen was naturally interested in hearing all about it. Jack wrote to him:

Since then, I've been facing my nature full in the face and the result is a purge . . . Remember that the earlier part of my life has always been spent in an atmosphere vigorously and directly opposed to this sort of atmosphere. It automatically repels me, thereby causing a great deal of remorse, and disgust . . . As to the physical aspects, which as you know, disgust me consciously, I cannot be too sure . . . whatever's in my subconscious is there.[26]

However, shortly afterwards, when Allen was on leave from Sheepshead Bay, he and Jack and Bill went together to the Everard Baths at 28 West 28th Street, a notorious gay hangout, with tiny bedrooms, a massage parlour, sauna and steam rooms and a swimming pool. Jack disappeared into the Turkish baths with a group of French sailors who gave him a blow job. Allen: 'I think he just dug the idea of a bunch of French sailors. He was quite sociable and happy . . . he was very gay about it.'[27]

Mostly, however, Jack concentrated his attentions on Eileen, utterly disregarding any effect this might have upon his friendship with Jack Fitzgerald. He also turned his attention to Céline Young, who was having second thoughts about her relationship with Hal Chase. Hal thought of Jack as a close friend and would have regarded Jack's behaviour as betrayal were he not so boastful of his own exploits as a 'cocksman'. Jack had less luck with Céline, who informed Jack that she was interested in him only as a friend and not as a lover, something that he complained to Ginsberg about at length in his letters. One thing he never mentions, and presumably did not think of, was that Céline was Edie's best friend and probably thought it would be a betrayal to have sex with him until Edie finally decided she wanted a divorce.

When Céline saw Jack at the beginning of September his job with Columbia Pictures had obviously filled him with enthusiasm for the motion-picture industry. He told her that he had been back to Columbia College to find out what credits he had as he was planning to go to college in California, 'because it's near Hollywood'. He began telling Céline how he expected to meet his ideal woman there, when Céline broke in and said, 'For God sakes, Jack, do you think you'll ever find another woman who understands you as well as Edie? You're a pretty moody guy and you'll never find another girl who can put up with them the way Edie can.' Céline told Edie: 'He sat up and looked surprised, as though a light had just dawned. You know, Edie, I think that was the first time that idea has ever occurred to him.'[28]

Hal Chase returned from his summer vacation in Denver and decided that he no longer wanted to live on campus. In late September he moved into Joan's apartment as a temporary measure until he found his own place. Though Hal was still keen, he and Céline appeared to be splitting up, so Jack renewed his attentions in her direction while, at the same time, becoming very close with Hal. Hal was annoyed by Jack's interference in his love life, both with Céline and his other girlfriends, and they discussed the matter.

Jack told him that he could have sex with a woman only if one of his friends had made love to her first. This was why he was so enraptured with Céline, who had been with two of the men he most admired: Lucien and Hal. It can be seen as a thread running through his life: the more he admired the man, the more likely he was to go after their women. Of his wives, Edie had previously been Henri Cru's girlfriend, Joan Haverty had been Cannastra's girl and Stella had the distinction of actually being Sebastian Sampas's sister. Of his serious girlfriends, they all appear to have been previously attached to one of Jack's friends: most significantly, Carolyn Cassady. All of this suggests the playing out of a form of homoerotic replacement of the desired male figure with the socially acceptable woman. Jack also discussed his bisexuality with Hal Chase, claiming that he was gathering material for his future writing. Jack recognised that he had sexual problems but didn't know what to do about them.

Jack's relationships with women were fraught with difficulty. Though he had strong sexual desires and wrote that women existed for him only as sexual playthings, he rarely made an effort to show his interest. There are many reports that women had to virtually rape him before he had the self-confidence to accept that they were genuinely interested in him. Perhaps the result of his self-image as thick and unattractive. In fact, Jack seems to have suffered from a form of what is now called social phobia, which can range from simple shyness to crippling paranoia. It is the third most common psychiatric problem in the Western world, after depression and alcohol problems, both of which are often linked with social phobia.

Doctor David Veale, consultant psychiatrist at Grovelands Priory Hospital in London says, 'When someone with social phobia goes to a party, they become so acutely self-conscious that they can't stop monitoring themselves. They want to be witty and intelligent but they are thinking about how others are responding ... They're lost in an inner world of negative self-evaluation and are no longer engaged in what's going on around them.'[29] Many of Jack's friends have commented that when sober he was shy, withdrawn and acutely self-conscious but that alcohol transformed him into a raging, garrulous, foolhardy drunk. It was, of course, something he was aware of and describes in his books.

Bill Burroughs rented a small, $15-a-week apartment on Henry Street, close to Bozo, Bob and Huncke's den of thieves, which he intended to use as a place to write. He stayed there occasionally but did not want to live that far downtown. He was a frequent visitor to 115th Street and got on with everybody there and so it seemed like a good idea for him to live there. Bill liked his privacy and was not normally the sort of person to share an apartment, but he would have his own room and, sometime in late September, he moved in.

Bill was engaged in hypnotherapy with Doctor Waldberg – referred to him by Doctor Federn, who felt that traditional Freudian methods were not achieving anything with a patient who had read so extensively on the subject that he was making his own interpretations. Doctor Waldberg placed his patients in a hypnotic trance in order to reach different layers of personality. The layers he discovered in Bill appear to have sprung straight from central casting: the fussy Saint Louis aristocrat; the English governess, always rapping people on the knuckles; the uptight Englishman; Old Luke, sittin' on his front porch in the bayou, watching the catfish swim lazily by, sometimes stirring himself enough to raise his shotgun from his knees to shoot a crow; the old red-faced Southern sheriff; and, beneath it all, the silent Chinese, sitting motionless, starving, by the banks of the Yangtse, completely *there*, with no pretences.

As soon as he moved in, Bill began to psychoanalyse Jack and Allen: fifty minutes each of free-association, lying on the couch, with Bill sitting in a straight-backed chair like Doctor Freud. Jack was at the flat three or four times a week for sessions and Allen did it whenever he had leave from Merchant Marine training. Allen wrote in his journal: 'Psychoanalysis is for me only an escape from decision. I must be serious in it. I am beginning to suspect Bill. Joan said, "Of course there are certain things he can't do. I don't suppose he could really analyse anyone's sex problems. He'd be too discomfited (or uneasy or embarrassed)." ' The analysis clearly did not go very deep because, even during analysis, Allen did not reveal to Bill that he was homosexual.

The sessions were of great interest, however, as everyone likes to talk about themselves. Bill also introduced them to 'routines': psychological parlour games in which they would all take on character roles. Ginsberg would become the 'well-groomed Hungarian' trying to sell worthless paintings to naive American tourists in post-war Europe: 'Beautiful Hungarian paintings from the 19th century, possessions of my family which, when I was forced to flee to exile, I brought with me here to Paris.' Burroughs would dress up in drag, with an old dress and a lady's hat, and come on like an old lesbian baroness whose job was to act as Ginsberg's shill, and lure unsuspecting American tourists into his apartment. Jack, of course, played the wide-eyed, slack-jawed American bumpkin, wearing a straw hat borrowed from his father, in Paris for the first time and amazed by European civilisation and sophistication.[30]

> Burroughs: 'I was playing an Edith Sitwell part. I got in drag and looked like some sinister old lesbian.'
> Ginsberg: 'You remember you had to bring the foolish, rich, young, ruddy-cheeked American to my art gallery?'
> Burroughs: 'Oh yes. You know Americans, they are so full of money. It is our duty to relieve them of a little bit, you know.'
> Ginsberg: 'He had a straw hat. He was an American named Kerouac. He was a nice boy, very nice boy. A writer.'[31]

5 Notes from Underground

n mid-September 1945, with the summer vacation coming to an end, Edie contacted Joan and asked if she could rent a room in her apartment at 115th Street. Jack was still dividing his time between Joan's apartment and his parents in Ozone Park, so when Edie arrived in New York at the beginning of October he found it convenient to simply slide into her bed once more. It is unclear whether Edie was officially living at Joan's, since her mother thoroughly disapproved: 'Shun that crowd as you would poison. They will degrade and cheapen you . . .'[1]

By living in close proximity to Bozo and Bob Brandenberg's apartment, Bill Burroughs had become friendly with Herbert Huncke. When Bill moved into 115th Street, he kept on his small Henry Street apartment, thinking he might still use it if he wanted privacy or to get away and write. Inevitably, Herbert Huncke moved in and Bill found himself inadvertently supporting him. Huncke knew a great deal about the criminal underworld and his account of his experiences interested Bill sufficiently for Bill to feel that this was an equal exchange, at least for a while. One afternoon in early October 1945, they were drinking coffee in Bickfords on 42nd Street when Bill invited Huncke to come back to the 115th Street apartment and meet his flatmates.

Huncke was attracted by the people at 115th Street, particularly Joan, and made strenuous efforts to ingratiate himself with them by telling them stories about the strange characters he had known. He began to spend a lot of time in the apartment, accurately predicting that middle-class kids would not throw him out even when he blatantly stole from them. He had them numbered as marks and, with the exception of Burroughs, they were. Huncke: 'I used to visit there constantly. Sometimes I'd stay overnight. Sometimes I'd cut out, stoned out of my gourd, at the crack of dawn, walk downtown, down to 42nd Street.'[2]

Jack: 'Then there was Herbert Huncke ... he's the greatest storyteller I've ever known. I don't like his ideas about mugging and all that stuff, but he doesn't do the mugging himself. He's just a little guy.'[3]

Herbert Huncke: 'I guess I represented the underworld. They were curious about the underworld and I was certainly much closer to the underworld than they were at that point, such as it was. Well, one thing they all had in common is that they wanted to write. They talked about writing and they knew of writers and so forth. They were very thoroughly trained academically.'[4]

Huncke reciprocated by introducing them to his friends. Of these, the one with the most drawbacks to his personality was Phil 'The Sailor' White, with whom Bill was already friendly. He and Bill had a shared need to find morphine and Bill briefly became White's accomplice as a lush-worker, picking the pockets of drunks on the subway. Months passed, and Huncke stretched the tolerance of the 115th Street roommates to their limit. By the spring of 1946, Phil and Huncke were using the apartment to stash stolen goods before mysteriously spiriting them away again. A chewing-gum machine would be dragged in and broken open, so there was free gum for weeks. They sometimes borrowed Bill's blackjack or his gun, and other times hid their own 'piece' there. Phil and Huncke worked together as a team, robbing stores and breaking into vehicles.

Years later, Kerouac described Phil as 'The Mad Killer of Times Square' and wrote that he had walked into a liquor store and shot the proprietor dead. The newspaper headline in the *New York Journal-American* actually read: 'Mad Dog Noonday Killer'. What happened was that Phil got very high on goofballs – a barbiturate marketed as Nembutal – and borrowed Bill Burroughs's .32 to hold up a store. He asked Huncke if he was coming but Huncke, seeing the deranged state Phil was in, declined to accompany him. He went to a furriers and pulled his gun. When the storeowner began to yell for help, White murdered him in cold blood. He and Huncke dismantled Bill's gun and dropped bits of it all over Brooklyn so that Bill would not be connected to the killing. Some months later, Phil White hung himself in The Tombs while awaiting transfer to another jail after squealing on a pusher. White knew that, as an informer, he would be beaten, tortured and possibly even killed when he reached a regular jail. Rather than face years of fear and violence he chose instead to kill himself.

Huncke also introduced them to Bill Garver, known as Old Bill Gains in *Desolation Angels* and *Tristessa* and simply as Gaines in

Book of Dreams. Jack got to know him best in Mexico City, when they both lived in Bill Burroughs's building, but it was in 1945 that they were first acquainted. William Maynard Garver was from Philadelphia. Like Huncke, he came from a well-to-do family. He was a tall, thin, distinguished-looking man with a gaunt face, sunken eyes, balding greying hair and a very elegant manner of speaking. He was thrown out of Annapolis Military Academy for drunkenness – 'It's for the good of the service' – and was paid $100 a month by his banker father to stay away from the family, apparently as the result of some reprehensible occurrence in his youth. Unfortunately this was not quite enough to maintain his drug habit, so he supplemented it by stealing overcoats. Huncke met him when he was allocated a bed next to him in the dormitory of Riker's Island jail (Huncke was doing a three-month stretch for robbery) and suggested that he look up Burroughs when he got out.

Garver lived at the Hotel Globe, a theatrical hotel at 42nd Street and 8th Avenue, in a $10-a-week room on the fifth floor and scored his smack around the corner at Bickfords and the Horn and Hardart. His was a specialised profession: he would take overcoats off the coat rack in restaurants and coffee shops and journey to the furthest parts of the city to pawn them. He could get $10 to $14 for a good $100 overcoat. Allen Ginsberg was particularly interested in him and would go and watch him operate. Allen sold Garver's pawn tickets to some of the students at Columbia, and even peddled one to his own unsuspecting brother, Eugene the lawyer. When Garver's father died, he came into $400 a month and moved immediately to Mexico City where such an income enabled him to maintain his habit in comfort.

To the flatmates at 115th Street, these were interesting glamorous people whose shortcomings they preferred to overlook. The victims of their crimes were not considered. When Huncke and Phil White were on board ship, they stole all the morphine syrettes from the lifeboat medical supplies and shot them up. Had the ship been torpedoed and injured men taken to the lifeboats, there would have been no morphine to ease their pain. Similarly, Garver had worked as a medical orderly in a mental hospital during the war and substituted milk sugar for the morphine given to suffering patients. He saw nothing wrong in causing them pain: 'After all, they're crazy anyway. They don't know the difference.'[5] Even Ginsberg who, only one year earlier had wanted to be a labour lawyer dedicated to helping the working class, was now aiding and abetting a thief who lived as a parasite, stealing the hard-earned overcoats of working people.

Through Huncke they naturally also got to know Vickie Russell, whom Jack called Vicki in *Visions of Cody* and Ricki in *Book of Dreams*. Jack was very attracted to her and they went to bed within hours of their first meeting. It was Vickie who introduced Benzedrine into 115th Street. She showed them how to unscrew the top of a nasal inhaler and take out the six white strips of paper soaked in Benzedrine and menthol and roll them into small balls. The idea was to swallow one of these, usually with coffee or juice to disguise the unpleasant taste. The effect came on very rapidly and would last for eight hours. It was very strong. The first time Jack took it Vickie gave him an overdose and he claimed to have lost thirty pounds in three days.[6]

Jack gives an account of how he and Vickie first met, in the tape section of *Visions of Cody*: a literal transcription of stoned conversations with Neal Cassady. Kerouac and Bill Burroughs were sitting on a park bench at 103rd Street and Broadway discussing how to score some junk. They took the subway downtown and went to Henry Street to see if Phil or Huncke were in. The door was opened by Vickie. She told Bill that no one was there except her, then turned her attention to Jack. Jack: 'Then she looked at me and dug *me*, physically, you know, because as I say, the next 48 hours I fucked her solid . . . "Come *in*!" she says . . .'

They all three took a cab to Times Square and on the way she gave them each a Benzedrine tube and told them to break them open and eat it. Three hours later, back at Bill's room on Henry Street she gave them two more. (Even Huncke would not normally use more than four strips – to take twelve on your first time was an enormous dose.) By this time Jack was so high he could hear a buzzing in his head. Vickie just laughed and told him, 'You're buzzing, man!' For the next 24 hours Jack, Vickie and Bill sat and talked. She told them about her $100 Johns – she had a small, select group of clients which meant that she didn't have to go out on the streets – and told them what each of the Johns liked to do. Bill went back uptown and Jack and Vickie took more Benzedrine before spending the next 24 hours in bed.

Vickie became very fond of Jack and at one point had three large photographs of men on her wall, captioned THE HEAD, THE HAND and THE HEART. Vickie liked to move in Harlem jazz circles and pianist George Handy was 'The Hand'. Charlie Parker was 'The Head' and Jack, standing looking romantic in his sailor's uniform, was 'The Heart'.

Back at 115th Street there were varied reactions to Benzedrine.

Allen Ginsberg found that it turned his writing into great spiderswebs of annotations and emendations which were virtually unintelligible. After trying it a few times he gave it up. Burroughs did not enjoy the effects but Joan developed a great partiality for it and soon graduated to a tube a day, speeding away as she tended to her little girl. Jack also liked it and found that it helped his writing. Large sections of *The Town and the City* were written on amphetamine and he continued to use it for writing purposes for the rest of his life.

Jack was no longer working for Columbia Pictures and was being supported by Edie, who had a job with an agency that supplied cigarette girls to the '21', Zanzibar and the Kit Kat clubs on Times Square. Since she was in work, Edie's mother did not feel so obliged to send her money, so she and Jack were trying to live off her meagre earnings. She sometimes managed to bring home steaks from the club, but often she and Jack were so poor that they would have to cruise the Fifth Avenue bars to eat the free food set out on the counters.

A poor diet, combined with too much amphetamine, caused a severe decline in Jack's health. Once, Jack was so pale that Vickie refused to go on the subway with him until she had applied pancake make-up to his face. His parents, of course, blamed Allen and Bill for leading him into bad ways and kept up a stream of invective against them both, despite the fact that Jack was four years older than Ginsberg. Jack knew what he was doing to himself, but he was so stimulated by the drug and by the conversations that everyone had on speed that he continued to use it. Most evenings they would sprawl on the beds and talk. There was much to talk about: the bombing of London, the dropping of the A-bombs on Hiroshima and Nagasaki, the Nazi concentration camps. The world was a very confusing place: all the old values appeared to have been swept away by the war but no new ones had yet been proposed to replace them.

One evening as they were all reclining on the huge double bed in Joan's room, chattering in a Benzedrine high, Joan's husband, Paul Adams, walked in fresh from fighting in Germany. He was shocked and appalled. 'Is this what I fought for?' he asked.

'Oh, why don't you get down from your character heights,' Joan snapped. Adams stamped out, disgusted at the scene.

To Jack, this was all material for his writing. His antennae were out, his eyes constantly roving. To Herbert Huncke he looked green because he was always looking around in amazement, like a farmboy fresh in the city, but it was all registering in his prodigious memory, waiting to be alchemised into the Duluoz Legend. Jack:

I was determined to be a 'great writer', in quotes, like Thomas Wolfe, see. Allen was always reading and writing poetry, Burroughs read a lot and walked around looking at things. The influence we exerted on one another has been written about over and over again. We were just three interested characters, in the interesting big city of New York, around campuses, libraries, cafeterias.[7]

In November 1945, there was an evening which became known among the group as 'The Night of the Wolfeans and the Non-Wolfeans'. This grew out of the charades and role-playing they had done together, and was a further definition of their individual characters. Thomas Wolfe was Kerouac's ideal writer and the Wolfean view of America was dear to Kerouac's heart. The nature of America was the subject of an argument between Wolfe and F Scott Fitzgerald at the Ritz Bar in Paris. Wolfe wrote afterwards: 'I said we were a homesick people, and belonged to the earth and land we came from as much or more than any country I knew about – he said we were not, that we were not a country, that he had no feeling for the land he came from.'[8] This was a neat summary of the divisions at 115th Street, which saw Kerouac and Hal Chase as the wide-eyed, innocent, insular, unsophisticated Americans, and Burroughs, Ginsberg and Joan as the urbane, sophisticated internationalists. Their homosexuality, cynicism and irony was un-American seen from this angle. Jack was firmly in the Wolfean camp. Wolfe's viewpoint became Jack's viewpoint. Wolfe wrote:

My conviction is that a native has the whole consciousness of his people and nation in him: that he knows everything about it, every sight, sound and memory of the people . . . it is the ten million seconds and moments of your life – the shapes you see, the sounds you hear, the food you eat, the colour and texture of the earth you live in.[9]

Jack took it as his credo and never deviated from it.

Wolfe wrote thinly veiled autobiography and, like Kerouac, his friends and acquaintances were easily identified in his books, leading to several libel actions, one of which cost him $5,000 in an out-of-court settlement (it was for this reason that Kerouac changed the names of his friends in his books). Wolfe also wrote quickly, with little revision, to catch the flavour, the first taste of experience. Writing in his daily journal about a drive from Denver to Boulder to

Portland in 1938, Wolfe wrote: 'The whole thing smacked down with the blinding speed and the variety of the trip . . . not taking too much time and putting it down from the beginning like a spool, unwinding at great speed.' Here we have the genesis of *On the Road*, of spontaneous prose, of the whole Kerouac take on the world. Read Thomas Wolfe and you know Kerouac.

'The Night of the Wolfeans' explored more than the obvious archetypes. They were all high on Benzedrine, sprawling on two beds – Hal Chase and Allen in one and Jack and Burroughs in the other. There was a definite sexual tension in the air – at least Ginsberg thought there was and remembered it almost twenty years later in his *Indian Journals*. Allen had fantasised about Chase, as he had about Jack and Lucien, and now, lying next to Chase on the bed, he was desperate for love and attention: 'That night in bed with Hal and Bill and Jack flirting on the 115th Street floor – on Benzedrine – talking about transparent waterfalls of cellophane – pure synthetic abstraction making me groan with desire to be kissed on the mouth . . .' For Allen, it seemed that they were telling him that to be a non-Wolfean was to be homosexual and Jewish, neither of which he could do much about.

The Wolfean and non-Wolfean polarity took the original Beats in two directions: Jack only ever felt really at home in America, whereas Ginsberg and Burroughs were world citizens. Jack's later pro-Americanism fitted well with the Cold War fifties, but he had no place in the psychedelic sixties, except late in the decade when the counterculture moved toward the land, communes and the beginnings of eco-consciousness. Then Jack's belief in the simple life, his opposition to consumer culture, his delight in the outdoor life, his religiosity and interest in Eastern mysticism were all seen as prescient. At its worst, Jack's Wolfean direction led to sentimentality about America and to a glorification of laissez-faire, do-your-own-thing anarchy, in most cases motivated by egotism and selfishness, which was perhaps best exemplified by Ken Kesey's Merry Pranksters, who were apolitical, ruthless in their attempts to blow everyone's minds with LSD, and equipped with a high-school notion of the meaning of freedom. Their freedom had little to do with responsibility; it was more the philosophy of the adolescent boy gang, an eternal puerile excitement. The Pranksters even named themselves after American comic-book heroes. It was very American and ultimately tended towards the right. Jack was horrified when he met them and could not see the connection between himself and their ideas.

The non-Wolfeans went in the direction of political international-ism: they were world travellers, anti-war and critical of America. Burroughs lived in self-imposed exile for 25 years writing serious – though sometimes slightly wacky – papers on how to smash the state and dismantle the control system. Ginsberg became a good-will ambassador, travelling the planet with a message of free love, meditation, homosexual law reform, and the legalisation of pot – an anti-authoritarian, anti-war, anti-nuclear-weapons position that became more and more international as he grew older.

In the sixties the polarity was exemplified by the difference in attitude towards LSD: Kesey's American mass-production, spike-everybody approach – a sort of Fordism of the psychedelic era – versus Tim Leary's east-coast scientific, carefully evaluated, spiritual approach, which smacked of elitism and the academy. Both strands of thought coexist in present youth culture, but maybe the non-Wolfeans presently have the upper hand.

Edie stayed with Jack on and off from Halloween until Christmas, but she was not having what she regarded as a good time because her lifestyle contrasted so sharply with that of the others. The 115th Street commune was deeply into drugs: Burroughs into morphine and the others taking Benzedrine. Jack was not only taking speed but drinking, and one night Hal Chase found him passed out in a bar unconscious from a mixture of Nembutals and alcohol, a potentially fatal mixture. Edie would get back from her stint as a cigarette girl and find them all too out of it to party. Edie also liked to eat and there was never enough food in the house. The lifestyle was not good for her health and when her teeth began to be affected by the amphetamine she called it quits and returned to Grosse Pointe. Years later, Jack told Al Aronowitz for the *New York Post*: 'The first wife was a rich girl from Grosse Pointe, Michigan, and we didn't have any money or anything. We kept eating mayonnaise sandwiches. "Well," I said, "go back to your family and eat good." '

Jack had ingenuously taken most of his friends home to meet his parents, with varying degrees of success. One night Huncke was in need of a place to sleep so he accompanied Jack on the long subway trip out to Ozone Park. When they arrived, Jack took one look at the expression on his mother's face, and Huncke found himself taking the long subway trip all the way back to the city. Hal Chase was a fine blue-eyed American boy so the Kerouacs liked him and made him welcome. They naturally disapproved of Burroughs, sensing his contempt of them, and were immediately suspicious of

Allen because he was Jewish. Jack's parents did little to disguise their anti-Semitism. Leo was small-minded, small-town, and frightened of Jack's big-city friends. Gabrielle was canny, superstitious and had the caution and conservativism of a peasant. People like Burroughs and Ginsberg worried her because, unlike Jack's girlfriends, they were an influence on her son that she was unable to counter.

In the autumn of 1945, Leo Kerouac fell terminally ill with cancer of the spleen. As Gabrielle was working, Jack began to spend more and more time in Queens to look after him. Leo's loudmouth, inarticulate rage at the world around him had run its full course, and he was now in a permanent black depression, convinced that his life had been worthless and that he had achieved nothing. In Gerald Nicosia's interview with Hal Chase for his book *Memory Babe*, Chase said Leo told him he knew Jack would become a no-good bum from the moment he had run gleefully up to him, aged four, to announce that Gerard was dead. Gabrielle saw her marriage to Leo as a failure and now pinned all her hopes on her Jack. Burroughs reported a chilling exchange when he visited Ozone Park with Jack in November 1945. Leo was in bed, in so much pain that he was hardly able to speak, while Gabrielle stuck out her tongue at him saying, 'Pretty soon I'm going to be saying ya ya ya to you and you'll be six feet underground.'[10]

Jack was living a double life: the Bohemian, intellectual, degenerate life of 115th Street and the miserable peasant existence out in Queens. He dealt with it by increasing his drinking and taking more drugs. In fact, Jack was turning into a speed-freak, as they were known in the sixties, and his health began to suffer. His complexion was sickly pale. He was run-down, thin, exhausted and tired, but so wired that he couldn't sleep. In the week before Christmas 1945, Jack, Allen and Hal Chase spent five days and nights up on Benzedrine, wandering at random all over the city, talking, talking, talking, rarely eating. Finally Allen and Hal were weak with exhaustion but Jack insisted on one last walk across the Brooklyn Bridge, in honour of Hart Crane's magnificent poem, 'The Bridge'. They got into an altercation with two policemen, which was not helped by Jack's excited yelling, but they extricated themselves and accomplished their aim. Heading back, Ginsberg was now too weak to continue, so Jack hoisted him up on to his shoulders and carried him a mile to the Seventh Avenue subway stop while Allen sang aloud Bach's *Toccata and Fugue in D Minor*. By the time they reached the subway, Allen and Hal's second wind had kicked in and they headed off to hear some music. However, this final amphetamine-induced burst of energy left Jack weak and powerless and he headed back to 115th Street on the verge of collapse. Next day he was confined to Queens Veterans Administration Hospital with thrombophlebitis: blood clotting in his legs caused by overexertion and excessive use of amphetamine. If a clot had travelled to his brain, he would have died. He lay for several weeks in a hospital bed, his legs wrapped in a cold compress, anxious and depressed. Allen wrote him a poem, 'To Kerouac in the Hospital', which did little to cheer him up: 'Death can make us gentle, pain will kill/The animal, subdue the aggressive/Pride of the disastrous healthy will.'[11]

While in the hospital Jack read Dostoyevsky's *The Brothers Karamazov* and *Nightwood* by Djuna Barnes. *The Brothers* took him seven months to read altogether: he was a very slow reader and liked to reread important passages to understand exactly how the author had constructed them. *Nightwood* impressed him tremendously and when he left hospital he used the style of Barnes's prose poem to write about his illness and hospitalisation. Unfortunately, when he showed his writing to John Kingsland, Joan's lover, he laughed uproariously, thinking it was a parody of modernism. Jack was not amused. Some of the flavour of *Nightwood* can be detected in Jack's later spontaneous prose, particularly in passages from *Visions of Cody*.

In Hal Chase's view[12] the painful phlebitis made Jack feel closer to his father because they finally had something in common. Now they could drink together to drown their pain and sorrows in a socially acceptable manner. Jack, for some reason, had told his parents that he was using marijuana, which had further convinced Leo that his boy was a write-off and would probably finish up in jail. Leo naturally believed all the adverse publicity about dope fiends put out by the FBI. Years later Jack still had terror dreams that his father caught him smoking pot. In one, reported in *Book of Dreams*,[13] Jack rolls a joint while talking excitedly under the influence of pot, forgetting that his parents are in the room. His father then stood up and said, 'He's not worried about marijuana? Eh?' and walked towards him. Jack saw him coming and went blind – the scene went dark – but Jack felt his father's touch on his arm: 'He may have an axe, he may have anything and I can't see – I fall fainting dead in the darkness, with a groan that wakes me up and prevents me being found dead . . . in my bed in the morning – for my blood stop't beating when that Shroudy Traveller finally got his hand on me . . . He's getting closer and closer.'

With Joan now clearly in love with Burroughs, her previous lover, John Kingsland, retired gracefully from the scene. Though Burroughs's sexual orientation was towards men, he had had plenty of girlfriends when he was a young man in Saint Louis and didn't rule out sexual relations with women. It was just that he preferred men. Bill had not had a steady boyfriend for several years and his closest friendship was with Joan, so it was perhaps inevitable that he and Joan would become lovers. Bill would recline on the long couch in the living room, talking, and Joan would sometimes lie down next to him and wrap her arms round his waist. Huncke was astonished by this new development: 'I was amazed to discover he had been physical with Joan.'

However, Bill, who was not one to boast, commented, 'One time she said, "Well, you're supposed to be a faggot. You're as good as a pimp in bed." Those were her very words.'[14]

Though no longer with Joan, Kingsland remained fascinated by the people at 115th Street, particularly by Burroughs, who allowed him to watch as he shot up in the bathroom, meticulously preparing his needle, the eyedropper, the spoon and flame. Bill was constantly trying to kick his habit and Kingsland would accompany him on various efforts, one time watching Bill swim endless laps at the Harvard Club to try and kick his habit through physical exertion, and another time spending all day in the steam rooms of the Turkish baths at the Biltmore Hotel as Bill tried to sweat the junk out of his system.

Kingsland's interest in Bill's life almost ruined his own. One day Bill gave Kingsland money to go and score for him on 103rd Street but the pushers mistook this fresh-faced college boy – Kingsland was still only seventeen – for a new pusher trying to muscle in on their territory and beat him up. The Columbia campus police took him in and, in order to confirm his innocence, sat him in Bickfords on 42nd Street for an entire afternoon to see if anyone approached him to try to score. He was suspended from Columbia, but he had been such a good student that his professors successfully circulated a petition to reverse the ruling and he was reinstated. Kingsland graduated in June 1946. Clearly going anywhere near the 115th Street circle was like hanging around The Rolling Stones in the seventies: it was very easy to find yourself out of your depth, without a life belt.

Herbert Huncke was sitting in Chase's Cafeteria in Times Square when an attractive young woman approached him and told him that a Professor Kinsey, from Indiana University, was doing research on sexual behaviour and would like to interview him. She gave Huncke the professor's hotel number and Huncke called him. At first Huncke naturally assumed that this was an elaborately planned sexual encounter, but the professor assured him that he just wanted to talk to him about his sex life: whether or not he masturbated, when he had his first sexual experience, if he had had any homosexual experiences, and so on. Huncke pointed out that he needed money and was assured that he would be taken care of, so he went along.

Kinsey wanted as wide and diverse a sample as he could get, so he worked from coast to coast and with all social strata. Kinsey himself conducted 7,985 of the approximately 18,000 sexual histories gathered by his research team.[15] Huncke proved to be invaluable to him. The pimps and pushers, hookers and hustlers of the Times Square area were an important potential source of data, but they were a very hard group for an academic like Kinsey to contact. Kinsey paid Huncke $2 for each person he brought to him. In this way Bill Burroughs, Allen Ginsberg, Jack Kerouac, Joan Vollmer and Vickie Russell, along with many of Huncke's other friends and acquaintances, answered the questions and – in the case of the men – allowed Kinsey to measure the length of their penis, both erect and detumescent. Their statistics were added to the pool and appeared, anonymously, among the tables of *Sexual Behaviour in the Human Male* when it was published in January 1948 by WB Saunders. (Its companion volume: *Sexual Behaviour in the Human Female* was not published until September 1953.) Kinsey was surprised and pleased to meet Burroughs, Jack and the others as he had not expected to encounter educated, articulate people in such a setting. On several occasions they all dined together along with several of Kinsey's assistants.

Leo's illness reached a critical stage early in 1946 and, with Gabrielle working in the shoe factory, it was up to Jack to nurse him during the day. Leo was in constant pain. Embittered and angry, he sat in his bathrobe with a blanket over his knees, looking thin and haggard. Everything he ate turned to water, and he had a catheter tube inserted into his urethra. One of Jack's tasks was to empty the vile-smelling water bowl. Every two weeks the doctor came to drain the fluid from his stomach while Jack waited in the next room, trying not to overhear his father's groans. When the doctor left, Leo would weep. Once he tried to stand but his thin legs had wasted away and he collapsed on to the floor. Here was the vain, loudmouthed braggart who stomped and yelled his way all over Lowell, lying in a wretched heap on the rug. Jack felt enormous compassion for him as he hauled him back into his chair.

As his father rested in the next room, Jack sat at the table working on *The Town and the City*, all his memories of his childhood flooding back to him as his father lay dying. One day in April, shortly after the doctor had packed away his bag and left, Jack was at his chair writing when he became aware that his father's snores were unusually loud. He went to investigate and found Leo dead in his armchair. The snores had been the death rattle of his last breath leaving his lungs. Jack stood in a daze looking at his father. He noticed his hands, permanently stained with printer's ink, the legacy of a life of work.

During the last weeks of his life, Leo had had two important messages to impart to Jack: 'Beware of the niggers and Jews' and 'Promise me that, whatever you do, you'll take care of your mother'. Jack promised, a solemn oath which he never broke, and which he always used as his explanation for living with her and not building a family of his own. It is unlikely that Leo expected Jack to actually live with Gabrielle and, in any case, it was Gabrielle who took care of Jack for the next decade, working in the shoe factory and paying him an allowance to enable him to write. Four decades later, on a BBC radio programme, Allen Ginsberg reflected upon Kerouac's life:

I don't think his nature was rebellion at all. Just the opposite. Every one of us was disappointed that he had family values and an old-fashioned artistic notion of himself as a novelist with a pipe and an armchair and a fireplace. Everybody expected him to be a rebel and an idiot and angry, and he wasn't that at all. He was a suffering Buddhist who understood a great deal and was able to live with his mother. That's not a rebel. Someone who takes a vow on his father's death bed cannot be considered a rebel, by any term that would be recognisable to a middle-class audience of the BBC.[16]

Back at the 115th Street apartment, things were going badly. Jack was not the only one who had developed a liking for Benzedrine. Joan's usage had continued unabated. Her skin was now covered with sores and she popped a Benny in her mouth as soon as she awoke. Herbert Huncke was back in jail, having been named by someone as a pusher. Unfortunately the police had arrested him in Bill's Henry Street apartment, so they were undoubtedly looking for him as well. Burroughs had continued his experiments with morphine and was now thoroughly addicted. He and Phil White came up with ever more implausible stories to get doctors to write morphine prescriptions for them. During a visit to a Doctor Greco, Phil White stole a blank prescription pad and Bill filled a couple of sheets out. He was arrested almost immediately because the alert pharmacist noticed that the 'doctor' had spelt Delaudid (synthetic morphine) inaccurately. Bill had foolishly given his real address on the script and two detectives came to 115th Street and took him off to The Tombs. There he was charged with violation of Public Health Law 334 – obtaining narcotics by fraudulent means – fingerprinted, had a mugshot taken, and was locked in a cell. He was forced to go cold turkey. Joan arrived the next day to bail him out and give him some goofballs to take the edge off his withdrawal. Joan wrote to Edie: 'The only way I could get him out on bail, unfortunately, was to call his psychiatrist, and he promptly informed Bill's family, which led to a good deal of unpleasantness.'[17] Once again Bill's father flew into New York City to bail out his delinquent son.

Bill was due in court in June, but in the meantime he still had a habit. He and Bill Garver decided to go into business as heroin dealers, taking enough for themselves and selling the remainder. For about three months Bill moved around the city, from one cheap hotel or rooming house to another, delivering the goods to the door. Unlike most dealers, Bill was punctual and gave a good deal: 16% pure, better than any other dealer in the city.

As Bill was a first offender, he was charged with a misdemeanour when his case came up in Special Sessions. The judge gave him a four-month suspended sentence with an unusual rider attached. He told Bill: 'Young man, I am going to inflict a terrible punishment on you. I am going to send you home to Saint Louis for the summer.' The judge could not have imagined how true his words were.

Joan now had trouble keeping the 115th Street apartment going: Edie had moved out at Christmas and Jack had helped her sister move her things when she finally came for them in April. Jack himself had moved out just after Christmas, first of all to nurse his father and then to attend his mother through the period of mourning. He took a job as a night clerk and elevator operator in one of the small campus hotels and went home to Ozone Park every day. Hal Chase moved out of 115th Street because he could see that it wasn't long before the whole place was going to be busted and himself with it.

Help came to Joan in the uncertain form of Herbert Huncke, who moved in with the intention of helping with the rent, although it is unlikely that Herbert contributed much in that direction. He did apparently bring some money into the apartment, even if it was illgotten. He and Joan sat up all night taking Benzedrine, talking, and picking at small creatures that their amphetamine-enhanced vision had enabled them to see burrowing under their skin:

> Allen Ginsberg: 'Huncke, you and Joan were once talking about those spore things coming out of your skin.'
> Huncke: 'Indeed we were! We sat up many hours at night.'
> Allen: 'There was a virus also, wasn't there?'
> Huncke: 'Well, in my case, and in both of our cases, a skin rash, frayed nerve ends, a complete rehabilitation . . . I thought all sorts of things were coming out of the skin, and that they couldn't be tracked. I spent hours looking for them.'
> Allen: 'This was a by-product of amphetamine.'
> Huncke: 'Well, yes. What amphetamine did was, as I understand it, was open up the pores to a large extent, thus the intake of certain things . . . ordinarily things would be shielded from you.'
> Allen: 'And frayed nerve endings?'
> Huncke: 'Yes, definitely frayed nerve endings . . .'[18]

The amphetamine had exaggerated a preoccupation with nerves. In a way this was a very American response. 'Nerves' and nervous disease were thought of as a particularly American phenomenon at the beginning of the twentieth century. In fact, neurasthenia was known as 'American nervousness' and was seen as a reaction against modern civilisation, which Americans thought was most advanced in their own country. It was characterised by depression, fainting and stammering.

Joan could see what was happening to herself and the apartment but seemed powerless to stop it. As she told Edie:

> [Bill going away] left me in rather a spot, emotionally as well as financially. Huncke stayed around and raised some money making parked cars for the luggage, and after a while we began taking in a few desperate characters as boarders, until before long I was running quite a pad. Everything in the darn place was hot, as were, of course, a couple of cars out front. Inevitably, people kept going to jail, until finally, due to that and also the ever-present back rent, we got tossed out. There simply wasn't an empty apartment in the city, so we bounced around from one hotel to another until Whitey, a sweet but stupid character with whom I was having a light affair at the time, blew his top and tried to lift a Howard Johnson's safe. He was picked up immediately.[19]

Joan found herself looking for a job, an apartment, a lawyer for Whitey (this was not Phil White, but a different young hoodlum) and money to pay the lawyer. As she was completely broke, she left Julie with her aunts on Long Island and went to stay with a young man she knew called McCarthy. Whitey insisted on having a particular lawyer, and Joan was finally able to pay for him even though, in her opinion, he was obviously no good. With the stress of being broke and homeless, and from taking so much Benzedrine, she finally landed in the psychiatric ward of Bellevue Hospital, the first incidence of amphetamine psychosis in a female that they had encountered. She was in hospital during Whitey's trial – he got five to ten years in Sing Sing.

Joan's father came down from Loudenville and took Julie to her grandparents while Joan tried to prove to the doctors that she was sane. The effects of the amphetamine wore off in a couple of days and she was normal again, but it took her a further ten days to convince the doctors that she was not completely mad. Then, with a masterful piece of timing, Bill Burroughs arrived back in town just before she got out. He swept her off to stay with his friends, Kells Elvins and his wife, in the Rio Grande Valley in Texas, where Bill's parents were going to buy him some land in the hope that life as a citrus farmer would keep him out of trouble.

Huncke, meanwhile, wrote to Allen Ginsberg from the Bronx jail, asking for him to send money: 'Also – paper and the bare necessities run into a bit of gold and I am completely broke – flat – taped – beat – busted and without.'[20] An early example of Huncke's use of the word 'Beat', the etymology of which has caused so much discussion in Beat study circles.

Allen Ginsberg:

I would say that Times Square was the central hangout for Burroughs, Kerouac and myself from about '45 to '48, probably the most formative period of early Spenglerian mind, where that language of 'Zap', 'Hip', 'Square', 'Beat', was provided over the Bickford cafeteria tables by Huncke. I would say Herbert Huncke is the basic originator of the notion of Beat . . . the ethos of Beat and the conceptions of Beat and Square. What they meant in our mouths was more or less what they meant in his mouth, because we heard it from him. I never heard the word hip until I heard him talking. And when I asked him where it came from he said, 'Oh, probably Chicago talk from the twenties. 'I'm going downtown. Have you got your hip boots on tight?'[21]

This was the period when Times Square was the centre of their world, a time described by Ginsberg as 'The diamond point of our youthful opening up, and probably the most determining experience'. They thought of Times Square as a 'big room', a giant living room lit by a smoggy neon glow in which they walked around, high on Benzedrine, like tiny mites, aware that they were just passing through. Ginsberg described it as giving 'a garish Technicolor intensity to the very heavens we were walking under and made it seem like some Biblical scene of the last of days'. The neon lights lit up the sky in a red apocalyptic glow above the cornices of the buildings. The play of neon lights on red bricks is an often repeated image in Kerouac. They felt that they were at the bottom of a well, looking up at infinite space – an oddly Gnostic awareness that Kerouac probably associated with his readings in the Egyptian Gnostics. As dawn broke over Times Square to challenge the neon and reveal the tawdry littered streets, they looked at the green pallor of the night hawks at Bickfords, with their mottled yellowish flesh. Under the influence of Benzedrine they developed an idea that everyone there was suffering from a radioactive disease, the cause of the small creatures that Joan and Huncke spent so much time probing for beneath their skin. It was a post-apocalyptic vision, set in the most urban, unnatural environment on the planet in the days shortly after the dropping of the A-bomb.

They hung out at the Pokerino, a 24-hour pinball palace on the Square, brightly lit with fairground fluorescent tubes and neon, filled with speed freaks, who were concentrating on the pinball machines with amphetamine intensity, gripping the tables, willing the ball to stay in play, while the crash and zap of the machine noises and the intense bright light made their heads spin. Jack called it the 'Nickel-O' in *The Town and the City*, incorporating into his text ideas and descriptions taken from Allen's piece, *The Pokerino*. But it was part of the New Vision to swap and exchange ideas. Only later did Jack complain that Allen had used his images in his work. Back then they pooled their experience to forge a new approach to art and literature.

Towards the end of 1946 the original group began its final split. With the collapse of 115th Street came the breaking apart of the original Beat group. Joan went off with Bill Burroughs and they eventually started a marijuana farm in east Texas. Allen moved in with an Irish family on east 92nd Street, but could not really entertain guests. Huncke moved in with Vickie Russell in an apartment at 89th Street and West End Avenue and, though Jack and

Allen were frequent visitors, they saw each other less than before. Jack spent most of his time at home with Memere, working on *The Town and the City*. Since she would not allow most of his friends in the house, and since he was prepared to go along with this stricture, it meant that the only friends Jack saw at home were those whom his mother liked, as if he were still a schoolboy. Hal Chase and Jack Fitzgerald were both invited to Thanksgiving dinner, but Allen Ginsberg – when he called to inquire after Jack's plans – was rebuffed. Bill's prediction that his mother would reel him in on her apron strings like a wriggling carp was already coming true.

Under the influence of his mother, Jack began frequenting a straighter, richer circle of Columbia friends. One of them was Allan Temko, an aspiring novelist whom Jack first met in 1944, but didn't really get to know until Temko returned to Columbia after serving in the Navy during the war. Temko thought that the 115th Street group were 'loathsome people', so he and Jack talked mostly about writing. Temko was fond of Hemingway whereas Jack still loved Wolfe, and this caused much good-natured bantering between them.

Another friend was Tom Livornese, a pre-med student at Columbia who had an extensive knowledge of jazz. Livornese was friends with many musicians and he and Jack often went to the 52nd Street clubs together, where Livornese introduced Jack to the latest developments in bebop as well as to the musicians themselves.

More and more Jack was feeling split apart by his two lives: the non-Wolfean big room of Times Square, versus his Wolfean home life with Mother. At his father's funeral, surrounded by the straightforward working people who were his relatives and his parents' friends, Jack was surprised to find that he felt a tremendous sense of belonging. This is one of the themes of *The Town and the City* but he was not yet a good enough writer to deal with it in a convincing way.

Jack's belief that he had to make a choice, rather than accept that life is multi-dimensional, was shaken at the end of the year by the appearance of a young man who seemed to embody both Wolfean and non-Wolfean traits. Neal Cassady, with his good-guy grin and bulging biceps was the all-American Western hero. He bore something of a resemblance to Jean-Paul Belmondo, with the same quizzical eyebrows and good-natured smile across his lips. He had the strong physique of a football player, with a thick neck and powerful chest. He and Jack Kerouac could have been brothers, as the famous photograph by Carolyn Cassady shows. In an earlier age, Neal would have been a cowboy. Instead he was a pool-hall hustler, filled with an exuberant energy and lust for life that was to captivate both Jack and Allen Ginsberg.

Neal Cassady was a friend of Hal Chase from Denver, Colorado. Hal had often entertained the 115th Street group with stories of this wild youth, whose father was a bum and who grew up in the flophouses and pool halls of Larimer Street, and had astonishing success both with the ladies and the gentlemen.

Neal was born on 8 February 1926. His parents separated in 1932, and he grew up with his wino father in a Denver flophouse. They slept side by side on a mattress with no sheets. In the morning, young Neal was woken at 7 a.m. by the clock on the Daniels and Fisher department store, dressed himself and ran to the communal washroom. His father usually remained in alcoholic oblivion. Neal went first to the Citizen's Mission, which gave breakfast and dinner to two hundred men each day. Neal was at least a dozen years younger than anyone else there. After a second cup of coffee, he made his way to school, bouncing a tennis ball through the alleys and backstreets of Denver, taking a different route each day. He appears to have got on well at school. He was big and strong and streetwise, so he was not bullied. He was also a voracious reader, which pleased the teachers. It was the movie, *The Count of Monte Cristo* that first introduced Neal to literature. He loved the Alexander Dumas story so much that he took the book out of the school library. He escaped from the squalor of his own life into the world of books and by the time he met Jack and the other Beats he had even read his way through Proust.

From the age of six, Neal accompanied his father across the country each summer, visiting relatives or following the fruit harvests, hitchhiking or hopping freight trains and travelling in covered boxcars in the proper hobo tradition. No doubt Neal's stories of hopping freights helped foster in Kerouac the romantic notion of the endless movement of people across America. Kerouac was himself to hop freights at the very end of the steam age.

They remained in Denver for the summer of 1934 because Neal Senior was living with a hard-drinking couple and their dozen children in an old barn. It was here, at the age of eight, that Neal received his initiation into sex by imitating the numerous brothers of the household. As he described it in *First Third*, 'I soon followed the leader in screwing all the sisters small enough to hold down – and those bold enough to lead.' By all accounts, sex for Neal was always something close to rape and it never occurred to him that his partner might also be entitled to some enjoyment.

It was inevitable that Neal would become a delinquent. He stole his first automobile at the age of fourteen in 1940, and claimed that by 1947 he had stolen about five hundred cars, most of which he used for joyriding, for picking up girls outside high schools or just for the sheer thrill of driving around the parking lot a few times before leaving the car back where he found it. Sometimes he was caught and he spent time in the reformatory but, when not in jail, he divided his time between the pool hall, the public library, and the pursuit of women.

It was this last activity that led him to meet Justin Brierly, a teacher and man-about-town who was on the board of the opera house and somehow also found time to practise law. Brierly was very taken by young Neal and took him under his wing, or, as Neal put it, allowed him to drive his cars in exchange for having sex with him.

Hal Chase got to know Neal in Denver, and fell for Neal's story about wanting to come east to learn how to be a writer. Hal was amazed by the energy and the flow of spontaneous thoughts in Neal's letters and showed them to all of his friends. They too were intrigued. Neal was not a genius, but his letters were something out of the ordinary: there was a special quality about his prose that set it apart. It was the use of everyday American speech, his unselfconscious use of swear words and total disregard for the normal conventions of English letter writing.

Neal was twenty when he arrived in New York City in the late autumn[22] of 1946 with his sixteen-year-old child bride, LuAnne, and a holdall containing copies of Shakespeare, Proust and a handful of clothes. They came from Sidney, Nebraska, where he and LuAnne had been staying with one of her aunts. Neal pumped gas and LuAnne worked as a maid but, within a few days, Neal remembered he had arranged to meet Hal Chase in New York. Neal stole her uncle's car while LuAnne broke open her aunt's safe and took $300. The car broke down in North Platte, Nebraska, so they blew the money taking buses all the way to New York.

It was their first time in the big city and, like the thousands of new arrivals before them, they left the Greyhound terminal and drifted to Times Square where for three hours they gawked, open-mouthed, at the giant billboards, neon lights, high buildings, and the huge Camel cigarettes billboard of a man who puffed clouds of real smoke into the square. They gazed at the vast selection of delicacies laid out in Hector's Cafeteria, everything glazed and highlighted and shining in the intense lights – something so memorably described later by Kerouac in one of his astonishing panoramic paragraphs – and spent half of their remaining money trying out the tempting array of dishes.

They spent the night in a hotel and the next day went in search of Hal Chase. Hal had told so many stories about Neal that everyone wanted to meet him. Neal was at his best dealing with just one person rather than in group encounters, where he felt compelled to put on an act. The first meeting with Jack, Allen and the others was not a success: Neal overplayed the part and the others were not impressed and soon drifted away. Allan Temko, Tom Livornese and Hal's roommate at Columbia, Ed White, dismissed him as a conman and thief and, though Allen Ginsberg pursued the friendship, he was more interested in Neal's good-looks than anything else.

Neal was a conman of the most transparent sort. Many people recognised this but liked him and were prepared to be conned; others were suspicious of him, disliked him and avoided his company. His way of ingratiating himself into someone's confidence was to focus totally upon them, listening intently to what they had to say so that they soon felt that Neal understood them on a deeper level than anyone ever had done before. If he could manoeuvre someone into a one-on-one confrontation, then he could charm the pants off them, particularly if it was a young woman. Neal described his method in a letter to Jack a few months later. He was on a long bus trip and on two occasions women made the mistake of sitting next to him: 'Without the slightest preliminaries of objective remarks (what's your name? where are you going? etc.) I plunged into a completely knowing, completely subjective, personal and so too "penetrating her core" way of speech; to be shorter . . . by 2 a.m. I had her swearing eternal love, complete subjectivity to me and immediate satisfaction.'

The second woman received the four-hour verbal onslaught from 10.30 a.m. the next morning until 2.30 p.m.: 'When I was done, she (confused, her entire life upset, metaphysically amazed at me, passionate in her immaturity) . . . I screwed as never before, all my pent-up emotion finding release in this young virgin (and she was) . . .' This ability to overpower the will of another person and impose one's control over them was most famously practised by Aleister Crowley, the 'Wickedest Man in the World', who, as part of his magical practice, would hang about Mayfair until he spotted a likely looking respectable young woman looking in a shop window. He would fix her eye with a penetrating stare, and within minutes would convince her to go with him into a hotel where, defying the prospect of divorce, disgrace and separation from children, they sometimes remained for up to three days before emerging shaken and ruined.[23]

With the obvious exception of his later wife Carolyn, Neal usually concentrated on young and inexperienced women, or, more often, women who were emotionally disturbed or had very low self-esteem, which made it easier for him to dominate them. Neal seemed to be the answer to their dreams. No one had met anyone like him before. Neal would be whatever anyone wanted him to be, concentrating on his subject with manic intensity: nodding his head, bobbing like a boxer in training and agreeing with their every word. Herbert Huncke was impressed: 'Cassady was very dynamic and had all that Irish charm.'

Hal arranged for Neal and LuAnne to stay in Tom Livornese's small flat on 103rd Street, near Columbia, as Livornese himself rarely used it, preferring to live at home and commute into college each day. Neal immediately sent LuAnne out to work. She found a job in a bakery shop but Neal couldn't wait for her to bring home the paycheck and asked her to steal money from the till. She was caught at once and dismissed. On her way home she got lost in Harlem and wandered around in a snowstorm in the darkness until one of Hal's friends found her. It was a traumatic incident for LuAnne which seems to have provoked a minor breakdown, causing her to have hallucinations of leaving her body.

Neal got a job parking cars at the New Yorker Hotel on 34th Street and, for some reason, took a cheap room in Bayonne, New Jersey, miles from the city. A few days later, the still shaky LuAnne lied to Neal by saying that the police had been around looking for him. Neal was dreadfully paranoid about being locked up again – he had already spent six terms in the reformatory – and freaked out. She immediately confessed that she had made it up, but although this was obviously a symptom of LuAnne's anxiety attack – she was only sixteen – Neal refused to believe that she had lied and left town at once on a bus for the Berkshires. By the time he recovered his composure and returned, LuAnne had left for Denver.

Shortly after this, Neal showed up in Ozone Park, saying that he wanted Jack to teach him how to write. Jack realised that this was a con and that Neal was just looking for somewhere to stay, but went along with the plan and, despite Memere's misgivings, let him stay for a few days.

As Jack wrote in *On the Road*:

He was simply a youth tremendously excited with life and, though he was a conman, he was only conning because he wanted so much to live and to get involved with people who would otherwise pay no attention to him. He was conning me and I knew it (for room and board and 'how-to-write', etc.), and he knew I knew (this had been the basis of our relationship), but I didn't care and we got along fine.[24]

Lucien Carr: 'I think Jack felt at home with Neal. Despite the fact that he admired Neal . . . he felt at home with Neal – he never felt at home with Allen, he never felt at home with me.' To Lucien, Jack was never at home with anyone except the guys who worked at the local gas station and some guy he could take back to Lowell to hang out with his old drinking buddies in the bars.

But, though they connected, Jack and Neal did not see much of each other because Allen commandeered most of Neal's time. Jack, Allen and Neal spent the night talking at Tom Livornese's flat and, since it was too late for Jack to take the subway to Ozone Park, or even for Allen to return to West 92nd Street, they all stayed over. Jack slept in Livornese's double bed with their host while Allen and Neal squeezed into the single bed. Allen was too fearful to make a move but Neal pulled him to him, precipitating an intense emotional affair between the two men that meant far less to Neal than it did to Allen, who fell totally in love. Allen relieved Jack of the task of teaching Neal how to write, monopolising all Neal's free time and attention. Jack resented this and relations between Jack and Allen grew frosty. Allen told writer Yves LePellec:

Jack was intimidated because I was sleeping with Neal. I remember once we were sitting around in New York. Neal, I think, just had a little Chinese dressing gown on, and I had my hand on Neal's thigh for about an hour, during a long conversation. Jack, finally, irritably said, 'Why don't you take your damn hand off his thigh . . . feeling him up all the time.' It was really funny. It was like his mother, an echo of his mother; which might have been God Knows What. Perception? Or jealousy? Or perception of my aggressiveness?[25]

Neal's request to Jack, and later to Allen, that they teach him all they know about writing was not entirely flattery or necessarily part of an elaborate con. At that time he did have a genuine interest in becoming a writer, and, as his letters had been passed around the circle of friends, they already knew his spontaneous style and admired him for it. His writing style was a direct extension of his speech – and Neal was a fabulous raconteur.

Jack, in particular, was very taken by the rhythmic, lyrical quality of his provincial Western twang. Neal told him long, detailed stories of his sex life and exploits in the pool halls and bars of Denver, including one about driving a car down a winding Rocky Mountain road while simultaneously having sex. It made Jack listen to actual American speech and realise that it was possible to write it down as it was spoken, like the transcription of an oral storyteller.

On 7 May 1947, Jack and Allen accompanied Neal to the Greyhound bus station. They were all three friends again, after spending Neal's last night in New York talking about their relationship. Allen recorded in his journals: 'I came out and talked soberly (and severely) and straight and vibrant to Jack, a la Cassady – and it worked! Jack and I in an unofficial rapprochement.' Neal left for Denver at 6.30 in the evening and Jack and Allen walked home with wildly different dreams in their heads. Allen was deeply in love with Neal, worried what the future might bring, but happy that he and Jack were friends again: '[felt] mostly a peace and grace which I attained with Jack that night'.[26]

Jack was now thinking that he too must go to Denver. He knew a lot of people from there and felt naive and inexperienced as he listened to their tales of travel all across the United States. This was partly precipitated by Beverley Burford, Ed White's girlfriend, who had become very close to Jack. Beverley had already flown around the States a dozen times, whereas Jack had barely left New England. He determined that he would hit the road as soon as he was able.

That May, Allen followed Neal to Denver. Hal Chase graduated early from Columbia and also returned to Denver, to continue his anthropology studies. Allan Temko and Ed White were planning to spend the summer there. Jack could not afford to go. He was stuck at home with his mother, living off her wages while he wrote.

6 On the Road

That June, Jack and Memere went on a two-week holiday to stay with Nin, who was now married to a missile technician called Paul Blake and living in the deep South. Seeking to impress Burroughs, Jack wrote him a letter about the snakes and alligators he had seen in the Okefinokee Swamp in Georgia and included some gratuitous racism, telling Bill that his sister and brother-in-law had an apartment 'near niggertown' and mentioning an incident when one Black girl chased after another waving a meat cleaver. Jack reported Paul Blake as saying, 'We better get out of here. I don't want to get brained by no nigger gal.'[1] It is interesting to see that Ann Charters chose to delete this racist passage from the letter when she included it in *Selected Letters*: part of the sanitising of Kerouac to make him safe and respectable, someone the good burghers of Lowell can be proud of, though this may have been done on the instructions of the Kerouac Estate.

Jack and Memere returned to Ozone Park, Jack still feeling dissatisfied. A holiday with your mother when you are 25 years old is not the same as going on the road. Then Henri Cru, his friend from Horace Mann, passed through town bringing with him a couple of thick sticks of Panama Gold, on his way to San Francisco where he had a job waiting for him as chief electrician on a ship. Henri thought that he could get Jack a job as an assistant electrician on the same ship. Memere thought the trip would be good for Jack's health and she gave the plan her blessing. Jack decided to hitchhike across the country and began to study maps and read biographies, histories and memoirs. As he said, 'My subject as a writer is of course America, and simply I must know everything about it.'[2]

He planned to take Route 6 which begins at Provincetown out on Cape Cod Bay and slowly meanders across the entire country to Los Angeles. On 17 July 1947, Jack Kerouac went on the road, hitchhiking up the Hudson to where Route 6 crossed the great river over the Bear Mountain Bridge. There was little or no traffic and he wasted an entire day standing around in the pouring rain. He finally took a bus back to New York and another all the way to Chicago. It was not an auspicious start. From Chicago he took a bus to Joliet to get away from the city traffic, and, back on Route 6 again, began to hitchhike. This was the beginning of his hitching saga as recounted in *On the Road*, though it is impossible to ascertain how accurate the novel is. *On the Road* is, in a sense, a transitional book and many events and conversations are fictionalised or else simply not true, placing it somewhere between a memoir and a novel.

It is the infectious enthusiasm of his hitchhiking accounts that encouraged thousands of young people to follow him down that road: the camaraderie among fellow hitchhikers, which does exist but was perhaps romanticised by Jack; the thrill of being on the open road; the freedom to go anywhere, as you please, each ride a potential friendship or adventure or change of destination.

The route Jack planned took him first to Denver, where he wanted to spend a few days visiting friends, and from there across the Rockies to San Francisco to join Henri Cru. When Jack crossed the Mississippi he was acutely aware of finally setting foot in the West. The sheer immensity of America always amazes anyone who travels across it by any means other than plane, though these days the superhighways have reduced the impact of cross-country travel. In Jack's day, most of the freeways were not yet built – they were part of the Interstate Military Highway System federally funded during the Cold War to enable men and materiel to be transported to any part of the country. It would now be difficult to repeat Jack's actual route.

He made good time on the thousand miles to Denver considering he was not yet an experienced hitchhiker. He made false starts, spent hours in remote lonely bus stations, ate plenty of apple pie and ice cream, and absorbed the conversations of the farmers and truck drivers who gave him lifts. He arrived in Des Moines at dawn and after breakfast he felt so tired that he looked for a room at the YMCA. It was full, so he finished up in an old hotel down by the freight yards. He pulled down the yellowing blinds and slept away the day as old steam locomotives clanked and puffed in and out of the nearby round house, filling the air with smoke and grime.

He woke in the late afternoon as the red sun was dipping towards the western horizon and for a moment he experienced a loss of identity. It was an epiphany: 'I was far from home, haunted and tired from travel, in a cheap hotel room I'd never seen, hearing the hiss of steam outside, and the creak of the old wood of the hotel, and footsteps upstairs, and all the sad sounds.'³ For about fifteen seconds he did not know who he was. He was not scared, he was just somebody else, a stranger. His life felt haunted, the life of a ghost, as he lay there in that red afternoon at the dividing line between the East of his past and the West of his future.

He went in search of apple pie and ice cream and watched the schoolgirls returning home from school before heading out to the road. He arrived at Council Bluffs at dawn and Jack, whose head was filled with the stories of the great wagon-train meetings there to decide whether to take the Sante Fe or the Oregon trails, was disappointed to find cute suburban cottages in the grey morning light. Across the Missouri River was Omaha, where Jack saw his first cowboy: walking through the meat-packing district looking like any Beat character to be found on the streets at dawn, except for his ten-gallon hat and cowboy boots. In Gothenburg he got the greatest ride of his life: two young farmers in a pickup who were stopping for every hitchhiker on the road. There were already six in the back when they slid to a halt in front of Jack. The farmers bought them all burgers and coffee at rest stops and for Jack it was the ride from heaven. He got into conversation with the other hitchhikers and reports several pages of dialogue verbatim in *On the Road*. The farmers were heading for Los Angeles and Jack was tempted to go all the way with them, but decided to get off at Cheyenne and hitch the ninety miles down to Denver where he was expected.

Jack called Hal Chase's house and his mother directed him to the Denver Art Museum where Hal was studying Indian basketwork. Hal intended to become an anthropologist and was taking his studies very seriously. Ed White also lived in Denver and his parents were away for the summer, leaving him the whole house to himself. Allan Temko had already moved in and they had a room reserved for Jack. The divisions between Jack's friends in New York were exacerbated when the Ivy Leaguers returned to their homes. Temko had become an aesthete, lounging about in a silk dressing gown while writing Hemingway-style short stories. Hal, Ed White and Temko were no longer friends with Neal Cassady and had also broken off with Allen Ginsberg. They knew they were both in town, but did not know where. Mostly they saw Beverley Burford and her brother Bob, who came from the same privileged, comfortable background as they did. It was a long way from the flophouses of Larimer Street where Neal grew up.

Allen was living in a basement apartment on Grant Street near the Capitol for $20 a month and had a night job at May Company vacuuming the second floor for $20 a week. Neal also worked for May Company, driving a shuttle bus at their other store.[4] Allen and Neal were having emotional problems. Neal was engaged in an almost impossible juggling act: he was having an intense affair with Carolyn Robinson, whom he later married, but was also still seeing LuAnne, despite the fact they were supposed to be filing for divorce. Neither Carolyn nor LuAnne knew of the existence of the other and he had devised a complicated schedule of visits as he ran between them, his job, and Allen's basement. He was also engaged in all-night Benzedrine-fuelled conversations with Allen, which he clearly found very stimulating despite having to constantly fend off Allen's advances. Neal was learning all he could from him, but did everything possible to avoid having sex with him more than the minimum required to keep Allen hanging on the line. Allen, for his part, wished fervently that they would stop talking and just go to bed, but Neal was no longer at all attracted to Allen physically, if he ever was. The sexual rejection and neglect almost brought Allen to a nervous breakdown.

Allen soon heard that Jack was in town and telephoned him. Jack's arrival calmed the tension somewhat, and Neal took the two of them on walks around Denver to show them all the houses that he had lived in as a child. He told them all the fantasies he'd had in each of the houses and in each alleyway. When he was really small he had lived in a big wooden house with many porches and an alleyway at the side. Allen wrote: 'So there were all sorts of bogeyman fantasies for that alleyway. Each bogeyman fantasy and each allegory had its own historical recollections.'[5] The telling of childhood fantasies and recollections led to both Allen and Jack telling their own, which had long been a favourite subject of conversation for them, and so the walks around Denver became associated not only with Neal but with the Shrouded Stranger of Allen's childhood and The Shadow/Doctor Sax figure of Jack's boyhood adventures in Lowell.

Despite his complicated schedule, Neal was also seeing two waitresses called the Gyllion sisters. They were also friends with Allen and had helped him find somewhere to live. Jack had a brief affair with one of them and they get a name-check in *On the Road* as the Bettencourt sisters. Away from the conservative strictures of his mother, Jack made a number of important choices about the direction he intended to go in his life. There was a dichotomy, as usual. On the one hand were the wealthy conventional Denver friends his mother approved of, with their good manners and sheltered homes. By cultivating their friendship he would have no doubt found himself in some comfortable situation. On the other side was the Beat Generation – though it had not yet acquired that name – represented by the fierce brilliant mind of Allen Ginsberg, whose awkwardness, sudden bursts of singing and laughter, and habit of walking around Denver in a swimming costume and formal white dinner shirt caused eyebrows to be raised.

Allen was already convinced of Jack's genius and constantly encouraged him to become a writer at the expense of everything else. In Allen's eyes, on the evidence of his letters, Neal was also potentially a great writer, and he still saw the core of friends fulfilling their task of ushering in the New Vision they had spent so many years planning and discussing. Jack found himself siding more and more with Allen and Neal, and feeling more alienated by the middle-class values of the others.

By the time Jack left Denver ten days later, he saw himself part of a group: a triumvirate of himself, Allen and Neal, to which Bill Burroughs would eventually be added. He had chosen his direction, but not yet his role. What was needed was a name: the Lost Generation, the Bloomsbury Group, the Brat Pack, Dadaists, Lettrist International . . . The group name is all important in achieving an identity and direction, whether in art, poetry, literature or rock 'n' roll.

Jack made two new friends in Denver. The first was Al Hinkle, a giant man of six foot six who was enthralled by Neal. Hinkle found Neal's manoeuvres and antics fascinating and followed him all over town just to watch him in action. Jack also got to know Carolyn Robinson, Neal's new girlfriend, to whom he felt an immediate attraction, but for once felt disinclined to win her favour. Carolyn came from a conservative bourgeois background and had been conned completely by Neal, who led her to believe he was a conventional college jock. Only later did she learn about the periods in jail and the hundreds of girlfriends. She was essentially monogamous, but there was one time during those two weeks when she realised how Jack felt about her. Carolyn wrote: 'Dancing with Jack was the only time I felt the slightest doubt about my dedication to Neal, for here was the warm physical attraction Neal lacked. This realisation disturbed me and was difficult to brush away. Jack's manner was tender without being suggestive, although he did betray some tension . . .'[6]

*   *   *

Jack was now completely broke. He telegraphed his mother to send him $50 and, when it arrived, he took the bus to San Francisco. He was two weeks late for his appointment to ship out with Henri Cru, but it transpired that the jobs had not materialised. Henri was still there, working as a security officer in Marin City, north of San Francisco over the Golden Gate Bridge.

Henri Cru:

> I recall on the morning of his arrival in Marin City – early morning – instead of using the door he came in the window of the shack that Dianne and I lived in and announced that he had just come through a picturesque little town named Sausalito. Jack said, 'There must be a lot of Italians living there.' I said, 'No, Jack, Sausalito is not Italian, the name is Mexican.'[7]

Henri had left a note on the door, three weeks before, telling Jack to climb in through the window if no one was in. It amused Henri enormously that Jack had climbed in anyway, even when they were both at home. Henri arranged for Jack to work with him at Morrisson and Knudsen and that summer Jack Kerouac became a police officer, working as a uniformed security guard in a barracks for an overseas construction company. He was sworn in as a special policeman by the Sausalito police chief, wore a police badge, carried a .32 automatic and a billy club. It was a good job at $45 a week and most of the time Jack could simply sit and type in the office.

Jack lived with Henri and Dianne, sending most of his earnings back to his mother so that eventually his hosts began to complain that he was not paying his way and began to pointedly hang up the grocery receipts on the wall. Though they were earning good money, Henri and Jack sometimes stole food from the kitchens of the barracks they were patrolling and the three of them lived quite well. Henri was prepared to let Jack stay because he was amused by him. Jack's naivety and his faux pas were a subject of constant levity, unless Henri himself was humiliated by him.

Sometimes they would go into the city, but here Henri was embarrassed by Jack's crude manners. Henri:

> The biggest mistake I ever made was introducing Jack to my father, Professor Albert L Cru. We had a date to meet at a restaurant in North Beach, San Francisco. Kerouac as per usual arrived over an hour late, drunk as a skunk as usual and in his usual lamentable way attempted to impress my father with

bastard Canadian French . . . translating literally he announced to my father, 'Je suis haut,' which Jack thought meant 'I am high'. Unfortunately, in French it translates into 'I am tall'. Jack was a lot of things but tall wasn't one of them. Needless to say my father didn't find Jack funny and in fact found him crashingly disgusting.[8]

Jack reported the incident in *On the Road*: Henri Cru was very much in awe of his father, the eminent professor, and borrowed $100 in order to wine and dine the old man in San Francisco. His girlfriend and Jack were supposed to give credibility to the stories he had presumably been telling his father in his letters about his success in life. Not only did Jack arrive late and drunk, but Allan Temko was in the expensive restaurant Henri chose and latched on to the party. Temko insulted Cru's father and was eventually thrown out of the restaurant for causing a disturbance. Henri was mortified and Jack, instead of trying to make amends, joined Temko in further hell-raising outside. His casual betrayal of his friends was already at work even in 1947. Amazingly, Cru did not throw him out of the cabin, but Jack at least had the sense to leave of his own accord a few days later.

He headed south to Los Angeles, reaching Bakersfield in just two rides, but, at midnight, and with a hundred miles to go and no likelihood of a ride, he went to buy a ticket at the bus station. While waiting for the bus he was struck by the dark beauty of a young Mexican woman and, typically, fell in love at first sight. When she boarded his bus, he plucked up the courage to sit across from her and engage her in conversation.

Her name was Bea Franco. She was a migrant worker who had left her husband because he beat her up. She had a seven-year-old son who was staying with relatives. By the time they reached Los Angeles, Jack and Bea had already planned to hitchhike to New York, where they intended to live together. Memere's reaction to this would have been something to see, but Jack obviously knew that these were fantasies that would never come true. He had clearly taken Cassady's lessons on how to pick up women on buses to heart. After spending the night together, they even got out on the road and attempted to hitch to New York but were unable to get a lift. Jack was acting a role and clearly saw the affair as a 'season'. (He and Allen Ginsberg often talked of having 'seasons', an idea taken from Rimbaud's *Season in Hell*.) Jack's relationship with Bea is described in 'The Mexican Girl', a fully formed section of *On the Road*, first published as a short story in *Paris Review*. It works perfectly as a stand-alone text and, in fact, some enterprising booklegger off-printed it as a booklet.[9]

The relationship lasted for fifteen days. It is unlikely that Bea saw it as a long-term thing either; to her Jack was a White American college boy who had for some reason taken a liking to her. They had fun while it lasted even though they were both completely broke. At one point Jack picked cotton with her, but he was only able to manage half a sack a day, for which he was paid $1.50, just enough to buy vegetables but not enough to even pay the rent on the tent they were living in. Through Bea he saw what real poverty was like, visiting her relatives, drinking with her five brothers, living day to day with a child to feed and no prospects, no safety net to fall back on. It put the claims of poverty and 'Beatness' of people such as Herbert Huncke into true perspective. These were the real *falaheen* that he saw himself as one of. Jack lasted for two weeks before his mother sent him $50 to take the bus back home. There is no question but that he used Bea Franco purely for 'experience': something to write about. It was another example of Jack's sometimes chilling disregard for the feelings and lives of others. His season was at an end, and he wrote: 'I was going home in October. Everybody goes home in October.' The bus took him to Pittsburgh, and he almost starved on the final lap to New York, literally having to panhandle the subway fare to get from Times Square to Ozone Park.

Neal Cassady, meanwhile, had spent several nights at Ozone Park, waiting for Jack, but had left for the coast two days before Jack returned. Neal had been helping Bill Burroughs with his marijuana harvest in east Texas and the two of them, together with Herbert Huncke, who had also been living on Bill's farm, drove back to New York with the pot. Neal, who normally talked a mile a minute, was virtually silent throughout the trip, intimidated by Burroughs's presence. This brings into focus the veracity of Jack's description of Neal, which is sometimes taken as literally true. Bill Burroughs:

Of course a writer's idea of a person is always a fiction in itself. Like Kerouac's picture of Neal Cassady. Well, I saw a very different Neal than the one he saw. You have *On the Road*, where Neal is always talking. Well, he had a great capacity for silence. I've driven with him for eight hours and he never said a thing.

Waiting for Jack on his dresser was the neatly stacked manuscript of *The Town and the City*. His life had changed enormously since he first began the book, and already he had many new experiences to write up. Sensibly, he restricted himself to fulfilling the original plan and saving the new material for a future volume. The cross-continental trip had changed Jack: he was more mature and now had a wider outlook on the world, which he longed to write about. But first he had to finish *this* book. He would tune into Symphony Sid, the first DJ to play the new sounds of bebop, and settle down for a night before his typewriter. Sid's all-night jazz show alternated a half-hour of records with live sets, which in 1948 were usually broadcast from the Royal Roost, a large, comfortable Broadway jazz club, the only one to charge admission, that had bars with names like the Cock Lounge where all the pimps hung out. Symphony Sid's announcement patter was quite stylised, with a forties intonation that he shared with American sportscasters of the period. Sid would also read the ads, one of which ran: 'When fate deals you one from the bottom of the deck, fall by Sunshine Funeral Parlours. Your loved ones will be handled with dignity and care, and the cats at Sunshine will not lay too heavy a tab on you . . .'[10], which would lead straight into the next number. There is a slight flavour of his speech patterns in some of the passages of *The Town and the City*, particularly the second half of the book where Jack describes his experiences in Times Square with Huncke, Allen and Bill. Jack would crack a Benzedrine inhaler and work all night with Charlie Parker, Cootie Williams, and Dizzy Gillespie filling his ears as he typed. He placed himself in a semi-trancelike state to write. He would work flat out, the carriage bell dinging so constantly it sounded like a doorbell. Then he would sleep, eat well, always starting his day with a big breakfast when he got up in the afternoon, then back to work again.[11]

Jack occasionally went into the city, usually to hear jazz with Tom Livornese, and also spent time with Ed White and Hal Chase, though he no longer saw his future as allied to theirs. Denver had reminded Jack of Lowell, and he began to make trips back to his hometown to see his old friends, sometimes taking Hal Chase with him. His previous left-wing stance, shown in his letters to the Prometheans, had now given way to something closer to his mother's position. He wrote to Ed White, bemoaning the state of the country, corrupt unions and the lack of old-fashioned family values: 'The family is the root of it . . . It will all fall apart like Rome if there isn't a renaissance in American feeling. Our modern art depicting life-dissatisfaction certainly isn't helping.'[12] His remark about 'life-dissatisfaction' was particularly amusing considering that this was precisely the criticism most critics levelled against the Beat Generation and their works when they were finally published a decade later.

Though he had missed meeting Neal in New York, they stayed in touch by letter. Neal was settled in California with Carolyn and was writing the manuscript which was to become *The First Third*. His letters to Jack often discuss the technical aspects of writing and there was one which particularly impressed Jack and contributed to the development of his writing style. Neal:

> I have always held that when one writes one should forget all rules, literary style, and other such pretensions as large words, lordly clauses and other phrases as such . . . Rather, I think, one should write, as nearly as possible, as if he were the first person on earth and was humbly and sincerely putting on paper that which he saw and experienced, loved and lost; what his passing thoughts were and his sorrows and desires; and these things should be said with careful avoidance of common phrases, trite usage of hackneyed words and the like. One must combine Wolfe and Flaubert – and Dickens.

Here again, coming from Cassady, an Irish Catholic, is the Celtic notion that writing is the telling of the tale, a chronicle of thoughts and impressions. It predates the sophisticated invention of the novel in which language is used to invent fiction. Neal's ideas and Jack's own rapid-fire writing technique were inexorably moving Kerouac towards spontaneous prose, though, for the moment, he was still essentially writing imitations of Thomas Wolfe.

The biggest influence upon Jack's life at this time, aside from his mother, was Allen Ginsberg. Allen and Neal's stay with Burroughs on his east-Texas farm had not been a success because Neal was utterly unable to return Allen's love, mentally or physically. After much manoeuvring and subterfuge, Allen conceded defeat and shipped out from Houston to mend his broken heart. He went to Dakar on the West African coast but, when he returned, he was still obsessed by Neal.

His obsession took on pathological dimensions and, in May 1948, Allen had an extraordinary series of aural hallucinations in which he heard the ancient voice of William Blake, reading poetry to him across the vault of time. Ever after, Allen was not sure if it was a nervous breakdown, a schizophrenic episode of 'hearing voices', or a genuine mystical experience. He eventually determined that it was genuine, and in 1984 maintained that it was 'probably the most real experience I've ever had'.¹³ Certainly it was an epiphany, or series of epiphanies, for the incidents occurred over a space of days, in which he saw the people on the streets, in the Columbia University bookshop and on Broadway, in all their trembling vulnerability, stripped of all pretence and armour, worried, anxious, terrified, sad, suffering as they went about their business. He felt waves of compassion for them, so strong that he scared himself. Whatever caused it, it gave Allen a powerful, deep insight into humanity that changed him for ever. It gave him the depth of understanding that was to lead him to become not only a world-famous poet, but a political activist, tirelessly dedicated to making the world a better place. Most of his friends, however, assumed that he'd finally flipped out and was following in his mad mother's footsteps.

Allen had returned to Columbia but was in a fragile state. He was actively exploring the gay bars of New York as well as mingling with the Columbia intellectuals – Allen was to become one of the greatest networkers of all time, though never with the intention of personal gain. He was writing dense, rather contrived, academic poetry which no one except Kerouac seemed to understand, though Allen's standing was high among his circles of friends and acquaintances as a literary critic. He was now extremely well read and his opinions were highly regarded.

Jack also constantly dropped literary references but they were usually gauche, and were confined to the works of Celine, Rimbaud or, naturally, Thomas Wolfe. Jack was a very slow reader and, although he eventually read many of the classics, he could not keep up with someone like Ginsberg, who had long ago overtaken him in his breadth of study.

Early in 1948, Jack showed Allen the manuscript of *The Town and the City*, which was now nearing completion in its first draft. Allen was so moved that he sobbed when he reached the end of it, now even more convinced than before that Kerouac was a genius. In fact, by the sound of it, the first draft was so modelled on Thomas Wolfe as to be a pastiche. Jack, however, was very pleased with it and himself. He quoted it in letters to people and, encouraged by Ginsberg, showed sections of it to critics and friends all across New York. He was most upset when people made critical comments; he was interested only in receiving praise for his achievement and did not want criticism, constructive or otherwise.

Allen extolled his work everywhere he went, and Jack reciprocated. Throughout 1948 they were a sort of double act, both convinced of each other's genius, endlessly promoting each other to anyone who would stand still long enough to listen. Their friends were impressed, as much by the fact that Jack had managed to write such a long manuscript as by the actual content of the book, but when it came to the world of commercial publishing things were different. In May 1948, Jack sent it to Scribners – Thomas Wolfe's publisher – who rejected it.

Jack habitually chose to allow someone else to decide his social life for him: when he was with Hal Chase, they saw his Denver friends; when he was with Allen, he saw the crowd that Allen was currently moving with. At this time they were mostly Columbia and ex-Columbia intellectuals, many of whom were hopeful writers. The roster included Gene Pippin and his wife Mary, John Hohnsbeen, Ed Stringham and Alan Harrington, a critic for the *New Yorker*.

Allen had sub-let an apartment from a theology student called Russell Durgin, and it was in his fifth-floor, walk-up apartment in Spanish Harlem that Allen had heard the voice of Blake. It was a very lively area, the streets filled with music and the aroma of spices and food cooking. On 4 July 1948, Allen threw a big Independence Day party. Alan Harrington brought along his friend John Clellon Holmes, and it was at this party that Holmes first met Ginsberg, Lucien Carr and Jack Kerouac. Holmes did not know anyone and so began looking at the bookshelves in the living room while the party raged in the kitchen. Durgin had a wonderful collection of eighteenth-century verse in fine editions, as well as an extensive library of scholarly religious studies, all neatly annotated. Regrettably, the best books in the library were subsequently stolen by Herbert Huncke, who sold them for a fraction of their real value.

As Holmes perused the shelves, he became aware of someone flopped out on the settee. It was Jack, who had withdrawn to the relative calm of the living room. He and Holmes began talking and immediately struck up a friendship. They met again the next day and found that they had a great deal in common. Two weeks after their first meeting, Jack stopped by Holmes's place with an enormous old leather doctor's bag containing the bulky manuscript of *The Town and the City* for Holmes to borrow and read.

There still remained a definite division between the aspiring New York intelligentsia, with their cocktail parties and endless talk about the *New Yorker* and editors and publishers, and the Beat circles of Allen Ginsberg, Bill Burroughs and Herbert Huncke. The New Yorkers did not take drugs, nor did it amuse them to spend all night sitting in the Royal Roost while Jack and Allen bopped their heads up and down to the beat. Holmes, however, was a transition figure between the two worlds, a genuinely open and honest individual, with a writer's eye for detail, but ultimately square and professorial, as his later career showed. He understood the nascent Beat Generation, understood where it was coming from, and for a while was a part of it – certainly as much as the San Francisco Renaissance poets of a decade later. In fact, without John Clellon Holmes the sobriquet Beat Generation would possibly not have been coined.

The Beat Generation was named in Holmes's small apartment at 681 Lexington Avenue, five flights up. Only two people were present: John Clellon Holmes and Jack Kerouac. Their accounts naturally differ. They both recalled the incident to Al Aronowitz ten years after the event. Jack:

> We were talking about the Lost Generation and what this generation would be called. And we thought of various names and I said, 'Ah, this is really a Beat Generation!' – and he leapt up and 'You've got it!' – see, just like that.

John Clellon Holmes: 'Jack and I never talked about the Lost Generation particularly. You see, when Jack used that phrase, we certainly didn't say, "That's it! That's it!" and make a big issue out of it.' Holmes gave a good description of the period in the late forties when Kerouac and Ginsberg were first flexing their muscles. The definition Beat then covered everyone who was part of their community, not just writers, because no one had yet published anything.
Holmes:

> In those days we were excited about everything and interested in everything. We were talking about where literature was going but, more important, we were talking about what everybody was feeling. Jack used to come over to my place on Lexington Avenue in the afternoon – he'd sleep there at night if he'd be in New York – and we would just talk. We would have some beers and we would play jazz records and we would talk talk all night. We talked for hours and hours and hours – I shudder to think of all the time we spent simply talking, not intellectual talk but exciting talk. As I said, we were very excited about life then.
> Jack knew a lot of different kinds of people that I didn't know, and this excitement was one thing they all had in common – a real hunger for life that had nothing to do with

ideas necessarily or education or intellectual trends but just with life itself. I felt that there was a great sense of identity and at this time we were all trying to put it into words, to label it, not just in terms of a generation – that came out accidentally. The phrase 'Beat Generation' – it wasn't about a group of writers because there wasn't any group of writers in those days.

Actually, what Jack said was, 'Everybody I know is furtive. They have a kind of furtiveness to them. They go along the street with a kind of interior knowledge on their faces which they're not admitting to. And, although they're reacting just like anybody else, inside they've got something new.' So for a long time I thought about this, and he did too, not with any plan in mind. And then one day he said, 'You know, everybody I know is kind of beat.' And that, as I recall, is the first time he used it in those days and just about the only time – oh, he'd used it in fun after that . . .

You see, everybody had hoped there would be a brave new world after the war, but it didn't work out that way. There wasn't even the decade of peace we had after the First World War. The Second World War ended in 1945 and by 1947 everybody was talking about the next one. By 1948, who could believe that any international organisation would be able to work this thing out? So that thrust you right back on yourself. What you felt yourself. Your eagerness for life, that was the important thing, and that meant jazz, liquor and fun.[14]

A name denotes an attitude: punks, hippies, teddy boys, existentialists; all are loaded terms. To define a generation is a brilliant move: as soon as it has been given a name, it exists. The term 'Beat Generation' created the Beats just as F Scott Fitzgerald wrote the Jazz Age into existence. Fitzgerald explained:

By a generation I mean that reaction against the fathers which seems to occur about three times in a century. It is distinguished by a set of ideas inherited in modified form from the madmen and the outlaws of the generation before; if it is a real generation it has its own leaders and spokesmen, and it draws into its orbit those born just before it and just after, whose ideas are less clear-cut and defiant.[15]

The term 'Beat Generation' has been the subject of much discussion, both in its origin and its meaning. Allen Ginsberg always credited Herbert Huncke with the use of the term 'Beat', which is no doubt the case. Allen:

> Huncke was a hipster, a thief, a junkie, but also a very romantic and Dostoyevskian character. I'm sure that, if you asked Jack about it, he would say that he associates the word Beat with Huncke, who was sort of a great visionary too. Because the point of Beat is that you get beat down to a certain nakedness where you are actually able to see the word in a visionary way, which is the old classical understanding of what happens in the dark night of the soul. If you want to understand the word beat as it is used by metaphysical hipsters, you have to look at Saint John of the Cross in his conception of the dark night of the soul. It's exactly the same thing as beat as it's used or as it can be used.
>
> I'd say that the primary fact of any beat writer of any interest is that each of them has individually had some kind of Kafkian experience of what would ordinarily be called the super natural – but which is not super natural, really: it's right there at the bottom of the universe . . .

This definition, made ten years later,[16] was closer to our present understanding of whom the term refers to. It has narrowed the perimeters to make it into a literary movement, rather than a social grouping, and by Ginsberg's insistence on an epiphanous experience, a taste of some sort of partial madness, he conveniently eliminates all the Harringtons, Stringhams and Livorneses from the group.[17]

Jack had an eventful summer in the city, with many girlfriends, drunken nights and brooding tortured days. He worked steadily on revising *The Town and the City*, already aware that it was out of date. Now that he knew the Times Square characters, had taken drugs and had crossed America by road, it was no longer an accurate reading of his mind. Though he introduced some of these elements, it was clear that the trip to California required a separate book.

His view of the world was now pretty much determined. He recognised his loneliness and seeming inability to establish a long-term, deep relationship with a woman. He had a profound awareness of death having watched his father fade and die, embittered and angry. Though he was controlled by his mother, whom he even allowed to read his mail, it was his father who was the role model. Lucien Carr always maintained that Jack wanted to be just like Leo – a big fish in a small pond – and there was a side of Jack that was a know-it-all, always pointing out the obvious to people as if they were dolts. Allen Ginsberg regarded Jack's relationship with his father as 'probably the central love experience of his life'. It was no surprise then that death of the father is the central drama of *The Town and the City*.

Jack also began work on two new books: *Doctor Sax: The Myth of The Rainey Night* and *On the Road*. He worked on both simultaneously, in the case of *Doctor Sax* working from a story outline which he had sketched out completely during the summer.

On 15 December, Jack received a telephone call from Neal in San Francisco, saying that he had just spent all his savings on a 1949 Hudson, and wanted to drive it to New York 'to break it in'. Neal proposed that he pick up Jack and return with him to San Francisco. Neal's friend from the railroad, Al Hinkle, was coming along for the ride, but there was one small flaw in the plan: they had no actual money. Jack promised to send them $10, and said that they should pick him up at his sister's place in Rockey Mount, North Carolina, where he and his mother would be spending the Christmas vacation. Neal called a few days later to give Jack a different address to send the money, which suggested that all was not well at home. Despite this, Jack appears to have had no qualms about the plan, which involved Neal leaving his wife, Carolyn, and their three-month-old baby daughter destitute in San Francisco while he made an utterly pointless trip east.

Carolyn, for her part, was frantic with worry. For the first time she saw Neal in his true light: he was prepared to abandon wife and child, squander their complete savings (most of which was her money), all for the sake of movement, for kicks. His carefully woven web of lies and deceit unravelled like an old sweater. She had been conned. Though he had talked her into it, there was no way that Neal was ever going to accept the responsibility of parenthood and marriage. In fact, the whole idea scared him witless. It was the beginning of a pattern that characterised their marriage: Neal would spend all their money and get into debt at the racetrack, have scores, even hundreds, of girlfriends – many of the liaisons near rape – then return home and confess all to Carolyn as if she were his priest. Her anger would make him feel comfortably guilty and able to start all over again. With a young child, Carolyn had little choice but to go along with his puerile behavior.

Carolyn:

A lot of people don't understand how conventional they were.

Neal was consumed with guilt because he couldn't follow the rules. He had a Catholic background; he was a family man, a hard worker. He always had a job on the railroad. My values were too strict in the other direction – too puritan. When he came home, I told him all the things he'd done wrong. Nag. Nag. Nag. That was what he wanted to hear so he could go out and do it again. It took me ten years to wise up.[18]

To raise sufficient funds for the trip, Neal and Al Hinkle hatched the plan of taking along Al's girlfriend, Helen, whom they thought had money. She was interested but refused to go off with Al unless they were married. It was the 1940s and certain proprieties had to be observed. A quick marriage was arranged and they set off. To Neal and Al's dismay, it turned out that Helen was not rich after all. She objected to Neal smoking pot in the car and demanded that they spend the nights in motels – it was, after all, her honeymoon. Neal wanted to drive all night, only stopping for gas and food, and relations soon soured between them. When they reached Tucson, Arizona, Helen ran out of money so they simply left her there. Al gave her his railroad pass, which he assured her would get her to New Orleans, and told her they would pick her up there in a week's time. Neal suggested she stay with Bill Burroughs, who was now living in Algiers, just across the Mississippi from New Orleans. Burroughs knew nothing about this, had never heard of Al Hinkle, and was not happy about being imposed upon in this way by a strange woman.

Neal, meanwhile, now detoured north to Denver with the intention of picking up his former wife, LuAnne. She was engaged to be married at the time, but her future husband was conveniently away at sea so she gladly came along on the trip, always open for an adventure. They roared off across America. The battered Hudson pulled up in front of Nin and Paul Blake's house on Christmas Eve and discharged its grubby occupants. Jack immediately invited them all to share their Christmas meal, much to his sister's surprise. Neal turned on the charm and proposed that he drive all of Nin's furniture to New York, as she and her family had decided to move in with Gabrielle at Ozone Park. It took two trips to transport Hinkle, Jack, LuAnne, Memere and the furniture to New York, trips which Neal accomplished in three days – more than 2,000 miles through the December weather.

Though Memere got on well with LuAnne, Nin and her family were arriving shortly, so Neal, Hinkle and LuAnne needed to find somewhere to stay. Allen Ginsberg was more than happy to have them invade his place so Neal and LuAnne quickly installed themselves in his new apartment on York Avenue. Allen was working the night shift at Associated Press so they were able to use his bed while he was out. Allen would crawl into bed with them both when he got home. After a few days Allen took time off work rather than miss any of the fun of being around Neal in New York. Allen was puzzled as to the point of Neal's round trip but, as neither Jack nor Neal would, or could, answer him, he shrugged and gave up, happy to enjoy their company. Jack was at York Avenue most of the time and life consisted of a round of holiday parties leading to the New Year. One memorable day they all went to visit Alan Ansen's wonderful house in the country, where Jack and LuAnne took a bath together and Neal went to bed with the host.

Back in New York, Neal sent LuAnne out to work while the men sat around stoned day and night. After a few weeks, Neal began to beat her. After he stole $2 from Lucien Carr it seemed as though the season in New York was coming to an end. It was time to get on the road. Jack was thrilled to be travelling with Neal and had his eye set on living with LuAnne when they reached the coast.

As the sun set over the New Jersey swamps on 19 January 1949, Jack, Al Hinkle, Neal and LuAnne set out for Washington DC on their way to New Orleans to collect poor Helen Hinkle, who was still trapped, penniless, with Bill Burroughs. Bill had been frantically sending cables and letters, demanding to know where her husband was but, despite his irritation, he could not resist a literary allusion in his letter to Allen: 'Mrs Hinkle is here for the past week. "Gathering her brows like the gathering Storm, Nursing her wrath to keep it warm." Tam O'Shanter – Robert Burns. Can't say as I blame her much.' Bill said he did not mind her staying as she was a most considerate guest, but 'I seriously consider this kind of irresponsible behaviour intolerable'.[19] After several cables, he wrote again, 'Does this Hinkle character expect to billet his wife on me indefinitely?'

The travelling party eventually pitched up in Algiers. Al and Helen Hinkle were reunited, apparently amicably, and decided to stay on in New Orleans while Jack, LuAnne and Neal headed west via Tucson, where they hoped to borrow money from Alan Harrington. Burroughs could not see the validity of the trip, like Ginsberg, except that he expressed his feelings more forcefully. In a letter to Allen he compared the trip, for its sheer compulsive pointlessness, to the mass migrations of the Mayans, then told Allen in no uncertain terms of his low opinion of Neal:

> . . . leaves his wife and child without $ one, cons other people (LuAnne, Kerouac) into sending a few $s for their support while he refuses to do a lick of work, or even send his wife a single letter. Then he arrives here and has the unmitigated gall to expect me to advance $ for the continuation of this wretched trip . . . I would not have contributed one cent, if I were wallowing in $s.

When Neal realised that Bill was not going to be conned, his friendly attitude towards Bill cooled considerably. But Jack managed to get $25 from Memere, so they were soon off again.

Bill regarded it as appalling weakness on Jack and LuAnne's parts to arrive in San Francisco penniless, depending on other people to look after them, and was sure that, any money they did raise, Neal would quickly con out of them. Jack was hoping to live with LuAnne when they reached San Francisco, but had not considered any of the practicalities. When Neal asked where they wanted to be dropped off, Jack was nonplussed. LuAnne gave the address of a hotel but Jack appeared to be in a daze. As soon as Neal left them, to return to the luckless Carolyn, Jack had deflated like a balloon. Whereas LuAnne wanted a strong man to take the lead, Jack was passive and needed a strong woman to make the decisions. He was penniless and guilty about spending his mother's hard-earned cash on this senseless trip. Jack spent the night sobbing in LuAnne's arms and withdrew so completely into himself that for the next few days she could not make contact with him. His mother sent him the bus fare and he returned to New York, stopping off for a day in Detroit to see Edie.

Back in Ozone Park, he resumed simultaneous work on *Doctor Sax* and *On the Road*, though he had not yet decided how to structure *On the Road*. He was still seeing a lot of Allen, who now had Huncke living with him at York Avenue. Allen seemed to have no control over his daily life and Huncke was stealing all his possessions and selling them. Despite his domestic chaos, Allen was still moving in intellectual circles, developing friendships and reading voraciously. Following Scribner's rejection of *The Town and the City*, Allen took the manuscript to Mark Van Doren, his English professor at Columbia, a Pulitzer-prize winner and a reader for Harcourt Brace. Van Doren was impressed and, after a meeting with Jack, telephoned Robert Giroux and recommended that Harcourt

Brace publish it. On 29 March 1949, Jack received a letter offering him a $1,000 advance on the book.

Jack was elated. He could pay his mother back – at least in part – for supporting him all these years. It meant that his confidence in himself as a writer was not misplaced. He sat down and wrote a long prayer to God, thanking him, writing it out in double-thickness letters, like a child, to emphasise his sincerity. Jack's imagination went into overdrive at the implications of being a published writer. He assumed that his book would be bought by Hollywood and envisioned himself sitting in the writers' block, working on the screenplay. He had fantasies of going to Paris and the Côte d'Azur.

He decided to use the money to move himself and his mother, accompanied by sister Nin and her family, to the countryside outside Denver, where they could live in the healthy fresh air, surrounded by good clean Western folk. Jack had now accepted that he was attached to his mother for ever; they were a couple even if she was not his actual wife. His obsession with her excluded the very idea that he might move to the West with a wife of his own to raise a family. His decision to leave New York City was also prompted by two unfortunate events involving Burroughs and Ginsberg. The former was arrested on a heroin-possession charge in New Orleans and the latter was caught with his apartment full of stolen goods: Huncke had been using it to store the spoils from his many robberies. Though Huncke would inevitably be returned to jail, Allen had not been on any of the robberies, nor did he stand to gain from them. It was, however, his apartment and he could not deny knowledge of what Huncke was doing. Intervention from the Columbia authorities in the shape of Van Doren and Lionel Trilling resulted in him spending time at the Columbia Psychiatric Institute instead of appearing in court.

Jack, meanwhile, was working during the day with Robert Giroux, editing *The Town and the City* into shape, and writing *On the Road* at night. The book seems to have taken a long time to edit, but Giroux was obviously very taken by Jack so he was probably in no great hurry to finish. Jack went to Denver to look for property but, with none of his old friends there, he suddenly felt lonely. Justin Brierly and one of his boyfriends helped Jack househunt and they eventually found a small house in the suburb of Westwood. Memere, Nin and Paul Blake were shipped out, complete with furniture, but Jack's mother hated it from the moment she got there. She was afraid that they would be caught in a mudslide off the nearby mountains and she was lonely. She had no one to talk to because Nin and Paul were at work all day, and Jack tended to sleep during the day and work at night. In addition, Paul began talking about returning to North Carolina almost as soon as he got there. The move was clearly not a success.

Robert Giroux visited Denver in July to work with Jack on the revised draft of *The Town and the City*. Together they hitchhiked in the mountains and went with Justin Brierly to the Central City Opera. Jack's mother returned to New York and, though his visit to Denver is in *On the Road*, Jack doesn't mention the fact that he moved there with his mother, who is undoubtedly the unconvincingly described, unnamed female in the book who slips him $100 to go from Denver to San Francisco.

Not surprisingly, Neal and Carolyn's marriage was not going well. Neal constantly two-timed her with a succession of one-night, or one-hour, stands, and continued to see LuAnne several times a week, while denying everything to Carolyn. Despite his own philandering and married status, he was jealous that LuAnne had other men, and in the course of an argument he threw a punch at her, missed her head and struck his left hand forcefully against the wall, breaking his thumb. The hospital inserted a traction pin which became infected and the tip of his thumb had to be amputated. In addition, a previous car-crash injury caused his nose to collapse and he also developed a cyst on his leg. To make their life even more complicated, Carolyn discovered that she was pregnant once more. When Jack arrived at 2 a.m. at 29 Russell Street in Russian Hill, Carolyn was distraught. Jack's presence always caused a major disruption in their life. He ignored her completely, demanding all of Neal's time, jealous of anyone else getting his friend's attention just as he was when other boys came to visit his brother Gerard.

Neal was in many ways a fantasy substitute brother, despite Neal being five years younger. Jack could not accept, or didn't even notice, that Neal had a wife, baby and responsibilities. Jack just wanted to go out to play and was unconcerned that his impact on other people's lives might be a negative one. Jack and Neal ran around town for a week, smoking pot, staying up all night in jazz joints, while Carolyn stayed at home and looked after the baby. Eventually Carolyn was unable to stand it any longer and threw them both out. Her relationship with Neal was at rock bottom: she was frantic with worry at the thought of yet another child to feed and unable to accept any of Neal's reassurances, knowing them to be lies. Instead of trying to help matters, Jack exacerbated the situation by inviting

Neal to New York, offering to pay his way with his advance money from Harcourt Brace, and suggested they go on from there to Italy.

Jack and Neal located a drive-away car to be delivered to Denver and, after a night of drinking, left San Francisco for Denver without even telephoning Carolyn to tell her they were leaving. Neal claimed he could not write with his bandaged thumb and had Helen Hinkle write a note saying he would not be back. Helen took the opportunity to tell Neal some home truths, which Jack dutifully reported in *On the Road*. Helen:

> You have absolutely no regard for anybody but yourself and your damned kicks. All you think about is what's hanging between your legs and how much money or fun you can get out of people and then you just throw them aside ... It nevers occurs to you that life is serious and there are people trying to make something decent out of it instead of just goofing all the time.

Jack lamely tried to defend Neal, claiming that it was Carolyn that threw him out.

In *On the Road* Jack's hopelessly sentimental image of Neal is revealed: 'That's what Dean was, the HOLY GOOF.' It is the word 'holy' that gives it away: any fool except Kerouac could see there was nothing remotely holy about Neal. Jack wrote, 'I suddenly realized that Dean, by virtue of his enormous series of sins, was becoming the Idiot, the Imbecile, the Saint of the lot.' Neal was in a near-psychotic state, presumably brought on by the prospect of another child and the responsibility that goes with it.

The car already had a driver and passengers when they signed on, but Neal convinced them to let him drive. The other passengers in the car were scared but Neal dismissed them contemptuously. He drove like a madman, deliberately engineering hair-raising situations from which he extricated himself at the very last moment, just as an enormous truck was barreling down on them. The car's original driver was a homosexual, with whom Neal had violent sex all night, treating the man 'like an old hen', as Ginsberg laughingly put it, but Neal was annoyed when the man didn't pay him.

In Denver, Neal went out of control: he attempted to seduce a neighbour's daughter until her mother appeared with a shotgun, and he tried the same with the fourteen-year-old daughter of the woman they were staying with. This time Jack intervened and Neal petulantly smashed one of the girl's records in a shabby act of revenge. At a fairground Neal followed a nine-year-old Mexican girl around, fantasising wildly. That evening, to prove his manhood, his youth, or just to show off to Jack, he stole six cars in a row, finishing up by parking a detective's car outside their front door. Considering his fingerprints were still on file from robberies past, this was a very stupid move and the next day they left town in a hurry.

They found a drive-away Cadillac to deliver to Chicago, which Neal cranked up to 110 mph before the speedometer broke. In Detroit they spent a week with Edie, living a life of luxury, but Neal was subdued and did not enjoy it, and Jack was so scruffy and dirty that he was picked up and frisked on the streets of Grosse Pointe. With Edie he could have had all the wealth and luxury he wanted, but he realised it was not for him, and in the course of a long serious talk they decided to have their marriage annulled, using Edie's father's lawyer.

Jack's mother had moved to 94-21 134th Street in Richmond Hill, Queens, near Atlantic Avenue and not far from their old place in Ozone Park. It was a small apartment and when Jack arrived with Neal she told him firmly that Neal was only allowed to stay for a few days. Jack meekly acquiesced.

It only took Neal a few days to find a girl to latch on to and within a week he was living with a New York model called Diana Hansen and they were planning to get married. He met her at a party. There were many parties, some of them for Jack, who was fêted as a soon-to-be-famous novelist, the first of the group. Though he was living at the Columbia Psychiatric Institute, Allen Ginsberg could be signed out for the weekend, so he did not miss any of the action. Sometimes he brought with him a new friend from the ward: Carl Solomon, to whom he would later dedicate his most famous poem 'Howl For Carl Solomon'.

Another new addition to the outer circle was Chandler Brossard, who, though he was never close friends with Jack and company, belonged to the same crowd. In fact, his first novel, *Who Walk in Darkness* is considered by some critics to be the first Beat novel. It is a passive observation of a month in the lives of a circle of Greenwich Village Bohemians at the beginning of the summer of 1948 – more or less the same Beat Generation crowd that both John Clellon Holmes and Jack were writing about. The publication of *Who Walk in Darkness* was held up by editor Delmore Schwartz, who thought he could detect portraits of Anatole Broyard (as Henry Porter) and Milton Klonsky (as Max Glazer) in the book, and insisted on changes being made to the text at proof stage. Portraits of Stanley Gould (as

133

Cap Fields), Bill Gaddis (as Harry Lees), and Seymour Krim can also be identified. But Brossard was not writing in the Kerouac manner and the characters were all composites. Brossard wrote: 'I am not into, nor was I ever into, the *roman à clef*, or any other such cleft palates, wop or otherwise.'[20]

Jack's book came out first. He had arrived back to find that Giroux wanted even more revisions, but these were completed on 18 November and publication was finally set for March 1950. That December, the core group whom Allen believed would change the face of literature – Jack, Allen and Neal Cassady – gathered at the mid-century New Year's party. Also present were Carl Solomon, Anatole Broyard and Philip Lamantia; they were the new generation waiting in the wings, waiting to take over.

As publication day drew near, Jack began to worry about what to wear when he was interviewed to publicise the book. His mother normally bought all of his clothes and he didn't even know his collar size. Jack was never known for his dress sense, nor, for that matter, were most of the Beats, despite the fact that these days they are used in advertisements for sports shoes and casual clothes. Jack was uncomfortable in anything other than a tartan work shirt and chino pants and was often so scruffy and dirty that he was mistaken for a bum. Lucien Carr, who was something of a snappy dresser, remembered Jack visiting him at UPI after the publication party for *The Town and the City*:

> Jack really was a fucking peasant. He never wanted to come up to UPI because he felt he was kind of a bum, you know. So he arrived, I guess, after they had a little party for that book and all of a sudden, man, he'd gone out and bought himself a suit! And son of a bitch. I mean it was like, *electric* blue. It was sort of black woven, iridescent . . . So there, he shows up, at UPI, in this suit . . . with his black-haired old stocky self, standing in this thing, and I'm supposed to say, 'Wow, Jack, you look . . .' and I say 'Holy Fucking Shit!', 'Je-sus, they've let the Cannucks in here!'. His colour was blue, his colour always was blue . . . Who could have put this suit on him? No one. No one but himself. He went and got this one, by himself.[21]

Perhaps because of Lucien's reaction, Jack asked Tom Livornese to help him buy a suitable outfit to wear on more formal occasions.

Critical reaction to Jack's book was not exactly ecstatic. The reviewers of course noticed the huge debt to Thomas Wolfe. How could they not when even the title was modelled upon *Of Time and the River* (1935) and *The Web and the Rock* (1939)? In the novel, Kerouac splits himself and his family into a number of brothers and sisters to describe his family history in small-town Galloway. His intention was to write a big *Bildungsroman*, like Thomas Mann's *Buddenbrooks*, a family saga on a broad canvas that dealt with generations and social history. Jack: 'It's not strictly autobiographical since I used various friends and girlfriends, and my own parents, to form a large family, the Martin family, who live in an old Victorian house on Galloway Road (which is actually Varnum Avenue).'[22]

In Virginia Woolf's *The Waves* the six characters were supposed to be different aspects of one individual but, as one of them says, 'How we suffered when we were divided'. The same could be said about the Martin family in *The Town and the City*. The division of himself into small parts, each corresponding to what he saw as different facets of his personality, was perhaps an unconscious recognition of the divided personality which was to cause him such misery. Certainly none of them really comes alive. Kerouac later repudiated the novel, saying:

> *The Town and the City*: that was mostly fiction. Fiction is nothing but idle daydreams. Look what I did with *The Town and the City* – I gave my father a nice big house. I gave my mother three daughters to help her wash the dishes. I gave myself four brothers. Bah! Idle daydreams. The way to write is with real things and real people.[23]

It is interesting that the three daughters and six sons of the Martin family correspond quite well to the Sampas family: Sebastian had six brothers and three sisters, one of whom, of course, Jack was later to marry. Sebastian gets very sentimental treatment in the book. He is portrayed as a great friend, a comrade, a confidant in the 'first glories of poetry and truth'. Jack described him as the first boy he met who was interested in books, who spoke of 'ideals', 'beauty', and 'truth', a boy who read poetry aloud in the streets with tears in his eyes.[24]

Maurice Poteet has pointed out the similarity in structure between *The Town and the City* and *The Delusson Family*, by Jacques Ducharme, 1939.[25] The narrator is called Peter in Jack's book; Pierre in Ducharme's. The death of the father is the strongest, most moving scene in both books. The cast of characters in both books includes a mother, a vagabond character who works the railroad or as a farm labourer, a young boy who dies in infancy, two independent strong-willed sisters, a college-educated son, and a son who moves away to work on a farm. Poteet also found a remarkable example of a 'found phrase' in a passage from *The Town and the City*:

> When all the family was stilled in sleep, when the streetlamp a few paces from the house shone at night and made grotesque *shadows of the trees* upon the house, when the river sighed off in the darkness, when the trains hooted on their way to Montreal . . .

Ducharme's next novel, published in 1943, was called *The Shadows of the Trees: The Story of French Canadians in New England*. Did Jack have it on his desk and did the words from its jacket unconsciously find their way into his narrative?

Jack's persona in *The Town and the City* is Peter Martin, who is the most completely described of all the characters in it. In attempting a large Wolfean canvas, Kerouac spreads himself too thin. The characters never successfully rise off the page, particularly the women, who are all poorly drawn. Sister Liz, for instance, is a charmless, artificial stereotype, as is the stocky homebody Rosie. By creating seven children, when he was really only describing the many facets of himself, he made them all one-dimensional and they become ultimately confusing and impossible to keep track of.[26]

The Town and the City shows why Kerouac stuck to reportage rather than develop his fiction. He clearly found it very difficult to write convincingly about anything other than actual events. His writing is strong when describing something that happened to him and weak when he attempts fiction: the death of Charley Martin in Okinawa is unconvincing, whereas the death of George Martin, Kerouac's father in the book, is awkward but ultimately plausible.

He is not successful in dealing with adult themes because he had so little experience of them himself. In his world, life is simple: his girlfriend Ann 'simply drifted away from her husband's home . . . There was no argument about the child; Anne simply went away and left the child in his care.' The welfare of the child or the psychological damage caused, a subject which most novelists would explore, simply does not occur to Kerouac. In fact, 'Francis felt the sheer delight and almost idiotic wickedness that truly indifferent men feel when they "steal" another man's wife without having given it much thought'. Jack was internalising Neal Cassady's way of using the world.

There are, however, beautiful passages describing the New England countryside, and, as it is a *Bildungsroman*, there is the obligatory growing self-awareness of the hero:

> He was a ghostly stranger, he was a dreaming forgotten thing, and he was an anguish-stricken humility, and nothing else . . . Peter almost with tears in his eyes late one night realized that other people were also strangers to themselves, and were lonely and troubled like him.

Jack throws all of his experiences into the book, from *The Shadow* to the Pokerino all-night slot-machine arcade on Times Square. The greatest interest in the book comes from Kerouac's introduction of the characters in the Beat pantheon: William Burroughs as Will Dennison, Allen Ginsberg as Leon Levinsky, and Herbert Huncke as Junky. Some of his fictionalised portraits are inventively handled. David Kammerer, for instance, is given only one arm, something William Burroughs regarded as a brilliant piece of writing, as it showed the emotionally crippled side of Kammerer by using a simple and direct device.

It gives a portrait of the original Beat Generation, seen in their mid-forties habitat around Times Square: Allen Ginsberg carrying the works of Rimbaud and WH Auden under his arm, smoking a cigarette stuck in a red holder; the scene in Times Square at four in the morning, all the cast-offs of society milling around under the horrible bluish glare of the intense neon lights, as seen with amphetamine vision – Jack wrote much of *The Town and the City* on speed.

Jack described how the lights illuminated every pore, every defect of the skin, making everybody look like a zombie, like a walking corpse. They looked, he said, as if all the neuroses, suppressed aggression, restrictive morality and scatological repressions had finally gained the upper hand on humanity: 'Everyone is becoming a geek!' The idea that the suppression of the sexual drive and the internalisation of restrictive morality could result in illness comes from the work of Wilhelm Reich, who was just beginning to be read in Jack's circle. Kerouac had not yet read *The Function of the Orgasm*, which was published in 1942, and *The Mass Psychology of Fascism*, published in 1946, but he heard the others discussing them.[27]

These passages of the book did not fit convincingly with the rest of it, but were the most indicative of work to come. They usefully capture the early exploits of the group. Allen Ginsberg: 'In the later sections on Times Square and New York you get some echo, some discussion of bebop and bebop consciousness and bebop paranoia and amphetamine use and Benzadrine and shuddering metropolitan hallucinations.' There were many more to come.

7 Visions of Neal

The *Town and the City* did not take off. In fact, by April, one month after publication, the sales had more or less stalled. Jack was devastated: he had naively been relying on royalties to pay for yet another trip across country. Nonetheless, he continued with the round of parties and socialising that went with the book launch. Robert Giroux bought him a tuxedo and took him to cocktail parties and the opera and introduced him to Carl Sandberg, who gave him a big hug.

On another occasion, Jack, John Clellon Holmes and Jay Landesman, the editor of *Neurotica* magazine, visited Birdland and ran into Artie Shaw. Jay:

> All Jack wanted to talk about was Shaw's terrific arrangement of 'I'm comin' Virginia' and Shaw, recently divorced from Katherine Windsor, only wanted to talk about Dostoyevsky. Holmes and I broke into laughter as we watched the two giants struggling to communicate.[1]

Less famous, but of more significance in Jack's life, was someone to whom Allen Ginsberg introduced him: a young Italian-American poet who was fresh out of jail after serving a term for robbery. Gregory Corso first met Allen Ginsberg in the Pony Stable, a lesbian bar on Sixth Street. Allen, always on the lookout for attractive young men, took him first to meet Mark Van Doren and then to see Jack. Gregory's memory of their first meeting is fleeting – Jack was dressed all in white: T-shirt, pants and Merchant Marine cap. When Allen said that Gregory was a poet, Jack asked him, 'What's poetry?'

'In everything,' replied Gregory.

Their meeting probably took place at Sara Yorkley's apartment. She was an editor at UPI, where she had an affair with Lucien Carr.

As usual, Jack had been attracted to a woman who had previously been with one of his friends, though in this case she was still going out with Lucien and never could make up her mind between the two of them. She and Jack had a serious affair, with ball games and jazz clubs and quiet romantic dinners at French restaurants. They watched the Easter Day parade together on the steps of Saint Patrick's Cathedral on Fifth Avenue. Jack divided his time between her apartment, where he was now hard at work on *Gone on the Road*, as it was now called, and his mother's house in Richmond Hill. He and Sara planned to marry and go to Paris for their honeymoon, but Jack had to go on the road again first and that was the end of it all.

The strangest thing for Jack about going on the road was leaving Neal behind in New York. Neal had a job parking cars in a lot at Madison Avenue and 40th Street and was comfortably settled with Diana Hansen, planning marriage and babies, despite the fact that Carolyn had given birth to another daughter that January.

Jack had no sooner reached Denver, and started making the rounds, when Neal arrived, having used his parking-lot savings to buy a car. He rushed in and immediately demanded that Jack accompany him to Mexico where he was going to get a quick Mexican divorce from Carolyn in time to legitimise the child that Diana Hansen was about to have. (Neal had yet another child somewhere in California who never figures in any of the stories about him.) Frank Jeffries, another Denver buddy, decided to join them.

They arrived in Mexico like typical loudmouth American tourists: flashing their money recklessly, looking for marijuana and cheap whores. A severely edited version of the story is used as the last trip in *On the Road*, including a long scene in a whorehouse with underage girls. In Mexico City they connected with Bill Burroughs, who was living there with Joan and the two children: Julia and their baby, Willie Jr, who was born when Joan and Bill lived on the farm in east Texas. Jack and Neal rented an apartment next door to them and immersed themselves in the Mexico City nightlife.

Jack came down with dysentery and was confined to bed, but Neal was desperate to get back to his various wives and had no time to stay and nurse him. Jack's description of Neal's departure in *On the Road* is ambivalent. On the one hand, he doesn't mention that he had met up with Bill and Joan, which makes Neal's leaving into more of a betrayal than it actually was, no doubt to show that Neal would let everyone down, not just his women; on the other hand, he didn't reveal that Neal stole money from both Jack's and Frank's wallets before he left. In the book Jack comments, 'When I got better I realised what a rat he was.'

Jack spent his time in Mexico City smoking very strong grass. He tried to work on *On the Road* but found that he was too stoned to write properly and so he postponed the project until he returned to the calm of his room in Richmond Hill. After about three weeks of wandering the streets and hanging out with Burroughs and Joan, he hitchhiked back to the States, fetching up in New York rather the worse for wear. He returned to find that Neal, true to form, had arrived back in New York, married Diana, and, two hours after the ceremony, boarded a train using his railroad pass to rejoin Carolyn in San Francisco. Whether Neal ever obtained a Mexican divorce is not known; certainly Carolyn never received any notification that she was no longer married to him, so there is a strong likelihood that the New York marriage to Diana was bigamous.

For the remaining weeks of summer and into the autumn, Jack spent most of his time at home smoking pot and working, prompting Allen Ginsberg to write to Neal: 'He has been strangely out of town the last several months, in retirement and brooding on T alone, and when he rejoined New York society he seemed to me to be more settled in reality, more sober.'[2]

Jack spent time with Beverley Burford, who passed through town on her way to Europe, and also went out with a woman called Rayanna, Allen Ginsberg's ex. Ever since he was released from the mental hospital Ginsberg had been making an attempt at a straight sex life. He described Rayanna to Neal as 'sharp, a real NY "on the town" pro type.'[3] She was evidently too sharp for Jack because the affair didn't last long.

That summer both Jack and Allen saw a lot of William Cannastra, a brilliant young lawyer who had been a part of their circle for several years. Cannastra graduated from Harvard Law School but had done his undergraduate work at the University of Michigan. He was a good friend of WH Auden and knew Howard Moss, the poetry editor of the *New Yorker*. He was said to be the model for the hero of Tennessee Williams's *Cat on a Hot Tin Roof*, and certainly Williams always stayed at his loft on West 21st Street whenever he was in the city. Cannastra was, in Ginsberg's description, 'young and damned'. Allen had been amazed to see him take a bite out of a wine glass at a party and chew the broken shards. It was Cannastra who 'danced on broken wine glasses barefoot' in Ginsberg's *Howl*. It was in Cannastra's loft where 'People made love in the bathroom (often, without realising it, for a circle of spectators looking down from the skylight)' in Alan Harrington's *The Secret Swinger*,[4] where Cannastra is called Bill Genovese.

Cannastra was like Lucien Carr seven years before, and Jack acted out the same Joe College pranks with him. Jack:

> I did a couple of collaborations in bed with Bill Cannastra in lofts, with blondes. He says, let's take all our clothes off and run round the block ... it was raining you know. Sixteenth Street off Seventh Avenue. I said 'Well, I'll keep my shorts on' – he says 'No, no shorts'. I said 'I'm going to keep my shorts on'. He said 'All right, but I'm not going to wear mine'. And we trot trot trot trot down the block. Sixteenth to Seventeenth ... and we come back and run up the stairs – nobody saw us. But he was absolutely naked ... about 3 or 4 a.m. It rained. And everybody was there. He was dancing on broken glass and playing Bach. Bill was the guy who used to teeter off his roof – six flights up you know? He'd go – 'You want me to fall?' – we'd say no, Bill, no. He was an Italian. Italians are wild you know. He says 'Jack come with me and look down through this peephole'. We looked down through the peephole, we saw a lot of things ... into his toilet. I said 'I'm not interested in that, Bill'. He said 'You're not interested in anything'. Auden would come the next day. Maybe with Chester Kallman. Tennessee Williams.[5]

On the evening of 12 October 1950, Bill Cannastra was out with three friends, Anna Adams, Howard Jones, and Jose Varges. The party left Anna's house on Spring Street, SoHo, after a night of drinking and wandering the streets, and took the IRT local subway, on their way to Lucien's to borrow money. Though Cannastra normally spent his time at the San Remo, he was also a regular at the Bleeker Tavern. As the train pulled out of Bleeker Street Station, someone mentioned Winnie, a large friendly Black woman who was a regular there, and Bill yelled, 'Let's go back and see her!' He stuck his head and shoulders out of the window as a joke, but apparently misjudged his lurch and found himself hanging unbalanced out of the window. Jose Varges grabbed hold of him to pull him back as the train roared into the tunnel but his coat ripped and Varges couldn't reach his shoulders as he was too far out. When Bill saw what was happening, he began screaming to be pulled back. He ducked, trying to avoid the pillars in the tunnel, but there was a sudden thud and he was dragged out of the window to the tracks. Anna pulled the emergency cord, but he was towed 55 feet down the tunnel before the train came to a halt. His head was cracked open and he died on the way to Columbus Hospital.[6]

Allen was particularly shocked as he had left the San Remo with him after a five-hour talk about death only a few nights before. Allen wrote to Neal:

> Everybody – Carl, Howard Moss, Ansen, Holmes, Stringham, everybody who knew him – so many – as well as those we don't know from the past – got all big theories and week-long drunks, everybody's pride was beaten for a week. As in Greek tragedy, the purging of pity and terror. The great question on everybody's soul was: was it an accident or did he do it on purpose?[7]

Bill Cannastra's behaviour had always been so self-destructive that an element of doubt would always hang over his death.

Though Cannastra had been becoming more homosexual in his sexual preference, he was also involved with a nineteen-year-old woman named Joan Haverty whom he met in the artists' colony of Provincetown, where he was taking a vacation as a scallop-boat fisherman. At the end of the summer of 1949, she followed him to New York City and lived in his loft, joining in his complicated sexual adventures.

After Cannastra's death, Joan tried to maintain the loft as a shrine to his memory. She was still only twenty years old. Ginsberg tried to have an affair with her, but she could see that he only wanted to sleep with her in order to move in and when she rejected him he quickly turned against her. Then Jack turned up one evening, under the impression there was a party on at the loft. He called up to the window and was surprised when a pretty girl stuck her head out and asked who it was. He told her his name. Cannastra had in fact tried, without success, to engineer a meeting between Joan and Jack shortly before he died. She recognised the name and invited him up for hot chocolate. In *On the Road*, Jack described the meeting: 'I went up and there she was, the girl with the pure and innocent dear eyes that I had always searched for and for so long. We agreed to love each other madly.'

Within two weeks, on 17 November 1950, to everyone's surprise, they were married. They were wed by Judge Lupiano at his residence in Greenwich Village, with Allen and Lucien as best men, attended by John Clellon Holmes and Liz Lehrmann, Lucien's girlfriend. They only invited a few people to their wedding party at the loft afterwards: Seymour Wyse, Alan Harrington, Carl Solomon, Alan Ansen, Wild Winnie from the Bleeker Street Tavern, John Hollender, and other Columbia friends. News of the party soon got around and two hundred people showed up, most of whom they didn't know, who ate and drank their way through everything in sight so that by the time they left the toilet was blocked, the beer keg had overflowed, and a platter of Vienna sausage had fallen behind the refrigerator.

Allen felt very ambivalent about the marriage. He was secretly still in love with Jack himself so resented anyone else's intimacy with him. His own advances towards Joan had also been cut short, causing him to write Neal a rather churlish letter about her:

> Kissed the bride, who's a tall dumb darkhaired girl just made for Jack. Not dumb really, since she's 'sensitive', and troubled (trying to be on own from family in the big city at age twenty), and has had men (Cannastra once for a short season), but full of a kind of self-effacing naivety, makes dresses as vocation; but I don't know her well, but in my opinion (strictly between you and me as I am on hands off policy as regards interference with process of others' free choice) she can't compare with Jack in largeness of spirit and so I don't know what she can give him except stability of sex life, housekeeping, and silent, probing sympathetic company while he's sitting around, and children.[8]

The marriage was doomed. Though in the early days it seemed to be based on love, Kerouac's views on marriage were reactionary and old-fashioned even for 1950: Kerouac thought wives belonged at home with the dishes and Joan was not allowed to accompany him when he went visiting his friends. She was not allowed to hold any opinions of her own, and if she dared contradict him or disagree he flew into a rage. He really believed that women were good only for sex and that their minds were inferior to those of men. When he told this to Ginsberg, Allen began sending him poison-pen letters, ridiculing his views. Many women have reported that Jack never listened to a word they said: his attention would wander and he couldn't wait to speak again himself. As Jack saw it, Joan's role in the relationship was to wash, cook and clean for him, as well as to keep them both from her earnings as a dressmaker. Jack was too busy being a writer to earn any money of his own.

To earn extra money, Joan took a job in a department store during the busy Christmas season, but Kerouac was lonely sitting at home writing and insisted that they give up Cannastra's loft and move in with his mother in Queens, so that he had someone to talk to during the day.

The move was a disaster: Kerouac and his mother spoke together in French most of the time so that Joan was unable to understand them. Kerouac spent a lot of his time going to Christmas parties and hanging out with his friends but Joan was not permitted to accompany him. Jack made her hand over her wagecheck to his mother each week and every morning Memere would give her her bus fare and lunch money. Memere regarded her as little more than a slave provided by her son to do all the housework. Jack insisted they sleep in his old room, which Memere had to pass through in order to reach her own bedroom, and each morning Memere would reach across Joan to hand Jack his morning glass of orange juice. Joan was not offered any. Memere did everything to make the young woman's life a misery. Everything had to be done her way and if Joan showed the slightest independence of mind by cooking or cleaning things in her own way there was trouble.

Jack wanted her to be Memere. Gerald Nicosia describes an incident in which Joan came home just before midnight, exhausted from a hard day's work, and Jack insisted that she bake him a spice cake. She had to rise early for work the next day and refused, whereupon Jack yelled: 'You should never deny your son anything!' Realising he had made a classic Freudian slip, he apologised, saying, 'You make a husband grouchy when you deny him things.' Joan went to bed while Memere prepared a spice cake and consoled little Jackey. In addition to all this, Joan had to listen to Memere's anti-Semitic ravings, calling Ginsberg 'a communist Jew' and muttering about Jews putting poison in the water supply.

It took only a few weeks for Joan to crack up. Early in January, she spent three days in bed, refusing to eat anything. When she did get up, it was to gather up her things and move back to Manhattan. She got a job as a waitress at Stouffers and took an apartment at 454 West Twentieth Street, in the beautiful Greek revival row that forms the south side of Chelsea Square between Ninth and Tenth Avenues. She was at work when the removal men came to take her things from Queens to Manhattan and she had given them strict instructions to take only what belonged to her. She told Jack that, if he wanted to come, that was up to him. During her lunch break she went over to West Twentieth to see how the move was progressing. She found Jack on the sidewalk in front of the apartment, sitting on the top of his rolltop desk, his slippers in his hand, as the removal men carried her things inside. She took him in.

Away from Memere, things seemed to improve and friends were astonished to visit and find a model of domestic tranquillity, with Joan sewing in one corner while Jack wrote at his rolltop desk across the room. However, things were not as placid as they seemed. Joan was not very impressed with *The Town and the City* – an opinion shared by most of Jack's friends, including Neal – and she objected to him lying in bed all morning while she got up and worked. His other literary friends such as Allen Ginsberg had jobs and she didn't see why Jack shouldn't contribute towards the rent as well. Eventually, Jack managed to get reinstated part time at his old job writing synopses of scripts at 20th Century Fox, but he didn't like it.

Jack was still unable to find a form for *On the Road*. He studied the great European novelists and experimented with a variety of different styles but nothing was satisfactory to him. He became bogged down with trying to create family backgrounds for his characters but was unable to write convincing fiction. Then, in March 1951, John Holmes showed Jack the completed manuscript of a book he had been working on about their group, called *The Beat Generation*. Jack was horrified at Holmes infringing on what he regarded as his territory. He claimed ownership of the term and suggested that Holmes call his book *The Beat Ones*, telling Holmes that he intended to write a book called *The Beat Generation* himself. Holmes left the term in the book, but agreed to use a different title. He called his book *Go*.

This was one instance where Jack was very concerned to claim paternity:

> In 1948 I said to John Clellon Holmes, 'This is really a beat generation.' He agreed and in 1952 published an article in the *New York Times* entitled 'This is the Beat Generation' and attributed the original version to me. Also, I had already called it the Beat Generation in my manuscript of *On the Road* written in May, 1951.[9]

Holmes began work on the book in August 1949, while Jack was still struggling with his Wolfean *The Town and the City*. Had Holmes not been such a nice guy, he could have used the title, which was already used in his book long before Jack wrote *On the Road*, but he valued his friendship with Jack and allowed him to have his own way. As it happened, when the beatnik fad hit in the late fifties, a quick-thinking Hollywood entrepreneur called Albert Zugsmith quickly copyrighted the name so in the end neither Jack nor Holmes got to use the term they invented.

In reading Holmes's manuscript, Jack was also concerned to find great chunks of his conversations with John reproduced verbatim in the book. Holmes had recorded the conversations in his journals and used them whenever appropriate. Jack later accused Holmes of plagiarism, despite the fact that Jack's own books use the same method and appropriate not only dialogue but entire life stories from other people. *Go* was published in the autumn of 1952 by Charles Scribner's, and has the distinction of being the first 'Beat' novel to appear.

At the end of December 1950, Jack had received a 23,000-word[10] letter from Neal which had astounded him. In it Neal attempted to set down the exact details of the events of his life, with no literary censorship and no attention to style or convention. He described normally controversial subjects like cock sucking and sex in a straightforward way as if describing the events to a friend in person. It was confessional, a heart outpouring with no attempt to hold back or shape the material into something more acceptable. Jack was amazed:

> I got the idea for the spontaneous style of *On the Road* from seeing how good old Neal Cassady wrote his letters to me, all first person, fast mad, confessional, completely serious, all detailed, with real names in his case however – being letters – I remembered also Goethe's admonition, well Goethe's prophecy, that the future literature of the West would be confessional in nature; also Dostoyevsky prophesied as much and might have started in on that if he'd lived long enough to do his projected masterwork, *The Great Sinner*.

Jack lavished praise on the letter which he described as 'the greatest story' he had ever read, that 'outmatches Celine, Wolfe; matches Dostoyevsky in its highest moments; has all of Joyce at its command . . .' He described Neal as a 'much greater writer than I am', something which was even more galling because Neal didn't regard himself as a writer, whereas Jack's whole identity was wrapped up in being a great writer. This was the fabled 'Joan Anderson' letter, named after the main character in the story, about a Christmas weekend in the pool halls, hotel rooms and lock-ups of Denver, 'with hilarious events throughout and tragic too, even a drawing of a window, with measurements to make the reader understand'. Jack described it to Ted Berrigan as 'the greatest piece of writing I ever saw, better 'n anybody in America, or at least enough to make Melville, Twain, Dreiser, Wolfe, I dunno who, spin in their graves.'

As it was lost overboard from Gerd Stern's houseboat in Sausalito we shall never be able to judge for ourselves its literary value but, if the surviving section published in Neal's *The First Third* is anything to go by, the writing is overblown and rambling, and Neal is being far from honest with himself. Certainly, with the exception of Allen, none of Jack's other friends could understand why Jack was so keen on it. The lost letter has now acquired an iconic significance in Beat Generation studies, akin to the stone tablets of Moses, the golden tablets of the Mormons, Buddy Bolden's original cylinders, and other missing sacred texts.

Annoyed that John Clellon Holmes had completed his book about their circle of friends, Jack was anxious to get his version down as quickly as possible. With Neal's letter in mind, he now decided to write the story down 'as it happened'. Joan had asked him on numerous occasions what exactly he and Neal had done together, trying to sort out the chronology and different trips, so Jack wrote *On the Road* as a letter to his wife. At first he kept getting blocked by the interruption caused by having to load new sheets of paper into his typewriter (a word processor would have suited him admirably). Then he got the idea of using the twenty-foot-long rolls of Japanese paper that Joan had brought from Cannastra's loft. The paper was almost transparent and the typing could be read through from the other side. He taped the rolls together and set to work.

This was how the Trotskyist intellectual and surrealist Victor Serge (the nom de guerre of Victor Lvovich Kibalchich) wrote, though Jack almost certainly thought of the idea independently. Jack fed one end of the roll into the carriage, set the carriage for single space, and began typing: 'I first mat (sic) met Neal not long after my father died ... I had just gotten over a serious illness that I won't bother to talk about except that it really had something to do with my father's death and my awful feeling that everything was dead.'[11]

It sounded like ordinary American speech – Joan had asked the question and he was giving her the story. He later changed the reference to his father's death and substituted that he met Neal after he and his wife broke up, attributing his illness to that – a fictionalising of the narrative which slightly weakened it. He was a fast, accurate typist, and worked from the handwritten notebooks which accompanied him everywhere, so many of the images in his writing were already formed.

He began work early in April 1951, working continuously, often with little sleep, and by 9 April he had already written 34,000 words. He typed furiously, fuelled by Benzedrine, soaking his white T-shirts in sweat. Periodically he would peel one off and wring it out, replacing it with a fresh one. Joan brought him coffee and pea soup. He was already writing when she left for work and still at his desk when she returned. He liked her to be near to him while he worked, so the bed was dragged over next to his rolltop desk and a screen put round it to shield her eyes from his desk light when she was trying to sleep. She could not drown out the clatter of keys and dinging of the carriage every second or so as the scroll fed steadily through the roller and the book took shape. By 20 April, *On the Road* was almost finished with over 86,000 words on the 120-foot roll, consisting of one long text with little punctuation except for a couple of lines' break when a new session began.

As the book neared completion, he transferred his typing to Lucien's loft next door. This way Joan was able to get some sleep, but some of the manuscript was lost when Lucien's dog chewed up the last four feet of the scroll. *On the Road* was written in twenty days flat. He felt elated and exhausted.

As soon as he had finished writing it, Jack gave the rolled-up scroll to John Clellon Holmes to get his reaction. Jack himself had not read it through. Holmes recorded his impressions in his journal a couple of days after he finished reading it, on 27 April 1951:

I was the first human being to read the book. Even he hasn't read it straight through, and I went down to visit he and Joan a nite ago to take the ms back to him and tell him my impressions. We had a nice evening, with beer, a spell at a waterfront bar, and even fifteen dark, cool minutes out on a cluster of pilings at the end of a pier watching a huge, lovely liner, all crusted with warm lights, steam slowly out of the harbor, her pinkish smoke stacks lit up. A beautiful, silent giant, dwarfing even the Jersey coast beyond. I told Jack that I could not entirely be objective about the book ... But I did, I think, communicate to him my enthusiasm about it, and my feeling that it will make exciting and stimulating reading when the few minor faults are wrestled out, and the line of it honed just a bit. The book had cleaned me out, exhausted me, because I read it straight thru without stopping for anything but cups of coffee. It took me a little over eight hours. The sections in Mexico are faultless, lovely, sad. There is much, much else.[12]

Jack later explained:

I wrote that for my new wife, to tell her what I'd been through.
It's directed towards a woman. That's why women like it. It's
sexy because it's addressed to a woman. But if I was writing for
my mother, I'd leave many things out. Of course I had to think
of Malcolm Cowley too, the Protestant Establishment. He was
literary advisor to Viking. Giroux said, 'My God, Jack, it's like
Dostoyevsky.' Harcourt Brace editor in chief Robert Giroux
had it first but said sales manager Ed Hodge 'does not approve
of the book'. I said all right, I'll take it to Viking, and they sat
on it for seven years. But I wrote it thinking of those guys. It's
not too dirty. And I wanted to give a poetic opinion of Neal.[13]

Jack had enthusiastically unrolled the scroll across Robert
Giroux's rug like a carpet seller in the casbah. Jack was mortified
when Giroux's first reaction was that 'it would be impossible to
revise such a manuscript'. Jack stamped out, calling him a 'crass
idiot'.

In fact, Jack already had a publisher. Allen Ginsberg's friend from
the madhouse, Carl Solomon, had gone to work for his uncle, AA
Wyn, at Ace Books, a cheap mass-market paperback publisher.
Through Allen Ginsberg, Jack had given Carl the forty-page section
of *Visions of Cody* beginning 'Around the pool halls of Denver . . .'
and on the strength of it Carl gave him a contract for *On the Road*
and a $250 advance. But, instead of writing in this style, which Jack
now felt was too rigid, he had gone for something more
improvisational. He set aside the first eighty pages of *Visions of Cody*
and wrote *On the Road* instead.

Jack brought the original dog-chewed scroll in to Carl. Carl:

My uncle said, 'Carl, it looks like your friend took this novel
out of his trunk. It's been sent around and been rejected
everywhere by its appearance. It looks like you're selling me a
false bill of goods, it looks like he took you in and now you're
taking me in.' So he turned it down.

Actually his innovative method threw me off: it was too
much for me to cope with, and I think all of us at AA Wyn.
Nobody wanted to cope with something as difficult as that.
How would you cope with *Ulysses* if somebody sent it to you
and you didn't have all the ballyhoo? . . . There was an editorial
meeting, and Arthur Wang, who is a well-known book editor

right now, former publisher at Hill and Wang – Wang was in favour but opinion was divided, Larry Hill was against it. Wang was the only one who was really for it but we overrode Wang. Turned it down. Gene Feldman was an assistant there who later edited *The Beat Generation and the Angry Young Men* and he put it down completely. He said Kerouac was a bum . . .[14]

Relations had never been smooth between Carl and Jack even before he brought in the scroll. Carl had a very fast mind and ran circles around Jack with his quick-fire jokes and literary allusions. Jack did not appreciate being the brunt of Carl's jokes and at one meeting over the book called him a 'Greedy Jew' and threatened to break his glasses. Though he did not go down in history as the publisher of *On the Road*, Carl did manage to get Ace to publish *Junkie*, Bill Burroughs's first book, and thus launch him on a long literary career.

John Clellon Holmes introduced Jack to his literary agent, Rae Everett, and at her suggestion he began to retype the scroll on conventional sheets of paper, changing the proper names as he went and making relatively minor changes to the grammar, spelling and punctuation. At the time of writing the scroll has not been made available to scholars, though it has been displayed in the Whitney Museum of American Art travelling show. Kerouac scholar Dave Moore's close textual analysis, based upon the photographs of the scroll that were published in Allen Ginsberg's *Friction* magazine, shows the kind of changes that normal copy-editing would provide.[15] Malcolm Cowley's later suggested changes were all structural, as one would expect, and so there is no way of checking on them at the present. In any case, Jack may not have regarded the removal or rearrangement of entire sections as editing his prose as such.

Though the book was composed in one long continuous draft, Jack had not yet formulated his theory of spontaneous composition and we know that the book went through many stages of revision. For instance, the most famous line in the book, 'The only people for me are the mad ones, the ones who are mad to live, mad to talk . . .', was inserted six months later during revision.

In his introduction to the first publication of a fragment of *Visions of Cody*, Kerouac described *On the Road* as 'a horizontal account of travels on the road'.[16] The book has a circular form: parts one, two and three all describe round trips to the coast and back, with part one being the longest and most detailed. Parts four and five together make a complete round trip and are even shorter. The narrator is Sal

Paradise, a young would-be novelist living with his aunt in Paterson, New Jersey. This substitution of Allen Ginsberg's home for his own is curious as no privacy was being violated by retaining his own address in Queens.

A friend has invited Sal to San Francisco, and, as many of his friends are spending the summer in Denver, he plans to go there as well. Denver is the home of the book's hero, Dean Moriarty, a quick-talking, wide-eyed, handsome, mercurial womaniser and car thief. Sal idolises Dean for being everything that he is not: ebullient, unselfconscious, unreserved, filled with the joys of life and possessing an easy confidence with women. The name Dean Moriarty has been the subject of much discussion: it has been suggested that Dean comes from James Dean, but this is not possible unless the name change was made after 1955, as Dean made no films before then (too early, also, for Dean Martin, though Neal was more like Jerry Lewis). Moriarty may well come from Sherlock Holmes's famous adversary in Sir Arthur Conan Doyle's stories of the great detective, which we know Kerouac loved very much.

The First Trip tells the story of Jack's travels from New York to Denver to San Francisco to Los Angeles. It is a straightforward account of his actual journey: his unsuccessful attempt to join Route 6 at Bearsville, the bus to Chicago and the thousand-mile hitchhike from there to Denver. His descriptions of the midwest landscape, the cornfields and the prairies, evoke the size of America and its easy-going friendly people, and are among the best ever written on the subject of the United States. Poet Lawrence Ferlinghetti said: 'He has a much more sweeping, greater vision of America than Hemingway.'[17] Ferlinghetti also compared him with Thomas Wolfe:

[Thomas Wolfe] is one of Kerouac's great heroes and the hero in *Look Homeward Angel*, Eugene Gant, saw America, saw the darkened landscape of America flash by from a train window whereas the same vision in Kerouac was from the window of a speeding automobile. But essentially it's the same vision of America and it's the 1930s America that no longer really exists. The America that exists now only in small Greyhound bus terminals in small lost, dusty towns.

When Sal gets to Denver he finds that his friends have divided into two camps: the Columbia College crowd, and Dean Moriarty and his friends, who include Carlo Marx, Kerouac's name for Allen Ginsberg. Sal has to choose between them and plumps for Dean. Sal continues on to San Francisco to stay with Remi Boncoeur – real-life Henri Cru – and goes from there to southern California. He tells the story of 'The Mexican Girl', and then returns to New York City alone.

The Second Trip is the story of his journey from Virginia to New York to New Orleans to San Francisco. Sal has arranged for Dean to pick him up in Testament, Virginia, where he is staying with relatives. He gives the story of LuAnne (Marylou) and Al Hinkle (Ed Dunkel) and Dean's complicated love life, including his wife Camille (Carolyn), who is back in San Francisco pregnant. He tells how Ed Dunkel left his wife, Galatea (Helen Hinkle), in Tucson and how they have to collect her from New Orleans where she is staying with Old Bull Lee (William Burroughs). The portrayal of Helen Hinkle is particularly mean. Old Bull Lee complains to Jack on the phone: 'Have you got this character Ed Dunkel with you? For krissakes bring him down and get rid of her. She's sleeping in our best bedroom and's run clear out of money. This ain't a hotel!'

In fact, Bill and Joan found Helen as ideal a guest as could be in the circumstances and, when Hinkle did finally arrive to collect her, they offered to let them both stay on. It was one of the many places in his books where Jack's misogyny made him distort the facts to show a woman in a bad light.

Carlo Marx (Allen Ginsberg) questions the reasoning behind the trips: 'What is the meaning of this voyage . . . I mean, man, whither goest thou? Whither goest thou, America, in thy shiny car in the night?'[18] When they reached New Orleans, Old Bull Lee (Burroughs) was even more direct: 'Now, Dean, I want you to sit quiet a minute and tell me what you're doing crossing the country like this.' But Dean can only blush and is unable to give a proper answer.[19]

In fact, Burroughs often complained about his portrait in *On the Road* because readers believed they were reading true facts. According to Bill, nothing could be further from the truth:

Kerouac described my orgone box in *On the Road* – a pretty good trick, as he never set foot on the south Texas farm. He had me taking a shot of morphine and going out to 'moon over his navel'. The fact is that I was not using junk at that time, and even if I had been I certainly would not have done so in an orgone accumulator. Kerouac even went so far as to write that 'Old Bull thought his orgone accumulator would be improved if the wood he used was as organic as possible, so he tied bushy bayou leaves and twigs to his mystical outhouse'. Like so much of Jack's writing, this makes a good story but is actually pure fiction.

When he visited me I was living in Algiers, across the river from New Orleans, in a little house laid out like a railroad flat and raised up on the marshy lot by concrete blocks. In Algiers I had practically no front yard at all, and was far too busy with a habit to build an accumulator.

Neal Cassady did visit me at the south Texas farm, but never used the orgone box. Since Kerouac presumably got the story of my first accumulator from Cassady, whose tendency to exaggerate rivalled Jack's, it's a wonder they didn't have me throwing orgies in the accumulator for the amusement of the wetbacks.

Sal goes with them to New Orleans to collect Galatea. As they leave, Sal writes: 'He hunched over the wheel and gunned her; he was back in his element, everybody could see that. We were all delighted, we all realised we were leaving confusion and nonsense behind and performing our one and noble function of the time, *move*.' This was the answer to Ginsberg/Marx's question and, in part, the reason for the immense popularity of the book.

In addition to being a portrait of Neal Cassady, the subject of the book was the car, the freedom of the open road, which is the subject of thousands of ads, radio shows and promotions. Jack wrote a celebration of Detroit Steel – he captured an era of middle-class youth striving for freedom from the dreadful conformity of the suburbs, from the constraints of Eisenhower morality. The success of the book when it was published in 1957 was very much to do with the glorification of the American road and the giant American car. These mammoth 400-horse-power monsters gave their owners an illusion of freedom, the power and ability to go anywhere, to take off and travel the open road. In reality they were used for the morning commute and for trips to supermarket where they stood in rows, great fin-tailed spaceships in a Flash Gordon parking lot. In *On the Road* Dean and Sal travel by Cadillac, not just in pick-up trucks. Though written about an earlier period, the readers assumed the cars in the book were the streamlined high-finned chrome machines which were then at the height of their fantasy/fetish period.

From New Orleans they set off for San Francisco, where Dean intends to return to Camille and get rid of Marylou by fixing her up with Sal. He had already tried in New York but insisted on watching while they had sex so their liaison was less than successful. Sal and

Marylou are happy to try out this arrangement but, without Dean's supercharger energy behind them, they drift into lethargy and Sal is unable to provide for them or make any decisions. Sal returns home.

The Third Trip is from New York to Denver to San Francisco and back. For the first time Sal goes to San Francisco to visit Dean rather than Dean visit him. Sal's arrival precipitates a break between Dean and Camille and he abandons his wife and baby daughter in order to get his kicks with Sal, who seems oblivious of the deleterious effect he has on the situation. Dean and Sal head towards New York with the intention of going to Italy. They hitchhike to Denver where they are able to find a drive-away Cadillac which they run into the ground on the way to Chicago. Some of Kerouac's best writing in the book concerns this stretch of the trip, speeding through America in the ultimate American-dream car.

The Fourth Trip is from New York to Denver to Mexico. Sal meets up with Dean in Denver and together they drive down to Mexico, in search of Kerouac's fabled *falaheen*. After a long scene in a brothel they reach Mexico City, where Sal gets dysentery and Dean deserts him to rush back to New York to marry his new girlfriend, who is pregnant.

The book ends with a short coda, in which Sal and his girlfriend attend the opera with Reni Boncoeur in a limousine, leaving Dean ragged and broke on the sidewalk. Just as it happened.

The frontier tradition, with its lack of women, has given America a literature and a popular culture filled with male companions – what the Australians call the cult of 'mateism': Huckleberry Finn and Jim, Ishmael and Queequeg, Batman and Robin, the Lone Ranger and Tonto, Cody Pommery and Dean Moriarty. Ann Charters points out that Kerouac's opening description of Dean Moriarty as a man whose 'wild yea-saying overburst of American joy' was 'an ode from the Plains, something new, long prophesied, long-a-coming' was a reference to Sebastian Sampas's concept of a 'new soul' being created in the great open spaces of middle America: 'A primitive man, crude, raw, unfinished – superb – is shaping in the heart of our land . . . In him coarse, rough-hewn, lie all our hopes – his will be the civilisation greater than all – all art will be an integral part of him.'[20]

The West is seen as a frontier, despite being opened fifty years earlier. Eleven times in nine pages Kerouac writes about this 'so longed for' West. *On the Road* is also a male initiation book: male bonding, male friendship, good buddies. Cassady is seen as a cowboy, 'who only stole cars for joy rides' rather than cattle. He was 'a car thief rather than a horse thief'.[21]

Kerouac's guilt-ridden sexuality meant that he never consummated his obvious sexual attraction for Neal, though Neal had an easy-going sexuality and was prepared to fuck anyone and anybody: friends, travelling salesmen, and of course, later in life, the many groupies surrounding the San Francisco rock 'n' roll scene. Allen Ginsberg, however, did not think there was an overt sexual attraction between the two men:

> Jack and Neal never made out together. They loved each other but they never made out and never were interested. What they had was so strong between them that a sexual thing was there also but it came out through the heart rather than through the genitals. It came out in actual physical thrills in the heart area as lovers have which is as strong as any kind of homosexual or heterosexual love feeling. Jack and Neal gave each other soul surrender.[22]

Carolyn Cassady:

> Jack was even closer than any woman was to Neal. They were soulmates. They both loved each other and they both hated themselves. Neal was a man of the most universal compassion. Whoever he was with became the centre of his universe. He'd try to make everybody happy, and you can't do that.[23]

> People seem mystified by the idea Jack and Neal could have this unconditional love and want either to break them up or make them gay. In our day everybody had a best buddy, doesn't that happen anymore?[24]

The move back to Manhattan gave a new lease of life to Jack's marriage to Joan, but he was not prepared to work at it and things quickly deteriorated once more. Jack's legendary meanness – he wouldn't even share his cigarettes with her – his infidelities, and the fact that she was still a domestic slave at home after working all day at Stouffer's as a waitress, combined to put intolerable pressure on the relationship. Despite the fact that Jack often slept at Carr's loft, Joan managed to get pregnant – something that they had been trying hard for in the earlier days of their brief marriage when Jack would even stand on his head before sex thinking that this would collect more sperm in his testicles to get Joan pregnant. When she informed Jack of her condition in early June he reacted with fear and anger at the news. Joan had retaliated against Jack's casual girlfriends by bringing a fellow worker at the restaurant home to her bed. Kerouac felt cuckolded and, despite his Catholicism, demanded that she get an abortion on the grounds that the baby was not his. Joan refused and threw him out.

Jack spent a few weeks brooding at Lucien's then went to join his mother in North Carolina, where she was staying with her daughter Nin and family. That July at Nin's house, Jack came down with a bad attack of phlebitis and spent two weeks sitting with his leg propped up on a chair, fussed over by his mother and playing with Nin's young children.

As far as Jack was concerned, his marriage was over and he later gave a flippant explanation of why it had not worked out: 'I didn't like her. She didn't like any of my friends! My friends didn't like her. But she was beautiful. I married her because she was beautiful.'[25] As during his marriage to Edie, he ran home to Mother every time things went a little bit wrong, and was not prepared to put any effort into making the marriage work. Memere, for her part, was always delighted when things did not work out and endorsed his decision.

Jack didn't stay away from the city for long because even before he and Joan broke up he had already embarked upon his next affair. Adele Morales was 25 when they got together: a stunning Latin beauty with short dark hair and a Bohemian reputation. Adele was a painter, but made a living by making store-window dummies. She had a cold-water flat on the fourth floor of a building on East Sixteenth Street. In the next building lived Ed Fancher, her ex-boyfriend, who, together with Daniel Wolf and Norman Mailer, later started the *Village Voice*.

Adele Morales:

> I was seeing Jack Kerouac while I was still with Fancher, since we both sort of did our own thing. I'd met him at a folk dance at the New School, where he came over and started talking to me. I was wearing a white off-the-shoulder blouse, and he told me I looked very beautiful. He was always very courtly, very gentlemanly, almost shy in fact. I guess I saw Jack over a period of a year but he was still a merchant seaman, so he'd be away at sea and I wouldn't hear from him for months. He said he was in love with me, and I think I was among the first of his friends to see the manuscript of *On the Road*.[26]

When she and Jack were drifting apart she met Norman Mailer and fell in love. They married and were together for a decade until

Mailer tried to stab her on the night he announced his candidature for Mayor of New York.

Shortly after Jack returned to New York from Nin's house he came down with another serious attack of phlebitis, this time so bad that he was admitted to the Veterans' Administration Hospital in Kingsbridge. However, this period of enforced hospitalisation had a very positive side to it. In 1962 Jack wrote to Hugo Weber:

> My stay in hospital in 1951 was actually the turning point in my system of narrative art – it was there, day after day in bed thinking, that I formulated all those volumes (16) I've written since (most of them save six so far published). But I mean I was *so happy* in the hospital.[27]

This was the actual planning out of the Duluoz Legend that he had first conceived of while reading Galsworthy's *Forsyte Saga*, on the SS *George Weems* on the way to Liverpool. He envisioned a series of books which would add up to a continuous record of his life, a map of his ever-changing consciousness. As he explained in a 1963 Farrar Straus and Cudahy press release:

> The final scope of the [Duluoz] Legend will be simply a completely written lifetime with all its hundreds of characters and events and levels interswirling and reappearing and becoming complete, somewhat à la Balzac and Proust. But each section, that is, each novel, has to stand by itself as an individual story with a flavour of its own and a pivot of its own. Nevertheless, they must all fit together on one shelf as a continuous tale.

He was truly setting himself one of the greatest tasks in literature. Percy Bysshe Shelley wrote:

> If it were possible that a person should give a faithful history of his being from the earliest epochs of his recollection, a picture would be presented such as the world has never contemplated before. A mirror would be held up to all men in which they might behold their own recollections and, in dim perspective, their shadowy hopes and fears . . . all that they dare not, or that daring and desiring, they could not expose to the open eyes of day . . . if the passage from sensation to reflection, from a state of passive perception to voluntary contemplation were not so

dizzying and so tumultuous, this attempt would be less difficult.[28]

In addition to the obvious progenitors of this form, one might add Ezra Pound, whose *Cantos* provide a graph of human development, and impose meaning on transient impressions, images and actions over a lifetime of experience,[29] and William Carlos Williams's *Paterson*, a long poem based on the idea that 'a man in himself is a city, beginning, seeking, achieving and concluding his life in ways which the various aspects of a city may embody . . . all the details of which may be made to voice his most intimate convictions.'[30]

Throughout the autumn, Jack continued to revise *On the Road*. Allen Ginsberg, Lucien Carr and the other friends who read the revised version all regarded the text as much improved. Though he was still seeing Adele Morales, Jack also had a short affair with Allen Ginsberg's girlfriend Dusty Moreland, called Josephine in *Visions of Cody*: 'Josephine wants to fuck and fuck and has been doing so with Irwin and me regular as pie'.

At the end of the summer, a large number of Jack's old friends had returned to the city and he found himself enmeshed in a furious social life involving Allen, John Kingsland, Lucien Carr, John Clellon Holmes, and Jerry Newman. He often saw Hal Chase's wife, Ginger, now separated from Hal, who was playing guitar and singing folk songs in the Village. She is the Peaches Martin who gets several mentions in *Book of Dreams*, which Jack began the next year.

Jack also saw his old friends Tom Livornese, Jack Fitzgerald and Ed White. On 25 October – Jack's sister's birthday – Ed White and Jack had dinner together at a Chinese restaurant on 124th Street in Harlem. Ed was training to be an architect and carried a notebook with him in which he made sketches of buildings. During the course of the meal, Ed suggested to Jack that a writer could do the same thing. Just as he was making a visual record in his sketchbook of what his eye saw, so it would be possible for a writer to make word sketches in the same way. That night Jack made the first of his sketches: a description of a bakery window in Jamaica, Queens, and an important new technique was added to his writing. For the next month Jack wandered around New York scribbling in his notebook and each evening he would go to Ed White's room to read his sketches aloud to him.

Allen Ginsberg: 'They were interesting improvisations. Ed White suggested that Kerouac carried a book around and did some prose sketches, like an artist's sketches, fast sketches of Hector's Cafeteria or whatever.' These are the sketches which constitute Book One of *Visions of Cody*, his next, and possibly greatest, work, which he began that October, 1951: the description of the diner, the El station on Third Avenue and 47th Street, Hector's Cafeteria, the bakery window in Jamaica, following alto sax player Lee Konitz down the street. These fragments are just a taste of what was to come. They are like listening to him tune his guitar or trim his reed.

Despite this great new breakthrough in his writing, Jack was anxious to leave town. Joan Kerouac had returned home to her overbearing mother in Albany, New York, who she had tried so hard to get away from. Pregnant, depressed and desperate for money, Joan threatened to sue Jack if he did not support her during her pregnancy. Jack, as usual, demurred, but when a writ arrived from the Domestic Relations Court he paid her five dollars a week for pre-natal care and began planning how to escape and avoid the responsibility for his child.

Adele Morales's memory of Jack going away to sea probably stems from that summer when Jack tried to join Henri Cru on a round-the-world voyage aboard the SS *President Harding*. Jack, wearing his white Merchant Marine cap, had gone to the National Maritime Union Hall to try to get a berth on her, but he was too late and there were no jobs left. Jack thought he might be able to get a position on the ship when she reached her first port of call, San Pedro in California, and began to plan his next trip, thinking that the Family Court would not find him in California. He was also anxious to see Neal. *On the Road* had not been enough; Jack was not yet done with his obsession with Cassady. He gave every impression of being as hopelessly in love with him as Allen had been. In a – presumably real – letter to Neal reprinted in *Visions of Cody*, he says, 'I'm completely your friend, your "lover", he who loves you and digs your greatness completely – haunted in the mind by you . . .'

Neal Cassady had telegrammed Jack back in August, inviting him to come to stay at their place at 29 Russell Street in San Francisco, a tiny one-block-long street off Hyde in North Beach. Neal said that he and Carolyn had fixed up the attic for him with a bed, a huge four feet by four feet sheet of plywood for a workdesk, a typewriter, paper, a radio, drugs, and a pair of bongo drums. Neal also had a tape recorder to use for 'experiments in new narrative techniques'. This was important news because Jack was already contemplating buying one himself. In *Visions of Cody* he tells Neal, 'Last night in the West End was mad, (I can't think fast enough) (*do* need a recorder, will buy one at once when the *Adams*[31] hits New York next

March then I could keep the most complete record in the world which in itself could be divided into twenty massive and pretty interesting volumes of tapes describing activities everywhere and excitements and thoughts of mad valuable me.'[32]

Neal told him that the Southern Pacific Railroad was hiring and that he could earn $400 a month. But it was not until 18 December that Jack finally arrived, long after the job on the railroad had gone. Jack worked for a few days in the railroad baggage department but blew most of his wages on prostitutes. The SS *President Harding* was due in San Pedro so Neal introduced him to the railroad guards on the Zipper, the express freight to Los Angeles, and he travelled south in comfort in the caboose.

He met up with Henri Cru and together they whooped it up in Santa Monica and Hollywood. Jack was treated to a Christmas dinner on board ship but there was still no work for him. They were hiring, but Jack's lack of seniority, and no doubt his record of having jumped ship, meant that he was passed over. He returned to San Francisco to live with Neal, Carolyn and their three children – their third child, a son, John, was born on 9 September. On his first night there, with rain sweeping in from the bay, Jack stayed up all night recording the story of Doctor Sax on Neal's tape recorder.

He settled into his comfortable attic room and plunged into the next section of *Visions of Cody*, his all-or-nothing attempt to fully explain Neal. Jack:

> I had a bed there. That was the best place I ever wrote in. It rained every day, and I had wine, marijuana, and once in a while his wife would sneak in. I wrote it mostly by hand, some typed on Neal's typewriter. No candles. The candles were for holy books, like *Tristessa* and *Desolation Angels*.[33]

Since Neal was obviously not going to finance him as well as accommodate him, Jack worked for a couple of months as a baggage clerk on the railroad and did his writing at night.

Visions of Cody opens with the sketches written that autumn, 1951, in New York, during which he contemplates his forthcoming visit to California to see Neal. Part Two starts with fifty of so pages of Neal's actual biography, beginning with his childhood in Denver, some of it taken from the New York sketches as Jack remembers their shared American background and experience. Jack brings the story up to date but keeps returning to his favourite subject; himself: 'I'm going to talk about these things with guys but the main thing I

suppose will be this lifelong monologue which is begun in my mind
– lifelong complete contemplation.'[34]

Part Three consists of meticulous transcriptions of actual
tape-recorded conversations with Neal: yet another attempt to
capture Neal's essence. Though it has no value as literature, per se,
at the time it was an important experiment. Jack:

> I typed up a segment of taped conversation with Neal Cassady,
> or Cody, talking about his early adventures in LA. It's four
> chapters. I haven't used this method since; it really doesn't come
> out right, well, with Neal and with myself, when all written
> down and with all the Ahs and the Ohs and the Ahums.[35]

Although not published until January 1973, after Kerouac's death,
the tape section was strangely prescient and shows Kerouac to be at
the cutting edge of the kind of experimentation which was to
characterise New York in the 1960s. For instance, it was written
many years before Andy Warhol's *a, a Novel*[36], which consisted of
458 pages of closely spaced transcriptions of tape-recorded
conversations, an idea Warhol later followed up with his 1989
Diaries[37], which were transcriptions of telephone conversations. This
paring down to the basics of communication, this search for honesty
in the presentation of thought and speech, unencumbered by
traditions of literature and conventions of literary and journalistic
presentation can also be seen in the unedited, straight question-and-
answer interview style of the underground press from 1966 onward
– common today in conventional newspapers – and in the use of
chunks of direct narrative, presented as unadorned dialogue in
novels. Long sections of William Kotzwinkle's *The Fan Man*[38], for
example, are presented like this without the endless use of 'he said'
or 'she said', and lacking descriptions of gestures and grimaces.
Jack:

> We did so much fast talking between the two of us on tape
> recorders, way back in 1952, and listening to them so much, we
> both got the secret of *lingo* in telling a tale and figured that this
> was the only way to express the speed and tension and ecstatic
> tomfoolery of the age.

Part Three of *Visions of Cody*, the section to do with the tape
transcripts, occupies the final two thirds of the book. This does
divide easily into sections so it seems more likely that Jack simply

forgot to label the divisions. Following the tape transcriptions comes a parody of them, clearly written on drugs, described by Allen Ginsberg as 'an imitation of the tape which is Joycean babble. Three hundred pages of this improvised strange dialogue, then an imitation of the tape in heaven, which is pure sound poetry for 40–50 pages, then it comes back to a narrative again toward the end. By this time being small type 3–400 pages.'[39]

The 'Imitation of the tape' section opens as a school essay: 'Composition . . . by Jackie Duluoz . . . 6-B'. It is clearly intended as parody. It is not an easy read. The words roll by like listening to a foreign language: how Jack must have heard English as a child, just registering the sounds, not getting the meaning. Pure sounds. It has been described as Joycean, but Joyce carefully crafted his invented words from notebooks to give them myriad references and multiple meanings, whereas Jack's are just sounds, like a saxophone solo or a George Shearing piano riff where the notes fall over one another. Jack's are American words, riffing, street-talking, goofing. It is word poetry. He is a master of transitions, after a long long sentence comes a sound, a space, an utterly unexpected word: 'By mires, and anon the, but you have to get real high before you can blow any kind of program, man, so listen to me there's nothin better in this big t – woops, now the typewriter's gone, it's thickening tremendously . . .'

Jack: 'Goddamn it, *feeling* is what I like in art, not *craftiness* and the hiding of feelings.' Allen Ginsberg:

> Kerouac was totally innovative. He broke through to a new realm of prose that nobody had ever tried before. Joyce had tried stream of consciousness as had any number of American novels or surrealists, but Kerouac was the only one with a theme which was something that was not just stream of consciousness but was a regulated flow of improvisation on fixed theme set forth in advance like a jazz musician blowing thousands of choruses on a fixed blues theme. So it was new innovation, the notion of writing and not looking back, not revising, but exhausting the mind by an outpouring of all the relevant associations.

It is Kerouac's theories of spontaneous composition that have caused so much rancour and criticism of his work. In retrospect it is hard to imagine why the critics and literary establishment felt so threatened. Part of it may have been the suspicion that he was getting away with something, with not learning his craft. His reliance on intuition and instinct to provide results automatically belied craft and tradition. In this he once again broke new ground. This disregard for the rules was most evident in the sixties, particularly with the rock musicians, with Bob Dylan being a supreme example. Lennon and McCartney were also loath to learn to read and write music in case it destroyed their songwriting ability. Spontaneity and intuition were valued above all else.

The idea has a long history in avant-garde literature. Beginning in 1919, in the uncertain period following the Great War, when for many artists and writers the known world seemed to have fallen apart, Andre Breton and Philippe Soupault – like Kerouac, writing under the influence of Lautréamont and Arthur Rimbaud – conducted a series of experiments in 'automatic writing' which are the direct predecessors of Kerouac's spontaneous prose. Breton and Soupault's first rule was that none of the words, phrases or sentences that reached the page were to be in any way altered or improved, 'with laudable disdain as regards their literary quality'.[40] They took great care not to interrupt the stream of consciousness and would on occasion devote themselves to it continuously for from eight to ten hours a day. There was no reflection, no correcting or editing, and the end of each section – as in Kerouac – was determined solely by the end of that day's work. The book which resulted from this extraordinary collaboration was *Les Champs Magnétiques* (The Magnetic Fields), which is generally thought of as the first systematic use of automatic or purely spontaneous writing, though it was not the first example. Breton himself cites Gérard de Nerval and Thomas Carlyle as predecessors, and both Horace Walpole and Carlo Gozzi are known to have used these techniques, though not in their final texts.

Jean Cocteau claimed that *Les Enfants Terribles* was 'dictated' to him at a rate of either seven or seventeen pages a day, whichever of his accounts one takes, and was not interfered with. He claimed not to have even altered the punctuation.

When Antonin Artaud was commissioned to write the biography of the third-century Roman Emperor Heliogabalus, he dictated the final draft in order to give the book a greater rhythmic force. Artaud wrote: 'I have written this life of Heliogabalus as I would have spoken it and as I speak it.'[41] Artaud was not however in favour of spontaneity in writing, which he thought should always be done with direction and intention. In this, he and Kerouac were opposites: Artaud disliked the lack of control represented by spontaneity because it left him vulnerable, Kerouac was attempting to achieve this very state of vulnerability.

Allen Ginsberg:

When Kerouac abandoned all revision he merged with the writer part of himself. The writer Jack Kerouac replaces the Jack Kerouac who used to be a man who wrote – he finally merged with his work, his sex life, his energy, everything was channelled into his writing. Like a hill farmer whose life and occupation are merged . . . a romantic, sacrificial approach to writing as prayer.

Jack Kerouac: 'By not revising what you've already written you simply give the reader the actual workings of your mind during the writing itself: you confess your thoughts about events in your own unchangeable way.' Spontaneous prose was the natural outcome of the Celtic storytelling tradition: a tape recording of the man at the bar telling a story to his drunken friends. But *Visions of Cody* is more than a tale told quick: it contains entire sections of word play and sketching which have no narrative and are just there for the pure pleasure of word sounds. It is when the two are combined that Kerouac is at his most sublime. Following on from 'Imitation of the tape' there comes a gem: 'Joan Rawshanks in the Fog'. Jack had unexpectedly encountered Joan Crawford filming in San Francisco.[42] Entranced, he wrote a long sketch of the filming, eighteen printed pages of long sentences and even longer paragraphs, writing until every aspect and association suggested by the incident was exhausted.

This is followed by more passages of pure sound with little or no narrative meaning until we get to an extended reworking of much of the material in *On the Road*. It is sometimes seen from a different perspective, but, as Gerald Nicosia points out in *Memory Babe*, it's almost always a faster, more condensed version, like the fast-forward, speeded-up sequence in the old Laurel and Hardy or Abbot and Costello films. Kerouac signs off like a crazed Hollywood director, flashing through an entire day in one page, beginning with a 'new day dawning' and ending, like the Lone Ranger leaving town, with the wonderful cinematic line: 'Adios, you who watched the sun go down, at the rail, by my side, smiling – Adios, King.'

8 Mexico City

Jack's life with the Cassadys in San Francisco, and later in San Jose, was probably the best time he ever had. Neal and Carolyn provided everything he needed as a writer as well as giving him all the advantages of a family with none of the obligations: he loved children and enjoyed playing with the new baby and telling elaborate stories to the two older girls. He had regular food on the table and delightful company. Carolyn:

> Jack's real interest was in being able to participate in family life without any responsibility. I knew early on that to get along with Jack you just listened. I wasn't very assertive, talking about my own ideas. I think most of the women he ran into were pretty independent females who had something they wanted to do or sell. I didn't.[1]

His best friend, Neal, was there for nights out on the town, visits to whorehouses and all-night drug sessions. But Carolyn was an equal attraction. On previous occasions Carolyn had been deeply suspicious of Jack. His arrival in her house always heralded a massive disruption of family life and usually ended in Neal walking out on her and the children. This time, however, they got to know each other and got along very well. The sexual tension between them, which they had both felt when they first met in Denver, began to develop again. At first neither of them was prepared to do anything about it. Then Neal's job took him away for a week. As he went out of the door he turned to them and said casually, 'I don't know about leaving you two – you know what they say, "My best pal, and my best gal . . ." Ha ha, just don't do anything that *I* wouldn't do – okay kids?' and left the question hanging. They were both so shocked at the suggestion that they spent the whole time he was away avoiding each other. When Neal returned, Carolyn asked him if he had really meant it. 'Yes,' said Neal, 'I thought it would be kind of nice if you got together.'

Carolyn came from a very strict, straight background and it seemed inconceivable to her that Neal could be so casual about adultery. But she was very attracted to Jack and knew full well that Neal himself had had dozens, scores and even hundreds of other woman, so this time she thought, 'If that's the way you want it, Neal, that's the way you're going to get it.'

Knowing that Jack was much too puritan to ever make the first move, she realised that she would have to seduce him. Carolyn: 'Jack had the Madonna and whore dichotomy about women. He had a hard time with any middle ground. He was terribly shy, guilty and difficult.'[2] She waited until Neal was away and then prepared a fine meal with wine and candles. It worked. Carolyn:

> Jack and I would never have done anything to hurt Neal. When he was home we never even touched each other . . . Neal knew of course, but it was never even mentioned . . . See, when Jack wasn't there, Neal and I tangled, but when Jack was there, Neal had enough freedom so he could do as he pleased without feeling guilty, and, of course, he loved being with Jack. Everything was nice and peaceful when Jack was with us but, when he went, Neal and I would start fighting and then he'd send for Jack. Jack did feel he was an interference, even though he was upset when we bought a new house and didn't have a room that would always be his. But as we got closer and closer, and it did get kind of heavy, there was the problem of the future, and there wasn't any future in it for him.[3]

The relationship continued for some time and Carolyn and Jack even discussed marriage and buying a house together. Carolyn:

> But I already figured out he was hopeless as a marriage bet. The thing was, in those days, you had to *talk* about marriage, because you could never admit anything was a casual affair. With Jack and I it had gotten so there wasn't any next step. You can't go on just loving somebody more and more and not doing anything about it, and Neal was the one I was interested in.

However, despite a certain amount of inevitable tension, most of her memories are of Jack happy: scat singing 'A Foggy Day in

London Town' and 'My Funny Valentine' or of an afternoon round the kitchen table with her and Neal while the children slept. In Carolyn's opinion, all that Jack ever wanted was 'home and kids and the picket fence and the station wagon. He wanted that desperately, and he began to realise as time went on that he could never handle the responsibility of that. His whole life was about escape . . . He was such a dreamer. It was escape all the time'.[4]

He could have had a family if he chose. All he had to do was pick up the telephone, but he was too scared. Joan Haverty had given birth to his daughter Jan on 16 February 1952, but Jack was not there. He remained in hiding in California rather than pay child maintenance, and his wife and child had to make do as best they could. His daughter grew up impoverished during the years of his greatest success. He felt that his first allegiance was to Memere, that if he had to pay child maintenance he would be unable to support his mother. He also made a feeble claim that the child was not his. He eventually admitted paternity in court when a blood test proved it, but by then his daughter was ten years old and had grown up without her father. It is likely that he knew all along that she was his child, particularly after she was old enough to show his distinctive features: Jan bore an uncanny likeness to her father as Allen Ginsberg, her godfather, informed him on several occasions. But Jack believed in Cyril Connolly's dictum, 'There is no more sombre enemy of good art than a pram in the hall', and put his writing before anything other than Memere.

How can a man deny his own child? Anyone who has had children knows the sadness and pain that even temporary separation from a parent brings. Where was Kerouac when he should have been reading his daughter bedtime stories, sharing with her his love for words? How could he play with Carolyn's children without a thought for his own? His fans claim that he had a great heart, that he was generous and sensitive, but he cared more for his cat than for his own daughter and there is all the difference in the world between sentimentality and sensitivity. He allowed Jan to become a junkie at thirteen, selling her body on the streets of the Lower East Side to buy drugs while he, wealthy from the worldwide sale of his books, drank himself insensate in the bars of Lowell and Florida. Kerouac may have been a great writer but, when it came to the human values of compassion, tenderness and care for others, he failed miserably. As a human being he was insensitive, selfish and cowardly, and must be held accountable for his daughter's misery.

Jack remained forever callow, a perpetual adolescent, and it is this immature view of the world that will always prevent his works from being truly world class: they do not address adult themes. It is, conversely, the very reason for his popularity with young people, who are able to relate to his awkward, half-formed, self-conscious stumbling progress through life. However, his rejection of his child would appear to stem from something more serious than a refusal to grow up. Plenty of adolescent couples have children and are able to deal with it. A Freudian view suggests that on an unconscious level Jack was unable to accept the child because Memere was not its mother. His deep-seated incest fantasy would demand that any child must be hers as she was his real wife.

Memere's own violent rejection of Jan would be explained by her related psychological problems, although both of them knew full well that the child was Jack's. If Jack had had the guts to admit paternity, and face up to his mother, Jan would probably still be alive today. His friends were ambivalent about his behaviour: these were the days long before the women's movement, and in Bohemian circles there was little reproach in getting a woman pregnant and then abandoning her. In Jack's case, however, he was married to Joan Haverty and the court saw no reason why Jack should not support his own flesh and blood. On hearing the news that investigators had burst into Lucien's apartment looking for him, Jack panicked and decided that he was not safe from the court's jurisdiction even in California. In April 1952, after living with Neal and Carolyn for four months, he set out to join Bill Burroughs in Mexico City.

Bill Burroughs was lonely, guilt-ridden and grieving, in the aftermath of a terrible event which had transformed his life. Joan was dead and their children, Willie Jr and Willie's half-sister Julie, were with their respective grandparents. Bill was responsible for Joan's death. The details of the now legendary story are that Bill had a .380 automatic that he had wanted to sell and had taken it over to his friend, John Healey, who had a buyer. Bill had recently returned to Mexico City from a trip to Ecuador with his reluctant boyfriend Marker and was in a very depressed state of mind because the relationship was going nowhere. That morning, he had taken a knife to be sharpened by the knife grinder in the street below and had found his eyes streaming with tears as he walked home.

Back at the apartment he had begun throwing back drinks and, by the time he and Joan went to sell the gun, they were both extremely drunk. A drinks party was in progress when they arrived and at some point Bill called out to Joan, who was across the room, 'Time for our

William Tell act!' She balanced a shot glass on her head and Bill took aim and fired. The gun fired low and the bullet struck her in the temple. She slumped to the floor and the glass fell to the floor and spun round, unharmed. She was pronounced dead on arrival at hospital. The whole thing was a tragic accident: they had no 'William Tell act' and, as Bill later said, it was sheer madness to fire at a glass in a crowded room – the flying shards of glass could have wounded any number of people quite apart from the danger to Joan. Bill was charged with 'criminal imprudence' and spent ten days in jail before his lawyer bailed him out.

Bill was living at Calle Orizaba 210, apartment 8, in a little courtyard apartment in Colonia Roma. He had written to Jack extolling the virtues of Mexico – in particular how one could live on very little money – and invited him to come and visit. Jack's presence cheered Bill up considerably. They walked in the mountains at Tenencingo with Dave Tercerero, Bill's morphine connection. They bathed in streams and went target shooting. Together they visited the Turkish baths and the Ballet Mexicano. Jack made frequent visits to teenage prostitutes, one of whom charged only one peso – twelve cents – and smoked 'three bombs a day'[5], the latter much to Bill's irritation. Not that Bill disapproved of drugs – as usual Jack had no money so Bill bought his pot for him and also gave him a couple of shots of morphine each week – Bill just wanted the drugs to be kept elsewhere.

Being out on bail placed Bill in a vulnerable position as the police were using possession of pot as an excuse to arrest Americans. He was already at risk because he had a morphine habit, so he did not want additional drugs on the premises. Bill did not relish returning to a Mexican jail just because Jack couldn't do without instant access to his marijuana stash.

Bill read the manuscript of *Visions of Cody* and was astonished at the great advances Jack had made in his writing since *The Town and the City*. He wrote to Allen Ginsberg: 'I am very much impressed by *On the Road*.[6] He has developed unbelievably. He really has tremendous talent, no doubt about it.'[7] At first Jack spent his time revising and sequencing *Visions of Cody*, and then mailed it, by the cheapest possible postage rate, to Allen Ginsberg.

Allen had a job in an advertising agency in the Empire State Building and a girlfriend, Helen Parker, and was trying to make it in normal New York society. After the departure of Rae Everett from MCA, Allen had been acting as both Jack's and Bill Burroughs's literary agent and was busy selling Burroughs's *Junkie* to Ace, as well as extracting an advance from them for Jack's *Visions of Cody*.

With *Visions of Cody* out of his hands, Jack now concentrated on his next book. *Doctor Sax* was a story that Jack had already worked out in his head in some detail. He had even told it aloud to a number of his friends and now, in Mexico City, he finally committed it to paper. *Doctor Sax* is his great *Bildungsroman*. It is a novel of late childhood although there is not much sexual awakening in it, despite the name Sax – sex? At the end a giant snake comes to life and uncoils itself from the deep, but sex is mostly restricted to the discovery of masturbation. The book is more a meditation on that curious hinterland between the end of the magic kingdom of childhood fantasy and dream, and the growing self-awareness of adolescence. Jack's Catholic upbringing provided him with a large vocabulary of hellish fears. For instance, as Doctor Sax enters his lair through a trapdoor the fires of hell shine out. However, the book mostly concentrates on universal perceptions, giving a name to thoughts and fears long-forgotten or only barely identified.

Burroughs tried to fill the emptiness of his life by seeing as many people as possible and the apartment was constantly filled with visitors, all talking and drinking, making it impossible for Jack to get any writing done. Jack retired to the lavatory where he wrote the book in pencil in several small notebooks, filling both sides of the page, while sitting on the toilet. Jack first began *Doctor Sax* in 1948 but he wrote most of it in May and June of 1952 in Bill's small apartment. On the title page of the first notebook was inscribed 'A Novella of Children and Evil, the Myth of the Rainy Night', which he later crossed out and replaced with 'Dr Sax'. Malcolm Cowley mentions that *Doctor Sax* is full of references to urine. Jack:

> Quite naturally it does because I had no other place to write it but on a closed toilet seat in a little tile toilet in Mexico City so as to get away from the guests inside the apartment. There incidentally is a style truly hallucinated as I wrote it all on pot. No pun intended. Ho. Ho.[8]

Another noticeable theme in *Doctor Sax* is that Jack, always a big eater, was obviously starving when he wrote the book. There are constant mouth-watering descriptions of food, including several pages where he and his sister simply discuss meals that they would like to eat. Jack had arrived with only $10 to his name and, though Burroughs was prepared to allow him to live there rent free, he resented having to pay for Jack's food as well. Jack ate everything in sight without leaving a share for Bill and Bill reacted by hiding the food.

The book opens with his famous description of his writing method:

> The other night I had a dream that I was sitting on the sidewalk on Moody Street, Pawtucketville, Lowell, Mass., with a pencil and paper in my hand saying to myself 'Describe the wrinkly tar of this sidewalk, also the iron pickets of Textile Institute, or the doorway where Lousy and you and GJ's always sittin and dont stop to think of words when you do stop, just stop to think of the picture better – and let your mind off yourself in this work.'

He has uncanny powers of recollection. All his schoolfriends lived on in his memory, the gang at the sand-lot, the kids at church, but they lived as part of himself, they were a part of *his* legend, he had absorbed and used them, they had no independent lives of their own.

A combination of Kerouac's theory of spontaneous prose and his copious use of pot makes *Doctor Sax* a very uneven book. We can see the words gallop away with him. Sometimes he would begin to type a word and hit the wrong key on the typewriter but, rather than revise, he would make this into part of the text, like a jazz musician covering for a bum note. 'Google giggle' is one example of hitting the wrong key, the next one on the typewriter, and keeping the word. This sometimes results in a number of long dreary paragraphs containing many made-up words where he obviously lost his train of thought but continued typing anyway. However, the book also contains some sublime passages, where the made-up words have a rhythm and potency and evoke an atmosphere. Since the book was originally written in notebooks, these typing accidents clearly represent a 'second draft', and it would be interesting to see how much the notebooks differ from the published text.

In 1987, Ginsberg in his role as teacher explained the character Doctor Sax to his class as:

> A mythological puberty fantasy figure of The Shadow superimposed on the boogie man: The shrouded stranger of the night plus William Seward Burroughs, WC Fields and a little bit of Sherlock Holmes. It contains one of the most beautiful passages by Kerouac around the evening of the snake's release when Dr Sax is preparing his magic powders. It is a parody of an apocalypse myth, as seen by a twelve-year-old child when the football coach takes the boy and they run through the backyards.[9]

Allen Ginsberg's poem 'The Shrouded Stranger' was composed towards the end of 1949 and was a major influence on Kerouac's composition of *Doctor Sax*, the latter part of which is the fruit of their closest collaboration. Jack had trouble with the end of the book and Allen made many suggestions which Jack used. He and Ginsberg had independently evolved this vision of the Shady Stranger which appears in many of Ginsberg's early poems as well as in Jack's work. Allen:

I had a series of related dreams [about the Shrouded Stranger] since I was three. . . . Kerouac had a very similar thing in Dr Sax; that in fact was *his* Shrouded Stranger . . . We'd discussed the book quite a bit, discussed how to end it and everything like that. That was one of my favourite books, because he enlarges on the Shrouded Stranger. It's an archetype, the boogie man, the Hooded Stranger.[10]

It is a novel of appropriation and childhood memories collaged with contemporary events, continuing the language experiments that Jack began in *Visions of Cody*. Burroughs features strongly in it as Jack was living with him and talking with him each day. Doctor Sax's high laugh, 'Mwee hee ha ha ha', was copied from The Shadow. He is caped and wears a slouch hat, and even has a personal rubber boat he can inflate, similar to the one used by The Shadow. He does battle with his enemy Count Condu, the Vampire, who lives in the Castle: a composite of the orphanage on the hill and a large private house on Wannalancet Street, Lowell. Count Condu came from Budapest, a vampire owing much to Count Dracula, and a little to the character of the well-groomed Hungarian that Allen Ginsberg would act out in the games of charades at 115th Street while Jack played the ingenuous country boy.

Sections fourteen and fifteen of Book One are given over to the Count, in a not very successful imaginary pulp story. The character Old Bull Balloon has certain similarities to William Burroughs and, after Doctor Sax and Old Bull play a long game of pool, Kerouac turns his attention to the search for hallucinogenic herbs with telepathic qualities; almost certainly a reference to yage, which Burroughs had searched for in the Amazonian jungles. The similarity of Sax to Burroughs becomes more apparent as Kerouac's 'mind-picture' gets distracted from Lowell and takes on more of his actual surroundings in Mexico City, and more of Burroughs's stories begin to leak through:

I sat in hot sun parks down in Peru, in the city of Lima, letting the hot sun solace me – In the nights I was every blessed time inveigled with some Indian or other type witch doctorin bastards to go into some mud alley in back of suspicious looking sewer holes dug in the ground, and come to some old Chinese wisdom usually with his arms hanging low from a big pipeful of World Hasheesh and has lazy eyes and says 'You gen'men want some-theeng?'[11]

Sax goes on about the hundred-foot-high vine trees before mixing up what Jack calls his glass ball with its 'terrible innocent looking morphine-powder-like spoonful' as if Burroughs was cooking up a fix right before his eyes, melting the morphine in a heated spoon before loading it into a glass eyedropper. At this point in the story, everything has turned blue, a sure sign that Jack has overdone it with Benzadrine – probably why his attention drifted from Lowell.

Sax changes from being Lamont Cranston into a parody of Bill Burroughs: there is talk of orgones – Burroughs was interested in the theories of Wilhelm Reich – and of two more of Bill's then favourite subjects, the calendar control system of the Mayan priests and giant centipedes, 'There's one of the Mayan spiders'. The section even reads with Burroughs's speaking voice. Late in the book, five pages from the end, Jack realised what he had done and commented, 'And his hair fell over his eyes, he looked a little bit like Bull Hubbard (tall, thin, plain, strange) . . .' Strangely, some of Bill's most characteristic lines are sometimes given to others: 'Edify ye mind, me bye,' says Gene Plouffe when he finds a big pile of *Shadow* and *Thrilling Detectives* magazines and shows them to Jack. This is what Burroughs said when presenting Jack with Spengler's *Decline of the West* not long after they first met. Kerouac never had much of an ear for dialogue and, when he did record it, he often gave it to the wrong character, as in this case where it clearly belonged to Sax.

The great flood of 1936 when the Merrimac flooded downtown Lowell is used as a fulcrum for the book. The action is concentrated towards the end of the book when the battle between Doctor Sax and Count Condu intensifies. The great snake – all the evil in the world in the shape of a hundred-mile-long snake coiled into a cavern deep below the old castle in Lowell – awakes and begins to make its way to the surface. There are masterful descriptions of the flood and the havoc it caused. At times the writing runs away with him, as in one description of Sax where even Allen Ginsberg makes a premature appearance and the language breaks down into gibberish:

Phanton Listener at My Window, Watcher With Green Face of
Little Jewish Boys in Paterson Night Time when phobus
claggett me gonigle bedoigne breaks his arse shroud on a giant
pitrock black Passaic weyic manic madness in the smoony snow
night of dull balls . . .

Kerouac's evocative descriptions of childhood in *Doctor Sax* are
among the most beautifully realised passages he ever wrote. They are
so accurate and universal that they transport the reader back through
the years, in an out-of-body experience, to familiar households of
childhood. But few women seem to enjoy Kerouac, perhaps because
the shared experiences, the universality of his writing, is confined
largely to boys: the comic books, the male heros, swimming in the
river, sports and pre-adolescent stirrings.

The book ends in a somewhat inconclusive way. Kerouac did not
know how to resolve the plot and it was Ginsberg's idea to have the
great worm turn into a husk of Shakespearean doves. Unused to
writing fiction, Jack was unable to structure the book to build to a
satisfactory finish, and the book ends somewhat abruptly, leaving the
reader to wonder what on earth all that was about with the snake,
Count Condu, a giant bird of paradise, and Doctor Sax spraying his
morphine mixture all over the place. All the evil in the world seems
to have been defeated by a nice big fix of morphine. One passage, a
pseudo-Shakespearean monologue at the end of Book Six, section
nine, is attributed to 'Doctor Sax's vacuumed powders' (Bill's
morphine?) and certainly reads as if Jack is feeling no pain.

Jack's casual disregard for Bill's security eventually placed a
tremendous strain on their friendship. Bill insisted that he keep his
stash out of the apartment except for what he was using. Instead,
Jack asked Dave Tercerero to bring him the whole bag so that Jack
could hide it in the apartment without telling Bill. Fortunately for
Bill, Tercerero informed him of Jack's plan. In addition, Jack's
constant raiding of the icebox caused further tension between them.
Jack had outstayed his welcome.

He began to feel paranoid. It seemed to him that everyone was
against him: the officers of the Support of Dependants and
Abandonment Bureau continually harassed his mother and friends,
trying to find his address; 'the Jews' of the New York literary
establishment were all ranged against him, not recognising his
genius, offering him paltry sums for his brilliant books; and his friend
John Clellon Holmes now appeared to be ripping off his ideas for his
own books. Jealous that Holmes's book, *Go*, was about to be

published, Jack was irate to find that Holmes now intended to make the jazz scene of the forties his next subject. In June, he wrote angrily to Holmes pointing out that the idea for a book called *Hold your Horn High*, the story of Lester Young and Billie Holiday, was his and that he still intended to write it: 'Find yr own Lester.'[12] But Holmes had already begun work on *The Horn*, which he had initially sketched out several years before and which was eventually published in 1958. Jack complained self-righteously to Carolyn: 'Holmes has started publishing jazz stories THAT I MYSELF TOLD HIM, imagine the gall,' seemingly unaware that he had done the self same thing with Neal.

Jack's dealings with John Clellon Holmes were very one-sided. Holmes was a loyal and true friend, and it was to him that Jack wrote some of his best letters: wild eager chronicles of his experiences and enthusiastic descriptions of his latest experiments with prose. Consequently, Holmes was also prepared to put up with Jack's sullen complaints and paranoia, and even his patronising and insulting remarks about John's own writing. Jack could be seen as being forthright and honest in expressing his beliefs – he never stinted in revealing his feelings – but, beneath that, there is a maddening naivety in the way that he never considers if he is likely to insult or hurt his friend. It is a naivety which stems from a deep-seated narcissism. Even Allen Ginsberg, who normally ignored or did not even notice behaviour which others found offensive, sometimes exploded with irritation at Kerouac's vanity.

As *Go* neared publication and his own *On the Road* (as *Visions of Cody* was still called) was rejected, Jack despaired. He was thirty years old, broke, anxious, bitter. He owned nothing in the world but a knapsack full of apparently unpublishable manuscripts and, far from keeping his promise to his father that he would look after his mother, the very reverse was true and she still slaved away at the shoe factory to pay for his travels and drugs and whores.

He borrowed Bill's last $20 of rent money, promising to pay it back as soon as he reached the USA, and set out to stay with his mother, who was about to move in with Nin in Rocky Mount, North Carolina. Two months passed and Bill had still not received his $20 or even a postcard. Bill wrote to Allen:

> To be blunt, I have never had a more inconsiderate and selfish guest under my roof . . . Unless he undergoes some radical transformation, I do not want him to visit me again . . . He needs analysis. He is so paranoid he thinks everyone else is

plotting to take advantage of him so he has to act first in self-defence. For example, when we were out of money and food, I could always rely on him to eat all the food there was if he got the chance. If there were two rolls left, he would always eat both of them. Once he flew into a rage because I had eaten *my half* of the remaining butter. If anyone asks him to do his part or to share on an equal basis, he thinks they are taking advantage of him. This is insane.[13]

Jack now directed his paranoia towards Allen and Carl, whom he thought had failed him. Allen was still trying to get AA Wyn at Ace Books to publish *On the Road*, but the situation there was complicated by the fact that, following the break-up of his marriage, Carl had gone crazy again. Carl attacked books with a knife, threw his briefcase at passing cars, flooded his apartment, smeared his walls with paint and screamed in the streets. He had been in and out of Bellevue several times and now Allen was faced with the task of presenting him with Jack's latest 'revision' of *On the Road* – the book we now know as *Visions of Cody* – which Allen received in June 1952 and which seemed to him to be unpublishable.

Ginsberg wrote to Jack:

I don't see how it will ever be published, it's so personal, it's so full of sex language, so full of our local mythological references, I don't know if it would make sense to any publisher – by make sense I mean, if he could follow what happened to what characters where.

The language is great, the blowing is mostly great, the inventions have full blown ecstatic style. Also, the tone of speech is at times nearer to un-innocent heart speech ('why did I write this?' and 'I'm a criminal'). Where you are writing steadily and well, the sketches, the exposition, it's the best that is written in America, I do believe . . . Wyn I'm positive won't take it now, I don't know who will . . . Will you be revising it at all? What you trying to put down, man? You know what you done.[14]

Though Allen admired the writing his chief criticisms were:

1. You still didn't cover Neal's history.
2. You covered your own reactions.
3. You mixed them up chronologically, so that it's hard to tell what happened when.

4. The totally surrealistic sections (blowing on sounds and refusing to make sense) (in section following taperecords) is just a hangup, hangup.

5. Taperecords are partly hangup, should be shortened and put in place after final trip to frisco.

6. Sounds like you were just blowing and taking things together, personally unrelating them, just for madness sake, or despair.

I think book is great but crazy in a bad way, and got aesthetically and publishing-wise, to be pulled back together, re constructed. I cant see anyone, New Directions, Europe, putting it out as it is. They wont, they wont.[14]

Allen was right. They didn't, and despite Herculean efforts it took Ginsberg twenty years to get the book published. He finally succeeded three years after Jack's death. Writing to Neal, Allen was somewhat more direct in his feelings about the book:

Jack's book arrived and it's a holy mess – it's great alright but he did everything he could to fuck it up with a lot of meaningless bullshit I think page after page of surrealist free association that doesn't make sense to anybody except someone that has blown Jack. I don't think it can be published anywhere in its present state.[15]

In North Carolina Jack took a job in the Rocky Mount Textile Mill. He was still on the run from the Child Support Agency, and he sensed resentment from his sister, who clearly thought he was a bum, wasting his life and sponging off their mother. Jack was unhappy and frustrated, but still continued to write. It was here that he began keeping the dream notebooks which became *Book of Dreams*.

There were few choices left for him. The only real home he had was with Carolyn and Neal, so he applied for a job on the Southern Pacific Railroad. Neal was enthusiastic and said he could pull strings to get Jack a job as a brakeman. He and Carolyn were about to move out of San Francisco to a large house in San Jose where he could have his own room and – Neal hinted – he could resume his affair with Carolyn.

Jack hitchhiked west with five dollars in his pocket. As he left he told Nin he would send her a present from China but she cynically replied, 'Never mind presents from China, just mail me fifty dollars room and board for the month of August.' Justin Brierly saved the day by wiring him enough to get to Denver and, while he was there, Neal sent him the $25 bus fare to the coast. He kept the money and hitched.

John Clellon Holmes's *Go* was published and was reviewed for the *New York Times* by Gilbert Millstein, a member of the same circle of friends that the book described. In *Go* Holmes used the phrase 'Beat Generation' and Millstein telephoned Holmes to ask him, 'What do you mean by Beat Generation? Do you want to do an article on it?' Holmes did, and it appeared in the *New York Times* Sunday magazine on 16 November 1952, under the headline 'This Is The Beat Generation'. Jack, in California, read the article and jumped and shouted in rage, yelling, 'That's my term! That's my term!' And, indeed, Holmes acknowledged it as such in the article, but not in his book.
John Holmes:

The phrase just slipped into my book. It described these people who felt such a lust for life, an excitement, a joy. In those days it was joy, it was celebration, it was let's stay up all night, let's drink, let's turn the volume louder, let's talk, talk, talk.[16]

Holmes explained:

We're all kind of furtive, we all walk down the street the same way. We're really beat, it meant being reduced to the essentials. It came out of the war when people had to live under continual tension and stress which was unnatural and the only way to do it was to no longer engage in attitudenizing and poses. Yes we're beat, so any energy you had left to do what you had to do was the important thing to preserve and all the crap went out of it.[17]

To exacerbate Jack's jealousy, Bantam bought the paperback rights to *Go* for $20,000 – a huge sum of money in those days. John generously mailed Jack $50, thinking he was probably starving somewhere. In fact he was earning $600 a month on the railroad but he appreciated the thought. Part of him was genuinely pleased at John's good fortune, but in his dream journals, calling Holmes 'James Watson', he griped: 'Now he has 20,000 dollars to my one.'[18] He also dreamt of Holmes stealing all his ideas and exploiting them: 'The big issues jazz will be, bop, and how Watson has already begun to capitalise on it at my expense (using my anecdotes, phrases etc. and in fact further battening on the sufferings of junkie musicians) – I feel horrified.'[19]

Life in San Jose was everything Jack had hoped for: he had the children to play with and take for walks, Carolyn to dance with and make love to, Neal to talk with all night and, of course, the tape recorder. Jack read *Doctor Sax* aloud to them, in a booming voice, sometimes putting on a WC Fields accent, Neal would read aloud from Proust, and on occasion they would pass out copies of Shakespeare and each take two or three of the parts. Sometimes Jack would record himself scat singing to the accompaniment of a tiny pair of bongos that Carolyn had given to him.

The only flaw in the arrangement was that, although Jack liked the romance of working on the railroad and carried his railroad handbook with him everywhere, even in New York, he was not very good as a brakeman. Neal chided him for his clumsiness, and the other railroad men called him nicknames – 'Hey, Caraway Seed!' – which he hated. Jack could not stand teasing: it hurt his pride.

There were ups and downs in the *ménage à trois*, as was to be expected, and at one point Jack sensed that Neal was regretting the arrangement. He moved to San Francisco and lived at the Cameo Hotel on skid row for a short time, engulfed in deep self-pity. He fired off a letter to Allen Ginsberg denouncing him and all of his friends in New York. All his pride and paranoia surfaced in one great rush: 'Why they publish Holmes's book which stinks and don't publish mine? . . . if you were men I could at least get the satisfaction of belting you all in the kisser – too many glasses to take off. Why you god-damn cheap little shits are all the same . . . Parasites everyone of you . . .' It was loyal Holmes that came in for the worst of it: 'The smell of his work is the smell of death – Everybody knows he has no talent . . . His book stinks and your book[20] is only mediocre, and you all know it, and my book is great and will never be published. Beware of meeting me on the street in New York.'

Allen was initially shocked but he was used to Jack's petulance and left it a few weeks to allow him to calm down before replying. Sure enough, two weeks later Jack sent him the manuscript of *Doctor Sax*, asking him to act as his agent in selling it. Jack often did his best work when he was depressed and it was at the Cameo that he wrote one of his gemlike masterpieces of pure spontaneous prose, 'October in the Railroad Earth'.[21]

It was not long before Neal sought him out and persuaded him to return to Los Gatos. Jack soon recovered once he was back in his own room at Neal and Carolyn's and he conveniently forgot all the insults he had heaped upon his friends. Early in December Jack got laid off but it did not concern him because he had already decided it was time for him to move on. His phlebitis had flared up once more and he planned to recuperate in Mexico City. He suggested to Carolyn that maybe she should have one husband at a time and asked her to come and stay with him in Mexico City for a while.

Neal was not at all pleased by this arrangement. He liked to be in control of things, but he compromised by saying that he would drive Jack to Mexico in order to buy a load of pot and then, when he returned, Carolyn could go and he would look after the children for however long she wished to stay. Carolyn knew, deep down, that she would never leave the children but she went along with the fantasy, and Neal and Jack took off.

Jack rented a $12 room on the top floor of Bill Burroughs's old building and bought a number of small luxuries to make the place feel like home. He then wrote to Carolyn, asking when she was coming. Back in San Jose, Carolyn was amused at the anguish Neal was going through at the thought of her leaving but she played him along for a while, remembering the countless times he had gone off with other women. Eventually she put him out of his misery. She told him she would not even consider going but, before she could tell Jack of her decision, she received a letter from him cancelling the arrangement: he was going to spend Christmas with his mother at his sister's house in North Carolina instead. The thought of being alone with Carolyn in a serious love relationship had evidently made him feel he was betraying his real wife, Memere. A few weeks after Christmas, Memere returned to Long Island and Jack went with her.

We have a very good account of Jack's arrival back in New York City from the journals of Judith Malina, who, together with her husband Julian Beck, founded the Living Theater. Jack was a contemporary of Julian Beck's at Horace Mann. Judith described New Year's Day 1953 when, just after midnight, Jerry Newman, John Clellon Holmes, Allen Ginsberg and Jack arrived to drink port and smoke pot. She wrote:

Jack Kerouac is a hero, a free-flowing spirit. He can't do anything except display his talent. Sardonic and handsome to a fault, he became raucous, drunk and incoherent as night wore on to morning. But a hero on a binge is still a hero . . . His false, coarse talk hides nothing. Of the intoxicated intellectuals he is the most interesting. Yet I am wary of him.

At seven or eight in the morning, Jerry Newman took Jack, Allen and Judith to his recording studio to listen to North African music. As their cab crunched through the snow-filled streets, Allen snoozed while Judith and Jack sang scat jazz. In the studio, Allen and Judith crawled under a piano to sleep while Jack continued. When they woke up, Jack had acquired a bottle of Sandeman port and was shouting obscenities. Jerry tried to play music, 'but in competition with Kerouac's cries, it is better stopped. He gets so loud and vehement that he scares me'.

It would appear that Jack was already, effectively, an alcoholic. Time and again we encounter descriptions of Jack, abusive, out of control, unhappy. He was acutely aware of the fact that he was now in his thirties and that most of his friends were engaged on a career path or at least settled in a relationship, whereas he, Jack, had nothing.

Gerald Nicosia suggests that it was the real love for Carolyn and his loneliness and longing while waiting for her to arrive in Mexico that caused him to come up with the idea of writing the story of his first great teenage love: Mary Carney, whom he called Maggie Cassidy. It is presumably no coincidence that she has Carolyn's surname. The book was written in Richmond Hill at his mother's apartment.

Jack was collecting railroad unemployment which enabled him to pay the rent. Memere worked at the shoe factory and bought the food and paid the bills. Written in early 1953, the first chapter of *Maggie Cassidy* was composed on the typewriter, and the rest was handwritten. It is one of the best examples of Kerouac's mature writing style, even though the subject is rather quaint by today's standards: an adolescent love affair in his home town. It is a *Bildungsroman*, but with little or no sex. It is the familiar story of the passage from innocence to experience. His composition is balanced and considered, the scenes laid out like a film script. It may have been spontaneous prose, but it was well-planned spontaneous prose.

The book opens with a group of boys dragging a drunken companion home through the snow on New Year's Eve, then immediately opens out into a panoramic description of the town and landscape before zooming into tight focus on their actual conversation, which in turn leads to a brief biography of each of the characters. Set in 1939 in Kerouac's beloved pre-war America it features some of his best descriptive prose. He uses small events like throwing a snowball at a car window to introduce childhood epiphanies. He describes winter – a subject he excelled at – and the two-storey wooden tenements of Lowell with their washing lines and porches and dim oil lamps on long dark evenings. His dialogue remains unconvincing, though it is often lyrical: '. . . as long as I live I'll have chains dragging me down to the oceans of sad tears that my feet are wet in already . . .' says Gus (George Apostolos).

It is the topographical obsessiveness, the description of walking home at night, the dark trees, the details of his high school, Maggie's house, his parents' living room, the wail of steam locomotives at night, that make the work ring true. The parochial details are a vehicle for a range of universal themes, feelings and observations, including a lovingly detailed description of devouring whole boxes of Ritz crackers smeared with peanut butter. Jack's mother was to prepare him snacks of half a pound of Ritz crackers spread with peanut butter throughout his life. Jack's diet was not unlike that of Elvis Presley.

The geographical specificity is crucial in creating this alternate reality – memory for him, fictional for us – and he describes the streets and buildings in great detail. The Kerouacs lived at 736 Moody Street from 1939 until 1941. On the ground floor of his parents' wooden apartment building was the Textile Luncheonette, often referred to by Kerouac as a lunchcart, a term which reflected the origin of traditional American luncheonettes as just that: carts pulled by horses and parked near workshops and factories for the workers to have a hot meal at lunchtime. It was all part of Jack's nostalgia for a long-lost America, as if everything associated with the lives of the first generation of immigrants were some great collective childhood, remembered and cherished by successive generations.

In *Maggie Cassidy* Kerouac succeeds in capturing the tender, self-conscious thoughts of adolescents. His thoughts are not unique; they are the quite ordinary perceptions that most teenagers have: the flashes of sudden awareness, the shifting of moods, the mystery of the distant stars, the night, an understanding that each little fragment of time is just a blink against the black universe seen overhead, and the awareness of life stretching on ahead, a sense of beginning. He describes first friendships and the sensitivity of teenagers: two buddies knew 'each other's most personal impossible interior hang-up pose core like they'd know their own or the marks of their own wounds'.

What is extraordinary is that he was able to remember these feelings and give them form. The book is heartbreakingly true in its descriptions of the awkwardness of adolescents dealing with sexuality. In this case it is the fumblings between two good Catholics back in the thirties, kissing for hours on end until emotional and physical exhaustion set in, all along carefully avoiding touching any erogenous zones.

This changes around the time of his seventeenth birthday. Jack's parents throw a surprise party for him but that night there is a fierce blizzard with snow twenty inches deep. It is the central pivot of the book: the moment of passage from childhood to adulthood. That night Maggie wants to go home with him, sleep with him, and get married. Jack, called Jack Duluoz in the book: 'I was beginning to sense her sexuality now and it was too late.' He finishes up in the Textile Lunch with his father and his friends and at 3 a.m. even manages to eat three hamburgers with ketchup and raw onions while the blizzard blazes outside.

Maggie is an upright Catholic and in that society the only way Jack could feel happy about having sex with her would have been to marry her:

> I'd reached my peak of love and fabulous success for a night or two – when? One night by the radiator in March she'd started huffing and puffing against me unmistakably, it was my turn to be a man – and I didn't know what to do, no ideal in my dull crowded-up-with-worlds brain that she wanted me that night; no knowledge of what that is.

Just after his birthday, still in the month of March, Maggie began to pressure him about getting married until he 'finally decided to hell with her my Ritz crackers and peanut butter would disappear. I pouted like a big baby over the thought of losing my home and going off into unknown suicides of weddings and honeymoons.' This decision was to stand throughout his life: he kept his crackers and peanut butter and never knew partnership with a woman. From then on, Kerouac was on the run from responsibility. In *Maggie Cassidy*, testosterone rages through him as he wrestles with his choices. There is also a darker side to the book where his ambiguous feelings towards women surface and he meditates on his changing perceptions of Maggie's volatile mood swings.

The book covers the period of Jack's year at Horace Mann School, and again he is able to capture the thrill and sense of wonder at spending his first ever night in the big city. He includes his innocent letters to Maggie in the book and in Allen Ginsberg's opinion these are almost certainly his actual letters to Mary Carney, once more blurring the difference between fiction and memoir.

In the book Jack describes how he tried to combine his two disparate lives and invited Maggie – Mary – to the Horace Mann Spring Prom, but the dance was a washout. Jack felt self-conscious and Maggie felt out of place among all the rich girls in their expensive gowns. Jack had fallen in with a new crowd and had a new life. Maggie returned to the Lowell which she never wanted to leave. Jack had made his decision to go to the big city to be a writer; she wanted to stay in Lowell and have children.

The book ends on a sour note. Three years later, after dropping out of Columbia and going into the Merchant Marine, he returns to Lowell, where he works for a while on a newspaper and in a garage. He telephones Maggie and in a strange switch to third person he describes himself: ' "Baby," he said out loud, "I'm sure gonna get you tonight – ain't gonna be like it used to be with you . . ." ' But the meeting is awkward: he is cold and distant and she accuses him of being cold-hearted. At two in the morning they thrash about in the back of the Buick, Jack drunk, fumbling unsuccessfully with her rubber girdle. She laughs in his face and he angrily drives her home then returns to the garage, driving recklessly, skidding all over the road.

There the book ends, abruptly, as if he gave up on it. A rumour has it that Jack and Mary Carney had a child, but little is known and it seems very unlikely. Jack regarded her as the only girl he ever really loved, holding a hopelessly romantic notion of the ideal girl, an innocent Irish beauty. However, his Lowell friend GJ says that there was never any real romance between Jack and Mary Carney, that Jack made most of it up. The real Mary Carney married twice, stayed in Lowell throughout her life and died in 1992, aged 72.

Mary Carney only gave one interview in her life, to Barry Gifford and Lawrence Lee for *Jack's Book*. She said that there was something deep between her and Jack that no one else understood or knew about, and that after *Maggie Cassidy* came out she had a lot of trouble from people telephoning her and neighbours gossiping. 'It was awful.' She described Jack as a sweet good kid and said that the people in Lowell didn't understand him. 'Nobody ever reads here.' In her opinion, all Jack ever wanted was a house and a job on the railroad.

Allen Ginsberg identifies a number of lines in the book that sound like Jack's mother speaking, even though they are attributed to Jack: 'You have to put up with life', 'Mixing up in the affairs of the world isn't for God'. Jack took dialogue from wherever he found it and gave it to the most unlikely characters in his books. Strangest of all is a prayer: 'Make my skull, my nose, soften, melt; just make me one piece knowing . . .'

Jack wrote the book in January and February, in Richmond Hill, Queens. It was quite a long composition time for him. He was in a peculiar frame of mind when he wrote it, torn by jealousies and self-doubt. John Holmes had bought a fourteen-room colonial mansion in Old Saybrook, Connecticut, with his book advance money. It was something that Jack would have loved to do, and Holmes's great success peeved him. Ace Books was preparing to publish Bill Burroughs's *Junkie*, which Bill had been working on while Jack was living with him. Although Bill only received a $1,000 advance, Jack could not help contrast his friends' situations with his own. Another irritant was that Gilbert Millstein, who had commissioned John Holmes's article on the Beat Generation for the *New York Times*, now rejected Jack's essay on the history of bop. It is possible that this is the same essay later published in 1959 as 'The Beginning of Bop', in which case it was probably rejected because of its many inaccuracies: Jack has Lionel Hampton 'jump in the audience and whale [sic] his saxophone at everybody with sweat . . .' Unusual behaviour from someone who was a vibraharp player. Malcolm Cowley, at Viking, expressed interest in several of Jack's books, but Jack was so disillusioned that he did not follow up Cowley's proposals. Upon completion of *Maggie Cassidy*, Jack took off for Montreal, intending to get a job with the Canadian Pacific Railroad.

Montreal was cold and unfriendly so Jack returned to his old job on Southern Pacific, living in a flophouse hotel in San Luis Obispo, 250 miles south of San Francisco. Jack had hoped to continue his affair with Carolyn Cassady, but Neal had broken his ankle in a railroad accident and was home all day, putting an end to Jack's plans and fantasies. Nonetheless, he moved to San Jose to work but insisted upon living in a cheap hotel in San Francisco.

He saved $300 and signed on with the SS *Carruth* to try to get away from it all. The *Carruth* was bound for Mobile, Alabama, New York City and Korea. Jack had a 'very easy and cool' job as a waiter in the officers' saloon but soon got into trouble for being so surly and uncooperative. In Mobile he was caught with a prostitute, drunk and half-dressed, walking down Main Street when he was supposed to be on duty. It was agreed that he would leave the ship when they reached New Orleans. He managed to save a further $300 during the voyage and arrived back in Richmond Hill a little wealthier if no happier.

The New York hipster scene centred on two Greenwich Village bars: Fugazzi's, a jukebox bar on Sixth Avenue, and the San Remo, on the northwest corner of Bleeker and MacDougal. Fugazzi's was the coolest of the Village bars, primarily because many of its patrons were junkies. The Bohemian types who congregated there, named 'Subterraneans' by Allen Ginsberg, included Gerd Stern, Stanley Gould, Mason Hoffenberg, Bill Keck, Anton Rosenberg, William Gaddis, Iris Brody and Jack's friend the poet Gregory Corso. The San Remo was a rendezvous of painters and poets, including Dylan Thomas, Willem de Kooning, Anatole Broyard and Franz Kline, but was used as an alternative by the Fugazzi crowd so there was a considerable crossover.

Jack spent a lot of time in both bars and usually spent the night afterwards at Allen Ginsberg's apartment on East Second Street in the Lower East Side, for which he had his own set of keys. In the summer of 1953, Allen had been seeing a young Black woman called Aileen Lee, but he was being pulled once more towards men as his sexual preference. Aileen was half-Cherokee, attractive, highly intelligent but, like many of her fellow Subterraneans, quite neurotic. She had already experienced several minor breakdowns, one of which had left her wandering naked at night in the Lower East Side. She was seeing an analyst to try to straighten herself out.

William Burroughs arrived in New York that August, bringing with him a large bag of yage, the hallucinogenic weed of the Amazon. He moved in with Allen and they began an intense love affair. Gregory Corso, who had also been staying at Allen's, was driven off by Bill's fierce glares as he slowly and methodically chopped up his yage with a machete. Aileen continued to visit and spent some considerable time typing up fair copies of Bill's second novel, *Queer*, and also his letters to Allen from the Amazon jungle which were later published as *The Yage Letters*.[22]

Aileen lived nearby in Paradise Alley, a courtyard of cold-water flats at 501 East Eleventh Street on the north-east corner of Avenue A in the Lower East Side.[23] This is the actual location of much of *The Subterraneans*, the novel that Jack wrote about his summer-long affair with her. Jack was drinking heavily through that August. In a hipster society where to be detached and icy cool was the optimum state, Jack was the epitome of 'hot'. He seems to have been in a manic state, loud, boisterous, and overbearing. Because of this he was not much liked at the San Remo and Fugazzi's. Aileen, however, was quite taken by him and they quickly fell in love, encouraged by Allen Ginsberg, who, although he liked her a great deal, saw this as a way of finally extricating himself from his own affair with her. *The Subterraneans* is the story of Jack and Aileen's love affair.

In addition to his involvement with Aileen, whom Jack called Mardou Fox in the book, this was also the time of Jack's famous tryst with Gore Vidal, which lasted for all of one night at the Chelsea Hotel. Though the 'Great Rememberer' describes picking up Vidal at the San Remo and suggesting that they get a hotel room together, he is coy about what happened. The next day he loudly told everyone at the bar of the San Remo that he had blown Vidal, but that is not how Vidal remembers it.

Gore Vidal first met Jack in 1949 at the Metropolitan Opera House. They were in full evening dress and Jack was with a publisher friend. Vidal was with a wealthy alcoholic writer, a friend of the publisher, who had paid both Jack and Neal Cassady for sex. This was at the time when Jack thought that the New York publishing world was dominated by homosexuals and was acting in such a camp manner that his friends accused him of acting like rough trade, which to an extent he was.

Jack and Gore Vidal met again on 23 August 1953 at the San Remo together with Bill Burroughs, and Jack began to flirt outrageously with Gore. Bill left in disgust after Jack began to swing around a lamppost like Tarzan. Jack put Aileen in a cab telling her he'd be back later, then he and Gore checked into one of the rooms of the Chelsea with a balcony overlooking 23rd Street. Jack later told various stories about what had happened, but in *Palimpsest* Vidal devotes an entire chapter to the event. In it Allen Ginsberg asks him, 'What did you and Jack do?' 'Well, I fucked him . . .' 'I don't think that he would have liked that,' Allen replied. Vidal said, 'I finally flipped him over on his stomach, not an easy job as he was much heavier than I.'[24]

Though Jack was much more interested in women than men, he had many dozens of male partners in his lifetime. Allen Ginsberg often discussed Kerouac's sexuality:

> Kerouac and Burroughs were in bed a couple of times. I think Burroughs would get desperate and say, 'Oh c'mon Jack!' and Jack'd say, 'How about blowing me?' and Burroughs would say, 'No, c'mon Jack!' the thing was so funny . . .
>
> I slept with Jack a lot of times. Mostly I blew him. He blew me once but mainly he was interested in getting blown, with men and women! Probably his main sex life with girls was getting blown too. It became a burden on our sexual

relationship because I wanted more response. Except I really loved him, so I was happy . . . so it was a very ambivalent relationship of him sort of denying interest but allowing it.[25]

Allen compared it to novelist John Rechy, who writes of the feeling of triumph if he could get someone to blow him and then refuse to blow them in return.

Jack's affair with Aileen was not disturbed by this incident. Their affair ended for the usual reason: that Jack was terrified of getting emotionally involved. Friends reported that he and Aileen were a wonderful couple, that they related to each other one on one, something that was rare for Jack, and that they seemed to be relaxed and close. According to *The Subterraneans* they were also a good team in bed. Jack had been reading Wilhelm Reich's *The Function of the Orgasm*. The problem arose when Jack began to fall in love with her, which in turn activated his neurotic urge towards self-destruction. He began drinking heavily, and the incident with Gore Vidal could be seen as an unconscious attempt to get Aileen to break off their relationship.

The book is the most astonishing confessional of the stranglehold of his Oedipal fixation on his mother and his inability to love any other woman. He describes his early doubts about marrying Aileen because she was Black, knowing that his mother would never approve. In the book this is described as the 'objections of my family, especially my really but sweetly but nevertheless really tyrannical . . . mother's sway over me'. Memere was an out-and-out racist: once, when she heard that Jack was going to see his Black friend Al Sublette in San Francisco, she sent him a newspaper clipping of a story of a Black man who raped a White woman on the subway, with a note saying 'There's your damned niggers!'.

It is a book in which Kerouac approaches and tries to define his Oedipal problems. This is indicated by his clever choice of name. Jack appears in the book as Leo Percepied. Leo was of course his father's name, with all that implies. Perce-pied literally means 'pierced foot'. The infant King Oedipus was ritually wounded in the foot (the name in Greek means 'swollen foot') and exposed on Mount Cithaeron, because of a prophecy that he would kill his father and marry his mother.

Despite the fact that he clearly recognised his problem, when Aileen tells him in the book that she doesn't think it is good for him to live with his mother always, he dismisses this as jealousy on her part and tells her: 'I really do really love her and love you too and don't you see how hard I try to spend my time, divide my time between the two of you – over there's my writing work, my well being.' He explains how much he enjoys having a Martini ready for Memere when she gets in from the shoe factory and the supper prepared for her so that she can get to the television by eight o'clock.

He reports his jealousy at seeing Aileen fool around on the couch with Gregory Corso, then in his early twenties, yet Jack had already spent three weeks plotting how to get rid of her without her being hurt. This was something he seemed to think was possible 'without her noticing', which gives an indication of how shallow his conception of love was. His stated aim was to 'get back to more comfortable modes of life', which meant staying at home and working all week, and coming into the city only for good times, 'if not to see Mardou then any other chick will do'.

It all ends in tears, with Jack crying down by the railroad tracks:

> ... weeping for my lost Mardou and so stupidly because I'd decided to throw her away myself, it had been a vision of my mother's love for me – that expressionless and expressionless-because-so-profound face bending over me in the vision of my sleep, and with lips not so pressed together as enduring and as if to say '*Pauvre Ti Leo, pauvre Ti Leo, tu souffri, les hommes souffri tant, y'aunque toi dans le monde j'va't prendre soin, j'aim'ra beaucoup t'prendre soin tous tes jours mon ange.*'

Jack translated this in the book as 'Poor Little Leo, poor Little Leo, you suffer, men suffer so, you're all alone in the world, I'll take care of you', but a literal translation would include 'I will always love you and take care of you for ever, my angel', which perhaps gives a more accurate idea of their relationship. He clearly blamed his mother for his inability to love another woman, but he had not the courage to fight against her stifling influence.

Jack wrote *The Subterraneans* in 'three full moon nights of October' while living with his mother in Queens. Jack:

> *The Subterraneans* is a true story about a love affair I had with a Negro girl in America. Only the names and identifying circumstances are changed. The book is modelled after Dostoyevsky's *Notes from Underground*, a full confession of one's most wretched and hidden agonies after an 'affair' of any kind. The prose is what I believe to be the prose of the future, from both the conscious top and the unconscious bottom of the

mind, limited only by the limitations of time flying by as your mind flies by with it. Not a word of this book was changed after I had finished writing it in three sessions from dusk to dawn at the typewriter like a long letter to a friend. This I believe to be the only possible literature of the free future, uninterrupted and unrevised full confessions about what actually happened in real life. It's not as easy as it sounds since it hurts to tell and print the truth.[26]

Jack's '*Notes from Underground* confessional madness' style[27] really was confessional in the deepest sense. Jack:

As to the style of *The Subterraneans*: this is the style I've discovered for narrative art, whereby the author stumbles over himself to tell his tale, just as breathlessly as some raconteur rushing in to tell a whole roomful of listeners what has just happened, and once he has told his tale he has no right to go back and delete what the hand hath written, just as the hand that writes upon a wall cannot go back. This decision, rather, this vow I made with regard to the practice of my narrative art frankly, Gentlemen, has its roots in my experience inside the confessionals of a Catholic childhood. It was my belief then that to withhold any reasonably and decently explainable detail from the Father was a sin, although you can be sure that the Father was aware of the difficulties of the delicacy involved. Yet all was well.[28]

As usual, it is difficult to know how true any of this is. There was plenty of material withheld from the Father: the details of his night with Gore Vidal, for a start, which Jack lamely said he 'forgot'. It is also not true to say that not a word was changed after he finished writing it because the book was originally set in New York City, using the locations where the events actually happened. In order to avoid a libel suit from Aileen, he was forced to rewrite the book entirely, changing the location to San Francisco. This was not simply a matter of changing a few street names: Lawrence Ferlinghetti and his City Lights Bookshop are included and some descriptions of jazz clubs are of actual San Francisco clubs, not transposed New York ones. At one point a fin-tailed Cadillac goes bouncing through the San Francisco streets and, though the Cadillac first sprouted a minor tailfin in 1949, it was not until the late fifties that it grew to become a noticeable feature, which is when Jack rewrote the book.

In the original manuscript, Jack ends the book with a fight with Gregory Corso but, in the published version, the fight becomes a daydream, a fantasy. Gregory: 'Aileen and me, we laid, just once, one sex shot. But he has it, he picks up a table, he's about to kill me! I said, "Don't say that. Don't end it like that," so he changed it!'[29]

Jack was proud of his achievement: 'Writing the Subs in three nights was really a fantastic athletic feat as well as mental, you shoulda seen me after I was done . . . I was pale as a sheet and had lost fifteen pounds and looked strange in the mirror.'[30] He excitedly gave the manuscript to Aileen to read, telling her that, if she didn't like it, she should throw it on the fire, but she knew he had a carbon copy at home. She hated what she read. She was shocked to read the physical details of their lovemaking and her sexual responses, and to find that her psychoanalysis and mental problems were all revealed on the page in stark detail. She complained that half the words he put into her mouth she had not said at all, nor were they even her opinions. They were said by someone else, in many cases by Jack himself. She felt her privacy was grossly invaded and her life violated and cheapened by Jack's description of their affair.

Jack definitely saw it as a biography of Aileen as much as the usual confessional autobiography of himself:

> *The Subterraneans* is an attempt on my part to execute the biography of someone else in a given circumstance and time, as completely as possible without offending the humanistic, in any case, human, tastes, of myself or anyone else, for the sake of entertainment, plus the suffering attention and edification of some reader by the fire of a winter midnight.[31]

The *roman à clef* is a very common literary form, particularly for first and second books. Kerouac continued to write them, having to go out and consciously experience adventures in order to give himself something to write about, but his approach was more than that. The Beats had a lot in common with the Surrealist group. With their common roots in Rimbaud and Lautréamont, they were 'in quest of the marvellous'. The Surrealists would not permit their members to write fiction with all its bourgeois concerns with plot and narrative development. They looked for writing which opened the door to the wonders of life, to the unconscious, to the surreal. Their prose work derived from the contemplation of real events and subjects and was an attempt to penetrate their surface reality. Good examples are *Paris Peasant*, Aragon's extended meditation on the then recently demolished Passage de l'Opera or Breton's wonderful *Nadja*, the dream girl of chance encounters which Kerouac's *The Subterraneans* parallels. Though there is no evidence that he was familiar with the work,[32] the book certainly had the same effect of making its subject feel violated. Nadja: 'How could I read . . . this distorted report of myself without rebelling, or even crying?'

Kerouac's view of African-Americans was hopelessly sentimental. There is no mention in his work of the fact that ten million Black people were living under segregation in the South, denied the vote, denied decent education and medical care, forced to ride in the back of buses, to use separate water fountains and to eat in Blacks-only cafes, unable to even watch Black entertainers except in Blacks-only venues. Of all the Beats, only John Clellon Holmes made any real attempt to write about African-American characters and their plight;[33] Kerouac wrote only of his *own* problems in falling in love with a Black woman.

The Subterraneans is written in spontaneous prose, with page-long sentences which do not obey strict rules of grammar but do retain a thread of meaning. This is Kerouac's spontaneous style at its best: perfected, mature, free-flowing, superb. Both Allen Ginsberg and William Burroughs were impressed with his achievement and wanted to know more about his method. They asked him to write a little brochure of instructions on how to write that way, which he did. The result was the essay *Essentials of Spontaneous Prose*, initially written for his friends but later widely anthologised as the manual of his method.

9 All Life is Sorrowful

Jack entered 1954 a sad man. He recognised that his drinking was a cover-up, a refusal to face the facts of his life. He now felt that he would never make it as a writer, even though he considered himself to be a genius. He knew that he would never have a meaningful relationship with a woman because of his Oedipal ties to his mother. He thought he would always be a bum, sponging off his family and friends till they finally tired of his constant demands, as some of them had already done. He was ripe for Buddhism, particularly the Four Noble Truths, the first of which, 'All Life is Suffering', he could easily relate to.

Jack:

How did I become a Buddhist? Well, after that love affair I described in *The Subterraneans*, I didn't know what to do. I went home and I just sat in my room hurting. I was suffering, you know, from the grief of losing a love, even though I really wanted to lose it. Well, I went to the library to read Thoreau. I said 'I'm going to cut out from civilisation and go back and live in the woods like Thoreau', and I started to read Thoreau and he talked about Hindu philosophy. So I put Thoreau down and I took out, accidentally, *The Life of Buddha* by Ashvaghosa.[1]

The scene in New York began to change. In December 1953, Bill Burroughs left for Athens and Tangier with no intention of returning, and Allen Ginsberg decided to quit the mid-town rat race and take off. He had saved some money and intended to go first to Mexico, to study the Mayan ruins and culture, and travel from there to California to visit Neal Cassady. Neal had also been writing to Jack, inviting him to visit, promising him a job and a place to stay. Jack thought a change of location would be good for him and took a Christmas job at the Post Office to save enough money for the journey. Jack dithered over the trip until the end of January, then set off in the freezing weather to hitchhike across the country. It took him several weeks and he was much the worse for wear when he arrived, having at one point been reduced to eating grass.

This time life was very different chez Cassady. Two things had happened which changed the situation. First, Neal had had an accident on the railroad and was suing for compensation. Carolyn and he talked endlessly about what they would do with the money when it came through: the new house they would get, the car, the presents for the children. The other, even more irritating thing was that they had both become followers of the late Edgar Cayce (1877–1945), the 'sleeping psychic' who placed himself in a sleeplike hypnotic state to provide answers to nearly any question imaginable.

Cayce's sleep-state responses are known as 'readings' and he gave over 14,000 of them, on more than 10,000 different topics, to people all over the world. They continue to be researched today by his followers at the A.R.E. Foundation: the Association for Research and Enlightenment. The last thing Jack wanted to hear about was reincarnation. He wanted to get out of this life as soon as possible and the thought of endlessly returning made him feel ill. As for some of Cayce's other beliefs, it drove Jack mad with rage to hear Neal, his all-American hero, babbling on about the Akashic records of Atlantis and second sight.

It is claimed that at an early age Cayce was able to master his school lessons by sleeping on his books. When he was 21 he developed a paralysis of the throat which threatened the loss of his voice. Doctors were unable to find a cause but Cayce entered the same sleep state which had enabled him to learn his school lessons years before, and was able to recommend a cure which successfully repaired his throat muscles and restored his voice. He quickly found that he could do the same for others.

Nearly 70% of the readings the 'sleeping psychic' gave were concerned with diagnosing illness and recommending treatment. He can be seen as one of the forerunners of holistic medicine since he believed that any complete approach to health needed to consider an individual's entire being rather than simply the illness. He usually proposed a well-balanced diet, regular exercise, and stressed the importance of relaxation and recreation.

Though most of his early 'readings' were to do with medical problems, people soon began asking him about such diverse topics as meditation, dreams, reincarnation and the lost continent of Atlantis. It is here many people lose him. Hundreds of readings deal with Atlantis, which, according to Cayce, was one of the most advanced civilisations the world would ever know. Naturally, Cayce was asked to interpret dreams, which he said were sent by God to give people insight into their lives. Cayce – via his readings – also believed in telepathy (mind-to-mind communication), clairvoyance (the ability to see with an inner vision), precognition (when one can see events before they occur), retrocognition (to see past events) and psychometry (to learn the history of an object and its immediate surroundings).

These were not special gifts; he claimed that everyone was psychic to some degree, because psychic activity was a 'natural ability of the soul'. Cayce also promoted a Western-style Christian meditation, essentially calming the mind. It is hard to imagine Neal sitting quietly in a chair focusing on the phrase 'God is love'.

Jack countered this with Buddhism, and their previously calm evenings were often shattered by violent philosophical disagreements. To further arm himself against the Cayce readings Jack went to the San Jose library where he found a copy of *The Buddhist Bible*, an anthology of Buddhist scriptures compiled by Dwight Goddard in 1932. Goddard wrote, '*The Buddhist Bible* is not intended to be a source book for cultural history and historical study [rather] it is designed to show the unreality of all conceptions of the personal ego.' He said that 'its purpose is to awaken faith in Buddhahood as being one's true self and nature; to follow the Noble Path, to become Buddha'. This was what Jack was looking for. These were the standard scholarly texts of old-school Buddhism which had withstood the test of time. A perfect counter to the rambling pronouncements of Cayce.

Jack found the sutras very appealing. The *Surangama Sutra*, for instance, appeared to be a direct affirmation of his theory of spontaneous prose: 'If you are now desirous of more perfectly understanding Supreme Enlightenment and the enlightening nature of pure Mind-Essence, you must learn to answer questions spontaneously with no recourse to discriminating thinking.'

Jack's reading on Buddhism was very thorough but, though he meditated, he was unable to sit in the lotus position or to sit still for very long because he had damaged his knees when he was a football player. Also, his Buddhism was academic rather than a dynamic part of his life. Unlike the other Beats who got involved with Buddhism, Jack never had the teacher-student relationship that is regarded as central to a proper understanding of Buddhism. He was never a part of a school and did not receive the oral tradition. His understanding was entirely autodidactic; it all came from books. Without a teacher, it is hard to imagine that he was able to meditate correctly, according to the Buddhist traditions. There are varying accounts of his actual understanding of Buddhism. Allen Ginsberg, ever generous towards Jack, thought Jack had a genuine understanding, whereas Gary Snyder, who later studied Zen in Japan, and Philip Whalen, who was later a Zen teacher in his own right, both thought that Jack understood very little. As for Lucien Carr, he said, 'That ol' Cannuck, he thinks the Buddha's the Pope.'

Despite this, the Four Noble Truths and the Eightfold Path became central to his thought for many years to come and were often cited in his books:

1. The Truth of Suffering. Birth is suffering; decay is suffering; death is suffering; pain, grief, despair, not getting what you want are all suffering.

2. The Truth of the Origin of Suffering. Suffering is caused by the craving for sensual pleasure, craving for eternal existence and craving for temporal happiness.

3. The Truth of the Extinction of Suffering. Suffering is extinguished by giving up this craving, forsaking it, and detaching oneself from it.

4. The Truth of the Path That Leads to the Extinction of Suffering. This is the Middle Way. Not to give oneself over to sensual pleasures nor to self-mortification. This is done by following the Eightfold Path:

1. Right Understanding.
2. Right Mindedness.
3. Right Speech.
4. Right Action.
5. Right Living.
6. Right Effort.
7. Right Attentiveness.
8. Right Concentration.

Things did not go well in San Jose. Jack and Neal argued over money – Jack was as mean as ever about paying for his share of the food – and the atmosphere became tense. Jack abhorred violence directed at children and was horrified when Neal knocked his daughter Cathy across the room. He quickly decided it was time to be moving on. In March 1954, he went to San Francisco and took a room at his favourite skid row hotel, the Cameo on Third Street at

Howard, which was in a funky neighbourhood of flophouses where the bus routes crossed, with the North Beach end of Market Street at one end and the railroad yards at the other. Jack was something of a connoisseur of skid row hotels, and stayed in many in San Francisco including the Swiss American on Broadway near City Lights, which Lenny Bruce also favoured.

Third Street inspired Jack to write another of his long impressionistic poems, 'San Francisco Blues', a cubist collage of images of bums and down-and-outs combined with a playful, joyous use of language, of bits of words and made-up sounds and rhythms. Kerouac described the method in some detail:

> In my system, the form of blues choruses is limited by the small page of the breastpocket notebook in which they are written, like the form of a set number of bars in a jazz blues chorus, and so word-meaning can carry from one chorus to another, or not, just like the phrase-meaning can carry harmonically from one chorus to the other, or not, in jazz, so that, in these blues as in jazz, the form is determined by time, and by the musician's spontaneous phrasing and harmonising with the beat of the time as it waves and waves on by in measured choruses. It's all gotta be non stop ad libbing within each chorus, or the gig is shot.[2]

Jack is using the term 'blues' somewhat loosely, but in these poems he is singing. Out of his pain and sadness comes a deep-felt sense of place, a compassion for its inhabitants, a delineation of his own mind, a richness of language, a joy. Although depressed and lonely, Jack was at the height of his powers.

Jack only stayed in San Francisco a month before returning home to Memere in Richmond Hill. He took a job on the Brooklyn Dock Railway but had to quit when his heavy drinking caused his phlebitis to flare up again. He had begun making notes from his study of Buddhist texts while he was in California, and he now extended this into translating texts from French and writing commentaries comparing Buddhism with Catholicism. This manuscript was growing rapidly and eventually became *Some of the Dharma*, finally published in the summer of 1997. He renounced sex, which he now identified as the primary cause of his problems, and began typing up his *Book of Dreams*.

Jack saw the dreams as another extension of spontaneous writing, almost automatic writing:

The style of a person half awake from sleep and ripping it out in pencil by the bed, yes pencil, what a job! bleary eyes, insaned mind bemused and mystified by sleep, details that pop out even as you write them you don't know what they mean, till you wake up, have coffee, look at it, and see the logic of dreams in dream language itself, see?[3]

It is always dangerous for a writer to publish his dreams as it opens the door to all kinds of interpretation, particularly Freudian interpretation. What Freud called 'the manifest dream' itself is often of little interest and it is hard for us to penetrate any deeper into Kerouac's psyche without knowing specifically when or where these dreams were written: we do not know what he was reacting to, or how he was feeling at the time. Freud wrote:

I have been concerned with the 'latent content' which can be derived from the manifest dream by psychoanalytical interpretation. A collection of dreams without associations and knowledge of the context in which it was dreamed does not tell me anything, and it is hard to imagine what it can mean to anyone else.[4]

Since we have a general idea of the context, we can identify dreams about his mother, and wet dreams about the girlfriends and wives of his friends. In fact, some of the most erotic writing Kerouac ever published is in this book, such as the 'Sex Dream of Marie Fitzpatrick or Somebody'.[5]

Several dreams concern 'Peaches', Ginger Chase, Hal's ex-wife who Kerouac had been seeing on and off the previous summer. There is also a notorious paedophile fantasy involving a seven-year-old girl he meets in a park who asks him to help her with her buttons: 'I feel guilt as deep as the sea.' There is one semi-homoerotic dream, in which Jack gets an erection sitting next to Neal in a double toilet when Neal begins talking about a gay actor, but there are surprisingly few dreams about his mother. He nowhere suggests that this is a complete record of his dreams, or that it has not been edited for interest and decorum, so perhaps those about Memere were left out.

He also experimented with science fiction, but the one story he wrote, *cityCityCITY*, showed that he did not have a feeling for it: it is a run-of-the-mill short story of an overpopulated totalitarian world in the distant future where individualism has all but been stamped out. Jack was floundering about; he had no prospects and delved more and more into Buddhism as the only way left open to him. He would become a *bikku*, a wandering mendicant. He spent the rest of the year dividing his time between increasingly out-of-control carousing in New York and quiet writing at his mother's house. In October Jack began *Book of Memory*, one of his attempts to 'delineate Lowell in its entirety', staying up late at night while his mother slept, brewing Nescafé with hot milk and puffing at a newly acquired corn-cob pipe in an attempt to cut down on the number of cigarettes he smoked. To aid his research, he took a bus trip to Lowell, where he checked into the Depot Chambers, a cheap hotel near the railroad yards, and set out to revisit his childhood homes and haunts.

He visited Mary Carney, but met with a wall of silent disapproval from her family. He was so distraught by the memories brought on by visiting his childhood friends that he went on a three-day binge, finishing up in the basement chapel of Sainte Jeanne d'Arc where he thought he saw the statue of the Virgin turn its head. It was here that he claims to have seen that the real meaning of the term 'Beat' was 'beatific', a somewhat different definition from Huncke's. Jack:

> In 1954, I went to Lowell, Mass., where I had lived as a kid. I got a room in skid row near the depot and walked 20 miles around Lowell every day. Went to my old church where I got my first confirmation – all alone, all alone in the church, and the great silence of the church. And I suddenly realised that beat means beatitude. Beatific. I was beatific in the church see. It doesn't apply to anybody else, I don't think.[6]

By the end of 1954, Jack was at the lowest ebb of his life: he was an alcoholic and a speed freak, he took Benzedrine each day even though he was liable to develop a fatal blood clot, and could not give up cigarettes. He was about as far from his Buddhist ideal as you could get, except for his vow of chastity. In addition, his nights on the town in New York had not gone unnoticed and he had been tracked down and arrested for non-support of his daughter. He appeared in Family Court in January 1955 where he was represented, for free, by Allen's brother Eugene, who provided the court with documents from Jack's physician saying that he was unable to work because of his phlebitis. The judge deferred sentence for a year.

Jack was now set in the pattern that continued throughout the rest of his life. He went on drunken binges which often caused his phlebitis to flare up, then stayed at home with his mother and recuperated. He had by now given up any serious ideas of living a life with a woman other than Memere and had begun to internalise many of her reactionary ideas. It was now, for instance, that Jack became a staunch supporter of Senator Joe McCarthy and his anti-communist witch hunt. From 1954 until his death, Jack's politics were about as far right wing as was possible, short of joining the American Fascist Party.

It is hard to understand Kerouac's defence of McCarthy because he was thoroughly discredited for unscrupulous, illegal and unconstitutional behaviour at just about the time Jack became his supporter. Both Joe McCarthy's rise and his fall were accomplished with astonishing speed. At the beginning of 1950 he was just another cheap, vulgar politician, then, on 9 February, he made a speech in Wheeling, West Virginia, in which he claimed that the Department of State was full of communists and that he and the Secretary of State knew their names. A Senate committee was immediately appointed to look into his astonishing allegation. He did not know any names, of course, and nor did the Secretary of State, but by the time this was revealed he was already famous. At the time when America was preparing for a war against communism in Korea, he had cloaked himself in the flag and was able to begin his fanatical campaign of hate, of baseless defamation and mudslinging, with impunity. His House of Unamerican Activities Committee became so powerful that it paralysed the Presidency. Neither Harry S Truman nor Dwight D Eisenhower, from early 1950 through till late 1954, could act without considering the effect of their plans upon McCarthy and the forces he led. Fear ruled the land: dozens of Hollywood screen writers were forced to live in exile, and even the kitchen staff at the Pentagon were investigated for subversive activities.

McCarthy claimed, in 1952, that 'McCarthyism is Americanism with its sleeves rolled', but to most Americans it eventually became a pseudonym for everything repressive, reactionary, anti-intellectual, illiberal and totalitarian in American life. He was finally brought down by Joseph N Welch, the lawyer representing the Army in the historic Army v McCarthy hearings to investigate McCarthy's allegations of communist subversives within the United States Army, the first major Congressional hearings ever to be wholly televised. Welch brought charges of improper conduct against the senator and his staff and McCarthy typically reacted by attempting to discredit Welch's law firm.

The climax of the hearings came on day 45 in a famous exchange between McCarthy and Welch. McCarthy attacked the alleged communist ties of one of Welch's associates, Frederick G Fisher, who had been a member of the National Lawyers' Guild while at Harvard Law School. Welch was outraged at this slur on his associate's character and delivered a powerful response to the senator, saying, 'Let us not assassinate this lad further, senator. You have done enough. Have you no sense of decency, sir, at long last? Have you left no sense of decency?' Welch's words were greeted with loud applause: it was as if the bubble of fear surrounding McCarthy was broken. He was discredited before a national television audience. The hearings continued for ten more days and ended with the Army's exoneration on all charges.

The Senate reacted and McCarthy was censured, or, in the language of the resolution, 'condemned' for conduct that 'tended to bring the Senate into dishonour and disrepute'. McCarthy's reputation collapsed like a house of cards leaving only his name in the language. Jack, however, remained a staunch supporter.

That April, *New World Writing* published an extract from *On the Road* called 'Jazz of the Beat Generation'. Jack was scared that the court would see the article and use it as evidence to make him pay child support so he published it under the pseudonym 'Jean-Louis'. Malcolm Cowley was furious with him: he had been actively pushing Jack's work to a number of New York publishers under his real name and now Jack had undermined his efforts. Jack was encouraged by its publication, even though both EP Dutton and Alfred Knopf had turned down *On the Road* and Little Brown had rejected *The Subterraneans*. *On the Road* was sent off to Dodd Mead with Cowley's recommendation. He promised Jack that, if they too rejected it, he would insist that Viking took it.

Memere was now retired from the shoe factory. She moved down to Rocky Mount, North Carolina, to live with her daughter, and invested all her savings in her brother-in-law's television business. Jack spent the winter and spring living at Nin's house but, as summer approached, he felt the usual need to move on. He spent the early part of the summer in New York, staying with Lucien Carr in the Village, seeing all his old friends and going on increasingly more self-destructive drinking binges, one of which caused a phlebitis attack which gave him a lump on his ankle the size of a tennis ball so he could barely walk.

Allen Ginsberg was creating an interesting scene around himself in

San Francisco and Jack wanted to join him. He set out to hitchhike there but, when he reached Texas, he once more felt the pull of Mexico and so continued south to Mexico City. Bill Garver, the overcoat thief, had retired to Mexico 'to cultivate a habit' and was now living in Bill Burroughs's apartment building at 210 Orizaba. Jack took a small cubicle room on the roof of his building. It had a clay floor and was reached by a precarious stairway with only a two-foot-high rail to stop him from toppling three floors into the central courtyard. To get the bedbugs out Jack had the local children burn the bedsprings while he fanned the flames with the mattress.

Jack had known Garver since 1945 and each afternoon he would take his bag of pot and go down to Garver's room with his notepad to idle away the day and write. Bill would sit in his easy chair in his purple pyjamas, high on morphine, and mumble about the Minoan civilisation and archeological excavations while Jack sat on the bed and wrote the poems which make up *Mexico City Blues*. Some of Bill's words filtered through, such as in 'Chorus 52', most of which is Garver's actual speech. Garver spoke very slowly, which enabled Jack to copy it all down. Garver was pleased and, not surprisingly, thought Jack's poems were very good. Allen Ginsberg had always said that Garver talked too much but Jack had the bright idea of listening to what he had to say. *Mexico City Blues* was written in three weeks in August and is generally regarded as the best of Kerouac's poetry books, though this may be because it is so well known: most of the others were not published in his lifetime and have yet to properly enter the canon.

Garver's morphine connection was a ravaged young junkie prostitute called Esperanza, the widow of Bill Burroughs's junk connection Dave Tercerero. Jack was using morphine, too, and she became the connection for both he and Garver. Each day she would make the connection in the slums and bring it to them. Jack: 'Poem 230 from *Mexico City Blues* was written purely on morphine. Every line in this poem was written within an hour of one another . . . high on a big dose of M.' He wrote on junk time: one line, wait an hour, write another line, wait another hour, another line . . .[7]

Despite his vow of chastity – or perhaps because of it – Jack fell in love with Esperanza. She was a waiflike young woman who had obviously once been very beautiful. In Kerouac's romantic eyes she still was: 'She was the most gorgeous little Indian chick you ever saw. Esperanza Villanueva. Villanueva is a Spanish name so she's half-Indian, half-Spanish . . . beauty. Absolute beauty. She had bones, man, just bones, skin and bones.'[8]

Unable to sleep in the August heat, Jack stayed up at night, writing about her in pencil in his notebook by candlelight. Esperanza means hope in Spanish, but Jack called her Tristessa in the book, which means sadness – a name undoubtedly taken from François Sagan's world bestseller of the previous year, *Bonjour Tristesse*.

Tristessa is Jack at his descriptive best, his infectious energy still burning. He describes the squalid shack in the slums which Tristessa shares with a dove, a hen, a cock, and her 'sister'. Her pimp is also there but Jack doesn't call him that. It is a cast of characters from a John Waters movie. People throw up, shoot up, they swig hi-balls as fast as Jack pours them, and the rain pours in through the cardboard roof. Then they hit the streets, high on morphine and booze. Saturday-night Mexico City, 2 a.m. in the hot rain: the bars, the taco stands, the dope dens – perfect Kerouac material. He sees it all from a completely passive standpoint, romantic yet uninvolved: 'Everything is so poor in Mexico, people are poor, and yet everything is happy and carefree.'

The book shows that Jack felt safe with her and, though he claimed to get involved emotionally, it was a conceit, an experience, like 'The Mexican Girl' in California, and had none of the gut-wrenching effect of an affair such as the one with Aileen Lee. He wrote of Tristessa: 'I love her, I fall in love with her. She strokes my arm with thin finger. I love it.' He was safe because he had sworn off lust, sworn off sexuality in order to live the chaste Buddhist life. Also, if he really loved her, he might have done something about her appalling circumstances.

Throughout August, as Jack wrote *Mexico City Blues* he sent the poems in batches to Allen in San Francisco. In return, Allen sent him the original manuscript of a poem he had just written. Across the top of the much annotated first page was written, in crimson pencil, 'Howl for Carl Solomon'. It was a radical change of style for Allen, and Jack instantly saw that it was a major achievement on Allen's part. He did not, however, like all the 'x-ings out and amendations [sic]' and complained to Allen about them, demanding that he stick to his original thoughts. He wrote 'Your HOWL FOR CARL SOLOMON is very powerful, but I don't want it arbitrarily negated by secondary emendations made in time's reconsidering backstep – I want your lingual SPONTANEITY or nothing . . .'9 Strangely, Allen had no memory of giving the poem a title, and thought Jack had just made that up – though why Jack would think of dedicating the poem to Carl Solomon is another matter as he and Carl were still not getting on. Jack sent the original ms on to John Clellon Holmes for him to read and it remained stored among Holmes's papers for thirty years.[10]

Allen had come into his own. Shortly after Bill left for Europe at the end of December 1953, Allen set off to investigate the Mayan remains in Yucatán, where he stayed for six months, living on a coffee finca in the middle of the jungle. When he finally arrived in California he stayed with Neal and Carolyn, but Carolyn caught Allen giving Neal a blow job and banished him from the house. He went to San Francisco where he quickly immersed himself in the literary scene, getting to know Kenneth Rexroth, Gary Snyder, Philip Whalen, Michael McClure, Lawrence Ferlinghetti, and the other poets of what became known as the San Francisco Renaissance.

Allen's poetry underwent a great change: he opened up, extended his breath length, became freer. The result was 'Howl' and its associated poems. When he first arrived in San Francisco he took a job with a market-research company and moved in with his new lover, Sheila Boucher. He enrolled in analysis and was told not to worry about his homosexual leanings. Shortly after this he met Peter Orlovsky and his life was transformed. Peter was to be his close friend and on-and-off lover for the rest of his life. He and Peter were living on Montgomery Street when Allen wrote 'Howl' but, by the time Jack arrived, Allen had taken a small cottage at 1624 Milvia Street, Berkeley, just across the Bay.

Jack left Mexico City on 9 September 1955, his knapsack filled with the manuscripts of *Doctor Sax*, *On the Road*, *Visions of Cody* and the first part of *Tristessa* – the second part was not written until a year later. He took a bus to El Paso and then hitched rather than use the money Allen sent him. He arrived in Berkeley just in time to be a part of the legendary Six Gallery reading on 7 October. Allen had been working with Gary Snyder and Kenneth Rexroth to put on a reading by the new group of poets. The postcard flyer was clearly Allen's work:

6 Poets at 6 Gallery: Philip Lamantia reading mss of late John Hoffman – Mike McClure, Allen Ginsberg, Gary Snyder & Phil Whalen – all sharp now straightforward writing – remarkable collection of angels on one stage reading their poetry. No charge, small collection for wine and postcards. Charming event. Kenneth Rexroth, M.C. 8PM Friday night, October 7, 1955. 6 Gallery 3119 Fillmore St. San Fran.

Allen had tried his hardest to get Jack to read from *Mexico City Blues* but he was too shy. On the day of the reading they took the bus across the Oakland Bridge and met up with Gary Snyder and Phil Whalen at Key Terminal. It was Jack's first meeting with them and they immediately related to each other. They became good friends: walking the streets, going to parties, staying up all night talking, so that when Jack finally returned to New York he left a note calling them 'the two best men I ever met'. Jack did not get on with everyone. He was loud and obnoxious when drunk, which made him unwelcome in many homes. He had not clicked with Kenneth Rexroth, who regarded himself as the *éminence grise* of the San Francisco literary scene and did not like Kerouac's disrespectful attitude.

At the reading Jack's shyness appears to have evaporated. He took charge of buying the wine, then sat on the edge of the stage, swigging from a whole gallon of red wine while another flagon circulated among the audience. Jack treated the reading like a jazz performance and tapped his jug in time with the rhythms of the poetry, and sometimes moaned or yelped out 'Go!' at an appropriate time, encouraging the poets to greater heights of expression. The poets liked it but Rexroth frowned in annoyance. When Allen read 'Howl', the whole audience joined in with Jack, yelling their encouragement, stomping their feet and cheering at the end of each fantastic, long, breath-length line. By the end of the evening, everyone present knew that something new had come into the world and that they had been present at a seminal event.

Jack was pleased and proud of Allen's success, but on other matters they disagreed: Jack disapproved strongly of Allen's affair with Peter Orlovsky, yelling at him that he shouldn't sleep with boys. He became so incensed that he slammed his fist into the bathroom door, splitting the wood.[11] Ginsberg: 'He was terrible about things like that.' Jack was in fact becoming more and more homophobic, and was to be increasingly so for the remainder of his life. He grew more disturbed by his own homosexual activities. Despite this, Jack and Peter became very good friends and always remained so.

Jack was astonished to find that most of the poets he met knew more about Buddhism than he did. 'Didn't you know everyone in San Francisco was a Buddhist?' asked Rexroth, condescendingly. California's position on the Pacific rim meant it looked east to the Orient as well as over its shoulder to the rest of America. The biggest difference between Jack and Snyder, Whalen, Rexroth and the others was that they were mostly interested in the Zen Buddhism of Japan whereas Jack stuck to the original Indian and Chinese texts. Jack continued to carry Dwight Goddard's *The Buddhist Bible* with him everywhere he went, just as he used to carry his railroad brakeman's handbook as an identity badge.

Philip Whalen:

I would argue with Jack about it a little bit, because a lot of the material he was reading was Theravadan on classical Buddhism, and I'd say, 'That's all very well and poetic but Buddhism is a lot simpler. You don't need all that goings on.' So we'd go around that. But I think he was interested more in the language of it than anything else. The ideas may or may not have done something for him but he was really attracted to the visionary, the descriptions of all these worlds and places and things and jewels and lights and music and so on. So, we didn't get into any acrimonious stuff. Gary tried to talk to him about it and Gary would try to get him to meditate but he'd wrecked his knees when he was playing football, so he couldn't bend his knees very easily, but he tried. But he couldn't sit still for very long, he was too jumpy.[12]

Allen Ginsberg, Phil Whalen, and Jack spent hours exploring the streets, both in Berkeley and San Francisco. Allen's 'Sunflower Sutra', which mentions Jack several times, was written on one such walk. They had strolled down Third Street in San Francisco, past Jack's favourite flea-pit hotel and down to the railroad yards at Townshend – the San Francisco Skyway approach roads were not yet built. They walked around the railroad yards down by China Basin, and sat down in the shade of a huge Southern Pacific steam locomotive to watch the sun set over Twin Peaks. In 'Sunflower Sutra' Allen wrote: 'Jack Kerouac sat beside me on a busted rusty iron pole, companion, we thought the same thoughts of the soul, bleak and blue and sad-eyed, surrounded by the gnarled steel roots of trees of machinery.'

Then Allen found a sunflower, covered with grime from the locomotives. Philip Whalen:

He found this thing, and he said, 'What is it? What is it?' and I said, 'It's a sunflower!' It had all gone to seed and was all black and sooty and he was completely enthralled. And Jack was wearing his little jacket with his hands in his pockets not picking up on the fact that Allen had discovered something or other but wanting another beer. Jack was always alternately gloomy or high, enthusiastically high. He was just interested in his own head and what he was seeing or hearing, or he'd be gloomy like Eeyore: glooming around about how he was going to leave, he was going to die, we were all gonna die. At one point he came up with the idea that he and Allen and Gary and I would all end up being some old bums under a railroad bridge by the river, years later. We would walk a lot of places, either in Berkeley or San Francisco. And in Berkeley it was usually Jack and I walking from the apartment in Milvia Street walking halfway across Berkeley to where there was a wine shop where we could buy cheap wine. Ten chances to one, either on the way out or on the way back we would be stopped by these young cops who would want to know what we were doing and where we were going. Jack would always say, 'Let me take care of this,' which was fine with me because I was scared of them. Anyway, he would kid them along and reassure them that everything was all right . . .[13]

These were happy days for Jack even though he was drinking too much. This was the life that Jack had intended for himself, living in a small cabin, possessions reduced to a minimum, studying the Buddhist scriptures, and all these people were already doing it. He really enjoyed the companionship of Allen, Phil and Gary and also that of Michael McClure, who initially kept his distance from the core of the group. McClure was astonished to meet someone even more acutely self-conscious than himself. He said that Jack felt that all eyes were upon him when he walked across a room.

It was Gary who influenced him the most. Eight years younger than Jack, he was a real Westerner, having been born in San Francisco in 1930 and growing up on a farm near Seattle, Washington. He was descended from 'punchers, miners, railroad men' and before that from Scots and Irish pioneers who fought with cougars and grizzly bears to open up Washington State. His grandfather was an organiser with the 'Wobblies': the Industrial Workers of the World, a socialist group with strong anarchist leanings who wished to 'form a new society within the shell of the old'. Snyder always held true to this philosophy, never wishing to destroy, only to transform. He grew up with a great love of the woodlands and animals. He studied folklore and American-Indian history. By the time his parents moved to Portland, Oregon, when he was twelve, he could already camp alone in the woods and sew his own moccasins. He went to Reed College in 1947 where he came under the influence of Ezra Pound and Robert Graves and began to write poetry. It was there that he formulated a personal philosophy based on American-Indian myths and Buddhist scriptures.

He worked for the Warm Springs Lumber Company in Oregon and as a trail crew worker in the Yosemite National Park. He was employed as a fire watcher in the Gifford Pinchot National Forest until the creeping tentacles of McCarthyism reached even into the Forest Service and he was fired as a security risk. With his independent views and left-wing background he could not be trusted to report fires in the forest. Whether Jack knew this is not known: it would have been interesting to see how he reconciled this with his continuing support for McCarthy.

Gary all along saw that ecology was the big issue. He felt that the problem stemmed from the Bible, which gave man dominion over the earth and set him apart from nature to rule over it. Instead of seeing ourselves as a part of nature and working with it, we regard it as there to be used, as raw material, as fuel. The Zen Buddhist teacher DT Suzuki wrote, 'Man makes use of it economically with no sense of kinship with it, hence with no sense of gratitude or sympathetic affiliation.'[14] This was a view that Jack understood and agreed with. He had always rejoiced in wearing simple, strong work clothes which could be repaired and would last. He loved his knapsack, his sleeping bag and travel equipment. He was torn between the simple life, in the woods with bare necessities, and the roaring all-night drunken excitement of the city. He never could decide between them, but with Gary he found his guide and mentor for the former.

Though Gary was studying Japanese Zen Buddhism, he and his girlfriend practised the Tantric Buddhist 'Yab-yum', literally 'father-mother', and a common name for depictions of male gods in sexual union with their female counterparts or *shakti*. In Tantric Buddhism it is used as a metaphor for enlightenment.[15] They arrived at Allen's cottage, stripped off their clothes, and invited Allen and Jack to join in. Jack was shocked and too shy to take off his clothes, but after Gary and Allen had achieved 'tantric union' he joined in, lying on the floor fully clothed, but finished up by taking a bath with the young woman.

Neal was also in San Francisco. He and Carolyn had more or less broken up and Neal was living in the city with a disturbed young woman called Natalie Jackson, visiting Carolyn and the three children only at weekends. The children were used to his frequent absences and so were not upset by it. Jack still had very strong feelings towards Carolyn and went to visit them in Los Gatos at the new house they had bought with Neal's insurance-claim money.

There was a garden and pool, but no spare room for Jack. He was devastated. He had always considered the Cassady household as his second home, somewhere like his mother's house, where a room was always ready waiting for him. Now this had been swept away. They had not even considered it when they bought the place but, watching Jack anxiously search the house for his room, Carolyn felt guilty at his obvious disappointment.

On the weekend of Jack's visit, a progressive bishop was giving a talk in Los Gatos and Neal and Carolyn had invited him to come back to their house afterwards. Neal drove to Berkeley to fetch Allen and Peter for them to meet him as well. The bishop arrived at the house with his mother and his aunt, whom Allen positioned on either side of himself on the settee. Allen leant forward asking pointed questions about sex while Jack sat at his feet, drunk, swigging from a bottle of cheap red Burgundy and repeating over and over to the bishop, 'I love you.' None of this seemed to phase the bishop. Jack appeared to be out of it but, as many people have said, he often pretended to be more inebriated than he really was. He was secretly taking it all in, mentally recording the details of conversation for future use. In this case he reproduced long sections of their dialogue in his play *The Beat Generation*, which became the script for the movie *Pull my Daisy*.

After the bishop left, Neal drove Allen and Peter back to Berkeley, leaving Jack and Carolyn to spend the night together. Carolyn, with three children, had little choice in those puritan days but to hope for a future reconciliation with Neal, but she was pleased to have Jack visit. Carolyn:

> Of course, their lifestyles were just appalling to me. I wouldn't have chosen to know any of these people . . . if I weren't already living with them. Neal would hurt me and I'd punish him. Now I think of him as a kind of sacrificial lamb for my education. What I learned in the end was how to love someone unconditionally; not to try to change them, but love them for what they are.[16]

She did the only thing she knew, which was to complain, and shame him for abandoning his family. 'Then he would feel guilty, as if he had gone to confession, and it was all right again for a while.'

For Jack, the greatest thing about his season in California was being invited to climb a mountain by Gary. Together with John Montgomery, a garrulous and disorganised librarian, they set off to climb Matterhorn in the Yosemite National Park. They drove to Bridgeport, near Mono Lake, up near the Nevada border. First Montgomery turned out to have forgotten his sleeping bag, so they had to borrow blankets from a lodge, then the next day, as they began their climb up the foothills above the lake, Montgomery remembered that he had forgotten to drain the radiator of his car. (In *The Dharma Bums* Jack says it was the crankcase but this seems less necessary. As a non-driver Jack knew little about cars.) He turned back and Jack and Gary continued alone. This was a fortunate occurrence because Montgomery's constant chatter had stopped them from talking. Now they exchanged intimacies and Gary taught Jack how to climb a mountain.

They made camp and waited for Montgomery, but it became clear that he would not reach them until the next morning. They made a huge fire beneath an overhanging rock which reflected the heat back on them, meditated, and then ate by themselves. Gary chilled a chocolate pudding in the snow. Jack felt like Han Shan, whose name translates as 'Cold Mountain', the Chinese sage who wandered the mountains, writing his poems on the cliff face. He had rarely been so happy and his enjoyment and exhilaration comes across in the book that he wrote about it, *The Dharma Bums*, his most accessible, positive and pleasing book.

Back in San Francisco Jack was filled with the idea of spending time on his own in the mountains. Gary had told him about his summer job as a fire watcher and Jack decided to commit himself to spending three months alone in a watchtower in the Cascades. There would be no way out until they came to get him, though he would be in radio communication each day with headquarters and the other watchtowers. Privately, Gary thought it would be good to make Jack follow through on an idea, instead of walking away as soon as things became sticky.

Neal had been gambling heavily and had persuaded Natalie to forge Carolyn's signature on $10,000 worth of bonds – Neal and Carolyn's life savings, intended for their children's education. The bank telephoned Carolyn because one paper had not been signed, but it was too late to get the money back. Neal had lost it all at the racetrack. The bank wanted to swear out a warrant for Neal and Natalie's arrest but Carolyn resigned herself to the fact that it would do no good. Neal thrived on punishment, just as he had in reform school. Natalie, however, was overcome with remorse and fear, convinced that the police were after her. On the night of Halloween 1955, Natalie, dressed only in a T-shirt and her bathrobe, went up on to the rooftop of 1041 Franklyn Street, where she lived with Neal, and slashed her throat with glass from a broken skylight. Someone saw her climb over the edge of the fire-escape walkway and called the police. The newspaper report read:

> Officer O'Roarke lunged through a window to grab her. 'All I could do was dive through and grab,' he said. 'I got a grip on one arm and her robe just as she tried to kick loose. But I couldn't hold her. All at once I was just holding the robe, and she had fallen.'

She fell three floors to her death. In her book *Off the Road*, Carolyn reported Neal explaining, 'Part of it was feeling so guilty about forging your signature – she's been agonising ever since – and she did that for me . . .' Natalie had tried, unsuccessfully, to cut her wrists the previous week. Carolyn, in a most magnanimous gesture, invited Neal to come home for a while to recover. Jack came to stay as well, but did not like sleeping on the settee with no privacy, and after a few days he set off to hitchhike to Rocky Mount to spend Christmas with his mother, sister and her family.

Before he left San Francisco, Jack had begun planning his next book; he liked to think them through in his head in some detail before he actually set them down, sometimes extemporising long sections of them to friends in all-night monologues. Philip Whalen remembered:

> He kept talking about Buddhism, but also, he would mix it, he would go back to talking about his brother Gerard and about what a saintly type Gerard was, and so on and then he would go on about all the buddhas and how marvellous that all was.

Once more settled in a room of his own, Jack began to write. Between New Year's Day and 16 January 1956[17], he wrote *Visions of Gerard*, surely the strangest book of his oeuvre. It was written at the kitchen table of his sister Nin's home in Big Easonburg Woods, North Carolina, from midnight to dawn, ending with 'refreshing visits to the piney barrens out behind the cotton field at sunrise. I did no rewriting or revising whatever, except for name changes and one important comma finally inserted somewhere, where I'd made a spontaneous mistake about it being needed, although I did reject a whole night's writing and started all over again on the section the next night. It was all written by hand, in pencil, in little notebooks. Certain kinds of stories seem to deny the rackety typewriter.'[18]

After Jack's sister and her husband went to bed Jack took over the kitchen, brewed tea and took Benzedrine. His sister wouldn't let him light candles so he used the regular light. Memere was not there, having gone to Brooklyn for the funeral of her stepmother. Jack:

If she'd been there, I wouldn't have written it. We'd have talked all night. But the funeral reminded me of funerals, my brother's funeral. The style of *Gerard* is directly influenced by Shakespeare's *Henry V*. The language is so windblown and Shakespearean.[19]

Jack may have supposed it was Shakespearean. It is certainly written in an extremely irritating style – when he was out of his head on speed, at the height of his spontaneous-prose period, using what he must have supposed to be Elizabethan scansion with lots of tis and twas, hearken, mayhap, rave lip't. 'He could feel the iron snap grinding his little imagined birdy bones and squeezing and cracking and pressing harder unto worse-than-death the bleak-in-life . . . For it's not innocent blank nature made hills look sad and woe-y, it's men . . .' Etcetera etcetera.

It is the sad story of a sickly little boy who loved his mother, cared for animals and yearned for heaven. Jack described it as 'a beautiful poem about death' and also claimed that it was true – 'My best most serious sad and true book yet' – and yet he had no memories whatsoever of Gerard except for one time when Gerard slapped his face, an incident which does not occur in *Visions of Gerard*. The book is a biography, of sorts, but not the first-hand reportage of Kerouac's other books. What Kerouac has done is effectively ghostwritten his mother's biography of her ever more saintly child. The detailed descriptions and the long passages of dialogue are assembled from the hundreds of stories she endlessly repeated to Jack throughout his life until he knew them all by heart.

The book is the resurrection of Gerard, reborn on the page, a final attempt by Kerouac to expunge his guilt for wishing Gerard dead, to prove his love for Gerard to his mother with a greeting-card portrait of the sick boy which is as cloying, sentimental and all-American as any Norman Rockwell cover for the *Saturday Evening Post*.

There are shades of Andy Warhol's mother here, who lived with him and sometimes did his lettering for him. Here Kerouac has finally internalised his mother's vision of Gerard and made it his own. He has become Memere and, in so doing, perhaps found some cathartic release for the abandonment and thus symbolic death of his own child.

The book consists of a series of sentimental, set-piece tableaux, each one a well-rehearsed story that he had heard time and time over. To these are added scraps of undigested Buddhist philosophy, peculiar Cannuck French and Catholic platitudes about Jesus, Mary and the angels and asides about 'the great American Saint Edgar Cayce'. Did he include them to please Carolyn? The pages and pages of dialogue are all invented, so on this level it is a fiction but, since it is based on fact, as filtered through his mother's extremely rose-tinted memory, it is a biography. Unlike the other books, it is not a *roman à clef*.

Gerard dominated Jack throughout his life, and when he appeared on a local Lowell radio station in 1962 he became quite emotional remembering a brother whom he could not really remember. He told the interviewers:[20]

> When Gerard was on his deathbed nine nuns of Saint Louis de France filed into the room and said, 'Gerard, repeat what you told us about Heaven.' They took down their notes and went away. He told my mother before he died that he was going to build her a little white cottage in heaven.

At this point Jack's voice cracked and he became weepy and sentimental.

Filled with the memory of his happy summer in the Bay Area, and still enthused with his climb up Matterhorn with Gary, Jack acted on the idea of applying to the Forest Service. In January he wrote off four letters to the Washington-district rangers applying for fire-spotting jobs. In February, slightly to his astonishment, he was accepted. He wrote joyfully to Carolyn: 'O boy, O boy, O here I go, I got the offer for the job watching fires on top of the mountains in the cascade country in northwest . . .'[21] He had to report for the job on 25 June and began planning his year in order to finish up in Washington on that date. Malcolm Cowley was teaching a creative-writing course at Stanford University outside San Francisco and Jack decided to join him there and complete the editing of *On the Road*, which was still being changed to meet the publisher's libel and obscenity standards, even though Viking had not yet committed themselves by signing a contract.

He also wanted to get away from Rocky Mount, where things were not going well. When Memere decided to invest her life savings in her son-in-law's television business, one of the conditions was that in addition to her living with them, and doing some of the housekeeping and childminding, Jack would also have room and board whenever he wanted it. Paul had initially gone along with this, but he found it intolerable that Jack could sit around the house all day, eating his food, drinking and meditating, while he was putting in a full day's work. He placed no value on Jack's writing, and was probably not aware of quite how late Jack stayed up writing. The two men probably put in the same number of work hours but to Paul they were not comparable. The situation became so bad that Jack and Memere seriously considered moving to California together to set up house away from Paul and Nin. Jack was now 34 years old, penniless and effectively homeless. The one definite thing in his life was the need to be in Washington in June so, on 17 March 1956, he borrowed $50 from his mother and set out to hitchhike the 3,000 miles to California.

The trip took him much longer than he had anticipated and, by the time he got there, Cowley's semester was over and he had returned to New York. Jack was outraged, even though he had fixed no actual appointments with Cowley, but at least he was closer to the Pacific northwest and he had arrived in time to visit Gary Snyder, who was leaving in May for Japan where he had been given a scholarship to study Zen. Gary was living in Mill Valley, near San Francisco, in a very basic wooden cabin rented from his friend Locke McCorkle, Sean Monahan in *The Dharma Bums*, who lived nearby with his wife and family. There was a spare room for Jack, who settled straight in.

Jack was very impressed with Gary's spartan lifestyle and learnt a great deal from him about survival techniques. Before Jack left to spend Christmas with his family in 1955, Gary had gone shopping with Jack to fit him out with a sleeping bag, backpack and all the necessary equipment to live in the woods. That winter in Rocky Mount, Jack insisted on sleeping on the back porch with all the windows open, snug and warm in his sleeping bag and parka. Together he and Gary camped in the woods near Mount Tamalpais and discussed Buddhism. One day Snyder told Jack, 'All right, Kerouac, it's about time for you to write a sutra.' Jack had already set down many of his thoughts about Buddhism in *Some of the Dharma*. Writing in pencil, with many revisions, 'because it was scripture. I had no right to be spontaneous'[22], Jack wrote *The Scripture of the Golden Eternity*. Philip Whalen described the text as 'to a degree, quotes, in his own extravagant language'.

Early in May, after a huge three-day party, Gary left for Japan, which was to become his home for the next thirteen years. Jack stayed on at the cabin for the next six weeks until it was time for him to head north for his fire-watching job. He invited friends to stay, one of whom was the poet Robert Creeley.

The Place was the main meeting spot for the poets in San Francisco, and it was here that Allen Ginsberg first introduced Jack to both Ed Dorn and Robert Creeley. Jack was very drunk at the time and, when they all went back to someone's apartment, Jack passed out on a bed. But they later got to know each other well, often meeting up at parties.

Robert Creeley: 'Jack and I would always find ourselves sitting on the sidelines and we have got some pots out of the kitchen and we'd be banging away ... But we were shy of dancing, characteristically, meantime Allen and Peter would be whirling by in delightful nudity.'[23] One night, at the cabin, Robert Creeley and Jack had both elected to sleep outside. Creeley was woken in the morning by Jack's face, inches from his own, asking, 'Are you pure?' Creeley responded at once: 'It's like asking water, "Are you wet?" ' Jack seemed satisfied with this.

After Creeley had left, Jack was alone and began to write. He told John Clellon Holmes: 'I've been finally doodling with an endless automatic writing piece which raves on and on with no direction and no story and surely won't do tho I'll finish it anyway.'[24] The piece was *Old Angel Midnight*, which Jack wrote, or at least began, on 28 May 1956. It was originally called *Old Lucien Midnight*, because it was an attempt to capture Lucien's sound, the rhythms and timing of his speech. Allen Ginsberg:

This is specifically Lucien Carr speech that he's parodying. It's really good. It's funny. It's just drunken talk, but all the sounds of talk, so you don't have to worry about what it means, except it's got this all sense of suggestions in the syllables and in the associations of the puns. Sunday afternoon in the universe with all the sounds of the universe coming in the window of the ear.

It is another work often described as Joycean because of its superficial similarity to James Joyce's *Finnegans Wake*. Kerouac himself described it thus:

My idea of how to make a try at a 'spontaneous Finnegan's Wake' with the Sounds of the Universe itself as the plot and all the neologisms, mental associations, puns, word-mixes from various languages and non-languages scribbled out in a strictly intuitional discipline at breakneck speed ...

In many ways he succeeds. Kerouac had clearly listened carefully to Joyce's sound, such as in this passage from the *Wake*:

It was when I was in my farfather out at the west and she and myself, the redheaded girl, firstnighting down Sycamore Lane. Fine feelplay we had of it mid the kissabetts frisking in the kool kurkle dusk of the lushness. My perfume of the pampas, says she (meaning me) putting out her netherlights . . .[25]

Kerouac has captured some of this, but Joyce goes for sound *and* meaning whereas Kerouac's work sacrifices all for spontaneous sound. There is none of Joyce's sophistication about Kerouac, neither in his work nor his person, but there is often more energy, more *élan vital*.

In the sense that Jack was looking for a sound, it is interesting to compare it to Gertrude Stein's early 'difficult' works, such as the long 1931 poem 'Winning his Way'[26], which was based on sound, with little regard to whether it made sense, or to her astonishing collection, *As Fine As Melanctha*: 'A chicken roasting and a gave stove pose. Rose leaning turn, I didn't think it would do it. I didn't know it was that shape. Always. Incredible, sound. Not a spot. She had a ring. I respect you Frederick.'[27]

Unlike Joyce, Stein's words occupy the furthest boundary of the language; they have the same tenuous hold on meaning. The words flutter by, sparking recollections, memories, causing fragmentary descriptions in the mind's eyes of objects, events, people and places, in a rush of images like birds' wings flapping or a railway station seen from a speeding train. Stein's words and phrases, like Kerouac's, progress in that most of American of forms, the sequence of frames in a comic strip: one may be a talking head, the next panel may be an overhead shot, the next a close-up or even a drawing of the whole city with a voice bubble coming from a tiny distant building. We construct meaning from the sequence; we are the ones who give it meaning. Stein used to write 'word portraits' which were not at all descriptive in the normally accepted sense: they were a Cubist construct of that person, done at the same time as Cubist paintings, using words and phrases as a Cubist painter would to build the image, except they worked in light and she, by the nature of the medium, in time and the rhythm and sound of words.

Jack had been introduced to the work of Gertrude Stein by Philip Whalen, who was a great admirer of her work. Jack, however, did not share his enthusiasm. He wrote to him: 'for God sake throw that

Gertrude Stein away she makes me puke with her dike cuteness concealing all that venom.'[28] For him to protest so much, Jack must have felt threatened by her, as if she were mining the same area and had already staked her claim. Certainly his word portraits use the same approach that she used decades before.

Jack arrived in the Pacific northwest and hitchhiked to the forest service station where he did basic fire-watching training. Jack enjoyed the easy camaraderie of the forest-service men, but when they left on their mules, after delivering him to his lonely eyrie on Desolation Peak, he began to wonder what he had let himself in for. He was alone in the wilderness with mountains as his only companions: brooding Hozomeen with its dark valleys and sudden storms, Sourdough, Jack, Golden Horn, row after row of peaks, as far as the eye could see. The boredom almost drove him crazy and, with no actual teacher to show him the way, his Buddhism was not much solace. After two months of staring at the sheer rock face of Hozomeen he began to feel waves of paranoia. The picture Jack paints of himself as a hermit *bikku*, happily meditating, cut off from the world for sixty days, is something of an exaggeration. According to his friends, the experience reduced him to a nervous wreck, desperate for human company, but Jack does merit credit for sticking it out, and for even trying it in the first place. Carolyn Cassady:

> Buddhism . . . everything's an illusion . . . I don't have to keep my feet on the ground. He had a yearning to get out of the earthly muck but, when he retreated to the top of that mountain, he was so miserable, he was so paranoid, it got so he thought even the bugs were after him.[29]

Kerouac always excelled at topographical writing and he had so much material from his two months in the Cascades that it dominated his next two books, spilling over from *Desolation Angels* into *The Dharma Bums*. After a prolonged binge in San Francisco he sought refuge with Carolyn in Los Gatos. He was disappointed that he not been able to handle sixty days of solitude, so he meditated in the woods by day and came home to the warmth of human friendship in the evenings, before unrolling his sleeping bag beneath the plum tree in the garden with flying clouds and stars above. Carolyn:

> Jack's basic thing was escape. Buddhism, the trips, the drink, the drugs, everything was an escape. All that bumming around;

if he wasn't high on something, he was miserable. He talked about solitude and when he tried it he almost lost his mind. He went on talking about solitude and meditating in the woods but he set it up so he could come back in the evening and watch television.[30]

With his fire-watching money, Jack took off to Mexico City where he could make his stake last a long time. He rented his usual rooftop room above Garver and spent his time walking around the city, patronising the fifteen-year-old prostitutes and drinking heavily. He naturally saw Esperanza again, but she was deathly ill and on the point of mental and physical collapse from taking too many goofballs. Jack's use of her was much more blatantly self-serving this time around and he only saw her when he wanted something new to write about. She certainly gave it to him when one night she introduced him to a gang of toughs who robbed him of his money, sunglasses, and even his notebook full of new poems. Jack's oath of chastity had lapsed and on this trip he had sex with Esperanza. Jack:

I didn't write in the book how I finally nailed her. She said, 'Shhhhhhhhhh! Don't let the landlord hear.' She said, 'Remember I'm very weak and sick.' I said, 'I know. I've been writing a book about how you're weak and sick.' But it was not a conquest. She was out like a light. On M. M., that's Morphine. And in fact I made a big run for her from way uptown to downtown to the slum district . . . and I said, here's your stuff. She said, 'Shhhhhh!' She gave herself a shot . . . and I said, 'Ah . . . now's the time.' And I got my little nogood piece. But . . . it was certainly justification of Mexico!

Lucien Carr's wife, Cessa, told him not to put that in the book because she said it would spoil it.

During those two months, Jack wrote the second section of *Tristessa* in what he called his 'ingrown-toenail-packed mystical style'.[31] It was written by hand by candlelight in his rooftop room. He had a ritual in which he wrote as long as the candle burnt but, when he blew the candle out, he had to stop. In the same sessions he also wrote Book One of *The Angels in the World*, later published as *Desolation Angels*, about his two months as a fire watcher.

Jack was waiting in Mexico for Allen Ginsberg, Gregory Corso, Peter Orlovsky and his younger brother Lafcadio. The plan was for them all to go to Europe, beginning their grand tour with a visit to

Bill Burroughs in Tangier. Allen and his gang arrived early in November and took a room next door to Garver and set out to explore the city. Jack no longer had any time for writing. Together they visited the pyramids of Teotihuacán and walked in the Floating Gardens of Lake Xochimilco, where Jack had once told Burroughs that he would one day write a book called *Naked Lunch*. Allen, with his wide network of contacts, knew people at Mexico City College and so they made the social rounds and met several old Mexican painters from the days of the great muralists.

Jack introduced them to Esperanza, but to the others she looked skeletal and sick from her morphine addiction. They simply could not see why Jack had such romantic fantasies about such a pathetic figure. Jack himself later saw her as tragic and years afterward he admitted: 'All I did was suffer with that poor girl and then when she fell on her head and almost killed herself . . . and she was all busted up and everything . . .' But at the time he did nothing to help her.

Gregory hated the poverty and squalor of Mexico. He moved into a clean tourist hotel and from there took a plane to New York, just as soon as his current girlfriend cabled him the money. One day, Allen and Peter picked up some young Mexican boys who took them home with them to play 'spin-the-bottle'. Jack willingly joined in the orgy, forgetting his rants and diatribes about homosexuality in the drunken thrill of the moment. Allen Ginsberg located someone who was driving to New York and they bought rides in the car: Allen, Peter, Lafcadio, Jack, the driver and a Puerto Rican who had already hired a seat. They quickly got on each other's nerves and it was a terrible ride for everyone. They arrived in New York City early on a Sunday morning with snow flurries blowing around the car. Allen asked the driver to drop them outside Helen Elliott's apartment building on Seventh Avenue across from the White Horse Tavern, thinking that Helen and her friend Helen Weaver might be persuaded to put them up, or at least allow them to wash and rest for a few hours. Allen: 'That initiated Jack's romance with Helen Elliott and then with Helen Weaver, which was quite a long-lasting romance. Two years or year and a half, something like that. They were all girls from Barnard.'

After finding a cheap hotel for Lafcadio, Allen and Peter moved in with Allen's on-off girlfriend, Elise Cowan, and her roommate Sheila in Yorkville. They pulled the mattresses into one room and slept all together in the bed. During the day Allen worked the literary scene, making connections, promoting the San Francisco poets and getting to know the younger New York poets, in particular Frank O'Hara.

Jack spent his days typing and drinking. Much of the time he was in a drunken stupor, often accompanied by Lucien. Much as Helen Weaver liked him, his meanness, his drunken rants and his total lack of consideration for other people resulted in her finally kicking him out of the apartment. Things came to a head when Henri Cru invited them both to dinner. He had cooked a magnificent French dish but Jack wouldn't touch it. All he wanted was wine. He sat and gabbled away all evening, not hearing a thing anyone else said. She realised that nothing could ever come of the relationship. Taking her typewriter with him, he moved into the Marlton, a cheap hotel on Eighth Street in the Village.

After so many years of revisions and changes *On the Road* now looked tired and worked over. With publication seemingly imminent, Jack now incorporated the latest changes that Malcolm Cowley wanted by retyping the book from the original roll. The homosexual incident between Neal and the travelling salesman was cut, as was Jack's visit to Edie in Detroit. The former for obscenity reasons, the latter because Cowley thought it slowed the pace of action. Then, after all the years of rejections and editing, on 11 January 1957 Viking finally signed a contract to publish *On the Road*.

10 The King of the Beatniks

llen was concerned for Jack's well-being and gave him the
telephone number of a girlfriend of his who he felt sure
would feed him and cheer him up. Allen wrote: 'Joyce
Johnson (née Glassman) was my girlfriend and then
Kerouac's girlfriend.'[1] Joyce Glassman was a writer, working on a
novel for which she had already received a $500 advance. Jack
telephoned her: 'Hello, I'm Jack. Allen tells me you are very nice.'
She happened to be at a loose end so she went along, thinking it was
hilarious to be fixed up with a blind date by Allen Ginsberg.

It was a Saturday night, early in January 1957, and they met at the
lunch counter of Howard Johnson's on Eighth Street in Greenwich
Village. Jack had ordered coffee which he was unable to pay for. He
had been short changed out of his last ten-dollar bill that morning so
Joyce bought him a dinner of frankfurters, home fries and beans with
ketchup. He asked where she lived. She had an apartment near
Columbia, an area that Jack always liked. 'Why don't you let me stay
at your place?' he asked. 'If you wish,' she replied. Joyce told the
story of their affair in her excellent memoir of the period, *Minor
Characters*, which is an often overlooked Beat Generation classic
(and one which was a little too truthful about Jack and Allen
Ginsberg for Allen's taste – he always disliked the book). Joyce liked
Jack but tried not to get too involved with him because he was about
to ship out.

He borrowed $200 from Allen and, on 15 February 1957, set sail
for Casablanca and Tangier, intending to visit Burroughs in Tangier
and spend his summer exploring Europe with Allen and Peter, who
were to follow later. When Jack arrived in Tangier, Bill was writing
the text which ultimately became *The Naked Lunch* and spent his
days typing furiously, cackling with laughter at his own jokes as they
appeared on the page. In the evening he took cocktails with his

friends in the hotel where he lived. One of them, Paul Lund, was a barkeeper with a colourful history as a professional thief back in England.[2] Bill had been living in Tangier for four years and had quite a circle of friends and acquaintances, including a number of Spanish boys. Bill had early on made the decision to patronise Spanish boys and not Arab boys and, as a consequence, he had still not learnt a word of Arabic.

He showed Jack around, took him to the casbah, went rowing in the bay and walking in the mountains. Jack took a small rooftop room in Bill's hotel, the Muniria, which cost him $20 a month. Food and wine were cheap, but the Arab whores were $3, which Jack regarded as extortionate. Jack helped type up Bill's messy manuscript. Bill had let the pages fall from the typewriter and go blowing around the room and out into the courtyard garden where the cats walked over them. Jack put them in order and made a neat copy, but Bill's stories and routines gave him terrible nightmares of huge bolognas coming from his mouth.

Kerouac: 'Burroughs is the authentic devil.'
Bill: 'Keep typing.'

Allen and Peter arrived on 22 March but already Jack was discontented. He hated the sanitary arrangements, hated the food, and already longed for America: 'All I wanted somehow was Wheaties by a pine breeze kitchen in America.'[3] These were the same complaints he had about Mexico.

Allen Ginsberg felt that, the more Bill led him away from suburban life, the more uneasy Jack became. This was first evident when Jack accompanied Bill in his exploration of the seedy bars of Eighth Avenue and Times Square, which Jack did not enjoy, even though he regarded it as valuable experience. When Bill enticed him into the 'sinister other world outside of America' Jack grew very paranoid. Allen:

Kerouac was great in America but, as soon as he got across the border, it was this big evil other world – European fairies lying in waiting! So Kerouac never got abroad really . . . Jack saw Burroughs as 'a sinister agent of facts'.[4]

In his homesickness, Jack thought of Gary and how happy he had been living the simple life in his cabin. He decided to act on the idea of moving to California with his mother: she could live quietly in

Berkeley while he would live in a small cabin in Mill Valley. This made him think that his next book should be about his experiences with Gary which, according to Nicosia, he already had a title for: *The Dharma Bums*.

Anxious to begin writing, he set off for home at once, even though Allen and Peter had only just arrived, leaving Tangier on 5 April for a perfunctory tour of France and Britain. He did not enjoy his journey through France because hitchhiking was forbidden and no one could understand his accent. In Paris all the cheap hotels were full and, though he met up with Gregory Corso, Gregory made him pay for an evening's drinking. Jack quickly moved on to London. At Dover he was stopped at customs because he arrived with only two dollars, but he showed a letter from his British publisher which mentioned a £150 advance, so they let him in. He sailed from Southampton on the SS *Nieuw Amsterdam*, getting into New York in late April. After two days with Joyce Glassman, 'now soft and pretty in a Springtime dress and glad to see me', he headed south to Orlando, Florida, where his mother had the furniture packed all ready to move.

Memere's belongings were shipped to California, care of Philip Whalen, and she and Jack boarded a bus on 6 May for the 3,000-mile trip. Memere remained the only woman that Jack went on the road with. His friends may have looked askance, but Jack loved her, she was his best friend and, at times, apparently, he also thought she was God.[5] Philip Whalen wrote to the poet Lew Welch: '[Jack] had brought his mama and is set up in an apartment down the street.'[6]

In May 1957, there was still some doubt over the title of Jack's forthcoming book, whether it would be called *On the Road* or *The Beat Generation*, but one thing was now certain: it would be printed by Viking that summer, for publication in the autumn. Extracts from it began appearing in literary magazines and there was a tremendous buzz about the book. Jack was less pleased about other publishing developments. Grove had agreed to take *The Subterraneans*, but his editor Donald Allen had corrected the punctuation and edited all the sentences to the same length. Jack insisted that they restore his original punctuation or not publish the book at all. Fortunately, they relented and returned the book to its original state.

Aileen Lee was also less than pleased. When Jack had asked her to sign a release form against libel, he lied to her that it was being published by *Evergreen Review*, 'a small West Coast literary magazine', which she assumed would only be seen by other writers

and literary people. Had she known that intimate details of her se
life – but not Jack's – would become a bestselling book, translated
into a dozen languages, she would probably have insisted on many
more changes.

Jack and Memere set up house at 1943 Berkeley Way on the
corner of Bonita just a few blocks from the beautiful mountainside
campus of the university. Jack worked at a furious pace: adding to
Lucien Midnight, expanding his *Book of Dreams*, writing up his
travels in Europe, composing more poetry and planning a massive
autobiographical novel called *Visions of Myself*. Memere kept him
healthy by cooking him huge meals but was not beyond criticising
his behaviour, and after one particularly bad lapse on his part Philip
Whalen heard her tell him, 'It should have been you that died, not
Gerard.' But Memere did not like Berkeley: she hated the hillside
looming above her and the morning mist which filled the Bay, and
she missed her daughter. And so, not many weeks after they arrived,
Jack decided they would move back to Florida.

Jack saw Neal, who was often in the company of LuAnne, but
Neal was interested only in gambling, chess and women. On the day
before Jack and Memere returned to Orlando, Jack received a box
of advance copies of *On the Road*. That afternoon, Neal and LuAnne
came to say goodbye. Seeing Neal at the door, Jack tried to hide the
books under the table but Neal soon ferreted them out. Jack was
embarrassed as they began to read, and started apologising for all the
things he'd said about them, but Neal was flattered, at least initially,
that Jack had found him an interesting enough subject to write about
at all, and he insisted that they go for a celebratory drink.

Jack felt cooped up in Nin and Paul's house in the Florida summer
heat, and went to Mexico City to wait out the weeks before *On the
Road* was published. But Mexico City had changed. Jack got off the
bus and headed straight for Orizaba, expecting to see Garver and get
his old room on the roof, even though he had told no one he was
coming. He was surprised to find the pane of glass in Garver's
window, which had been broken as long as he could remember, had
now been repaired. He asked the landlady where he was. 'Señor
Garver *si murio*,' she told him. Garver had stolen his last overcoat.
He had died the month before. Jack went to his old room on the
roof, but a young Spanish woman was living there and it had been
cleaned up and whitewashed. It was no longer his.

Despite looking in the usual places, Jack was unable to track down
Esperanza, who, he later found out, had married a policeman. With

no contacts or friends, Jack checked into an expensive, marble-panelled, downtown tourist hotel, and spent the next two weeks sitting in his room or visiting young prostitutes. He clearly did not take his usual precautions because by the time he left he was in terrible pain from swollen testicles. Back in Orlando he felt drained, utterly lacking in enthusiasm for anything or anybody. He wrote to Burroughs that he never wanted to leave the States again and complained angrily about his friends and family. The tension of waiting for the first reviews of *On the Road* was getting to him.

The Viking publicity department had interviews lined up, including one with *Time* magazine, and could not understand why Jack was not in the city. Joyce Glassman cabled him the $30 Greyhound bus fare from Orlando, and he arrived in New York on 4 September 1957, the day before the book was published. Joyce had only moved into her new apartment two days before, but already the phone was ringing for Jack.

That evening, they went to the newstand at 66th Street and Broadway, where the next day's *New York Times* usually arrived a little before midnight. They knew this would be an important review, but did not know how important. Fortuitously, the *Times*'s usual book reviewer, Orville Prescott, was away on holiday and *On the Road* had been given to Gilbert Millstein to review. Millstein was a friend, a regular at the San Remo. It was Millstein who had reviewed John Clellon Holmes's *Go* and commissioned him to write the article 'This is the Beat Generation' for the *Times*, so for him to write the review was ideal. Millstein put his reputation on the line. The prescient review opened by saying:

> *On the Road* is the second novel by Jack Kerouac, and its publication is a historic occasion in so far as the exposure of an authentic work of art is of any great moment in an age when the attention is fragmented and the sensibilities are blunted by the superlatives of fashion ... The fact is that *On the Road* is the most beautifully executed, the clearest and the most important utterance yet made by the generation Kerouac himself named years ago as 'beat', and whose principal avatar he is.
>
> Just as, more than any other novel of the Twenties, *The Sun Also Rises* came to be regarded as the testament of the Lost Generation, so it seems certain that *On the Road* will come to be known as that of the 'Beat Generation' ... There are sections of *On the Road* in which the writing is of a beauty almost

breathtaking. There is a description of a cross-country automobile ride fully the equal, for example, of the train ride told by Thomas Wolfe in *Of Time and the River*. There are details of a trip to Mexico (and an interlude in a Mexican bordello) that are, by turns, awesome, tender and funny. And, finally, there is some writing on jazz that has never been equalled in American fiction, either for insight, style or technical virtuosity. *On the Road* is a major novel.

It would have been virtually impossible to get a better review, or in a better place. Joyce Johnson, in *Minor Characters*, gave a succinct description of his reaction:

Jack kept shaking his head. He didn't look happy, exactly, but strangely puzzled, as if he couldn't figure out why he wasn't happier than he was.

We returned to the apartment to go back to sleep. Jack lay down obscure for the last time in his life. The ringing phone woke him the next morning and he was famous.

Viking sent over a case of champagne. People everywhere wanted interviews but they had not read the book carefully enough: they thought Jack would be like Neal Cassady, not realising that he was Sal Paradise, the narrator, the passive fly on the wall. Gauche, self-conscious Jack modelled himself on Neal in his loud enthusiasms when drunk, and on Gary with his knapsack wanderings, but when forced to be Jack Kerouac, the writer, he did not know how to behave. Carolyn Cassady:

He was shy and introverted but his upbringing had trained him to be macho. He was sensitive, tender and compassionate but these were the qualities that he had been taught not to show so he put on a macho bluff much of the time. Neal, however, was spontaneous male macho without any effort. One was an introvert, one an extrovert. Jack wished he had Neal's prowess with women and loved watching Neal do it.

Jack explained to the press that Dean was not himself but another, even telling them his name. He told the *New York Post*:

Neal is more like Dostoyevsky than anybody else I know. He looks like Dostoyevsky, he gambled like Dostoyevsky, he

regards sex like Dostoyevsky, he writes like Dostoyevsky. I got
my rhythm from Neal, my Okie rhythm, see. 'Now look h'yar
boy, I'm gonna tell you what, see' – that's the way he talks.
Neal was a great Midwest poolroom saint. Neal Cassady and I
love each other greatly.

But now his public expected him to be Dean and, with Allen and
Gregory in Paris, Burroughs in Tangier, Gary in Japan, John Holmes
in Connecticut, Phil Whalen in San Francisco, Jack had only Lucien
and a few old friends in New York to help him and was very
ill-equipped to handle the situation. Jack clammed up completely on
the *Nightbeat* television show, giving terse, noncommunicative
answers to interviewer John Wingate. Jack: 'I just kept saying no,
like a kid dragged in by a cop. That's the way I thought of it.'[7]

The book was a publicist's dream: they went so far as to wrap an
additional dust wrapper around the review copies with a long blurb
about the Beat Generation for reviewers to quote:

> *On the Road* is about Sal Paradise, Dean Moriarty, and their
> friends – one moment savagely irresponsible and the next
> touchingly responsive and gentle. The narrative of life among these
> wild Bohemians carries us back and forth across the continent and
> down to New Orleans and Mexico. The characters buy cars and
> wreck them, steal cars and leave them standing in fields, undertake
> to drive cars from one city to another, sharing the gas; then for
> variety they go hitchhiking or sometimes ride a bus. In cities they
> go on wild parties or sit in joints listening to hot trumpets. They
> seem a little like machines themselves – machines gone haywire,
> always wound to the last pitch, always moving, drinking, making
> love, determined to say Yes to any new experience.

Not all critics agreed with Millstein. Three days later, in the *New
York Times Book Review*, David Dempsey urged caution:

> As a portrait of a disjointed segment of society acting out of its
> own neurotic necessity, *On the Road* is a stunning achievement.
> But it is a road, as far as the characters are concerned, that leads
> nowhere and which the novelist himself cannot afford to travel
> more than once.[8]

The newspapers saw the Beat Generation as a wonderful new
topic, a potential fad like the Hula-Hoop or Davy Crockett hats, a

gossip-column filler for the silly season when hard news is always scarce. As well as talking to Jack, *Time* sent someone to Paris to interview Allen. Everyone wanted to talk to Jack, not about the book but about the Beats. Who were they? What did they stand for? Were they a threat to government, to established religion? Jack assured Jerome Beatty for the *Saturday Review*, 'The Beat Generation has no interest in politics, only in mysticism, that's their religion. It's kids standing on the street and talking about the end of the world.'[9] And he assured his old friend Bruce Cook: 'I wasn't trying to create any kind of new consciousness or anything like that. We didn't have a whole lot of heavy abstract thoughts. We were just a bunch of guys who were out trying to get laid.'

The book hit America just at the right time: coinciding with America's great love affair with the automobile and with the birth of rock 'n' roll. Readers did not know that the book was written about events which occurred in 1948 and 1949; to them it was in the present. They did not know it was autobiographical; they saw brilliantly realised characters. When they read about the Cadillac trip to Chicago, in their mind's eye they saw the massive fish-tailed 1957 Cadillac swooping along the road, not a rounded blimp car of the forties. When the radio blared, they heard Elvis Presley and Little Richard, and the characters themselves they thought of as young. The 'teenager' had just been invented, a rebellious, insecure, self-conscious figure, epitomised by Elvis 'the Pelvis', the singing truckdriver with the swivellin' hips who was regarded as so debauched that Ed Sullivan would only allow his cameramen to film him from the waist up.

On the Road had it all: teenagers, nightclubs, fast cars, sex. It was the first rock 'n' roll book and it sold like hot cakes. Jack complained bitterly when the press made comparisons between juvenile delinquents – known as JDs – and the Beat Generation, but they saw the hero of *On the Road* as a fictional character, and how else can you describe someone who is a car thief, a joyrider, who steals fuel from gas stations and food from trusting Mom and Pop stores, who seduces underage girls and endangers the lives of everyone on the road with his reckless driving? Dean Moriarty was a juvenile delinquent just as much as the street gangs that the press fulminated over so vehemently.

Jack protested that the Beat Generation were not violent, but certainly David Kammerer and Joan Vollmer died violent deaths and, for that matter, Jack found himself in plenty of bar fights, often in the company of Lucien Carr. Herbert Huncke, the epitome of Beat, was known to mug people, and it was Burroughs's gun that Phil White used to murder a storekeeper in a hold-up.

Beat certainly originally meant to be like Huncke or Garver, a miserable unsuccessful petty thief, but by the end of the fifties Jack had redefined it to mean beatific:

> Beat doesn't mean tired, or bushed, so much as it means beato, the Italian for beatific: to be in a state of beatitude, like St Francis, trying to love all life, trying to be utterly sincere with everyone, practising endurance, kindness, cultivating joy of heart. How can this be done in our mad modern world of multiplicities and millions? By practising a little solitude, going off by yourself once in a while to store up that most precious of golds: the vibrations of sincerity.[10]

This was a definition that Allen Ginsberg ran with until it meant positively pacific, leaving everyone confused. Jack also saw Beat as a celebration of individualism:

> It's a humerous, sentimentally flavoured type shot of life as it's lived ... Youth in the past has frequently been called wild, or flaming, or what you will. In the 1940s, when I was in my twenties, the term 'beat' seemed to apply to me and the people I knew. But we were individualists compared to the wolfpacks of today. There is no relation between the pranks of the lonesome, talkative Beat Generation of the 40s and the concerted desecrations of this new delinquency hounded generation of the 50s ... The so-called 'Beatniks' of San Francisco wouldn't even talk to me when I was wailing through there in the late 40s.[11]

In the course of the many interviews Jack gave about *On the Road*, he was naturally asked about his writing technique, which gave him a chance to explain his theory of spontaneous prose. Jack maintained that *On the Road* was published with no rewrites or editorial changes. He wrote to John Clellon Holmes:

> *On the Road* is just as originally written on that block long (around the block?) sheet of Cannastra's drawing paper (secret: Viking thinks it's a 5 year extensive rewrite job I gave them, it's the pure shining original by God) and that's the way to write, I say, who wants everything hidden under a bushel.[12]

Clearly this is not the case, as the items Viking wanted removed for libel reasons are not in the final book and the compressions they suggested were made, but until the roll is made available to scholars by the Kerouac Estate we shall not know how much the versions differ. It irritated Malcolm Cowley to be made the villain of the piece by Jack, who had enthusiastically agreed to the editorial changes that Cowley proposed. For instance, at the time of the Six Gallery reading, Jack wrote to Cowley: 'Any changes you want to make okay with me. Remember your idea in 1953 to dovetail trip No. 2 into Trip No. 3 making it one trip? I'm available to assist you in any re-arranging matters of course.'[13] Cowley's belated response came in *Jack's Book*:

> Jack and his memory are very, very unfair to me. Blaming me for putting in or taking out commas and caps and what-not in *On the Road*. I didn't really give much of a damn about that. I knew that Jack wrote well naturally ... Jack did something that he would never admit to later. He did a good deal of revision, and it was very good revision. Oh, he would never, never admit to that, because it was his feeling that the stuff ought to come out like toothpaste from a tube and not be changed, and that every word that passed from his typewriter was holy. On the contrary, he revised, and revised well.[14]

Allen, who was never a complete convert to spontaneous prose, had remained all along impressed that Jack had Cowley as an editor to work with:

> The first manuscript of *On the Road* was one single long sentence, marked by dashes. It was later doctored, by Malcolm Cowley, no less, who was a great critic of the twenties and a friend of Hemingway, Wolfe, Fitzgerald and the Paris group of bohemians of the twenties so the lineage of Kerouac's editorship is remarkable.[15]

Nonetheless, Allen regretted the editorial changes that had been made. In an article in the *Village Voice* he wrote of:

> A magnificent single paragraph several blocks long, rolling, like the Road itself, the length of an entire onionskin teletype roll. The sadness that this was never published in its most exciting form – its original discovery – but hacked and punctuated and

broken – the rhythms and swing of it broken – by presumptuous literary critics in publishing houses. The original mad version is greater than the published version, the manuscript still exists and someday when everybody's dead be published as it is. Its greatness ... the great spirit of adventure into poetic composition. And great tender delicacy of language.[16]

Jack had always longed for fame and acceptance but, now that it had arrived, it threw him over the top and he became insufferable. His drinking increased so that most of the time his talk was little more than incoherent babbling. People laughed at him behind his back and he became something of a standing joke as well as someone to avoid. He would listen to no criticism: as far he was concerned his belief in himself as a writing genius had been vindicated, and he intended to tell everyone how great he was. The partying went on for weeks.

Despite living with Joyce, he had sex with dozens, possibly scores of women. He made no effort to attract them; he was totally passive, waiting to be carried off to bed by literary groupies. In fact the drinking had made him more or less impotent. All he really wanted was a blow job and he was not fussy about where it came from. He once claimed to have had sex with 245 women[17] (double Casanova's 122; it is typical that Kerouac would have kept a tally). Though he never revealed how many men he had sex with, it was certainly dozens.

Throughout the madness of the publication celebrations, Joyce continued to take him in whenever he turned up at her door, drunk, battered, beaten, his clothing torn. She gave him a bed, cleaned him up and mended his clothes ready for another night's revels, until even she became exhausted, and, realising that the affair was entirely one-sided, decided to break from him. He used so many people like this, particularly women. He was a manipulator, a controller of people's lives, as if they were his to play with but not his responsibility. His writing came first, all else was subjugated to it, but his friends did not realise just how expendable they were to him. They were used when it was convenient. They were there to stay with, to praise his genius, to listen to his drunken babble, to feed him, to drink with him, to keep him out of trouble and to have sex with, but he had little interest in their lives, their ideas, their writing or work, unless he could use it as raw material for his writing.

He casually used pages from Joyce's book manuscript as writing paper. He would turn up at 4 a.m. at a friend's door unannounced with several hangers-on, expecting to party. Friends became used to the 4 a.m. drunken phone call, to vomit on the floor and their booze all gone. Some, like Lucien, were stalwart – he enjoyed a drink himself – but others bowed out; they could take no more. Jack had become a danger to himself and a nuisance to have around.

Meanwhile, the publishing industry was suddenly interested in 'The Kerouac Phenomenon'. In that year, 1957, *New Directions Annual* published an excerpt from *On the Road*.[18] The second *New Editions Anthology* published 'Neal and the Three Stooges'. 'October in the Railroad Earth' appeared in the San Francisco edition of *Evergreen Review*, with a smaller earlier draft appearing in *Black Mountain Review*. Sections from *Lucien Midnight, Mexico City Blues* and *San Francisco Blues* appeared in literary magazines, as did his manifesto 'Essentials of Spontaneous Prose'. His great store of unpublished material was finally being unleashed. He even published a short piece about Christmas in the *New York World Telegram*.[19]

But Jack's fame and success was not as a writer; it was as the self-proclaimed spokesman for the Beat Generation. The press were not much interested in writing and literature. They saw Jack not as the author of *On the Road* nor a proselytiser of spontaneous prose, but as an advocate of what seemed to them a nihilistic, rebellious, hedonistic lifestyle which included petty theft, the use of illegal drugs, and the seduction of underaged girls. Jack found himself in the front line as the establishment began its counterattack. John Clellon Holmes:

> He realised he wasn't famous. He was notorious, and that's quite different. When you are notorious you are news. When you are famous you are some solid thing in the landscape that people try to avoid and have difficulties in assessing immediately but take seriously. Jack Kerouac was never taken seriously while he lived. They weren't looking in the right place; they weren't looking at the work; they were looking at their image of the man, an image which they derived from the few works which they had read. They kept mixing Jack up with Dean Moriarty, in other words with Neal Cassady. They kept thinking he was Dean Moriarty but he wasn't.[20]

Jack finally staggered back to Florida, exhausted, in mid-October. Viking now saw that they had a valuable property on their hands and encouraged him to write something more accessible as a follow-up.

Rather than try to place *Doctor Sax* with them, Jack concurred and set to work to write *The Dharma Bums*, his most straightforward, most accessible, and possibly his most influential book.

Despite his terrible physical condition, Jack hammered out *The Dharma Bums* in ten sittings. He would take amphetamine, settle himself at the typewriter, and write between 15,000 and 20,000 words at each exhausting session. Then he would take to his bed to recover. By the end of November 1957, it was completed. Jack had been very concerned about the connection made between *On the Road* and juvenile delinquency and told the *Detroit News*:

In my new novel, *Dharma Bums*, which is coming out this fall, there isn't even one sentimental hubcap stolen. It's really a book about religious vagrants – young guys wandering around smiling, with rucksacks on their backs, drinking wine in the moonlight like Li Po, the Chinese poet, climbing mountains to pray for the final safety of all living beings. Why? What more decent activity?[21]

Jack told Ann Charters that Malcolm Cowley made him take out the best part of *The Dharma Bums*, which was an argument between him and Gary Snyder. Gary said, 'You old son of a bitch, you're going to end up asking for the Catholic rites on your deathbed.' Jack replied, 'How did you know, my dear? Didn't you know I was a lay Jesuit?' which made Gary angry with him.[22]

Kerouac himself wrote the jacket copy for the Viking hardback, but it was not used on the subsequent paperback editions. It gives a good insight into Kerouac's own intentions and his assessment of the book:

Dharma is the Sanskrit Word for Truth. It may also be translated as The Duty, or The Law. *The Dharma Bums* is a surprising story of two young Americans who make a goodhearted effort to know the Truth with full packs on their backs, rucksack wanderers of the West Coast, hiking and climbing mountains to go and meditate and pray and cook their simple foods, and down below living in shacks and sleeping outdoors under the California stars.

Although deeply religious they are also spirited human beings making love to women, relishing poetry, wine, good food, joyful campfires, nature, travel and friendship. The hero is young Japhy Ryder, poet, mountaineer, logger, Oriental scholar and dedicated Zen Buddhist, who teaches his freight-hopping friend Ray Smith the Way of the Dharma Bums and leads him up the mountain where the common errors of this world are left far below and a new sense of pure material kinship is established with earth and sky. Yet it is the ancient Way of all the wild prophets of the past, whether St John the Baptist in the West or the holy old Zen Lunatic Hanshan in the East. Japhy and Ray adventure in the mountains and on the trails, and then they come swinging down to the city of San Francisco to teach what they have learned, but the city will not listen. 'Yabyum' orgies, suicide, jazz, wild parties, hitchhiking, love affairs, fury and ignorance result, but the Truth Bums always return to the solitude and peaceful lesson of the wilderness.

In this new novel, Jack Kerouac departs from the 'hipster' movement of the Beat Generation and leads his readers towards a conception of 'continual conscious compassion' and a peaceful understanding truce with the paradox of existence.

The Dharma itself can never be seen, but is felt in this book. It is the strangest of tales, yet an honest, vigorous account depicting an exciting new Way of Life in the midst of modern despair. The rolling pages of the novel are filled with original descriptions of the High Sierras, the High Cascades, the Northwest, the South, the desert, and the American road. There is also an account of the night of the birth of the San Francisco Poetry Renaissance.

Through these pages pass hoboes, blondes, truckdrivers, poets, hunters, Negro preachers, Mexicans, librarians, hound dogs, children, janitors, forest rangers, loggers, cowboys and Zen thinkers in a bewildering and delightful verity as the story races true to life to its conclusion.

Read slowly and see.

In the autobiography of Alan Watts, *In My Own Way*, Watts claims that his essay 'Beat Zen, Square Zen and Zen'[23] is regarded as being largely responsible for the 'notorious "Zen Boom" which flourished among artists and "pseudointellectuals" in the late 1950s, and led on to the frivolous "beat Zen" of Kerouac's *Dharma Bums*, of Frank Kline's black and white abstractions, and of John Cage's silent concerts.'

Many people would not think this was a bad thing at all, as Kline and Cage are both recognised as having produced many beautiful and important works. As for Jack's *The Dharma Bums*, which was published after Watts's essay came out, it is one of his most popular books and, if it led some readers to examine a few Buddhist texts, then there can be little wrong with that. It is true that there was a 'Zen Boom', and for a while every Bohemian with a beard and set of bongos also claimed to be a Zen Buddhist. Zen became yet another excuse for existential disengagement, though very few of them did any serious meditation and even fewer took a teacher.

Watts was not criticising Gary Snyder, who, as Japhy Ryder, was the hero of *The Dharma Bums*; it was more a case that he regarded the portrait of Snyder as 'a characterisation which hardly begins to do him justice'. Nonetheless, getting in on the Zen Boom himself, Watts's 'Beat Zen, Square Zen and Zen' was published as a pamphlet by City Lights and became one of the essential source books of the time.

On the Road inspired many young people to go out on the road and explore but, by the time it was published, the traditional routes Kerouac described were being rapidly replaced by the superhighway programme. *The Dharma Bums* added a new dimension: it was not a celebration of speed, of movement and travel for the sake of it; the 'Zen Lunatics' were in search of spiritual experience. They hitchhiked but were more at home in the woods, exploring nature, climbing mountains. *The Dharma Bums* heralded the so-called 'rucksack revolution', which was to take tens of thousands of young people to San Francisco and other centres of hippie culture, prophesied in the book by Japhy Ryder in a much quoted passage:

> . . . a world full of rucksack wanderers, Dharma Bums refusing to subscribe to the general demand that they consume production and therefore have to work for the privilege of consuming, all that crap they didn't really want anyway . . . I see a vision of a great rucksack revolution, thousands or even millions of young Americans wandering around with rucksacks, going up to mountains to pray, making children laugh and old men glad, making young girls happy and old girls happier, all of 'em Zen Lunatics who go about writing poems that happen to appear in their heads for no reason . . .

It was a prophecy which came true a dozen years later when a large segment of the hippie movement moved to the land, establishing tens of thousands of country communes, sharing land, sometimes sharing children, living in old farms, in tepees or geodesic domes, their rejection of consumer society more complete than Gary

Snyder or Jack Kerouac could ever have imagined. This is why Kerouac is important: he prophesied and popularised these ideas and these two books, *On the Road* and *The Dharma Bums*, became handbooks for the new, uncharted sixties lifestyle which made up its own rules as it went along.

In terms of literature, *The Dharma Bums* is not his greatest work. In fact, the book falls apart after the hero, Japhy, leaves for Japan. But it does have many beautiful passages describing mountains and nature, and also captures the social scene he was moving in. It is the story of the birth of the San Francisco Poetry Renaissance and as such it is an important historical record.

One reason that Jack wrote it in such a hurry was that he had been offered $500 to read at the Village Vanguard jazz club in the Village in the week before Christmas. Allen Ginsberg wrote from France to warn him that it was bound to end up as a drunken fiasco and Jack must have known that, but he still went ahead. Howard Smith reported in the *Village Voice* that Jack was very nervous and read in a thin, high voice but the first-night audience was with him and applauded loudly. However, Allen's prediction came true as Jack got increasingly intoxicated on each subsequent night, sometimes reading other people's poems, or mumbling from his own pencil-written notebooks, running with sweat as the audience talked loudly among themselves. In the end no one was listening and his friends stopped coming to give support because they were so embarrassed. David Amram:

> When Jack first read at the Vanguard he was really kinda flipped out because it was so formal. His formal stuff he'd do with us. He would read some poetry, make up songs, sing, scat-sing, play the piano. Then he ran out during intermission and drank wine with all the poets – he had a very broad definition of poetry, and that included anybody with a wine bottle or some reefer, or both ... His thing at the Vanguard actually didn't come off that well because he was too nervous and got drunk.

Though it was an opened-ended residency, he lasted just one week. One good thing came from it, however. Steve Allen was in the audience and, through Gilbert Millstein, who had arranged the Vanguard gig, Jack and Steve Allen went on to cut a record together.

While the adverse criticism of the Beat Generation and of Jack in particular continued, Jack retired to Florida to type up a fair version of *The Dharma Bums*. It was perhaps unfortunate that the next book of his to be published was *The Subterraneans*, which Grove released in February 1958. It was everything the establishment hated: an affair between a Black woman and a White man, drugs, irresponsible behaviour, drunken rowdiness. Jack's head was handed to them on a plate. The bad reviews, the celebrity and notoriety caused Jack to drink so heavily that even his mother, who enjoyed a drink herself, yelled at him to stop before he killed himself. That January, Jack told Mike Wallace of the *New York Post*: 'It's a great burden to be alive. A heavy burden, a great big heavy burden. I wish I were safe in heaven, dead.'[24]

Jack was earning good money: *The Subterraneans* was a paperback bestseller and MGM bought the motion-picture rights for $15,000. He was getting royalties from *On the Road* and Viking was about to give him an advance for *The Dharma Bums*. Nonetheless, he still refused to pay back the $225 he owed Allen Ginsberg, who was virtually starving in Paris. Allen also desperately needed the money to get Peter back to the States to look after his brothers. Peter wanted to get Julius out of the mental hospital and prevent Lafcadio – who appeared to have gone mad – from being sent to one. At Allen's request, Jack went out to visit Lafcadio in Northport, Long Island, where the Orlovsky family lived in a converted chicken coop. He liked the town so much that he bought a home there for himself and Memere: a large wooden house at 34 Gilbert Street, with porches at both front and back. The town had a small harbour and a bar where the clam fishermen gathered. There were sand dunes, white New England clapboard houses and groves of trees. Though only 45 miles from New York, it was an escape from the temptations of the city. Jack was an alcoholic, and was always drunk, but there was a big difference between his everyday steady sipping and his big-city binge drinking. He knew that he was a danger to himself, so he tried to avoid the city as much as possible.

Henri Cru:

Anyone of any importance I introduced him to he alienated in seconds after I introduced him; when he gained a measure of renown he became intolerable. He would either call his best friends dirty Jews or fag bastards. He got carved up pretty good by two acquaintances of his; one was wearing a large ring with a large sharp Chinese monster on it. On this occasion he made the *New York Times* after suffering half a dozen stitches in his face round his nose.[25]

This was when a gay boxer, who felt himself libelled in *The Subterraneans*, encountered Jack and Henri drunk at the San Remo. Jack's arm and nose were broken and he finished up at Saint Vincent's Hospital in the Village. Allen Ginsberg:

> Kerouac kept saying he couldn't come to Manhattan. He was afraid he would get drunk and bang his head and break his skull on the sidewalk curb. That's something that did happen to him when he came in, drank, and got into arguments and fights in the San Remo Bar. And he was incapable of fighting back. Not that he was weak, but he simply wouldn't strike another person, he believed in the Lamb, and so lived that through. There were situations where people attacked him, out of inquisitiveness or jealousy or natural alcoholic anger or irritability – jealousy primarily. Then there was one incident where he actually was down on the sidewalk with a big huge man literally banging his head on the sidewalk, Kerouac said it 'did something to his brain', scrambled his brains permanently. So he was afraid to come into the metropolis after that.[26]

Even Huncke had his doubts about Jack:

> He wasn't geared to withstand the pressures of the society in which we live any more than *most* of us are, without some kind of outlet, so he had started drinking and drinking was acceptable. That was the thing about Jack that always irritated me – that business of trying to stay within the bounds of good behaviour while indulging in a sort of dual role, of living with these people who were all either shooting up or taking Benzedrine or smoking pot regularly. He didn't even really like to smoke pot. But drinking, since it was legal . . . you see he always catered just a little bit to the standards of the government, the establishment, the society in which we live. I suppose that's maybe to his credit.
>
> It was my one complaint with him for the simple reason that he was this gay, Bohemian, freedom-loving character in one breath, and then a very conservative person in the other. Somehow or other the two don't mesh together. You're either one or the other.
>
> One of the saddest things I can recall seeing, as far as people are concerned, is Jack blown up like a balloon, his face just huge and round and red and stubble-covered, with an old shirt

half-hanging out of his pants like an old Turk. That's what he looked like, like an old Turk, with a pair of carpet slippers on, sitting, feeling extremely sorry for himself, swimming in alcohol and sort of gazing up with tears streaming down his face at the absurdity of everything. It really touched my heart very deeply because he'd been an extremely handsome man and no one likes to see anyone destroyed so obviously. And there were, of course, his sycophants or his followers, waiting for him to move on to another place, to buy another drink. But there was just something very pathetic about him, and I didn't like to be in his presence when he was like that towards the end.[27]

Neal also rejected him, though for more complex reasons. They parted ways after the publication of *On the Road*. Carolyn: 'Jack's portrayal of Neal was too close for comfort.' But it wasn't entirely that. Neal himself was hopelessly torn between the demands of his family and his other life as a compulsive gambler, dope fiend and womaniser. On the one hand he held a job on the railroad for ten years to provide for his children, but on the other he was known as the Johnny Appleseed of North Beach, handing out pot to one and all, which had naturally brought him to the attention of the narcotics squad. He had apparently knowingly given policemen joints. Neal understood this self-destructive behaviour in himself and hated to see Jack fall apart in the same way.

Neal also had a natural horror of lushes because his father was a wino and he grew up surrounded by puking drunks. Carolyn: 'Neal didn't contact Jack personally for so long because it was too painful for him to watch Jack destroy himself drinking. He stopped communicating but he never stopped caring; that lasted all their lives.'[28]

At one of the many parties surrounding *On the Road*, Jack met the Swiss photographer Robert Frank. Frank had received a Guggenheim fellowship in 1956 and spent the money driving around America with his wife, Mary, photographing empty highways, shabby motels, jukeboxes, bleak cemeteries; the antithesis of the America shown on the 'highest standard of living in the world' billboards. He shot the sullen faces of the poor Blacks and the uncomprehending White trash. He and Jack had a similar sensibility and intuitively understood each other. In April, Robert drove Jack to Florida to bring Memere up to Northport, shooting photographs all the way. Jack insisted on staying in the tackiest, most run-down motels they could find. When Grove published Frank's photo essay, *The Americans*, in the USA, Jack wrote an introduction for it: 'The humour, the sadness, the EVERYTHING-ness and American-ness of these pictures! ... Anybody doesnt like these pitchers dont like potry, see?'[29]

The Beat Generation proved to be a more long-lasting fad than Hula-Hoops and had not gone away. In fact, the phenomenon grew and grew, both in New York City and in the North Beach quarter of San Francisco, where the term 'Beatnik' was coined on 2 April 1958 by *San Francisco Chronicle* columnist Herb Caen. Six months after the Soviet Union won the space race by launching Sputnik into earth orbit, Caen ran a story that *Look* magazine was preparing a photo spread on San Francisco's Beat Generation. Caen wrote that *Look*: 'hosted a party in a No. Beach house for 50 beatniks, and by the time word got around the sour grapevine, over 250 bearded cats and kits were on hand, slopping up Mike Cowles' free booze. They're only beat, y'know, when it comes to work.' It was a term just waiting to be invented. The very next day the *San Francisco Examiner* ran a headline about a 'beatnik murder' and the word entered the language. 'Beatnik must have been spinning around in my subconscious,' Caen said, 'and it just came out. I fell into it. To my amazement, it caught on immediately.'

Caen claimed in an interview: 'I ran into Kerouac that night at El Matador. He was mad. He said, "You're putting us down and making us sound like jerks. I hate it. Stop using it." And onward into the night.'[30] This seems unlikely as Jack did not go to the coast that year.[31] Nor could it have been Allen as he was still in Paris.

In San Francisco the police were not unaware that they had a sizeable community of 'Beatniks' or that many of them smoked pot. In February, Neal bragged to his friend Al Hinkle that he had 'split a joint with a Narc', but this boasting was to lead to tragic results for him and his family. In April he was arrested for giving two joints of marijuana to undercover narcotics agents and, on 14 June, he was sentenced to five years in prison, most of which he spent in San Quentin. The authorities were convinced that he was a part of an organisation that brought in marijuana from Mexico and shipped it up to San Francisco by train. We will never know the truth, but Neal was still compulsively trying to work his 'system' at the racetrack so it is possible that he found himself deep in debt and was forced to participate in something like that. He certainly always had huge quantities of pot which he distributed freely to virtually everyone he met.

Jack was horrified and wondered if the notoriety that came to Neal because of *On the Road* was responsible, but Neal was well known to the drugs squad before the book was published and, in any case, most people thought it was a novel. There is no doubt, however, that they associated Neal with the 'Beatniks', the new scourge of North Beach. 4 May 1958 saw the beginning of a full-scale police clampdown on the eighty or so Bohemians living in the North Beach area, fuelled by a series of vicious attacks on the North Beach community by June Miller, a reporter for the Hearst morning paper, *The San Francisco Examiner*. This was all the excuse the police needed to begin a dramatic crackdown on all Beat establishments, and the previously relaxed atmosphere of the neighbourhood was destroyed.

In Paris, Allen read the news clippings sent to him by friends and was thankful that he had escaped. He was living at the Beat Hotel, engaged in a massive correspondence with poets and little literary magazine editors all across the USA and Europe, promoting Jack's work, as well as that of Bill, Gregory Corso and his other friends. Two of his letters were from Jack's mother. Allen had written to Jack while high on cocaine, not realising that Jack's mother opened his mail. Knowing that Allen was due back in the States that summer, Memere fired off several vitriolic letters to Allen demanding that Allen not write to Jack at the house nor through anyone else, nor even try to get in touch with him. She told Allen she had read his letter and 'I don't want an immoral lout like you around us. You are not fit to associate with us Christians'. She reminded Allen that her husband had made her promise to keep Allen away from Jack. Nor did she want Burroughs to write to Jack: 'You miserable bums, all you have in your filthy minds is dirty sex and dope.' She told him she had given his name to the FBI so that when he got back to the USA they would be on his tail.

> And another warning, don't ever mention Jack's name or write any more about Jack in your 'dirty' 'books' I'll sue you and have you in 'jail' . . . I raised Jack to be decent and I aim to keep him that way . . . we don't want sex fiens [sic] or dope fiens [sic] around us . . .[32]

Since she knew no better, she only put a 6¢ stamp on the letter. It went sea mail and Allen had returned to New York before it reached Paris. It was forwarded by Burroughs from the Beat Hotel, who had instructions from Allen to read his mail and send on anything important. Bill commented:

The woman is mad ... a stupid, small-minded vindictive peasant, incapable of a generous thought or feeling ... In your place I would show Jack the letter. If he is content to be treated like a child and let his mother open his mail and tell him who to see and correspond with, he is a lost cause.[33]

Jack knew about his mother's letters, and wrote to Allen what he must have thought was an explanation of it, also sending his letter to Paris too late to catch Allen before he shipped out. Amazingly, Jack approved her demands: 'It's nothing new from Ozone Park 1945 hangups only now I more agree with her not because what she says, but I have withdrawn ... and want to live my own kind of simple Ti Jean life ... I'm just a Buddhist-Catholic and want no more shit nonsense . . .' He said he wouldn't dream of interfering in Julius Orlovsky's problems – Allen was engaged in trying to get him released from the mental hospital – or in 'Neal's fall'. He told Allen, 'I agree with my mother on the point of your not using my name in any activities of yours (other than pure poetry and prose) such as politics, sex, etc. "action" etc etc. I'm retired from the world now ... that's why I've made no effort to see poor Peter or even Joyce any more.'[34]

Burroughs was furious:

I herewith forward Jack's weak and cowardly letter. Like some cat explaining to former friend how he 'can't have him to the house anymore because of the little woman don't like Jews, and after all I am out of "all that" now ... not that we can't meet now and then (not too often) for a glass of beer someplace, maybe, etc.' Weak and Cowardly. 'And of course you understand I can't help out with Neal or Julius.' After all, why should I involve myself. Must consider Mother first. She is easily upset you know, and I *did* warn him after all. And a Catholic-Buddhist yet. My God! She really has him sewn up like an incision ... You can tell him from me that no one can achieve the fence straddle he attempts. No one can simultaneously stand behind those filthy letters of Mrs Kerouac and be in any meaningful sense a friend of the person to whom those letters were addressed. Jack has reaped fame and money telling Neal's story, recording his conversation, representing himself as Neal's life long friend ... In any case he has sold Neal's blood and made money. Now he will not lift a dollar to help. I don't see it, Allen.

Bill said that Gregory had written an angry letter to Jack but had decided not to send it. The next day, Bill added a postscript, his feelings running higher than ever:

> I don't like the way he shrugs off the horrible injustice of Neal's imprisonment. All he wants is security for himself. A weakling, no a coward who cannot be trusted under any pressure. He doesn't want *his* name mentioned. What about your name and Neal's and mine in his books?? This P.S. is written day after the letter. More I think about it the *less* I think of him, and the less desire I have to have to see any more of him.

This was effectively the end of Bill and Jack's friendship, though it had already taken a battering when Jack had been such an inconsiderate guest while writing *Doctor Sax* at Bill's place in Mexico City. They saw each other twice more, briefly, the last time being ten years later, in 1968, at a hotel before Jack appeared on the *William Buckley Jr Show*. Bill advised Jack not to go on in his drunken state and declined to come along to the show.

It was the beginning of the end of the Beat Generation as a group of old friends with a common vision. From now on, Allen's relationship with Jack was entirely one-sided, with Jack using Allen and giving nothing in return. He stayed with Allen in the city but Allen was forbidden to visit him at home. Neal had withdrawn from Jack after the publication of *On the Road*, confused and embarrassed by the fame it brought him, but also with a distinct sense that he had been used, his energy and stories wrung out of him, leaving him like a limp rag.

After the publication of *The Dharma Bums* there was a spell when Gary Snyder broke off correspondence with Jack. Gary felt his privacy had been invaded and did not like his portrait as Japhy Ryder. The last time they saw each other was at the docks when Gary's ship sailed for Japan in 1956. Just as the Beat Generation was becoming well known, it had died. It was similar to John Lennon leaving The Beatles but asking them all to keep it a secret because they were negotiating a new record contract. Jack still wanted to be the King of the Beats; he just didn't want the Beats anywhere near his home.

Jack traded heavily on his fame and recognition, asking complete strangers if they knew who he was, and lording it over his remaining friends. Fame also made him attractive to women and he wrote to Philip Whalen:

I have a slew of girls in NY now and screwing them all and wish Gary were here to help, just too many. One night I was in bed with 3 girls. I'm getting too old for this. I try to serve the Bodhisattva's role for them, but this ole Bodhisattva gettin tired.[35]

That October Jack met the artist Dody Muller at Robert Frank's apartment and through her he got to know the New York artists' scene. She gave him painting lessons and took him to the Cedar Street Tavern on University Place and introduced him to Willem de Kooning, Kline and the others. Jackson Pollock was often barred from the Cedar Street and it was not long before Jack joined him. In Jack's case it was for pissing in the sink. They would both look longingly in through the open door, hoping that the bartender would relent.

Jack's week-long drinking sessions that autumn precipitated something like a nervous breakdown and he cancelled a number of readings and interviews that had been planned by Viking. There was one event, however, that he was persuaded to attend: a symposium called 'Is There a Beat Generation?' organised by Brandeis University at Hunter College Playhouse on 6 November 1958. Jack didn't know what a symposium was and had expected to give a speech by himself, which he prepared beforehand.

On the panel were Jack Kerouac, as the spokesman for the Beat Generation; James Wechsler, editor of the *New York Post*, as a spokesman for the 'unreconstructed radical' generation then fighting for civil rights and to end segregation in the South; Ashley Montagu, a British anthropologist teaching at Princeton who was certainly not antagonistic towards the Beats; and Kingsley Amis the British novelist, author of *Lucky Jim*, described by the press as a member of the 'Angry Young Men', who claimed that his real interests in life were 'films, drinking, women's breasts, American novels, Jazz and Science Fiction'.

The hall was filled to capacity, with many people standing and many more crowded outside, unable to get in. Kingsley Amis said that Kerouac did his best to make him feel uneasy by greeting him with 'Hello, my dear', but Jack was probably trying to be funny. When they first went on stage, the audience cheered Jack, who responded by what Amis described as 'weaves, bobs and a chimpanzee shuffle or two'.

James Wechsler was delayed at the door until he proved he was on the panel and as he entered, Jack, who spoke first, was already in full flight. As Wechsler approached the stage down the centre aisle, Kerouac glared at him and stopped in the middle of one of his long paragraphs to complain: 'You ruined my sentence.' Jack was wearing his usual lumberjack shirt unbuttoned at the neck and a pair of baggy work pants. He sipped from a glass of brandy, which he made several trips to the wings to refill.

Unfortunately, the only way Jack could get through the ordeal was to behave as a show-off drunk, playing to the audience, which consisted almost entirely of young people. He launched into his speech[36], gesturing and waving his glass:

> Live your lives out, they say; nah, love your lives out, so when they come around and stone you, you won't be living in any glass house – only a glassy flesh. What is called the 'Beat Generation' is really a revolution in manners ... being a swinging group of new American boys intent on life. James Dean was not the first to express this. Before him there was Bogart and the private eyes. Now college kids have started using the words 'hung up' ... I'm hung up, you know – words I first heard on Times Square in the forties. Being Beat goes back to my ancestors, to the rebellious, the hungry, the weird, and the mad. To Laurel and Hardy, to Popeye, to Wimpy looking wild-eyed over hamburgers, the size of which they make no more, to Lamont Cranston, The Shadow, with his mad 'heh-heh-heh' knowing laugh.

> And now there are two types of beat hipsters – the Cool: bearded, sitting without moving in cafes, with their unfriendly girls dressed in black, who say nothing; and the Hot: Crazy, talkative, mad shining eyes, running from bar to bar only to be ignored by the cool subterraneans. I guess I'm still with the hot ones. When I walk into a club playing jazz, I still want to shout: 'Blow, Man, Blow!'

By this point in his speech Jack had overrun his time and the moderator, the Dean of Brandeis, Joseph Kauffman, tried to interrupt him, but to no avail. Jack read his speech to the end, for about forty minutes, amid cheers and hoots from the audience. Then Amis told the audience that the 'Angry Young Men' did not exist:

> [It] is an invention of literary middlemen, desperate journalists who thrive on classifications and clichés, who put writers in pigeonholes and save people the trouble of reading. This

nonsense can also be traced to the Anglo-American cult of youth.

Then Montagu, looking amused by the whole thing, told the audience:

James Dean symbolised the Beat Generation. His death was consistent with the Beat Generation philosophy – life is like Russian roulette. Their only conformity is non-conformity. The Beats give personal testimony to the breakdown of Western values. These are the children who were failed by their parents. Compassion, not condemnation, is called for. The Beat Generation is the ultimate expression of a civilisation whose moral values have broken down.

Kerouac meanwhile had dashed on and off stage a dozen times. Now he dismissed Montagu, saying that he'd seen him on the *Jack Paar Show* but that he had nothing new to say. When it was Wechsler's turn to speak, Jack was even less civil.

Of course, the audience did not know that Kerouac was a right-wing Republican, so when he attacked James Wechsler, the editor of the *New York Post* whose whole life had been devoted to social causes, they did not realise that this was because Jack saw him as a communist – even though he most certainly was not:

Kerouac: 'James Wechsler. Who's James Wechsler? Right over there. James Wechsler, you believe in the destruction of America, don't you?'
Wechsler: 'No.' (The audience laughs, thinking Kerouac is joking.)
Kerouac: 'What do you believe in? Come here, come here and tell me what you believe in. You told me what you don't believe in. I want to know what you do believe in.' (Yells of 'That's right!' from the audience.) 'This is a university, we've got to learn . . . I believe in love, I vote for love.' (The audience applauds.)
Wechsler, confronted by such a question, found it difficult to avoid a pretentious reply: 'I believe in the capacity of the human intelligence to create a world in which there is love, compassion, justice and freedom. I believe in fighting for that kind of world. I think what you are doing is to try to destroy anybody's instinct to care about this world.'

> Kerouac: 'I believe, I believe in the dove of peace.'
> Wechsler: 'So do I.'
> Kerouac: 'No you don't. You're fighting with me for the dove of peace. You came here prepared to attack me.'

This was not true at all. Like most of the audience, Wechsler had come mainly to see Kerouac in the flesh, to try to find out more about this new social phenomenon. His sixteen-year-old son was very taken with the Beats, and Wechsler, far from coming to attack, had come to learn.

Jack then played dog in the manger, distracting the audience by taking Wechsler's hat, putting it on his head and flopping into his seat in the same position as Wechsler had been in. The irritated editor objected, which only encouraged Jack, who then wandered around the stage wearing the hat. Wechsler, who, as editor of the *Post*, attended President Eisenhower's weekly press conferences and spent his professional life interviewing and arguing with some of the most obdurate philistines in America, told the audience:

> After listening to Mr Kerouac I understand less about what they stand for than before. I see no virtue in organised confusion. The issue is not whether there is a Beat Generation, but whether civilisation will survive. There is no valour in their kind of flight and irresponsibility.

But this annoyed Jack, who angrily pushed Dean Kauffman aside to grab the microphone and denounce Amis, Wechsler and Montagu as 'a bunch of communist shits' and give a dire warning that, if they got what they wanted, 'the Sovietization of America', there would be no more meetings like this one. Amis, considering his politics, was justifiably insulted by this, as were the others, and an argument ensued. Jack had resorted to the last resort of the demagogue: name-calling.

He continued to play the boorish drunk: he dragged Allen Ginsberg on stage, then began playing the Warsaw Concerto on the piano, stopping from time to time to pose for photographs before switching to boogie-woogie.

Kerouac had been very ambivalent about appearing, changing his mind several times until the promise of an honorarium of $100 plus a limousine decided it. Some critics have suggested that Kerouac was set up, but there was no way the organisers could know Jack was an alcoholic, and they clearly considered Amis, as a so-called 'Angry

Young Man', to be a fellow rebel, and Montagu and Wechsler to be rebels of an earlier generation (though there were only eight years between Wechsler and Kerouac). Jack:

> Afterwards I went all the way up the spiral staircase backstage with two coloured guys and we turned on, and we were looking down on the stage, and I said, 'I am the Phantom of the Opera, boys!' And they were all screaming on the stage, see![37]

After the event Jack wrote to John Montgomery that he 'went off stage and played the piano in the back and insulted photographers and generally acted like a mad drunken fool just off a freight train which is precisely the way I am and precisely what I think of universities.'[38]

This attempt by the academy to present a public discussion on a subject so hotly and hysterically debated in the press was laudable but ill-conceived. It is understandable that they wanted Kerouac, but he was not capable of a formal discussion: he felt cowed and intimidated by intellectuals, he was nervous at speaking in public, and he was an alcoholic. They would have been better served by Allen Ginsberg, who sincerely wanted to spread the message of the Beat Generation, and in fact became its loudest, most vociferous proponent.

This forum has been interpreted in widely different ways. It has been used to show that Kerouac was the only hip one on stage and the others were all hopeless old squares; it has been used to show that Kerouac was the only right-wing Republican on stage and the others were all Democrats, with greater or lesser commitment to the public good; and used to show that Kerouac was incapable of coherent debate. In Allen Ginsberg's view, Kerouac was presenting koans to the panel and audience to enlighten them. Unfortunately, the plain fact is that Jack was blind drunk and virtually incapable of stringing a sentence together. The press and public came away with the impression that the Beats were nothing more than little boys showing off.[39] Jack called himself a representative of the 'Beat Generation' and defined it as a revolution of manners – in this instance bad manners, a return to the manners of the kindergarten.

Essentially, all Jack was offering was old-fashioned right-wing American individualism of the type advocated by Ayn Rand. This had been tarted up a bit with Oriental ideas, though by this time Jack had more or less renounced Buddhism in favour of his native Catholicism. Allen Ginsberg, ever the apologist, explained Jack's ch and behaviour as that of a guru. Allen saw it as: 'a call for phanies, of awareness, of the vastness of space, of oceanic feelings manifesting your own soul by language. He meant tolerance, compassion, empathy, humble, humility.' The trouble was that Jack had just demonstrated that he possessed none of those qualities.

It is hard now to imagine how shocking the Beatniks were to the average American. This was the era of conformity, when the White middle class lived in identical houses in far-flung suburbs, the woman ran the house and the men, in grey flannel suits with identical crew cuts like cadets from the Prussian Military Academy, took the commuter trains into the city each day. To not wear a necktie was regarded as the height of casual dressing. As to sex before marriage, drugs, bare lightbulbs, mattresses on the floor, abstract painting, poetry that didn't rhyme, beards ... It was all too shocking to contemplate.

The original Beats were themselves quite formal in their dress. Photographs from a 1959 art opening show Kerouac, Robert Frank, Allen Ginsberg and others with short hair and wearing neckties. Burroughs did not stop wearing a three-piece suit and hat until the eighties, when he moved to Kansas and his desire to remain anonymous in a crowd made him switch to jeans and a baseball cap. Lucien Carr, who worked for a major news agency, wore normal work attire. It was the Beatniks who extended their rebellion into the streets by adopting the clothes of the European Bohemians: the Breton fisherman's shirt, the beret, paint-splattered jeans, and sandals. Women wore black clothes, baggy sweater, tight toreador pants or jeans, and their hair long, like Juliette Greco. As for Jack, he was always being mistaken for a bum rather than a Beatnik, with his red face, stubble, unkempt hair, check flannel shirt and baggy chino pants.

Jack wanted nothing to do with the Beatniks, whom he thought had stolen his thunder and bastardised the original ideals of the movement. Jack:

Do you know what a Beatnik is? Usually some guy who says, 'I hate my father. I hate my mother.' So they leave home in Indiana and they come to New York. They write a line of poetry, type it up in a great big expensive five-dollar binding book, put it under their arm, put on sandals, grow a little goatee, walk down the street and say they're poets. It's just kind of a fad. It was invented by the press. Listen, I'm a railroad brakeman, Merchant Marine deckhand in wartime. Beatniks don't work. They don't get jobs.[40]

That November, Memere went to Florida to stay with Nin, so Jack was able to have Dody come and live with him. It was like a schoolboy having his girlfriend over when his parents go on vacation. Even Allen was allowed to visit. While she was there, Dody made some sculptures out of candlewax which she left behind when Memere was due to reappear. Memere found them and thought they were gypsy curses. When Jack brought Dody to dinner Memere was horrified: Dody wore her long hair loose and went around the house barefoot. Convinced that Dody was a witch, she waited until Dody had cleaned up the kitchen after cooking and then cleaned it again, to remove any spells she might have cast. When Dody returned to the city, Memere sent her a series of poisonous letters, demanding that she stop trying to steal her son away from her.

Though Jack was embarrassed at the rumours and jokes circulating about his relationship with his mother, and usually tried to downplay her, he did allow *New York Post* reporter Al Aronowitz to interview her for his series on the Beat Generation:

Memere: 'He's a good boy. Once he took me over to this publisher's house, Barney Rossett, because this publisher from France, Claude Gallimard, wanted to meet Jack and we were all talking French . . .
Jack: 'We had a big screaming dinner and then we started, my mother and I, started roaming up the street, hitting all the bars . . .
Memere: 'Gosh, I'll never do that again. Oh, I might as well come out with it. I had too much to drink, but I was having a big time and I was with him . . . Yes, he drinks a little. I think a little too much for his health . . . But I like his friends, even Neal – he's a little eccentric. But that other guy, I won't let him in my house.'
Jack: 'She means Allen Ginsberg.'
Memere: 'That's right. And I'm afraid of him. And then one time I read the letter he sent to Jack, and he was insulting priests. Catholic priests that had befriended him . . .'
Jack: 'He was telling Franciscan monks to take their clothes off.'
Memere: 'That's right. And my husband couldn't stand him either. Before he died, he made me promise not to let Ginsberg . . . well, I'll go downstairs and make some sandwiches.'
Jack: 'Awww. She doesn't like my girlfriend either. My girlfriend Dody Müller. Because she has long long hair and

doesn't tie it up. Because she likes to go barefoot. Because she's an Indian. She's 95% Indian, and my mother calls her *la sauvage* – the savage. She's a very Bohemian painter, you know. She's teaching me how to paint.'

Allen Ginsberg:

His mother hated all his men and women friends. She monopolised him. She was a very difficult woman. Just an old battleaxe. He thought that she was completely crazy, but he didn't want to abandon her. He had sworn to his father, on his father's deathbed, that he would take care of his mother, and it was like an old French-Canadian peasant family oath, so he did take care of his mother until he died. She ordered around all of his wives and dominated them and bossed them and insulted them, as well as forbidding me to come to the house, as well as Burroughs and Neal Cassady and all of Kerouac's life-long friends.[41]

Northport was close enough to New York for Jack to sneak away from Memere and come into town; in fact, it was more a case of her letting him go out to play. His life was more and more conducted on her terms and he allowed himself to be infantilised and cowed by the invisible adult presence of his father. Allen Ginsberg, never one to give up on his friends, insisted on visiting Jack in Northport and was quite shocked at what he found:

We sat by the television set and there was a retrospective news broadcast about Hitler and the concentration camps. Kerouac and his mother were both drinking. She was also a great tippler, both were drunk, and they began arguing among themselves. And then some German refugee came on the screen and talked about the Holocaust and Kerouac's mother said in front of me, 'They're still complaining about Hitler, it's too bad he didn't finish them off.' Kerouac agreed with her. I sat there and nodded. Then he said to her, 'You dirty cunt, why did you say that?' And she said, 'You fucking prick, you heard me say that before.' And then began an argument of such violence and filth I had never heard in any household in my life. I was actually shocked.
I suddenly realised the relationship between them: they were a bunch of drunks together, actually, talking totally uninhib-

itedly like down-home peasants, not restrained at all in their family squabble fired by alcohol. Not a calm maternal scene but a weird companionship. Many of his friends 'disapproved' and thought he would do better out in the world with us. I even bought a farm in New York State as a refuge for him in case he were able to make his break from the family. But poet Philip Whalen pointed out to us: 'There's nobody else that could take care of him except his mother.' So it's probably a good thing that he's there with her, because otherwise he might die in the city.[42]

But Memere didn't want Jews in her house and insisted that Jack keep them out. He told Allen never to visit him at home again. Allen was naturally insulted and offended, but Jack couldn't even understand why. He wrote to Gary Snyder: 'Do you hear from Ginsberg? . . . he's mad at me because my mother doesn't want him in the house here, never did . . . don't know why . . . she doesn't want Burroughs either, thinks they are both "murderers".'[43]

Henri Cru had the same experience as Allen while visiting Northport, and was just as shocked:

Jack and I had a lot of fun in Hollywood before he became famous. After he became well known he was never worth a damn. He drank whiskey by the full quart and as a guest in his and his mother's home I witnessed him abusing his mother verbally, calling her an old whore. She always treated me like her own son and spoiled me rotten. I have a long playing record where he praised his mother as a heavenly being. It's the most beautiful poem I ever heard.[44]

Jack had finally achieved the position he always wanted: he had become Leo Kerouac. Lucien Carr: 'He really wanted to be that old fart that was his father. And he wanted to sit on top of the hill and say that's who he was . . . and boast about all the famous and interesting people he knew.'

11 Madman, Bum and Angel

More money was now coming in than Jack had ever had before: the so-called 'men's magazines' wanted in on the Beat Generation action to show how hip they were and in 1958 Jack had pieces in both *Playboy*, and *Esquire* (which then featured pin-ups) as well as magazines like *Holiday*, *Jubilee*, *Pageant* and the newly launched *Village Voice*. The next year, he continued to contribute to *Playboy* and *Esquire*, but also began a regular column in the supposedly hip men's magazine *Escapade*. Often he did not have the time to write a new piece so he would use something from his huge store of manuscripts.

Through his friendship with Robert Frank, Jack became involved in film making. The project got off to a poor start when Robert Frank, his co-director Alfred Leslie, and Dody Muller drove out to Newport to examine Jack's manuscripts for a potential script. Jack went out and bought takeaway enchiladas for Robert and Al to eat before he and Dody slipped out to spend some time together. Memere appeared and ordered Frank and Leslie out of the house because they were Jews, then disappeared into her room. Robert went off to a restaurant but Al decided to heat up the enchiladas for his lunch. As he finished eating, Memere appeared screaming, 'Hey, you Jewboy! You look for my whiskey? No whiskey for you, Jew!' and locked her liquor cabinet. Leslie staggered outside, shocked, and threw up on the lawn. When Jack returned he was irked and asked why Leslie didn't use the neighbour's lawn.

Amazingly, they still wanted to work with Jack and chose the third act of his play, *The Beat Generation*, as their script. This was written in 1957, based on the visit by the progressive bishop to Neal and Carolyn's house in California. Jack read them the script to a background tape of a Symphony Sid jazz broadcast and they knew they had just what they wanted. Filming was to begin on 2 January 1959.

Financier Walter Gutman raised the money: 'It all came from Wall Street. The largest investor was Jack Dreyfus of Dreyfus Fund fame. He put in half but never saw a screening. He never realised, as far as I know, how beautiful it was.' The film cost $15,000, which was a lot of money in 1959, and many meetings were required. There is a photograph by Robert Frank of Gutman and Allen Ginsberg having coffee at the Bankers Club: Allen sitting in a high-backed chair in suit and tie, clean-shaven, short-haired, looking for all the world like a young financier.

In his financial newsletter, Gutman also revealed how Jack gave him a tip for the stock exchange:

> I met him at an opening of an exhibition. He jumped up from the chair in which he had been drinking and said, 'Oh Walter – Walter, I think US Borax is the thing to buy.' He held his hand up in excitement – 'I had a dream a few months ago and I dreamed about boron – at the time I thought boron was God, but now, after reading your last week's Letter, I think US Borax is the thing to buy.' In his letter Gutman then dutifully discussed the pros and cons of buying boran.[1]

It quickly emerged that they could not call the film *The Beat Generation* because, incredibly, a Hollywood entrepreneur called Albert Zugsmith had copyrighted the title for a cheap exploitation film for MGM. He wrote the script himself about a Beatnik rapist and also dashed off a cheap paperback version for Bantam Books: 'The shocking and revealing novel about a generation gone wild.' They had to find another name and took as a title a poem that Jack and Allen had jointly written back in the forties called *Pull my Daisy*.

The film was shot between January and April 1959, at Al Leslie's Fourth Avenue studio at Twelfth Street using just one camera and 16mm black and white stock. The brief exterior shots were done at a Brooklyn warehouse on the East River. The soundtrack was added later. It was intended to overdub the dialogue, but preliminary experiments showed that this would be impossible largely because the 'actors' had no previous experience. A monologue by Jack was used instead.

For 28 minutes the audience watches everyday life in Milo's (Neal Cassady's) house. Milo's wife (Carolyn) feeds the child and gets him off to school. Allen Ginsberg, Peter Orlovsky and Gregory Corso show up and cavort around, playing the flute, drinking beer, reading poetry and talking – they all play themselves.

Typically, none of the women have names, not even Milo's wife, who plays an important role in the film. Carolyn is played by Delphine Seyrig, who holds the film together. She was the only professional actress in the film and was later to star in *Last Year at Marienbad*. Impeccably dressed, her scenes are like clips from a French *nouvelle vague* movie, with the same beautifully framed moody close-ups. Ginsberg and Corso's scenes, in contrast, are like a home movie, with Allen self-consciously acting the fool much of the time, and Gregory looking as if he'd rather be somewhere else, except when they share a huge joint (which Kerouac, in his narration, sensibly does not mention).

Milo, played by painter Larry Rivers, comes home and the bishop, accompanied by his mother, played by the painter Alice Neal, and his sister arrive and are interrogated by the poets – 'Is baseball holy?' 'Are alligators holy?', 'Have you ever looked at girls in their tight dresses?' – causing chaos. Mooney Peebles as the bishop has a stab at acting and there is a nice moment when the camera focuses on Peter Orlovsky looking at Sally Gross's knees with great interest – she played the bishop's sister.

The bishop leaves and Milo's wife remonstrates with him for allowing the bishop to be treated with disrespect. The others quietly leave. After a short sharp argument, Milo joins the boys to go out on the town, leaving the wife at home in tears to look after the child. 'She'll get over it,' comments Jack and the film ends with the boys rushing out on the town; 'Let's go, let's go. Off they go!'

Jack's script is revealing for its stereotypical Beat attitude to women. The nameless woman is seen as the housewife, the mother and the pernicious influence stopping her man from having fun with the boys. Jack's contempt for woman is shown in his monologue: 'They're sitting round the table. They're getting kind of congenial. By God, even the woman feels good!'

Robert Frank's camera work is superb, moving in the way the human eye would move, catching little actions and events with the flick of an eye. Jack's overdubbed monologue has flashes of inventiveness and interest, but is mostly pedestrian and would have been better had he written a proper text to accompany the final edited version of the film instead of improvising. Most of the time he resorts to describing what we can see perfectly well on screen: 'Fallin' on the couch' (Gregory falls on the couch), 'Look at all those cars out there' (cut to view from window of a passing car) . . .

He is better when he makes up dialogue: 'They're sitting there talking about Empire State Building and dooms of bridges . . . Their secret naked doodlings do show, secret scatological thought. That's why everybody wants to see it.' He usually extemporises from some action on the screen. Allen rolls on the floor and pretends to play a violin: 'What cha want to play violins for? Don'cha know that Empire State has fallen underneath the Gowanas Canal?'

The film is now seen as one of the earliest examples of the sixties New York underground film movement but, several years after it was released, co-director Alfred Leslie deflated the myth of the film as 'spontaneous documentary' and revealed that the film had a script, that the shooting schedule was planned, the set was carefully arranged, each scene was rehearsed before shooting, the floor positions were marked and the footage slated. Leslie said that the Kerouac improvisation was in fact recorded four times – not two – and that all four versions were edited together in the final mix.

David Amram, who played the music on the soundtrack, maintains in an interview with Uri Hertz,[2] that it was recorded in two takes. It was agreed that Jack's original reading of the script was far better than any of the takes, but they were unable to use it because of the Symphony Sid background which posed impossible copyright problems. The film was probably considerably less improvised than most people thought but, whatever its merits, these days it is a wonderfully evocative piece of footage which captures an era better than virtually any other Beat artefact. Sadly, all of the hours of outtakes from this remarkable film were destroyed in a fire. At the time Allen Ginsberg said:

> I didn't think much of the movie as a movie. I thought it was relatively sweet – innocuous. But I thought Kerouac's narrative did a great deal – integrated it – made it beautiful – gave it a point that it might not otherwise have had.[3]

It is generally agreed that without Jack's narrative the film would not come off. The soundtrack was recorded in a five-hour session at Jerry Newman's recording studio with David Amram and Kerouac jamming together, Jack with earphones on while Amram played the piano. Amram: 'Jack's narration, of course, was almost like a great jazzman ... he played around the chords or played around the situation, improvised on certain given things, and just made a beautiful tapestry out of nothing.'

People often expect to see Jack himself in the film but he was barred from the set shortly after filming began, after he arrived, inebriated, expecting to party and accompanied by a particularly smelly, drunken bum he had found in the gutter in the Bowery. Al

Leslie told him to get out. During the filming of *Pull my Daisy*, Jack spent quite a bit of time on the Bowery nearby, drinking with the bums. Feeling compassion for them, he would drag three or four back to a friend's house, usually Dody's studio, for a good meal and a sleep. This generosity illuminates two sides of Jack's personality. He was genuinely concerned about the plight of these unfortunate men, but he would never have considered taking them back to Northport. He thought nothing of invading Dody's studio, however, because he valued no one else's work and did not even consider that having four rowdy, and quite likely mentally unstable, alcoholic street people in her studio would disrupt her work, inevitably result in damage and theft and possibly put Dody herself in danger. For Dody this was the last straw and in February she broke with him. Jack continued to come round and plead with her, but she was firm in her resolve. From then on they saw each other only at art openings and parties.

But Jack's generosity was selective: when Huncke got out of Sing Sing after a five-year stretch, Jack refused to help him. Only after Allen's entreaties, did Jack grudgingly write a $25 check, but he insisted that Allen be responsible for Huncke paying it back as soon as possible. Because Memere opened all of Jack's mail, she found out about Allen's involvement in all this and fired off more of her poisonous letters to him, accusing him of involving Jack with 'bums'. Allen could only laugh. Jack was the biggest bum of all: he was the one who liked to lie in the gutter on the Bowery and commune with the angels he met there.

Though Jack knew better than to bring Bowery bums to Allen's apartment, he still treated Allen in a most cavalier fashion. Though Allen was banned from his house, Jack thought nothing of bursting into Allen's at 4 a.m. waking everyone up. Allen:

> Once Kerouac came to visit Peter Orlovsky and me in East Second Street in New York, in 1959, very late at night, drunk, banging on the front door disturbing the household. Peter Orlovsky's sister Marie, who was studying to be a nurse, was living in the little side room off our kitchen, and Kerouac made a lot of drunken noise, then opened the door to the room of this young, innocent, virgin girl and frightened her. I got outraged and told him to shut up and behave himself and he fell down on the floor laughing at me and said, 'Ginsberg, you're a hairy loss!'

This traumatised Marie, who genuinely thought she was being attacked, and may have been a contributory factor in her later mental breakdown. Allen later cited the line 'Ginsberg you're a hairy loss' as an example of Kerouac's gurulike cutting through ego, but only Allen could be generous enough to see it that way.

Jack continued to abuse Allen's friendship. He had taken to drinking with the clam fishermen at Gunther's bar in Newport where he became friends with a Sicilian called Leo. One night he took Leo into the city and they went to visit Allen, unannounced. They knocked on the door but Allen yelled 'Get lost!'. Jack ordered Leo to break the door down, which he did. As they burst in, a young man quickly leapt from Allen's bed, grabbed his clothes and ran. Allen was furious with Jack, but didn't throw them out.

Of the new generation of poets, Jack particularly liked Ray Bremser, who had just been released from jail after doing six years for armed robbery. Ray Bremser was first made aware of the Beat scene by John Clellon Holmes's novels *Go* and *Horn*. Ray: 'He was a seminal influence on me when I was in the reformatory.' LeRoi Jones had published Ray in *Yugen* magazine and, when he got out of jail, LeRoi gave a party for him at his house. Jack Kerouac, Frank O'Hara, Kenneth Koch, Joel Oppenheimer, Al Feinstein, Franz Kline and Larry Rivers were all there. Ray:

> I was trying to hit on Diane di Prima when Jack and Larry Rivers trussed me up and threw me in the back of Larry's panel truck and took me to Lucien Carr's where Allen was. And I was trying to be nice to Helen Elliott, and I remember Allen hovering above me, reciting Hart Crane's 'Bridge' and I was saying, 'Will you beat it? I'm trying to score here . . .'[4]

This was the time of the 'mimeograph revolution', little literary magazines and coffee-house readings. John Rappanic organised some of the first of the Beat poetry readings at the 7 Arts Coffee Gallery upstairs at 43rd Street and Ninth Avenue in Hell's Kitchen. Ray Bremser remembered one evening when Gregory Corso persisted in badgering a Black man in the audience, saying, 'Oh you beautiful black angel!' The man smacked him. Ray:

> Gregory got so mad he broke everything he could see: he broke the dishes, he knocked over the table. I was sitting with Jack Kerouac and he said to me, 'Let's get out of here, this place is getting pretty tough.' We went across the street to a bar while Gregory was fending for himself. Those were the good poetry readings![5]

Jack Kerouac

On 2 March 1959, there was a reading by Frank O'Hara and Gregory Corso at the Living Theatre on Fourteenth Street at Sixth Avenue. Though the audience was small – about sixty people – it was star-studded: Willem De Kooning, Allen Ginsberg, Peter Orlovsky, Franz Kline, Morton Feldman, Willard Mass, Julian Beck. In his description of the event,[6] Brad Gooch said, 'Most of the trouble was caused by a drunken Jack Kerouac.' Jack jealously yelled at O'Hara, 'You're ruining American poetry, O'Hara.' O'Hara's riposte was immediate: 'That's more than you ever did for it.' Despite an acrimonious intermission, in which Kerouac again told O'Hara that he didn't like his poetry, when they resumed the reading Jack insisted on joining them on stage, sitting on a chair with his back to the audience. Jack's continual heckling irritated Frank O'Hara so much that he gave up trying to read 'The Unfinished' and made a speedy exit through the back door, calling back to the audience, 'This may seem uninteresting but it's no more uninteresting than Jack Kerouac's wanting to read.'

Allen was mortified. He had carefully orchestrated a rapprochement between the Beats and the School of New York poets to present a united front against the poetry establishment. He saw them all as having the same spirit but Kerouac was ruining everything. Ginsberg told Gooch, 'I was shrivelled in my seat, embarrassed for my friend Kerouac and at the same time sympathetic with O'Hara . . . I think the problem was alcohol, alas.' Allen persuaded Kerouac to visit O'Hara with him and apologise. They were let in but O'Hara was not there. Kerouac left a typewritten note saying, 'Dear Frank, The reason I was so extraordinary that nite I was jealous of Gregory liking your poetry – J.K.' O'Hara was not impressed.

Those in the New York literary establishment were not the only ones to loathe the Beats. Joe McCarthy may have slipped from view, but the government still took a grim view of what they thought was unAmerican behaviour: to them the Beats were hardly Mom and apple pie. At one of Jack's readings in Greenwich Village, he was surprised to see in the audience the homosexual boson who had caused him to jump ship in 1944, looking out of place in a crew cut and tweed suit, recording the proceedings on a tape recorder. Jack had a few drinks with the man, who was now working for the government, and agreed to go to the officer's room and tape an interview. The man told Jack that the FBI were concerned about communist involvement in the Beat Generation. Jack was no doubt happy to inform him of his own Republican sympathies and is reported as saying, 'You know how the tape ends? I was fucking him in the mouth! That's the FBI for you. Take that to J. Edgar Hoover!

It's all on tape. He's got the tape.' As a closet queen, Hoover would have no doubt enjoyed the tape very much. Nonetheless, in 1961 – slightly after the fact – Hoover announced that the Beatniks were one of the three greatest threats to America.[7]

On 30 April, Grove Press published *Doctor Sax*, which garnered more terrible reviews for Jack. However, publishers still regarded him as a commercial proposition and Avon paid him an advance of $7,500 each for *Maggie Cassidy* and *Tristessa*, the former due for publication in July. Jack's manuscript stock was getting low and he began looking around for something to write about. He wrote to Gary Snyder, with whom he was back on letter-writing terms:

I figured I might as well go on completing my 'Duluoz Legend,' that is to say, those true stories like *Dharma Bums* in which in later collected edition of my work, 'Ray Smith' will be 'Jack Duluoz' and I'll have to figure new name for you – Bums, Road, Cassidy, etc. all chapters in one long story literally the Kerouac Legend – why not? – nice system – only the true stories are getting harder and harder to confess . . .[8]

He had made notes and researched every period of his life, but none of it looked very commercial. He concluded that the obvious thing to do was write up the David Kammerer murder.

Lucien had changed considerably in jail and when he got out he applied himself to keeping a low profile. He had taken a job at the UPI news agency and stayed there, working his way into a position of authority. When Allen dedicated *Howl* to him – alongside many other friends – Lucien thanked him, but insisted firmly that he wanted his name removed from all subsequent printings. Now Jack was threatening to bring the whole business of 1944 up again and perhaps endanger Lucien's job. Lucien was furious, and his wife Cessa got hysterical every time Jack mentioned it, thinking that Jack was deliberately trying to break up their marriage. Jack had always been jealous of Cessa because Lucien's commitment to his wife, children and job had meant that Jack could no longer drag Lucien out for all-night drinking sessions any time he pleased. Allen also wrote to Jack, telling him not to write about the affair as Lucien really did not want it. Jack acquiesced for the time being.

That June, Memere enacted her usual seesaw between New England and Florida. They sold the Gilbert Street house and Memere went to Orlando, leaving Jack to stay in occupation until the new owners took possession, before following her south.

In July *Maggie Cassidy* was published, to the usual bad reviews: in the *Saturday Review* John Ciardi called it 'one of our boy's earliest scrolls'. Jack saw no reason to stick around New York since he only got drunk there and was not exactly a part of the literary world. He had been invited into their circles but had made a point of rejecting them, such as the occasion when Tom Payne from Avon Books introduced Jack to Anaïs Nin at the Cedar Street Bar. Nin was a supporter of the Beats, and later wrote: 'The most valuable contribution of American writers has been in the realm of rhythm. There was rhythm in Kerouac's *On The Road*.'[9] But when she was unable to keep up with his drinking Jack simply walked away and left her. In the end the publishers and editors gave up trying to be friendly.

Nor was Jack welcomed any more by the painters, who had grown tired of his drunken tirades and had been offended by his treatment of Frank O'Hara. That July, Jack, surrounded by an entourage, arrived at a party given by the painter Lee Krasner – Jackson Pollock's widow – at her house in East Hampton.

'I thought this was an open party,' he said.

'Not *that* open,' replied Lee. 'Ouuutttt!'[10]

Jack's plan was to go to Florida in August, but Nin and Paul were having problems with their marriage so Memere returned to Northport. As there was nowhere for her to return to, Jack quickly bought a house at 49 Earl Avenue, one block from Main Street. Jack initially used the basement as a study and writing room, but it became too damp in winter so he had a workroom built in the attic. Nicosia reports that Jack and Memere carefully priced the work and in the end determined that it would be cheaper to hire a crew at an hourly rate. A few days into their work, Jack took the entire crew on a two-day drinking binge. They enjoyed themselves enormously as he was not only buying the drinks, but paying them for their drinking time. Memere was not happy. Nor was she pleased when he brought home four of the clammers from Gunther's and they almost wrecked the place. But Jack had made his choice of whom he wanted to be with and he felt more at home with Bowery bums, clammers and provincial barflies than in the competitive atmosphere of the New York literary scene, where he felt dull and stupid in the face of their intellectual conversation.

He wasn't missing much. A good example of the state of the scene came that winter when Norman Mailer appeared, together with Dorothy Parker and Truman Capote, on David Susskind's television talk show, *Open End*, to discuss literature. Naturally, the Beat Generation writers came up. Capote, the master of the sound bite and snappy phrase, dismissed them all, saying, 'None of them can write. Not even Mr Kerouac . . . [It] isn't writing at all – it's typing.' This phrase was to dog Kerouac for the rest of his life. Mailer's rebuttal, regrettably, has long been forgotten.

It was a jibe which many people thought had a grain of truth in it, even the normally loyal Carolyn Cassady, who remarked, echoing Capote: 'I can remember thinking that Jack was wrong in not structuring things more. Those tapes he used in *Visions of Cody*: that isn't writing, that's typing.'[11]

The media remained interested in him, however, and, when Jack was offered $2,000 to read from *On the Road* on the Steve Allen television show, Memere insisted that he do it. The show had 35 million viewers, and she knew it would help sell the book. Jack was understandably nervous, being very far from that world. When he went to buy new clothes in Newport to wear on the show, he looked so scruffy in his rumpled chinos with his shirt hanging out that the clothing store owner thought he was a mental patient from the nearby Pilgrim State Hospital and tried to evict him. Only after he showed papers to prove his identity was he allowed to spend his money.

The show was on 16 November and Jack dithered so much about going that he had to fly to Los Angeles, despite the fact he had already bought train tickets because he hated flying. Jack was looking good and had curbed his drinking, knowing how important the show was. He gave a satisfactory reading, albeit restrained and obviously nervous. Afterwards he threw up. The footage of Jack on *Steve Allen*, still looking surprisingly handsome and athletic, is the most widely seen film we have of him, and contributes largely to our image of the man. Jack stayed on in Los Angeles and a few days later he got drunk with Al Leslie and insisted they went to visit Steve Allen in his office. For some reason they bought a foot locker as a present but Steve Allen was busy and embarrassed, and had nothing to say to them. As they left, Jack gave Steve Allen – his 'millionaire hero' – the finger. Afterwards he felt embarrassed by this gratuitous drunken insult but never had the courage to write to apologise.

Jack and Al went up to San Francisco, where they stayed with Phil Whalen and his two roommates, Albert Saijo and Lew Welch, both of whom were poets. They got on well: Saijo was a Buddhist and Welch was a woodsman, happiest while living in a remote cabin. Welch was also a heavy drinker, so he and Jack had a lot in common.

They so enjoyed each other's company that Welch and Saijo offered to drive Jack back to New York in Welch's Jeep station wagon. The journey was like a return to old times for Jack, with Saijo meditating in the back and all three of them making up haiku, having a good time. They arrived in New York, where Jack arranged for them to stay at Allen's East Second Street apartment. They hit the bars, and Lew and Jack met at least one willing girl. Lew wrote to Gary: 'We shared a very sexy girl. It was a relief.'[12] Jack relished their company and, unusually, invited them to come and stay in Northport overnight. Memere liked them because they were polite to her.

While in New York the three of them visited photographer Fred McDarrah's house to be photographed for *The Beat Scene* anthology he was assembling for Corinth Press. They sat round a table in the living room and made up a collective poem – later published together with their road haikus as *Trip Trap* – while McDarrah snapped away. The photographs of Jack, in full-flight creativity, wearing his red plaid peaked cap and signature check flannel shirt, became almost iconic. Five years later, when Allen Ginsberg went to a poetry cafe in Prague, huge blow-ups of those photographs were on the wall.

Jack had a new girlfriend, Lois Sorrells, who came from Northport but lived in New York. They first got together when Memere was away before Jack bought the Earl Avenue house. When Memere returned, Jack would sneak Lois up to his attic workroom where he was not to be disturbed. Memere, in any case, sometimes turned a blind eye to Jack's sexual adventures, knowing he could not be expected to remain celibate. Jack sang Sinatra songs to Lois and played records. They danced and made love. Jack sometimes saw her in the city and some weekends she would come to Northport and stay over. Then they lived like a married couple and Jack would bring her breakfast in bed – something his other wives never got. They seemed so well matched that they began to consider marriage.

Jack's drinking grew worse and Memere showed concern because he was no longer eating properly, and Jack had always been a big eater. He fell down in Penn Station and hurt his elbow, and a month later, in May, he went on a week-long binge which culminated in him falling on his head in the Bowery among all the bums. But he continued to write. He would lock himself away in his attic workroom, feed a teletype roll into the typewriter and get to it. He had the perfect set up: a desk, an electric typewriter with a reading light wrapped in silver foil to direct the light on to the typewriter carriage, a tape recorder with a large collection of jazz tapes, books and papers, all neatly filed. In Northport he usually got up around midday or one o'clock, stood on his head for eight minutes, which he believed was a cure for phlebitis, and then did some writing before having breakfast: 'That's the best time for writing.'

The headboard of his bed had a light fitting attached to it and next to it, on the wall, sheets of paper were spiked on a hook where he could grab them in the night: 'I call these bedside sheets. I use them to write down dream thoughts. I hear them in a dream and wake up and turn the light on and write them down.' These were the notes that Lawrence Ferlinghetti published as *Book of Dreams* in December 1960 but, as it was a paperback original, it was not reviewed.

Bob Thiele, the producer of the album that Jack made with Steve Allen after the Vanguard date, wanted to record a follow-up. He asked if Jack wanted to use Allen again. Jack said no. He wanted to use his two favourite tenor saxophone players: Al Cohn and Zoot Sims. Thiele was dubious: he didn't see how Jack could read against a pair of tenormen, but Jack insisted that this was what he wanted so Thiele went ahead and booked them for a session. The recording went well, with Jack able to hold his own against the saxophone riffs. At the end of the session, Cohn and Sims packed up their horns and left. Bob Thiele found Jack in the studio, leaning against the wall, crying. Bob Thiele:

He said, 'My favourite saxophone players left me. They don't even want to listen to these playbacks.' We went down to a bar on Eighth Avenue and he started to throw beer bottles at the taxi cabs on Eighth Avenue. I split.[13]

It is interesting that Kerouac described Cohn and Sims as his 'favourite tenormen'. Though he obviously admired the black horn players who invented the genre, Jack appears to have felt more at home with White players like tenormen Allen Eager and Brew Moore, both of whom he wrote about. It is interesting that Zoot Sims, Al Cohn, Allen Eager and Brew Moore recorded an album together in April 1949 called *Four Brothers*, which we can assume Jack had in his collection and may be the reason he requested these musicians.

Jack's phrasing on the record owes much to the original hard bop players – it was Allen Ginsberg who characterised Kerouac's writing as 'spontaneous bop prosody' – and the Cohn–Sims recording mimics the phrasing of Dizzy Gillespie, whose 'Salt Peanuts' was one of Jack's favourite sides.

Jack had a great, instinctive love of jazz and he really understood its rhythms and inner tensions. He told Mike Post of the *New York Post*:

> Jazz is very complicated. It's just as complicated as Bach. The chords, the structures, the harmony and everything. And then it has a tremendous beat. You know, tremendous drummers. They can drive it. It has just a tremendous drive, it can drive you right out of yourself.[14]

Allen Ginsberg:

> Bop musicians were adapting their music to the cadence of actual Black street talk, talking to each other with their instruments, using street talk. Kerouac returned it to speech using rhythms more interesting than existing printed poetry and prose to get the emotions of spoken language into the written language.[15]

Despite a succession of bad reviews, Jack entered the sixties in a strong position as a writer: *Mexico City Blues* had recently come out from Grove, New Directions had published a 120-page extract from *Visions of Cody* as a signed limited edition, City Lights was planning publication of *Book of Dreams* later that year, Corinth Books were to publish *Scripture of the Golden Eternity* that spring, *Tristessa* was due from Avon and McGraw Hill had arranged to release *Lonesome Traveller* in September.

Lonesome Traveller is a collection of articles from *Holiday* magazine, assembled by McGraw Hill editor Gray Williams. Jack had a good relationship with both Ted Patrick, the editor of *Holiday*, and John Knowles, the assistant editor, and they used to pay him $1,500 to $2,000 for each one. Maybe Jack was conforming to the house style, but he comes over as the stereotypical American tourist: friendly, wide-eyed know-nothing with a very shallow understanding of what he sees, and little interest in learning about it. The book only really livens up during the Tangier piece when Burroughs makes an appearance.

In his introduction to the collection, Kerouac distances himself from the Beat movement, saying:

> Always considered writing my duty on earth. Also the preachment of universal kindness, which hysterical critics have

failed to notice beneath frenetic activity of my true-story novels about the 'beat' generation. Am actually not 'beat' but strange solitary crazy Catholic mystic . . . Final plans: hermitage in the woods, quiet writing of old age, mellow hopes of Paradise (which comes to everybody anyway) . . .

Jack discouraged visits to Northport from most of his old friends but, when Henri Cru received a commission to rewire the high-school auditorium across from Jack's house, he naturally wrote to Jack. He commented to Edie Parker:

Since I had fed and boarded Jack in Marin City, California in years gone past I assumed, mistakenly, that Jack would put me up for a couple of weeks as a paying guest. Instead he wrote me an insulting letter telling me that I imposed on him more than anyone else in this world. I tore up the letter and filed my memories of Jack in the garbage can with the torn letter. His turning me down turned out to be a blessing in disguise. (Job fouled up.) I would have never lived down this catastrophe had I participated in this ill conceived project.[16]

Ferlinghetti was one exception to the visiting rule. He went to Northport in April to discuss *Book of Dreams* and look through Jack's remaining manuscripts. It was just after Jack's fall in Penn Station and he was red-faced and sweating profusely. Lawrence thought he looked in terrible shape and offered him his cabin in Bixby Canyon, Big Sur, to rest and recuperate. Jack gladly accepted.

Jack was actually in need of more experience to write about. He had virtually exhausted his Beat Generation memories, and as he was no longer close to Burroughs he could hardly resurrect his project to write a portrait of him. Ginsberg never appealed to him as a suitable subject, and Allen's portrayal in Jack's books was always unsatisfactory. Allen was too deep a character and there was not enough action in his life to make the sort of book Jack wrote. A trip to Big Sur might provide a subject. Jack arranged to leave Northport on 17 July to spend three months in Big Sur.

Jack asked Lawrence not to tell anyone that he was in San Francisco as he wanted to slip quietly away to the cabin and write, with no distractions. Of course, as soon as he arrived he went on a two-day drinking binge, ending up in a skid-row hotel, and by the time he took the bus to Monterey he was already in a terrible state. A cab dropped him at the Bixby Canyon Bridge in the dead of night and, using his brakeman's lantern, he walked down the precipitous track to the canyon below. Once in the gorge it was pitch-black and his lantern was of little use.

It is easy to see how Kerouac, given his fragile state, was unsettled by Bixby Canyon. The morning mist does not burn off until about midday, and the thousand-foot-high canyon walls are claustrophobic, even in the strong Californian sunlight: sheer rocky bluffs with pines clinging to whatever foothold they can find, with thick verdant tree cover at the bottom. Ferlinghetti's small cabin was a very basic wooden structure, with a porch, sleeping pallet and a small potbellied stove. Standing nearby was the old wooden privy where Jack wrote graffiti on the rough unpainted walls – 'Useless, useless,/The heavy rain/Driving into the sea' – in his distinctive script. On the north side of the cabin ran the little Bixby Creek, to which he rushed continually to drink great drafts of water to compensate for his alcoholic dehydration.

The path to the beach follows close by the stream. Bixby Creek has cut a deep narrow gorge which ends in a wide white sandy beach, strewn with great tendrils of kelp torn from the sea bottom, twisted round each other heaped on the fine sand in tangled mounds. A thousand feet above the beach, US 101 crosses the canyon over the single span of the Bixby Canyon Bridge. At the foot of the cliffs lay the wreck of one car that didn't make it.

The creek wandered aimlessly in an ever-changing path across the final stretch of sand to the ocean and the sodden wrinkled heads of seals could sometimes be seen bobbing around the offshore rocks. Beyond the white sand, beneath the waves, lay an immense pebble bank. After each breaker came the sound of millions of pebbles grinding together in the undertow.

Each night, after cooking himself supper, Jack would make his way down the track using his brakeman's lantern and sit on a rock, listening to the sea, scribbling his notes in a small secretarial notebook, his hands and the notebook protected from the spray by a large, clear, plastic bag. It was a conscious attempt by him to fulfil James Joyce's unresolved plan to re-create the sounds of the ocean by using syllables and words arrived at through stream of consciousness. It was a great success.

> Which one? Which one? Which
> one? The one ploshed –
> The ploshed one? The same,
> ah boom –

Jack used the poem, 'Sea Sounds of the Pacific Ocean at Big Sur'[17] as a coda to the main text of *Big Sur*. It is superb, one of his most brilliant pieces of writing. His careful analysis of the exact components of the sound – the breeze, the sustained hiss of the breakers, the roar of the grinding pebbles, the foaming at the water's edge, small splashings among the rocks – and his rendering of them in language using onomatopoeic words which convey not only the sounds but the sense and feel of the place is masterful. Jack:

Proust and Joyce are the greatest twentieth-century writers, and Joyce was gonna sit by the sea – he was blind, remember. He was seventy years old and he was gonna sit by the sea and write the sounds of the sea, and he died and he didn't do it, so I did it for him.[18]

The poem owes much to Michael McClure's 'Beast language' poems, and McClure along with his wife and child were among Jack's visitors at Big Sur.

After three weeks of living alone, the demons in Jack finally got to him. On the beach one day he took a deep breath of the bracing sea air and passed out. He walked back to the cabin, packed his rucksack and returned straightaway to San Francisco, where he took a room in skid row. He cashed $500 in travellers' cheques and set out on a serious binge, starting out with Philip Whalen and other friends, but entering a critical phase when Lew Welch joined the entourage. They drove down to visit Neal and Carolyn but by this time Jack was so out of it that, when Carolyn went to greet him, he just snarled at her and pushed her to one side. However, in the morning, when he awoke under the plum tree in the garden, he was able to recall all the events of the previous night and scribbled them in his notebook.

The party went on day and night. At one woman's apartment Jack was incontinent and pissed all over her bathroom. She called him a 'son of a bitch' and threw him out. At Al Hinkle's house, Helen Hinkle had to hold him up while he urinated because he could hardly stand. Since Jack appeared to have had enough solitude, Ferlinghetti decided to make a party of it and invited everyone down to the cabin for the weekend. Ferlinghetti, Victor Wong, Phil Whalen, Michael and Joanna McClure and their daughter, and several others. The party ended after a bonfire on the beach, with dawn approaching, and Jack reading aloud from Robert Louis Stevenson's *The Strange Case of Dr Jekyll and Mr Hyde*, one of the series of uniform red-bound classics that Ferlinghetti kept in his cabin. Victor Wong suddenly realised that Jack was no longer reading from the page but was improvising, and began to join in. The two of them exchanged choruses until the candle finally guttered and the dawn lightened the horizon above the forest.

The weekend over, everyone went home, leaving Jack to recover from an attack of DTs. The following Friday, the party started up again with the McClures, Neal, Carolyn and all their children. Afterwards, Jack returned to Los Gatos with the Cassadys because Neal had promised him his latest mistress, a woman called Jacky Gibson. In his drunken stupor Jack sometimes called her Lucien because she looked very like him. He spent a week in her apartment in San Francisco, during which he killed her goldfish by pouring wine into their tank, ran up a huge phone bill with calls to Paris, and finally broke her armchair which collapsed under him while he was drinking. She had a precocious four-year-old son called Eric, and when she and Jack had sex she encouraged Eric to watch. The little boy was horrified and beat on Jack's bare back with his fists as he fucked her.

Jacky was very needy, and Jack's attraction to her quickly turned to aversion. Nonetheless, he took her with him to the cabin, along with Lew Welch and his girlfriend, the poet Lenore Kandel. The combination of drinking and a woman making demands on him resulted in Jack cracking up. He had the worst attack of delirium tremens in his life and accused them all of being communist spies sent to poison him or drive him mad. That night as he lay trembling and shuddering he had a vision of the cross, the only thing left that he could trust and hang on to.

Shaken, Jack returned to San Francisco where he stayed with Lawrence Ferlinghetti, who shaved him and cleaned him up before sending him home to Mother.

In January 1961, Joan Haverty began new court proceedings to make Kerouac contribute money towards the upkeep of his daughter. She was living in dire poverty in the worst part of the Lower East Side of New York and didn't see why Jack's daughter should grow up in a slum when he was now wealthy. Jack grew hysterical with rage, encouraged by Memere, who convinced him that Joan was only after his money. He denounced Joan, Jan and women in general. Though in San Francisco he had boasted to Victor Wong's father that he had a daughter, Memere's fury so convinced him that Jan was not his that he agreed to take a blood test. His friends kept trying to calm him and get him to accept the truth. She was obviously his child: Jan looked identical to him, but he would have none of it. Represented once more by Eugene Brooks, he went to court. Whether his feelings of persecution by women had anything to do with it is hard to tell, but at this point Jack was probably seeing more men than women sexually. His drinking meant that he was unable to have normal sex and, in any case, he had always preferred a blow job. He laughingly told Allen Ginsberg that he was ready to turn 'queer' and Allen says that they had sex a lot in these years. Certainly, when Jack's girlfriend Lois went looking for him, he was often to be found in Allen's bed on East Second Street (just a few blocks from where his daughter lived).

He seemed obsessed with homosexuality and the small size of his own penis. Ginsberg told a story which illustrates this:

There was an adventure with the writer Paul Bowles, Tennessee Williams and John Gielgud the actor, at the very elegant Johnny Nicholson's restaurant in 57th Street sometime in the early sixties, where he insisted that the very dignified gay musician-writer Paul Bowles show everybody his prick. Kerouac would talk about nothing but that for the whole elegant supper. He got underneath finally and overturned the entire marble round table still yelling that Bowles should show his prick. Alas Bowles didn't have the courage or the amusement to do so and satisfy him.[19]

Or the courage to call the maitre d' and have Jack thrown out.

Jack's utter lack of comprehension of what it meant to have a relationship with another person, man or woman, is shown in *Big Sur* where he reports an argument with Jacky. She defends her right to have another boyfriend and tells Jack: 'He's much kinder to me than you'll ever be: at least he gives of himself.' To which Jack replies, 'But what's all this giving of ourselves, what's there to give that'll help anybody?' 'You'll never know, you're so wrapped up in yourself,' she tells him. And yet elsewhere in the book he wonders:

Can it be I'm witholding from her something sacred just like she says, or am I just a fool who'll never learn to have a decent eternally minded deep-down relation with a woman and keep throwing that away for a song at a bottle?[20]

That January, Allen Ginsberg began helping Dr Timothy Leary, then a psychologist at Harvard University, to conduct a series of tests to see the reaction of creative people to the drug Psilocybin, also known as magic mushrooms. Allen gave the pills to Charles Mingus, Thelonius Monk, Barney Rosset, the owner of Grove Press, and Robert Lowell. Timothy Leary was visiting New York when Allen gave them to Jack at East Second Street. Leary was immediately uneasy when he met Kerouac and described him as: '. . . scary. Behind the dark good-looks of a burly lumberjack was a New England mill-town sullenness, a Canuck-Catholic soggy distrust. This is one unhappy kid, I thought.'[21]

Jack took the pills, along with Allen and Timothy, but Jack also continued to drink. He talked nonstop, ranting and raving, striding round the room, jumping on chairs and making up poetic babble. He leapt on the settee and declaimed: 'I'm the King of the Beatniks. I'm Francois Villon, vagabond poet-rogue of the open highway. Listen while I play you hot-lick, spiral improvisations from my tenor typewriter . . .' Jack's best line of the night came when Allen asked if he had sensed any greater reality from the pills and Jack replied, 'Walking on water wasn't made in a day.'

Leary had taken trips with more than a hundred people, 'but no one had tried to control, dominate, overwhelm the experience like Kerouac. He was imposing his saloon style on it, and for me it was too much . . . Kerouac had propelled me into my first negative trip.'

At dawn Jack was still shouting and guffawing, so Leary decided to join him and together they went to buy cigarettes. A blanket of pure untouched snow covered the grimy Lower East Side and Jack immediately threw a snowball at Tim, just missing his head. Leary threw one back and together they danced whooping down the street, their breath making great clouds in the crisp fresh air. The corner bar was just opening so they had a few beers and played the jukebox before buying freshly baked Italian bread to take back to Allen's apartment, throwing snowballs to each other in long looping football passes as they went. Leary:

> Throughout the night Kerouac remained unmovably the Catholic carouser, an old-style Bohemian without a hippie bone in his body. Jack Kerouac opened the neural doors to the future, looked ahead, and didn't see his place in it. Not for him the Utopian pluralist optimism of the sixties.

12 Good Ol' Boy

n April 1961, after Jack's drinking caused him yet another painful attack of phlebitis, Memere said that they would move back to Orlando, Florida, where the sunshine might do him some good. The Northport house was sold, and off they went once more. They bought a house two doors from Nin and Paul at 1309 Alfred Drive in a new suburban development.

Once Jack had settled in, unpacked and arranged all his papers, he flew down to Mexico City to spend a month completing *Desolation Angels*. He had been trying to finish it for some time, but each time he hammered out a section there was something wrong with it and he would dump it. With Jack's system it was all right to have another go at a text, you just were not allowed to alter it. Of course, by the fourth try, some of the better phrases and words from earlier drafts must have stuck in the memory, but Jack didn't discuss that.

It took three rejected drafts, and 40,000 words before it was finished. It is easy to see why he had trouble with it: the book lacks a centre, it feels empty and this is because it is not a portrait book. Kerouac's most successful books are all portraits – not biographies – of someone: Gerard, Mary Carney, Aileen Lee, Gary Snyder and, of course, Neal Cassady. Without a strong central character the book lacks direction. Jack's own role in it is diluted by his adventures with Allen Ginsberg, Peter Orlovsky and Gregory Corso, who all have a strong presence but none of them is central enough to hold the book together. The book opens with Jack on fire-watching duty in Desolation Peak, and ends, after travels through Mexico, New York and Tangier, back in Mexico City. It appears to be an arbitrary slice of his life which could have been shorter or longer depending on how many pages he had typed. The book is interesting because it chronicles, in some detail, the lives of these major Beat Generation figures, but if the reader did not know who they were then it would not make much sense.

There is a lot of careless writing in the book mixed in with the good. Kerouac by now is writing without any regard for his reader: in section eleven he describes a dream in which a murder victim sits in his father's chair 'just about on Sarah Avenue location'. He has never described his childhood home on Sarah Avenue, and even a reader familiar with his biography could not know the placement of the furniture in a house that Kerouac lived in from 1935 to 1939, so what is the point of this piece of information? It illustrates the pitfalls of spontaneous prose, particularly Jack's approach to it:

I have a nice method for writing. I call it spontaneous prose. I don't fumble for words – that's a stumbling block. Some writers, when they come to a place where they can't think of the proper word, they just stop. I don't do that. If I can't think of the proper word I just go blublublublublu ...

Many of his friends felt that he was heading up a cul-de-sac by insisting on writing in that manner because it was making him sloppy. Lucien Carr said that he thought Neal's influence on Jack's writing was bad:

Well I shouldn't have said 'bad' – 'unfortunate' ... I'm talking about language. I think Jack's language tended to get cheaper as it went on, and by 'cheap' I mean easily come by ... it became cheaper and cheaper, which is a shame ... I mean, to a man who loved each word in the English language more than you love your wife ... it became, plastic blither blither ... I'm thinking of what Kerouac had to say, as he went on ... the words that came out of his mouth. Jack tended, later on, to classify people into categories ...[1]

That October, Jack fed a new roll of teletype paper into his electric typewriter and, fuelled by Benzedrine, banged out *Big Sur* in ten nights. It was written in what Kerouac described as telling 'a plain tale in a smooth buttery literate run'.[2]

Ferlinghetti, who apparently did not like the description of himself as a literary businessman, described *Big Sur* as a 'tired old book by a tired old alcoholic',[3] but the book has much to recommend it in structure, language and narrative.

Structurally it is very straightforward: it opens with his arrival in San Francisco and ends with his departure, a chastened man. In its language there are many beautiful passages of observation, though as usual it is marred by his excessive use of action adjectives: 'crazy', 'rushed', 'goof', 'mad', and so on. It is one of the most powerful, painful, detailed, soul-baring descriptions of someone going through a complete alcoholic breakdown ever written. It is confessional, almost in the sense of a church rite, but, ultimately, though he clearly sees that he is on a self-destructive path, he seems to learn nothing from the writing of the book. As if, by confessing it, no more needs to be done and the personal problems that caused his breakdown do not themselves have to be addressed. At times he even gives the impression of being proud of how far he had fallen and of how appalling his behaviour was, as if he is being brave at confessing it.

In the book he is distraught and upset at receiving the news from his mother upon his arrival in San Francisco that his cat, Tyke, has died. He explains that he identified cats with his brother and says that, when he was three or four years old, he and Gerard would lie on the floor on their stomachs to watch them lap milk. These must be stories he heard from his mother but they make him equate the death of Tyke with that of Gerard and precipitate a drinking binge which results in his crack-up. Ferlinghetti noticed his overreaction to the news and suggested that he return to the cabin alone for a few weeks to get over it, knowing that otherwise Jack would drown his sorrows in drink.

When his girlfriend, Jacky Gibson – known as Willamine 'Billie' Dabney in the book – digs a garbage pit the same size and shape as a grave for her four-year-old son, Jack comments: 'We've all read Freud sufficiently to understand something there.' But what was there? Did Jacky really wish her son was dead? It would be interesting to know if it was really coffin-shaped. Jack had been up all night having paranoid fantasies that the others were out to kill him so maybe it his own grave he saw. Or, more likely, the grave of his cat, Tyke, whose death was constantly upon his mind. This would make the grave not that of the four-year-old Eric, but the nine-year-old Gerard. The book ends a few pages later with an image of Tyke's grave in his mother's backyard. The death of Tyke frames the book: a pair of bookends, beginning with the cat's death and ending with its burial. Possibly Jack thought that his breakdown had finally freed him from the guilt of Gerard's death. That would explain the surprisingly anodyne ending to the book: 'Something good will come out of all things yet – and it will be golden and eternal just like that. There's no need to say another word.'

Jack bought himself a case of Cognac to celebrate the completion of *Big Sur*, which he regarded as his most 'honest' book yet. He recovered consciousness in hospital two weeks later with no memory of the intervening days. He visited friends in New York but he felt guilty about yet again invading the privacy of his friends and atoned for it with a four-week binge. He ran into Burroughs while he was there but Bill was cold and formal towards him. As far as Bill was concerned, their friendship was over.

Jack's paternity case reached court on 20 February 1962, when he had to take a blood test. He met Jan and her mother in Brooklyn where they went for hamburgers. Jack kept telling Jan she was not his daughter until the ten-year-old disarmed him by saying, 'I don't care if you're my father or not – I'll still love you!'

Jan Kerouac described seeing her father for the first time:

> The first meeting was in Brooklyn, New York, and the whole purpose of the meeting was for a blood test to determine whether he was my father or not and it turned out positive. My mother was filing a paternity suit to try and get money from him. I was unaware of that at the time and I just thought it was great fun and our blood was being tested and I thought that we had some special blood or something that people wanted to know about.
>
> He had his own crazy reasons for not admitting that he was my father, mainly that he was afraid of his own emotions. I know that he lived with his mother most of his life and that he was kind of a baby in many ways because of that, and that he relied on his mother a lot and I know he felt strange about knowing that he had a daughter somewhere and yet he never sought me out. He spoke to a lot of his friends, like Allen Ginsberg, and mentioned certain feelings that he had about me but he would never have the courage to actually talk to me about them. It was partly because he was busy being a baby himself, I think.[4]

Joan Haverty reported that, after Jan saw Jack, the deep belly laugh she used to have as a child reappeared, 'a belly laugh I hadn't heard since she was four'.

Despite a positive reading on the blood test, Jack still denied paternity in court. Judge Benjamin Fine took Jack into his chambers and told him that, no matter what his feelings were towards Jan's mother, he should not deny his daughter her name. He offered Jack a deal: if he would acknowledge her, he would only have to pay the minimum in child support – $52.68 a month. Jack agreed, but back in court he blustered that he was only recognising her name, not her. His legal fees were $2,500, which would have enabled Joan and Jan to move out of the slums. Eugene Brooks: 'There were Family Court proceedings in which Jack "conceded the paternity" but there was some difficulty in getting Jack to settle the case. His mother kept saying, "It's not yours! It's not yours!" ' So did Jack, but he admitted privately to Allen that the photographs of Janet bore a remarkable resemblance to himself.

At the various Kerouac conferences one hears how Jack was so sensitive, compassionate and tender. Ginsberg particularly talks of his 'great heart', but his rejection of his daughter negates all this, if his constant betrayal of his friends had not already done so. Jack was cold-hearted, obdurate and callous. He took no interest in Jan's welfare, even after it had been proven that she was his child. Each month he begrudgingly sent off the cheque, but did nothing to help her off drugs or to get her off the streets, though he was fully apprised by Allen Ginsberg of the life she was leading in the Lower East Side. The ill-health caused by this life killed her when she was still young, a tragic and unnecessary end to a talented young woman. Jan Kerouac herself showed more generosity of spirit than her father ever had when she recognised that Jack was infantilised by his mother and unable to behave like an adult: he was trapped for ever as a guilt-ridden, carousing, Catholic college jock.

Jan recorded her experiences in two painfully honest autobiographical volumes of hippie life in the sixties: *Baby Driver* and *Trainsongs*. Whereas Jack always had his mother to fall back on, who telegraphed money to him whenever he needed it, Jan had no safety net. Her story of being on the road is the real thing.

In the spring of 1962, *Visions of Gerard* was accepted by Farrar Straus and Cudahy, and to Jack's pleasure he found himself once more working with Robert Giroux as his editor, who this time agreed to make no editorial changes. Jack did not expect good reviews, nor did he get any. In fact, the critics slaughtered him.

The sixties was a period of inexorable decline for Jack: his blackouts became more frequent; his DTs became more ferocious; his health declined; his hair began to fall out; and he was clearly now drinking himself to death, gulping down a quart of Cognac or whiskey a day, followed by beer chasers. He was now a confirmed anti-intellectual and refused to allow any serious discussion near him. He would holler and yell and play the clown rather than discuss literature. His sexual encounters were now almost exclusively with men. His views became openly anti-Semitic and he had taken on all his mother's racist opinions. This was the most shocking new development because, previously, apart from a few occasions when Jack had refused to go to parties in New York 'if negroes were going to be there', he had not embraced all her prejudices. He had always enjoyed Black jazz and counted among his friends the Black poets LeRoi Jones and Ted Jones. Now he sided with the most reactionary of all Southern racist organisations, the Ku-Klux Klan.

In the summer of 1962, he got his fourteen-year-old nephew Paul to help him build a cross from two-inch-by-four-inch wooden posts which he then covered with cloth. They drove to a wall which roughly divided the Black neighbourhood from the White section of Orlando. There Jack soaked the cloth in kerosene, stood the cross on the wall, and set fire to it. As his home-made fiery cross burnt, Jack danced up and down, yelling racist obscenities.[5]

Exhausted by the sweltering Florida summer, Memere decided that yet another move to New England was in order and asked John Clellon Holmes to help Jack househunt. Jack arrived in Old Saybrook on 9 September and flopped into Holmes's armchair, where he spent the next week drinking a quart of Cognac a day, listening to jazz, reading through Holmes's collection of Balzac, and talking at top speed about anything and everything that came into his head. For the last three days he remained unwashed and unshaven, slumped in his T-shirt and pyjama bottoms. The final day, John had to bring him a Cognac in bed before he could get up. He had finally managed to go on a drinking binge without leaving his chair.

Ashamed, Jack straightened up and even managed a few hours' househunting before hitting a bar at lunchtime. That evening he was back on the Cognac and decided that he wanted to go to Lowell, which he had not visited for eight years. John Holmes's wife, Shirley, finally found a taxi driver who was prepared to drive him the 150 miles for $60. He left carrying a storage jar filled with enough brandy and soda to last him through the trip. He arrived, unannounced, at GJ Apostolos's house, Jack's boyhood chum, who was now a respectable businessman with a family. When Jack tried to dance on top of the piano he was thrown out.

Jack established himself at the Sportsmen's Athletic Club where, for the next week, he performed for the locals, signing autographs, singing, talking a mile a minute, mixing Shakespeare with Sinatra, and poetry with racist and anti-Semitic snarls. He sat in the street outside the club, wearing a filthy mackintosh, swigging from a bottle, and read his poems to a crowd which eventually numbered about a hundred people, blocking the road and stopping the traffic. Calling himself the 'King of the Beatniks', he managed to make the Lowell gossip columns each day with his antics.

He presented himself to Stella Sampas, the unwed sister of his boyhood friend Sebastian, and told her he had come to marry her. She asked her brother Tony to take care of him as he was obviously barely capable of standing. Not surprisingly, Jack made lots of new friends in Lowell and he arrived in New York on 24 September in the company of one of them, Paul Bourgeois, who had convinced Jack that he was the Chief of the Four Nations of the Iroquois. Conveniently, one of the tribes was called 'Kirouac' and another 'L'Evesque', Memere's maiden name. Jack naively took the whole story on board, and it was only when he began planning a book about it that Bourgeois confessed that he had made it all up. But Jack would not listen: he insisted on taking Bourgeois with him to Orlando. Memere didn't believe a word of it but Jack put Bourgeois in the spare room and together they hit the bars. Bourgeois was a French-Canadian thief who had spent twelve years in jail. He was tough and knew how to handle himself in bars. One night Jack stepped out of line and Bourgeois threw him through the window. When Jack got up the next day, Bourgeois was gone. Memere had put him on the train back north.

Jack's health deteriorated further and Memere decided to move to Long Island again where he seemed happier. It was Memere who made all the decisions now and together they moved back to Northport, to a luxury house at 7 Judy Ann Court, off Oak Street, with two bathrooms, a fireplace, and an enclosed garden with mature trees. They arrived on Christmas Eve 1962 in the snow, carrying their cats in carry cages.

The cost of the house shocked Jack, prompting him to try for a bestseller. In February 1963, Jack asked his editor how he could be a bestselling author like John Le Carré and was told he needed to write about something sensational. 'How about a murder?' asked Jack. He now intended to fill in the last remaining gap in the Legend of Duluoz, the period covered in fictional form in *The Town and The City*, and, incidentally, covering the Kammerer murder.

Jack was by no means broke. In a letter to Philip Whalen that February Jack said his only worry about money was 'the promise I made in my dying father's house, to take care of his wife, his wife not mine. HIS wife, not MINE, to take care of her for HIM, my father in Heaven . . .'

Jack was becoming more and more defensive about his relationship with his mother. He told his friend, the Japanese-American painter Matsumi, about an occasion when his mother had tried to have sex with him. Matsumi suggested that he probably should have done it, and that it might have made him feel better, but his reply outraged Jack, who smashed some of Matsumi's bowls and threatened to kill him. Jack tried to explain his relationship with her to the press, telling Van Duncan at *Newsday*:

> I've always been 'settled with my mother' who supported me by working in the shoe factories while I wrote most of my books years ago. She's my friend as well as my mother. When I go on the road I always have a quiet clean home to come back to, and to work in, which probably accounts for the fact that I've published twelve books in the last six years.[6]

He neglected to say that most of them were written long before that. Jack's mother was the one constant in his life, the only fixed point. As a child, when they moved home every two or three years, she was always there. Jack never had a place of his own without her. Home was with Mother. Lou Reed once asked Bill Burroughs what had happened to make Kerouac finish up sitting in front of the television set, drinking beer with his mother. Bill told him:

> He didn't change that much, Lou. He was always like that. First there was a young guy sitting in front of television in a T-shirt drinking beer with his mother, then there was an older fatter person sitting in front of television in a T-shirt drinking beer with his mother.[7]

It was surely Jack's great physical strength that enabled him to survive so long. His years as an athlete and football player stood him in good stead and enabled him to take the daily punishment he meted out to his body. DTs, blackouts, tiredness dogged him. Sometimes he would disappear for days and be found sleeping in the woods where he had passed out. He was no longer capable of doing much writing and even an article now took him weeks. He was to survive another six years, during which time his drinking increased and his health deteriorated. Doctors warned him that he was killing himself but he did not heed their advice.

Allen and Peter returned to America in December 1963, and went to Northport to see him. Memere would not let them into the house, and Jack acceded. He had written to Allen in Japan, requesting him to cut his hair and shave off his beard before visiting him, neither of which Allen was prepared to do.

In November 1964, Jack met Neal Cassady for the last time. Neal had arrived in New York City with Ken Kesey and the Merry Pranksters, driving the famous psychedelic bus. He wanted Kesey to meet Jack, to join together the two halves of his life. Allen Ginsberg gave him the address and Neal drove out to Northport to get him and bring him to the big apartment on Park Avenue where they were all staying. It was not a happy meeting. The Pranksters had spread a large American flag across the settee in his honour, but Jack carefully folded it up before sitting down as an object lesson on how to show respect for the flag. Jack was withdrawn and silent; he refused offers of pot and Acid, and contented himself with slugging from the bottle he brought with him. Novelist Robert Stone, author of *Dog Soldiers* (1974), described the meeting:

> Kerouac had reached the stage of being very alcoholic and embittered – boy, he hated us. He was jealous that Ken Kesey had grabbed Neal as a bus driver. These people were just a bunch of California hippies. He did not see us as angels, seraphs, and all the terrific things that he saw his own generation as. It's true, in a way we were the opposite – we were a lot healthier and California-like; we were just not a New York number. There was a lot of the hayseed, cowboy element in Kesey that clashed with the Eighth Street commando – and East/West Coast cultural clash of ages. Kerouac was eloquent on what jerk-abouts we were.[8]

In 1965 Jack wrote *Satori in Paris*. This is a piece of travel writing, originally serialised over three issues of *Evergreen Review* before being published in book form. It is a lamentably poor piece of writing, obviously written in an alcoholic haze. It was described by Jack as 'Really the first book I wrote with drink at my side – Cognac and malt liquor'.[9] In it Kerouac flies to France from Florida, intending to trace his genealogy, first in Paris, then Brittany, London and Cornwall, but instead he gets hopelessly drunk. After five days he was homesick and the book is a drunken account of being thrown out of libraries and bars for obnoxious behaviour. It is a catalogue of disasters. He saw nothing of Paris but the inside of bars, beginning the day with beer before his morning coffee and ending it trying to pick up whores. He was so busy drinking at the airport that he missed the plane to Brest and a day or two later missed his train back to Paris for the same reason. Even while in Brittany, he made no effort to see the sights or even to contact members of his supposed family. When he found he could not fly direct from Brittany to London, he returned to Paris and went straight back to Florida, having accomplished nothing. There was no satori; nothing was revealed at all. The boyish buoyancy is gone, replaced by the kind of stumble-bum monologue, complete with pointless digressions, with which he enthralled his drinking partners in Lowell and Saint Petersburg, Florida, during the last years of his life. After one of his digressions, he states quite clearly, 'But I'm not a Buddhist, I'm a Catholic,' finally setting the public record straight.

By 1966, Kerouac's contact with his old friends was limited almost entirely to phone calls. Allen Ginsberg:

> Late at night, toward the end of the sixties, most of our communication was in the form of telephone calls, usually in the middle of the night. Sometimes 2 or 3 a.m. He would be alone, home, lonesome, drinking, and finally get up the spirit to pick up the phone to make long long-distance calls to his friends.

He telephoned John Clellon Holmes, Lucien Carr, Robert Frank or, when he felt lonely and regretted his lack of a wife, he would call long-distance to Carolyn Cassady. He would call her drunk, at 2 a.m. California time. Sometimes she would talk about old times, but often she would bury her head under the pillow while the phone rang and rang.[10]

Allen Ginsberg, with his years of experience with his disturbed mother and Peter Orlovsky's family, would always take Jack's calls and not only tolerated his rudeness but, in his lifelong belief that his friend was a genius, managed to find some value in Jack's abuse:

> Usually the calls were mockingly abusive, insulting. He'd constantly rag me for being a city intellectual Jew, make fun of my eyeglasses, ask me to suck his cock on the telephone. The older he got, the more gross in alcohol, the more insistent he was that I get down and suck his cock. The more he stank, the more fat, the more obese, the more drunken, the more insistent he was.
>
> In the phone calls, along with insults, were very intelligent trenchant remarks always. Finally I realised he was toying,

playing, trying to see if he could get a rise out of me, trying to see if he could get me angry. Usually he did, but at one point I realised that this was almost like a Zen Master's tactics for trying to break through my sense of self-importance. And so finally I said, 'Kerouac, if you don't shut up, I'll call your mother on the phone and tell her that her cunt is full of shit.' He said, 'You will?' And I said, 'Yes, bring her over to the phone.' Then he started laughing. And, from then on, the conversation was very serious about Rimbaud and literature. So this was a seemingly vicious but playful mask. He was capable of a kind of bone-deep humour, but as I remember it, by hindsight, despite my irritation at the time, it was always a lesson such as I learned from another great drinker, the Tibetan Lama Chogyam Trungpa.

There is a trenchancy in that alcoholic insight that sometimes is useful and in the hands or mouths of someone like Kerouac for me was always a teaching rather than pure insult. What that kind of bitterness or black humour did to him is nothing I can account for, and obviously it killed him. But on the other hand there was always an intelligence there that was really sublime, actually, as I saw it. When I began insulting his mother, he began to ease off and take it easy and start talking straight. But, until I was willing to counter his insult with a direct insult to him, he would pursue it and pursue it. I think that is characteristic of many drinkers.[11]

Ginsberg still made the effort to see Jack on his own turf now that he was too far gone as an alcoholic to be allowed into the city by himself. Allen:

There were a few times when I and other friends wanted to come see him in mid-sixties and late sixties – once with the poet John Weiners who had just come out of a mental hospital. We called ahead by phone every half-hour to Cape Cod where he was living and he kept encouraging us to come because I hadn't seen him for a year. But, when we got there, all the lights in the house were out and he wouldn't answer the door. Later, he said it was because his mother refused to admit anybody and so Kerouac went and hid in the backyard, frightened among the garbage bins, afraid to appear at the door and turn us away, but trapped between his mother's obsessions and his own openness. He actually did want to see us, but was afraid of his mother and what he said to me later was: 'My mother is as crazy as your mother was, except I'm not going to throw her to the dogs of eternity like you threw yours.' So he was guilt-bound to stay with her and take care of her, participate and empathise with her and exercise enormous generosity of temperament which in some respect was suicidal for him.

Jack's Italian publishers, Arnoldo Montadori, were about to publish their 500th book, and decided to give the honour to a translation of Jack's *Big Sur*. Jack was sent $1,000 to visit Italy and take part in the celebrations. On the plane he acted the redneck ugly American by making passes at the air hostess and, when one of the other passengers told him 'Don't make an ass of yourself', he reacted by drinking even more heavily. He staggered off the plane so drunk that he lost his suitcase. He was taken to his hotel where someone gave him a shot of morphine to try to calm him down. In his paranoia he thought he was being given poison and frantically telephoned Fernanda Pivano, his Italian translator, and said he wanted to go home – he would pay back the $1,000, he just wanted to get back to America.[12] The visit was a nightmare. Fernanda Pivano:

> I had to interview him for the television. He tried to recuperate some energy and so he was very arrogant. He didn't answer the questions. It was very difficult. Then he went to the press conference and didn't say a word and then he went to a party and spent the evening just drinking without speaking with anyone. The publisher was very resentful.

In Rome the television crew made another attempt at an interview but it was no use. Fernanda: 'He was there on the stage under a flood of spotlights, very sad, very desperate, defeated, completely defeated.' It was a poignant scene: Jack in his scuffed work shoes and lumberjack plaid shirt, surrounded by the fashionable Italian literary critics, well-dressed in their smart grey suits. Fernanda: 'They were looking at him like a wounded lion.' Worse was yet to come. At a nightclub afterwards he tried to make a pass at a girl but she didn't know who he was and wanted nothing to do with him because he was so drunk. Smart Italian nightclubs were a world that Jack and the other Beats knew nothing of.

Back at the hotel, Jack spoke for two hours with Fernanda Pivano on the telephone, talking about his mother who had been paralysed by a stroke the day before he left. He didn't know what to do with her. He had not yet solved the problem of how to look after her and kept repeating: 'I came because I had to pay the rent for my mother's house.'

The next day he went to Naples but was so befuddled that he couldn't even walk and had to be supported on either side. At a public meeting in southern Italy, he defended the American war in Vietnam and was jeered off stage by the young audience. Fernanda: 'He died three years later. He was still very handsome but somehow swollen in his face, but his eyes were still beautiful, his voice was still beautiful.'

Jack and his mother were living in Hyannis when her stroke occurred. Jack was obviously incapable of looking after her so, in a marriage of convenience, he asked Stella Sampas to marry him and come to act as housekeeper. They had known each other since high school. Stella had never married and presumably thought that this was better than the life she was presently leading. They were married in the Hyannis Ridgewood area of Cape Cod in November 1966 by Judge Philip Boudreau. Jack's mother was a witness. While Stella phoned her friends and family in Lowell, Jack sat in his study and sipped Johnny Walker Red. No family and no friends were present and the only other person there, apart from Town Hall officials, was Frank Falacci, a reporter from the *Boston Herald*.

In January 1967, they moved to 271 Sanders Avenue, out near the Mount Pleasant Golf Club, the most fashionable and expensive part of Lowell. Nick Sampas, Stella's brother, found the house for them. Nick had a bar called The Three Copper Men which quickly became Jack's favourite hang-out. Jack now became a part of the Sampas family. When he was invited to do an interview, in French, with Radio Canada in Montreal, it was Nick who drove him there. They stopped to pick up a bottle of Scotch en route, then another, and were stopped near Montreal by a trooper. Jack, speaking in French, managed to talk his way out of it. Nick claimed that they went to fifteen jazz clubs in one night while they were there.

During the two years he lived in Lowell, Jack had his phone taken out because he spent too much money making long-distance calls while drunk, so even this contact with his old friends ceased. As he didn't have a car and he didn't drive, he would send new friends like Joe Chaput postcards to say he wanted to go out for an evening and they would come by and pick him up. They would usually drive to somewhere away from Lowell and its bars, to a club or restaurant, and get home at 3 or 4 a.m. when Jack would play his friends jazz records by Parker, Young, Ellington, staying up through the night. In the morning he would cook them all breakfast.

In 1967 Kerouac wrote his last full-length book, *Vanity of Duluoz*, subtitled 'An Adventurous Education, 1935–46'. He addressed it to his wife, just as he had done with *On the Road*. Kerouac:

> Finally I decided in my tired middle age to slow down and did *Vanity of Duluoz* in a more moderate style so that, having been so esoteric all these years, some earlier readers would come back and see what ten years had done to my life and thinking . . . which is after all the only thing I've got to offer, the true story of what I saw and how I saw it.[13]

This was the only period left to write about. He had covered it in *The Town and the City*, but he did not regard that book as a proper part of the 'Duluoz Legend' and wanted to rewrite it in a non-fictional form. There was also the commercial consideration of finally writing about the Kammerer murder which, up until then, Lucien Carr and Allen Ginsberg had always managed to dissuade him from doing. It would have been a very different book had he written it a decade earlier for then it would have been a long romantic myth of his colourful past. The title tells the whole story: *Vanity of Duluoz* is all about his vanity, a look at his youth from beyond the grave. Allen Ginsberg gave a very good description of it:

> Everybody's beauty was a vanity. Everybody's tolerance was egotism. So it's a late disillusioned version and a very precious one for that, because it's a view of youth seen from the advantage of illness and age and total realism, no longer clinging to the favourite images and archetypes and loves of youth. It's really washed out of that. You rarely get a view of youth from old age which is still tender, but judged accurately on the basis of experience.

Once you get past Jack's school grades and sports results, the book is easily his most accessible work and is the source of most people's received knowledge of the early days of the Beat Generation. It embodies the story of Edie Parker, of meeting Lucien Carr, Allen Ginsberg, Bill Burroughs and Huncke. It retells the well-known anecdotes of the 115th Street commune and, of course, the tragic story of the death of Kammerer. The book ends with the slow painful death of his father, which was also the end of Kerouac's youth.

When Ted Berrigan, Aram Saroyan and Duncan McNaughton arrived at Kerouac's house in Lowell to interview him for *Paris Review*, Jack welcomed them in, pleased to finally be afforded recognition by the magazine that had interviewed the likes of Celine, Ezra Pound, Eliot, Huxley and Graham Greene. But, before they could get through the door, Stella, described by Berrigan as 'a very determined woman', seized Jack from behind and demanded that they leave at once. Berrigan sweet-talked her into permitting them to stay for twenty minutes, provided there was no drinking.

Jack explained his right-wing political stance and told them: 'I'm pro-American and the radical political involvements seem to tend elsewhere . . . The country gave my Canadian family a good break, more or less, and we see no reason to demean said country.'[14] He also railed against the experiments taking place in the arts as the sixties got under way:

I'm bored with the new avant-garde and the skyrocketing sensationalism . . . I like to hang around with non-intellectuals, as you might call them, and not have my mind proselytised, ad infinitum . . . The Beat group dispersed in the early sixties, all went their own way, and this is my way: home life, as in the beginning, with a little toot once in a while in local bars.[15]

Allen Ginsberg:

As Jack grew older, in despair, and lacking the means to calm his mind and let go of the suffering, he tended more and more to grasp at the cross. And so, in his later years, he made many paintings of the cross, of cardinals, popes, of Christ crucified, or Mary: seeing himself on the cross, and finally conceiving of himself as being crucified. He was undergoing such crucifixion in his mortification of his body as he drank. Nonetheless, he did have this quality of negative capability, the ability to hold opposite ideas in his mind without 'an irritable reaching out after fact and reason' which John Keats proposed as the true mind of the Shakespearean poet.[16]

One example of this was his attitude to so-called 'draft-dodgers'. Though he told Ginsberg and Peter Orlovsky that he would like 'to shoot anti-war protesters down from the trees' he did not hold the usual right-wing views about those who avoided the draft, perhaps because he remembered his own unfortunate dealings with the military. When young Paul Jarvis was due to be called up, he searched out Kerouac, who knew his father, to ask his advice. He found Jack at the Copper Kettle Bar and poured his heart out to him about his reluctance to go to Vietnam. Kerouac took him home and woke up Memere at 3 a.m. to meet him, saying, 'This is Paul, he's a real honey lamb.' Memere didn't seem to mind being woken up. Jack encouraged him to follow his heart and avoid the draft, which he did.

In November 1967, Jan Kerouac, then aged fifteen and pregnant, showed up in Lowell with her boyfriend, John Lash. They were on their way to Mexico and thought they might be away for some time. Though Jack paid her the $52 a month in child support she did not even know his address. She telephoned all the Kerouacs in the Lowell phone book and soon found herself surrounded by relatives, all astonished to find that Jack had a daughter. Jan looked exactly like him: the same deep-blue eyes, thick black hair, the full lower lip. They trooped around to Sanders Avenue and burst in.

Jack was sitting in his rocking chair wearing an old blue plaid shirt, nursing a bottle of Johnny Walker whiskey, watching *Beverly Hillbillies* on television. Her image of him was of a chubby baby, rocking in his crib, sucking on his bottle. Jack was acutely embarrassed to find her in his house, surrounded by his relatives, who were all demanding to know why they had not met her before. He yelled for someone to turn the television off, even though he was the one sitting next to it, and shooed the relatives out of the house. When Jack found out that her boyfriend was waiting outside he roused himself from his chair and went to fetch him. 'Ahh Genghis Khan, eh?' he commented, seeing John's hair tied up in an Oriental topknot.

Jack invited her to sit next to him on the settee and Jan asked to see his hands. Her mother had always told her that she had Jack's hands. She thought they were the same. Jack demurred. He took her over to the wall and proudly showed her a portrait he had done of Pope Paul VI in his papal regalia which he claimed he had painted from a 'vision' he'd had while the Pope was still Cardinal Giovanni Montini. Also on display was a portrait of his brother Gerard.

John told Jack that they were on their way to Mexico to live. Jack looked at Jan and told her, 'Yeah, go to Mexico an' write a book. You can use my name.' After they had been talking for a few minutes, Memere began stirring in her wheelchair and called out, 'Is Caroline there?' and, 'Foreigners! All foreigners!' Stella then asked them to leave, saying that they were upsetting the old woman. Jan wrote in *Baby Driver*: 'So we left, and I felt cheated out of time. I had an idea that my father would have loosened up if I continued to talk to him . . .'

There was another paternity claim made on Jack the next year, when he was invited to appear on *The William Buckley Show*. Jack loved Buckley for his right-wing politics, his pretentious fluency with language, his devout Roman Catholicism and the fact that they had been at Columbia University together. In the elevator at the television station was another of Buckley's guests, the poet, musician and anti-war activist Ed Sanders. Ed recognised Jack and said, 'Hello, Dad!' Jack turned and snarled, 'I'm not your father, you son of a bitch.' Joe Chaput, who was acting as Jack's minder, had to get between them.

During the show, Jack lolled in his chair and explained that he and his mother had always voted Republican, while Buckley smirked at him with ill-disguised disdain. The most interesting incident was the exchange between Jack and Ed Sanders:

Jack: 'You make yourself famous by protest.'
Ed: 'Who does?'
Jack: 'You.'
Ed: 'Not me. I make myself famous by singing smut.'[17]
Jack: 'I make myself famous by writing songs and lyrics about the beauty of the things I did, and ugliness, too. You made yourself famous by saying, "Down with this, down with that. Throw eggs at this, throw eggs at that." I cannot use your abuse. You may have it back.'[18]
Ed: 'OK.'

But, later in the show, Jack leant over to Ed and joked with him, telling him he had recently been arrested 'for decay'. Allen Ginsberg had accompanied Jack to the studio, and was sitting in the audience looking worried. Jack made a point of telling Buckley not to associate Ginsberg's name with his own. During the commercial break, the producer tried to substitute Allen for Jack, but Allen refused. It was the last time Allen saw Kerouac alive.

In order to pay for yet another move to Florida, Jack sold his correspondence with Allen Ginsberg to Columbia University's Butler Library, making enough money to buy a house in Saint Petersburg for Stella, himself and Memere. He bought a large, hurricane-proof, modern, Spanish-style villa with a glassed-in porch and a lawn. Trees and tropical plants grew in the yard, which was fenced in to keep sightseers away.

Away from his Sampas-family minders, Jack soon got himself into trouble. In September 1969, he foolishly took a retired Swedish Air Force Lieutenant to a Black bar downtown and got into a fight with the house band. At the hospital he was given four stitches over his eye before the police arrested him for drunkenness. He wrote to Edie Parker that he couldn't come and visit her in Detroit because he had two black eyes, bruised arms and a twisted knee.[19] Instead, he invited her to Florida, saying that Stella would not like it but she should come anyway. But 'no moochy moochy'. She did not visit but they continued to telephone and correspond with each other until his death. Eight days before he died he wrote to her, 'You'll Be Okay.'

At 11 a.m. on 21 October 1969, Jack began throwing up blood while watching *Galloping Gourmet* on TV, after opening a can of Falstaff beer. His liver could take no more. Jack died an hour or so later at Saint Anthony's Hospital.

The funeral Mass was celebrated by Father 'Spike' Morissette, the man who encouraged the teenage Jack to become a writer. It was held at Paroisse Saint Jean-Baptiste Church on Merrimack Street, Lowell, at 11 a.m. on Friday 24 October 1969. It was the church where Jack worshipped as a boy and where he had realised that 'Beat' meant 'Beatific'. Jack was buried in grave 1, lot 76, section 96 of the Edson Cemetery on Gorham Street, Lowell, Massachusetts.

Allen Ginsberg: 'So he drank himself to death. Which is only another way of living, of handling the pain and foolishness of knowing that it's all a dream, a great, baffling, silly emptiness, after all.'[20]

Postscript

I n June 1988 the City of Lowell dedicated the Jack Kerouac Commemorative, a $100,000 granite monument occupying a one-acre park on the Eastern Canal, once the site of a mill. It is a sad state of affairs that Kerouac, who loved the language of Shakespeare, should be honoured with such a piece of bad grammar. A commemorative what? 'Commemorative' is an adjective, not a noun. There was more suspect language at the dedication ceremony when Jack himself was described by Mayor Richard Howe as: 'a man who has become a cultural resource'. Mayor Howe proclaimed 25 June as Jack Kerouac Day in Lowell and Lowell City manager James Campbell informed the assembled crowd that the park was a part of a $60,000,000 development project for downtown Lowell.

This unlikely event came about through the intervention of Allen Ginsberg. Early in 1985, when Allen returned to New York after teaching in China, he told Lowell resident Brian Foye: 'In China, they know Lowell because they know Kerouac. Most people know there's nothing in the city celebrating him. What you should do is put a plaque on one of his old houses. Or maybe a small statue near the river.' Allen was thinking along the lines of the blue commemorative plaques on historic buildings in London.

Allen agreed to do a benefit reading in Lowell to raise money for such a scheme. Brian Foye, together with Roger Brunelle and Reginald Ouelette – both of the same French-Canadian background as Jack – formed the Corporation for the Celebration of Jack Kerouac in Lowell. Allen gave his reading and the sell-out crowd of 400 drew the attention of the Lowell Preservation Commission.

The computer industry had brought a new wealth to the city, attracting many new young professionals who were active in the Lowell Historic Preservation Commission. The idea quickly mushroomed out of Brian Foye's control and soon became part of a multi-million-dollar revamping of the entire historic city centre. The turning point came at a meeting of the Lowell City Council on 30 December 1986, when the idea of a memorial was first put to the vote. The ex-mayor, Brendon Fleming, was opposed to the idea. 'I'm not saying anything about his writing, but what we would be doing is glorifying his lifestyle. I'm worried about a role model for our kids.' But Councilman Ray Rourke rejoined, 'The man has been gone for a number of years now. Let God be the judge of his human frailties.' The council voted for the monument by seven votes to one.

It was decided to raze the old Morton warehouse on the Eastern Canal, described by Kerouac as 'the great grey warehouse of eternity', to create the new $3,500,000 Eastern Canal Park, the first urban national park dedicated to preserving the history of the Industrial Revolution. The Hilton Hotel had wanted the park directly across from their front entrance, but thankfully that plan was averted.

The memorial itself consists of eight three-sided stone pillars, like the monolith in Kubrick's *2001*, though Texan sculptor Ben Woitena claims that his inspiration was Stonehenge. These are made from polished, red South Dakota granite, engraved in Minnesota with passages from Kerouac's books and arranged to make a mandala. Their triangular cross section creates a circle within a square within a diamond, but gives the impression more of a war memorial than anything else. The City Council stipulated that the opening paragraphs from Kerouac's Lowell books be used: *The Town and the City*, *Doctor Sax*, *Visions of Gerard*, *Maggie Cassidy* and *Vanity of Duluoz*. The last paragraph from *On the Road* is there, a biographical passage from *Lonesome Traveller* and a poem from *Mexico City Blues*.

The ex-mayor was not the only one who objected to the idea. The critic Norman Podhoretz had long waged a personal war against the Beats and was responsible for some of the most damning articles on them in the late fifties. Thirty years later, Podhoretz remained unrelenting in his criticism. Writing in what Ginsberg called his 'chief sourpuss'[1] mode, Podhoretz fulminated against the idea of a memorial. 'A Strange Honour for a False Prophet' ran the headline of his syndicated column in the *New York Post*,[2] whereas the *Washington Post* pulled the line 'Kerouac and Ginsberg once played a part in ruining a great many young people' as a sub-head.[3] Podhoretz was amazed by the Lowell City Council decision to dedicate a new park to the memory of Kerouac: 'To Kerouac, the only people in America who could be considered really alive were those outside the system – bums, thieves, whores, junkies and anyone

lucky enough to possess a dark skin. Such people he celebrated . . .'
This is, of course, manifestly untrue. Kerouac's books are filled with
celebrations of 'ordinary people', of truck drivers, railroad men,
waitresses in lonely highway diners, shop clerks and woodsmen.

It was Jack's rejection of the conformist, middle-class suburban
America that Podhoretz hated. Podhoretz blustered:

Within a very short time, the values celebrated by Kerouac,
Ginsberg and all the other Beat writers had established
themselves as the orthodox dogmas of what came to be known
as the 'counterculture'. Dropping out, hitting the road, taking
drugs, hopping from bed to bed with partners of either sex or
both – all in the name of liberation from the death-dealing
embrace of middle-class conventions – came to be as 'in' among
the middle-class young of the 60s as early marriage and the
pursuit of career had been 10 years before. This, then, is what
the City of Lowell is inescapably honouring in building a
monument to Kerouac.

On dedication day there was a tour bus to take visitors to all nine
houses where the Kerouacs lived and the tourist office produced a
helpful brochure giving directions to Kerouac's grave, inviting the
visitor to make a rubbing of the stone like the brass-rubbings of the
tombs of saints. Allen Ginsberg, Robert Creeley, Lawrence
Ferlinghetti and Michael McClure gave a poetry reading, and
Kerouac biographers Regina Weinreich, Ann Charters, Gerald
Nicosia and John Tytell attended a panel discussion. Pointedly not
invited to the ceremony were Jack's daughter, his ex-wife Edie Parker
Kerouac, and Joyce Johnson, who lived with him and cared for him
through the first hectic days of the fame brought about the
publication of *On the Road*. Eventually Brad Parker at the Lowell
Corporation for the Humanities arranged for Jan Kerouac to get to
Lowell from New Orleans, but Edie Parker and Joyce Johnson had to
pay their own way. None of them were invited to contribute to the
discussions and celebrations. Already the Kerouac camp was divided,
with the Lowell faction firmly in control.

How would Kerouac have felt about it? Father 'Spike' Morissette
writing in 1979 quoted Jack as complaining, 'After all I did for this
goddamn town, the citizens should have erected a statue in my
honour. It should be right in front of City Hall in place of "Winged
Victory", which doesn't mean a thing.' Jack's feelings about Lowell
were mixed; he clearly had a sentimental attachment to his home

town, but he spent his life trying to escape from it. A dream about Lowell, printed in *Book of Dreams*, shows his ambivalence. In the dream his Canuck landlord has just finished some repair work and is leaving him a form that he is to deliver downtown:

> they begin dreary Lowell street instructions – the prodigal returner – I experience momentary despair and bleakness of being back and subject to 'laws of Lowell' again ... bleak wintry city streets of Lowell Canada – not a happy or even interesting dream.[4]

Lowell was not the only city to honour him. On 25 January 1988, the tiny stretch of Adler Alley, running between City Lights Bookstore and the Vesuvio Bar, was renamed Jack Kerouac Street, as part of the implementation of a proposal by Lawrence Ferlinghetti to rename twelve San Francisco streets to venerate authors and artists associated with the city. Other new streets included Bob Kaufman Street, Kenneth Rexroth Place, Isadora Duncan Lane, William Saroyan Place and Jack London Street. Jack's back alley appropriately leads to a bar.

According to an article published in the London *Sunday Times*,[5] the day before he died Kerouac wrote to his nephew Paul Blake, Nin's son, telling him that he was planning to divorce Stella or have her marriage to him annulled. He explained that he had changed his will to leave everything to Memere, and in the event of her death, to Paul. Kerouac vowed his estate should go to a direct descendant or a descendant of his sister Carolyn or of Paul's mother. Kerouac was quite clear that he did not wish to leave anything to his wife's family. His daughter Jan was not mentioned.

When Memere died in 1973, she appeared to reverse Jack's wishes by naming Stella Kerouac as her sole heir. Matters were further complicated by Stella Kerouac leaving her assets to her family when she died; so, notwithstanding Jack's wishes, Kerouac's estate went to the very individuals Jack seemed to be trying to guard it from. In 1994 Jan Kerouac contested Gabrielle's original will, alleging that it was a fake. A complex lawsuit followed which is still ongoing.

Jack had always meticulously filed his papers and annotated his correspondence with the obvious intention of providing a complete archive for future scholars. Jan Kerouac continued her fight to gain control of the estate, believing that the collection should go to a research institution.

Jan's death, on 6 June 1996 in Albuquerque, New Mexico, only seems to have made matters worse. She named Kerouac biographer Gerard Nicosia her literary executor and her long time boyfriend John Lash her general executor, but the two of them disagreed on what approach they should have to the Jack Kerouac Estate. This dispute, which is ongoing at the time of this writing, split the community of Kerouac scholars into several warring factions.[6] Hopefully, when Kerouac's archives are finally ensconced in a university rare book department, the situation will be defused and the various factions will be able to make peace again and return to the original focus of the arguments: Kerouac's writing.

So, apart from an unseemly squabble over his estate, which is now valued at many millions, what did Kerouac leave behind? To quote William Burroughs: 'Kerouac and I are not real at all. The only real thing about a writer is what he has written, and not his so-called life. "And we will all die and the stars will go out, one after another." '[7]

Kerouac left a substantial body of work which will eventually find its place in the American literary canon. He is probably not as good a writer as his many fans would like to think, nor are his books anywhere near as bad as his numerous detractors would have the world believe. He is destined to remain known mainly for his association with the Beat Generation rather than for his own work. This is already how he appears in many memoirs and essays, including some published before his death, such as Alan Watts's autobiography *In My Own Way* (1960), which says:

> Jack Kerouac, Lawrence Ferlinghetti, and especially Gary Snyder and Allen Ginsberg were now among our friends. Jack – a second Thomas Wolfe – was a warm and affectionate dog who eventually succumbed to the bottle, but the others were more serious artists and, speaking at least of Gary and Allen, more disciplined yogis.

Almost forty years later the wider literary world has more or less reached the same conclusion as Watts. Kerouac is now regarded as a serious writer, though perhaps not the best of the Beat writers. *On the Road*, at least, is regarded as a classic, but much of Jack's work is still seen as marginal and his dream of a grand set of Duluoz Legend volumes seems as far away as ever. Jack wrote:

> My work comprises one vast book like Proust's except that my remembrances are written on the run instead of afterwards in a

sick bed. Because of the objections of my early publishers I was not allowed to use the same personae names in each work. *On the Road*, *The Subterraneans*, *The Dharma Bums*, *Doctor Sax* and the others including this book *Big Sur* are just chapters in the whole work which I call the Duluoz Legend. In my old age I intend to collect all my work and re-insert my pantheon of uniform names, leave the whole long shelf full of books there, and die happy. The whole thing forms one enormous comedy, seen through the eyes of poor Ti Jean (me), otherwise known as Jack Duluoz, the world of raging action and folly and also of gentle sweetness seen through the keyhole of his eye.[8]

The harmonisation of proper names would still create a very uneven series. Unlike Proust, Kerouac uses radically different styles in each book and not all of his books qualify for inclusion. *The Town and the City* was dismissed by Kerouac himself as fiction and was essentially rewritten as *Vanity of Duluoz*. Though the central relationship of *The Subterraneans* is an authentic memoir, its entire location was changed from New York to San Francisco, which denies it a place in the legend, unless, of course, the original text is published. The main character in *Pic* is entirely fictional and much of *Doctor Sax* is a reworking of old Shadow stories and childhood fantasies. *Visions of Gerard* was essentially written by Kerouac's mother, with Jack making up dialogue to fit the stories, so this should not be included. The 'Legend' then consists of *Maggie Cassidy*, *Vanity of Duluoz*, *On the Road*, parts of *Visions of Cody*, *The Dharma Bums*, *Tristessa*, *Desolation Angels*, the relevant pieces of *Lonesome Traveller*, parts of *Book of Dreams*, *Big Sur* and *Satori in Paris*. They do not fit together easily.

We have to determine Jack's importance by other means. His articulation of mood and disposition was exceptional: he was able to describe very precise variations in temperament, to give form to the vaguest of feelings. This came from his acute self-consciousness. Like Narcissus he was a man constantly examining his own reflection. Kerouac never forgot himself: he watched himself see things, he watched himself experience things. Other people become involved in activities, act unconsciously, but Jack only experienced his own consciousness of these activities. Everything was seen through this consciousness, at a remove, smaller, less involved, but tightly focused, as if seen through a magnifying lens. Because of this, his experiences seemed to him to be more intense than those of other people.

His view of life stemmed from his earliest feeling of alienation: that his brother Gerard was loved and he was not. At some point there must have been a sudden awareness of himself as a separate entity from the family, an individual, an 'other'. Jack always saw himself as different from other people, never part of the mass, out of reach of their feelings. Jean-Paul Sartre discussed this self-conscious remove from other people when writing about Baudelaire, who shared this same self-consciousness and was even more fixated upon his mother than was Kerouac. Sartre described this assertion of 'otherness' as a gesture of defiance, as a defence mechanism which in the child takes the form of pure self-consciousness:

> It is an heroic, and aggressive choice of the abstract, a desperate stripping of oneself, at once an act of renunciation and affirmation. It has a name and its name is pride. It is a stoic pride . . . This form of pride is as unhappy as it is pure because it revolves in the void and feeds upon itself. It is always unsatisfied, always exasperated and exhausts itself in the very act of asserting itself. It is founded on nothing; it is entirely in the air because the sense of being different, which creates it, is an empty concept which is universal. Yet the child wants to enjoy his sense of being different from other people; he wants to *feel* that he is different from his brother . . .[9]

Sartre describes how the child watches and examines his desires and his anger, that which he enjoys and that which makes him sad, in the hope of discovering the secret of his own nature. It is through this undivided attention to his moods that he develops a permanent self-fixation.

Because Jack was so aware of his feelings, he felt a compelling desire to express them. In the early forties he and Allen Ginsberg attempted a complete revelation of feelings and emotions, a total communication of being, something which became the basis of the Beat Generation ideal of confessional writing. Jack attempted the same thing with Neal Cassady, trying to pinpoint the origins in memory or fantasy of each thought and change of emotion, exploring every level of consciousness. All of this Kerouac recorded in his notebooks and word portraits, introducing a level of candour previously unknown in modern literature, and written at a time when 'real men' were strong silent types who didn't cry or even say very much. A German friend of mine recalled that when he first read *On the Road* he was shocked and revolted at the idea of Moriarty and Sal telling each other their personal feelings, consciously trying to communicate completely with each other, to tell everything, no matter how embarrassing or personal. This was something completely unknown among his family and friends. In this, Kerouac helped usher in the sixties ideas of openness, frankness, total honesty, of 'Letting it all hang out', erasing much of the formality and stiffness which had previously inhibited intimacy between people.

Kerouac introduced the same informality in his subject matter, sweeping away conventions of what could and what could not be written about. His subject matter was literally everything that he experienced: 'What I have written so far ... has been what I saw with my own eyes ... I'm writing about what actually happened ... I just write about what happened. In life there is no plot ... You just take a spate of time.'[10]

Hanif Kureishi, for instance, was inspired by *On the Road*:

The book's grammar was loose, the structure slung-together and repetitive, the plot nonexistent. But it contained no modernistic devices and the style was intimate, as if secrets were being told to friends. Unlike a book by Robbe-Grillet you could actually read it. With its unfastidious relish for life, *On the Road* was pop writing at its best. It changed the way I saw the world, making me yearn for fresh experience and helping me understand that no subjects were especially 'literary'. The possibilities of fiction were all around, whether sex, drugs, music or hitchhiking.[11]

Kerouac helped pave the way for a new freedom in writing and was part of a great wave of ground-breakers, including Henry Miller, Jean Genet, William Burroughs, Alexander Trocchi, Vladimir Nabokov, who all showed that anything can be the subject of a book and that it can be written in any style you choose. Without these writers, John Rechy's *City of Night*, Hubert Selby Jr's *Last Exit to Brooklyn*, and Jan Cremer's *I Jan Cremer* could not have been written. Kerouac's most obvious impact was on the 'New Journalism' of Tom Wolfe and books such as Michael Herr's *Dispatches*, Norman Mailer's *Armies of the Night* and, of course, Hunter S Thompson's 'Gonzo' journalism. This tangent later developed into the Lester Bangs school of rock writing, encountered weekly and monthly in the music press but also found in Albert Goldman's *Elvis*, and Marlon Brando's confessional autobiography *Songs My Mother Taught Me*. A book like *Please Kill Me*, Legs

McNeil and Gillian McCain's oral history of punk, takes the tape-recorded section of *Visions of Cody* to the limit of personal revelation.

Jack's other great bid for freedom was less successful. Spontaneous prose was not a new invention and was normally used for rapidly written pulps and romance novels. There is nothing inherently artistic or expressive about not correcting one's prose. Ian Fleming, describing how he wrote the James Bond 007 books, said, 'I never correct anything and I never look back at what I have written, except the foot of the last page to see where I have got to. If you once look back, you are lost. How could you have written such drivel?'[12]

The essential flaw in spontaneous prose, as well as its great virtue, is that it gives a rather accurate picture of the state of mind of the writer. In Kerouac's case, as he was often drunk, his prose sometimes disintegrates into the literary equivalent of the grunts and whistles of the totally intoxicated. Other passages clearly show the effects of Benzedrine, particularly when he is attempting his saxophone-solo stream of word associations, rather than writing a description.

Like any improvised solo, some are good and some are bad. In live performance the audience applauds the good and politely ignores those that led nowhere. In the studio, musicians usually record a number of takes and choose the one with the best solos, or even edit the best bits of the various takes together. Most saxophone players also have a pretty good idea of how their major solos are going to develop. In literature, writers usually edit and correct in the same way. By not doing so, we get to see how bad a writer is as well as how good. Spontaneous prose was a dead end for Kerouac, particularly when he began writing while drunk. Jack was writing books, not telling the stories in a bar. However, it was as a storyteller that he saw himself, and for his stories we thank him.

Q: What does Jack Kerouac think of Jean Kerouac?

A: Ah! What do I think of myself? I'm sick of myself. Well, I know I'm a good writer, a great writer. I'm not a man of courage. But there's one thing I know how to do, and that's write stories. That's all![13]

Acknowledgements

Although writing a book is a largely solitary affair, and in literary biography the primary sources tend to be books, letters and manuscripts, I have received help and advice from a number of people to whom I am indebted. The late Allen Ginsberg first encouraged me to set some of my thoughts on Kerouac down on paper and I consulted with him a number of times during the writing of this book. I have quoted him extensively, often from texts to which he directed me in the course of our conversations as well as from our talks, and I am very much obliged to him. I had already discussed Jack with the late William Burroughs on a number of occasions and, in the course of interviewing him for a future project, I asked him questions about Jack. I have also used material taken from interviews I conducted with Michael McClure, Philip Whalen and Lucien Carr for my Allen Ginsberg biography.

I would like to thank Ann Scott for her thoughts on my amateur psychology and for her explanation of the Oedipus complex. However, the views expressed here are entirely my own. Jim Perrizo's chronology of Edie Parker Kerouac's days with Kerouac was invaluable. As usual, Gordon Ball provided some helpful insights into Kerouac, and in particular his relationship to Allen Ginsberg. Victor Bockris clarified my ideas in a number of areas and gave me some useful clippings. Thanks also to Carolyn Cassady, Simon Caulkin, Felix Dennis, Leslie Dick, Raymond Foye, James Grauerholz, Jay Landesman, Paul McCartney, William McPheron at Stanford University Libraries, Bill Morgan, Bob Rosenthal, Jon Savage, Steve Turner, Regina Weinreich and Peter Wollen.

Asher Levi's Literary Kicks web site and the Bookzen web site were both very useful, in particular for details of the controversy over Kerouac's literary archives and Jan Kerouac's treatment by the

Jack Kerouac

Kerouac Estate. Kerouac's Canadian origins and name were researched at The London Library.

Special thanks go to Michel Bulteau at Editions du Rocher for first proposing the book; to Sally Holloway at Virgin for taking the English-language edition; to my agent, Andrew Wylie, and Victoria Scott at the Wylie Agency, London; to my assistant Polly Timberlake; and finally to my wife Rosemary Bailey for offering a multitude of valuable suggestions.

Notes

Preface
1 William Seward Burroughs, 'Remembering Jack Kerouac', *The Adding Machine*, Seaver Books, New York City, 1986.
2 3407 N. Paulina, Chicago. Tel: (773) 348 4321, as of December 1996.
3 'Rebel Without a Clue', directed by James Whitmore Jr, NBC Television, 1991.
4 'True Brits', *Guardian*, 20 December 1996.
5 Ann Charters, *A Bibliography of Works by Jack Kerouac*, Phoenix, New York, 1967 and 1975.
6 *Le Nouvel Observateur*, 29 October 1969.
7 Whitman, 'The Song of the Open Road' in *Leaves of Grass*.

Chapter 1
1 Kerouac incorrectly places Saint Hubert in the adjoining Temiscouata County. He probably liked the sound of the name and substituted it.
2 *Visions of Gerard*, Penguin, New York, 1958, p78.
3 *Newsday*, 18 July 1964.
4 JK interviewed by Ted Berrigan, 'The Art of Fiction XLI: Jack Kerouac', *Paris Review*, no. 43, 1968.
5 *Visions of Gerard*, op. cit., p14.
6 John T McGreevy, *Parish Boundaries: The Catholic Encounter with Race in the Twentieth Century Urban North*, University of Chicago Press, Chicago, 1996.
7 Donald Warren, *Radio Priest: Charles Coughlin, the Father of Hate Radio*, The Free Press, New York, 1996.
8 Father Armand 'Spike' Morissette, 'A Catholic's View of Kerouac', *Moody Street Irregulars*, no. 5, 1979.
9 The haricot has been important in Brittany only since the ancien régime. Before that the broad bean was the staple.
10 Interviewed by Jerome Beatty in *Saturday Review*, no. 22, September 1957.
11 *Visions of Gerard*, op. cit.
12 In an interview with the author.
13 Don Allen, ed., *New American Poetry*, Grove, New York, 1960, p268.

14 Quoted in James Steranko, *The Steranko History of Comics*, Supergraphics, Reading Penn., 1970.
15 Ibid.

Chapter 2
1 Walter Gutman, *The Gutman Letter*, Something Else Press, New York, 1969.
2 JK to Sebastian Sampas, 15 March 1943.
3 JK to Sebastian Sampas, 25 March 1943.
4 Allen Ginsberg in conversation with the author, 1984.
5 This was the reason given by Allen Ginsberg. It could also have been his involvement in the Carr-Kammerer affair which resulted in his unwanted status.
6 JK to Sebastian Sampas, 15 April 1941.
7 However, he told Edie Parker that he first had sex in a confessional in Saint Jean Baptiste church in Lowell, the church where he was baptised and his funeral was held.
8 Scotty Beaulieu quoted in Gifford and Lee, *Jack's Book*, St Martin's, New York, 1978.
9 Alfred G Aronowitz, 'Jack Kerouac', *New York Post*, 10 March 1959.
10 JK to Sebastian Sampas, no date (mid-September 1941).
11 In conversation with James Grauerholz and others, tape transcript in the Ginsberg Archives.
12 JK to Norma Blickfelt, 15 July 1942.
13 JK to Sebastian Sampas, 26 September 1942.
14 JK to Al Aronowitz, *New York Post*, 10 March 1959.
15 Taken in part from Allen Ginsberg, 'West End Bar', *Work in Progress* MS, Ginsberg Archives, c1944.
16 *Kerouac Connection*, no. 13, 1987.
17 Edie's brother was to die in the war.
18 *Kerouac Connection*, no. 13, 1987.
19 Henri Cru to Edie Parker, 25 June 1983.
20 Edie Parker interviewed in Lerner and MacAdams, 'Kerouac', *Arena*, BBC Television, 1988.
21 Edie during a panel discussion at the Jack Kerouac Conference, Naropa Institute, 1982.
22 *Kerouac Connection*, no. 3, 1984.
23 Described in *Desolation Angels*, Granada, London, 1972, pp38–41.
24 JK to Al Aronowitz, *New York Post*, 10 March 1959.
25 JK to Cornelius Murphy, no date (spring 1943).
26 JK to George Apostolos, 7 April 1943.

Chapter 3
1 From Charlie's diary (Edie's sister), who was also present.
2 Not June, as most of the standard biographies state.
3 *Vanity of Duluoz*, Paragon, New York, 1979, p198.
4 Edie to Mrs Parker, c29 December 1943.
5 *Vanity of Duluoz*, op. cit., p222.

6 In conversation with James Grauerholz and others, tape transcript in the Allen Ginsberg Archives.

7 Interview with Ted Berrigan, 'The Art of Fiction XLI: Jack Kerouac', *Paris Review*, no. 43, 1968.

8 Conversation between Lucien Carr, Lawrence Lee, Barry Gifford and James Grauerholz, William Seward Burroughs's bunker, 6 February 1977.

9 *Vanity of Duluoz*, op. cit., p237.

10 Allen Ginsberg, 'Literary History of the Beat Generation', lecture 2, Naropa Institute, Boulder, Colorado, 14 June 1977. Unpublished.

11 From US Military Internet sources.

12 Edie Parker to William Seward Burroughs and James Grauerholz, 26 June 1992.

13 JK to Alfred Aronowitz, *New York Post*, 10 March 1959.

14 William Seward Burroughs in conversation with the author, c1972.

15 *Lawrence Journal-World*, 10 September 1987.

16 JK to Edie Parker, 18 September 1943.

17 Interview with Bill Gargan in *Catching Up With Kerouac*, Phoenix Az, 1984.

18 Edie Parker to William Seward Burroughs and James Grauerholz, 26 June 1992.

19 Ibid.

20 John Antonelli, *Kerouac*, Mystic Fire Video, Amsterdam, 1986.

21 Journal entry for 4 January 1944, quoted by Ann Charters in *Selected Letters*, Viking, New York, 1995.

22 Carolyn (Nin) to JK, 12 July 1944.

23 Based on the 17 August 1944 *New York Times* report of Lucien Carr's confession to the district attorney, 'Columbia Student Kills Friend and Sinks Body in Hudson River', and the *Saint Louis Post-Dispatch* report of the same date headed 'Lucien Carr Stabs David Kammerer to Death in Fight'. Additional details taken from the 16 August 1944 *New York Journal-American*, 'Accuse Student in River Death', and *New York World-Telegram*, 'Student Admits Killing Teacher'. Additional information taken from the 17 August 1944 reports in the *New York Daily Mirror*, 'Gashed Body Found in Hudson, Student Held'; *Daily News*, 'Student Accused as ' "Honor" Slayer'; *New York Herald Tribune*, 'Student is Held in Death of Man Found in River'; *New York Journal-American*, 'Youth Tells How He Killed Prof'; *PM*, 'Columbia Student is Held in Killing of an Instructor'; *New York Post*, 'Columbia Student Kills Ex-Instructor, Rolls Body into River'; *New York World-Telegram*, 'Clash Marks Hearing of Student in Slaying'; *New York Sun*, 'Student Arraigned in Slaying'.

24 William Seward Burroughs in conversation with the author, c1972.

25 Allen Ginsberg in conversation with the author, 1984.

26 *New York Times*, 18 August 1944, 'Student is Silent on Slaying Friend'.

27 *New York Herald Tribune*, 18 August 1944, 'Student is Held Without Bail on Slaying of Man'.

28 *Saint Louis Post-Dispatch*, 18 August 1944, 'Sailor Says Carr Confided

Jack Kerouac

in Him After Murder'. Also reports in that day's *Spectator*, 'Lucien Carr Arraigned in Homicide Court for Riverside Park Murder'; *New York Daily Mirror*, 'Student Mum at Slaying Hearing'; *Daily News*, '"Honor" Slayer Held Without Bail'.

29 *Saint Louis Post-Dispatch*, 25 August 1944, 'Another St Louis Man Knew Carr Killed Kammerer'.

30 *New York Journal-American*, 24 August 1944, 'College Student Held in Slaying'. Also reported in *New York World-Telegram*, 24 August 1944, '2nd Witness Held in Teacher Killing'; *New York Times*, 25 August 1944, 'Student is Indicted in 2nd-Degree Murder'; *New York Daily News*, 25 August 1944, 'Honor Slayer Faces Trial in Second Degree'; *PM*, 25 August 1944, 'Columbia Student Indicted in Slaying of Ex-Teacher'; *New York Daily Mirror*, 25 August 1944, 'Indict Student in Murder Case'.

31 *New York Times*, 31 August 1944, 'Witness in Slaying Freed'.

32 John Antonelli, *Kerouac*, Mystic Fire Video, Amsterdam, 1986.

33 Henri Cru to Edie Parker, 1 August 1982.

34 Gabrielle Kerouac to JK, 15 September 1944.

35 *Saint Louis Post-Dispatch*, 15 September 1944, 'Lucien Carr Pleads Guilty of Manslaughter'. Additional reports in *New York Journal-American*, 15 September 1944, 'Carr Admits Fatal Knifing'; *New York World-Telegram*, 15 September 1944, 'Student Pleads Guilty to Killing Ex-Teacher'; *New York Times*, 16 September 1944, 'Guilty Plea Made by Carr in Slaying'; *New York Daily Mirror*, 16 September 1944, 'Student Pleads Guilty in Killing of Former Teacher'; *Daily News*, 16 September 1944, 'Student Cops Manslaughter Plea in Slaying'.

36 Céline Young to JK, 1 October 1944.

37 *Saint Louis Post-Dispatch*, 6 October 1944, 'Lucien Carr Gets Indeterminate Term For Killing'; *New York Journal-American*, 6 October 1944, 'Carr Sentenced to Reformatory'; *New York Sun*, 6 October 1944, 'Young Slayer Is Sentenced'; *New York World-Telegram*, 6 October 1944, 'Carr Sentenced to Reformatory'; *New York Times*, 7 October 1944, 'Student Slayer Sent to the Reformatory'; *New York Herald Tribune*, 7 October 1944, 'Carr Is Sentenced, Judge Urges His Rehabilitation'; *New York Journal-American*, 9 October 1944, 'Student Slayer Carr Off to Reformatory'; *New York World-Telegram*, 9 October 1944, 'Slayer to Reformatory'; *New York Times*, 10 October 1944, 'Young Slayer Goes to Elmira'; *Saint Louis Post-Dispatch*, 10 October 1944, 'Lucien Carr Begins Term For Killing Kammerer'.

38 Allen Ginsberg to Eugene Brooks, not dated (October 1944).

39 Interview with Ted Berrigan, op. cit.

40 Ann Charters, *Kerouac*, Warner, New York, 1973 and 1974.

Chapter 4

1 Allen Ginsberg, 'Literary History of the Beat Generation', lecture 1, Naropa Institute, 9 June 1977. Unpublished.

2 Edie Parker at the Jack Kerouac Conference, Naropa Institute, 1982.

3 Martin Gardner, *In the Name of Science*, New York, 1952.

306

4 Alfred Knopf, New York, 1926 and 1928. Burroughs gave Jack the first one-volume edition, complete, New York, 1932.
5 Charlotte Parker to her daughter Charlotte, 13 January 1945.
6 Interview with Ted Berrigan, 'The Art of Fiction XLI: Jack Kerouac', *Paris Review*, no. 43, 1968.
7 JK to Caroline Blake (née Kerouac), 14 March 1945.
8 Howard Brookner, 'Burroughs', *Arena*, BBC Television, 1984.
9 JK to Caroline Blake, 14 March 1945.
10 Freud, 'The Economic Problem of Masochism', *PFL*, vol. 11, p425.
11 *Scattered Poems*, City Lights, San Francisco, 1971, p13.
12 *Book of Dreams*, City Lights, San Francisco, 1960, p123.
13 Anna Freud, 'Indications and Contraindications for Child Analysis', *Problems of Psychoanalytic Training: Diagnosis and the Technique of Therapy*, Hogarth Press, London, 1974. See also Ann Scott, *Real Events Revisited: Fantasy, Memory and Psychoanalysis*, Virago, London, 1996.
14 Allen Ginsberg, 'Literary History of the Beat Generation', lecture 19, Naropa Institute, 27 April 1981. Unpublished.
15 Herbert Huncke always insisted that the bar was called The Angler but Ginsberg remembered it as The Angle. The name is given variously in books about the Beats.
16 Fritz Lang, 1931.
17 Marcel Carné, *Les Enfants du Paradis*, 1945.
18 Marcel Carné, *Le Quai des Brumes*, 1938.
19 Jean Renoir, 1938.
20 Julien Duvivier, 1936.
21 Ibid.
22 Allen Ginsberg, 'Literary History of the Beat Generation', lecture 4, Naropa Institute, 21 June 1977. Unpublished.
23 Allen Ginsberg to JK, no date (early summer 1945).
24 JK to Allen Ginsberg, 17 August 1945.
25 Ibid.
26 JK to Allen Ginsberg, 6 September 1945.
27 Allen Ginsberg in conversation with the author.
28 Céline Young to Edie Parker, 6 September 1945.
29 Quoted by Judy Sadgrove, Health Page, *Guardian*, 10 December 1996.
30 Allen Ginsberg, 'Literary History of the Beat Generation', lecture 32, Naropa Institute, 13 April 1982. Unpublished.
31 Allen Ginsberg and William Seward Burroughs play-acting for the Howard Brookner film, 'Burroughs'.

Chapter 5

1 Charlotte Parker to Edie Parker, 19 September 1945.
2 Herbert Huncke interviewed by Stewart Meyer and Mel Bernstine, *Newave*, April 1981.
3 JK interviewed by Al Aronowitz in the *New York Post*, 10 March 1959.
4 Huncke interviewed in *Newave*, April 1981.
5 Reported by Ted Morgan in *Literary Outlaw*, Henry Holt, New York, 1988.

6 *Vanity of Duluoz*, Paragon, New York, 1979, p291.
7 Interview with Ted Berrigan, 'The Art of Fiction XLI: Jack Kerouac', *Paris Review*, no. 43, 1968.
8 Thomas Wolfe to Maxwell Perkins, May 1930.
9 Cited in A Scott Berg, *Max Perkins: Editor of Genius*, E.P. Dutton, New York, 1978.
10 Reported by Ted Morgan in *Literary Outlaw*, op. cit.
11 Unpublished.
12 As reported by Gerald Nicosia in *Memory Babe*, Grove, New York, 1983.
13 *Book of Dreams*, City Lights, San Francisco, 1960, p131.
14 Howard Brookner, 'Burroughs', *Arena*.
15 Kinsey Sex Institute web site.
16 Interviewed by Hugh Sykes, *Rebels*, BBC Radio Four, 24 April 1987.
17 Joan Adams to Edie Parker, 29 December 1946.
18 Huncke interviewed in *Newave*, April 1981.
19 Joan Vollmer to Edie Parker, 29 December 1946.
20 Herbert Huncke to Allen Ginsberg, 23 September 1946.
21 Allen Ginsberg, 'Literary History of the Beat Generation', lecture 1, 9 June 1977. The etymology of 'hip' is unclear. It is usually thought to derive from 'hep' in its American Black slang usage for cool, laid back, in the know, from which came hep-cat and hipster. It has two other sources. In the seventeenth century it meant depressed from 'hyp' or 'hip', from which we get hypochondria and the cry to animals hip-hip-hurrah. In German, 'hepp' doubled as a cry to animals and as a signal for an attack on Jews.
22 In the document 'Notes on Characters in Ginsberg Letters as They Occur Almost Chronologically' by Neal Cassady, attached to the collection of letters sold by Cassady to the University of Texas in Austin in August 1965, Casady notes: 'Vickie Russell turned me on to tea Aug 46 along with Kerouac.' This would seem to place him in New York City that summer. However, autumn seems the most likely date.
23 Tom Driberg MP in conversation with the author, 1966. (Driberg was a friend of Crowley.)
24 *On the Road*, Penguin, Harmondsworth, 1972, p6.
25 Interview transcript among Ginsberg's papers, date unknown.
26 Allen Ginsberg, unpublished journals.

Chapter 6
1 JK to William Seward Burroughs, 14 July 1947.
2 JK to Hal Chase, 19 April 1947.
3 *On the Road*, Penguin, Harmondsworth, 1972.
4 Interview with Allen Ginsberg by Drew Becker, *Sunday Denver Post*, 12 August 1979.
5 Allen Ginsberg, 'Literary History of the Beat Generation', lecture 16, Naropa Institute. Unpublished.
6 Carolyn Cassady, *Off the Road: Twenty Years with Cassady, Kerouac and Ginsberg*, Black Spring, London, 1990.
7 Henri Cru to Edie Parker, 8 June 1982.

8 Henri Cru to Edie Parker, 28 January 1982.
9 *The Mexican Girl*, Pacific Red Car Press, Brighton, no date.
10 Quoted by Ross Russell in *Bird Lives!*, Quartet, London, 1973.
11 Allen Ginsberg in conversation with the author, 1983.
12 JK to Ed White, 17 September 1947.
13 Allen Ginsberg in conversation with the author.
14 John Clellon Holmes interviewed by Al Aronowitz for the *New York Post*, 9 March 1959.
15 F Scott Fitzgerald, 'My Generation', c1938. Unpublished until *Esquire*, October 1968.
16 Allen Ginsberg interviewed by Al Aronowitz for the *New York Post*, 13 March 1959.
17 From conversations with Allen Ginsberg, I believe his final definition of who was a genuine member of the Beat Generation was a narrow list consisting of himself, Kerouac, Burroughs, Joan Vollmer, Corso, Carr (honorary), Huncke and Solomon.
18 *Guardian*, 5 June 1987.
19 William Seward Burroughs to Allen Ginsberg, 10 January 1949.
20 Chandler Brossard, 'Tentative Visits to the Cemetery: Reflections on My Beat Generation', *Review of Contemporary Fiction*, spring 1987.
21 Lucien Carr in conversation with James Grauerholz and others at William Seward Burroughs's bunker.
22 Ann Charters, *A Bibliography of Works by Jack Kerouac*, Phoenix, New York, 1967 and 1975.
23 JK interviewed by Charles Jarvis and James Curtis, WCAP Lowell, 8 October 1962.
24 *The Town and the City*, Grosset and Dunlap, New York, 1960.
25 Maurice Poteet, 'The Delussons and the Martins: Some Family Resemblances', *Moody Street Irregulars*, no. 5, 1979.
26 See Luther Blissett, 'The Many Images of Jack Kerouac', *Changing Faces Anthology*, Neoist Press, London, 1985.
27 Ginsberg and Burroughs had read both books by this date, as had Ginsberg's father. Kerouac read *The Function of the Orgasm* in the spring of 1953.

Chapter 7
1 *Independent*, 6 April 1988.
2 Allen Ginsberg to Neal Cassady, 18 November 1950. 'T' is marijuana.
3 Allen Ginsberg to Neal Cassady, 31 October 1950.
4 Alfred Knopf, New York City, 1966.
5 Interview with Ted Berrigan, 'The Art of Fiction XLI: Jack Kerouac', *Paris Review*, no. 43, 1968.
6 Reports on 13 October 1950: *New York Herald Tribune*, 'Man Killed Climbing Out of Subway Train Window'; *New York Daily Mirror*, 'Prank Costs Him His Life on IRT Train'; *Daily News*, 'Climb From Subway For Drink Kills Rider'; *New York Times*, 'Knocked Out IRT Window Man Killed When Crushed Between Train and Tunnel Wall'.
7 Allen Ginsberg to Neal Cassady, 31 October 1950.

8 Allen Ginsberg to Neal Cassady, 18 November 1950.
9 *San Francisco Examiner*, 5 October 1958.
10 It has also been described as being 40,000 words long. We will never know since it is unlikely that anyone actually counted and the letter is no longer extant.
11 Eight of these words were changed by the time the book was published, proving that *On the Road* was subjected to considerable revision.
12 John Clellon Holmes, 'First Reader of *On the Road* in Manuscript', *Moody Street Irregulars*, no. 5, 1979.
13 Ann Charters, *A Bibliography of Works by Jack Kerouac*, Phoenix, New York, 1967 and 1975.
14 Carl Solomon talking to Ginsberg's Beat Generation class at Brooklyn College, 30 March 1987.
15 *Kerouac Connection*, 10 April 1986.
16 Introductory note in *Excerpts from Visions of Cody*, New Directions, New York, 1964.
17 *Friction*, no. 2/3, 1982.
18 *On the Road*, Penguin, Harmondsworth, 1972.
19 Ibid.
20 Sebastian Sampas to JK, 26 May 1943.
21 RJ Ellis, 'I Am Only a Jolly Storyteller: Jack Kerouac's *On the Road* and *Visions of Cody*', A Robert Lee (ed.), *The Beat Generation Writers*, Pluto Press, London, 1996.
22 Allen Ginsberg, 'Literary History of the Beat Generation', lecture 18, Naropa Institute. Unpublished.
23 *Sunday Times*, 25 October 1987.
24 *Time Out*, 14 October 1987.
25 To Alfred Aronowitz in the *New York Post*, 10 March 1959.
26 Peter Manso, *Mailer, His Life and Times*, Simon and Schuster, New York, 1985.
27 *A Jack Kerouac ROMnibus*, Penguin Electronic, New York, 1995.
28 Quoted by Richard Holmes in *Shelley: The Pursuit*, London, 1974.
29 Kerouac claimed on the first page of *The Subterraneans* that his group 'knew all about Pound'.
30 *Paterson*. Kerouac was introduced to the poem by Ginsberg, who knew Dr Williams. *Paterson* Books One, Two, Three and Four were published in 1946, 1948, 1949 and 1951 respectively, so Kerouac may not have seen Book Four. Paterson was where Ginsberg grew up but Williams's poem may have been an additional reason to give that city as his home in *On the Road* instead of Queens.
31 The SS *President Harding*.
32 *Visions of Cody*, Part Two, McGraw-Hill, New York, 1973.
33 Ann Charters, *A Bibliography of Works by Jack Kerouac*, op. cit.
34 *Visions of Cody*, Part Two, op. cit.
35 Ann Charters, *A Bibliography of Works by Jack Kerouac*, op. cit.
36 Andy Warhol, *a, a Novel*, Grove, New York, 1968.
37 *The Diaries of Andy Warhol*, Simon and Schuster, New York, 1989.
38 William Kotzwinkle, *The Fan Man*, Avon, New York, 1974.

39 Allen Ginsberg, 'Literary History of the Beat Generation', lecture 21, Naropa Institute, 4 May 1981. Unpublished.
40 *The Magnetic Fields*, translated by David Gascoyne, Atlas Press, London, 1985.
41 *Artaud Collected Works*, vol. 7.
42 She was probably filming *Sudden Fear* (1952), which was set in San Francisco.

Chapter 8
1 *Guardian*, 5 June 1987.
2 *Sunday Times*, 25 October 1987.
3 *Time Out*, 14 October 1987.
4 *Sunday Times*, 25 October 1987.
5 JK to Neal Cassady, 27 May 1952.
6 As Jack was calling *Visions of Cody* at that time.
7 William Seward Burroughs to Allen Ginsberg, 15 May 1952.
8 Interview with Ted Berrigan, 'The Art of Fiction XLI: Jack Kerouac', *Paris Review*, no. 43, 1968.
9 Allen Ginsberg to his class at Brooklyn College, 16 March 1987.
10 Ekbert Faas, *Towards a New American Poetics: Essays and Interviews*, Black Sparrow, Santa Barbara, 1979.
11 *Doctor Sax*, Grove, New York, 1959.
12 JK to John Clellon Holmes, 3 June 1952.
13 William Seward Burroughs to Allen Ginsberg, 13 July 1952.
14 Allen Ginsberg to JK, 12 June 1952.
15 Allen Ginsberg to Neal and Carolyn Cassady, 3 July 1952.
16 John Clellon Holmes to Alfred Aronowitz in the *New York Post*, 9 March 1959.
17 John Antonelli, *Kerouac*, Mystic Fire Video, Amsterdam, 1986.
18 *Book of Dreams*, City Lights, San Francisco, 1960, p61.
19 *Book of Dreams*, op. cit., p90.
20 Allen Ginsberg, 'Gates of Wrath', *Collected Poems*, Viking, London, 1985.
21 *Lonesome Traveller*, Andre Deutsch, London, 1962.
22 *The Yage Letters*, City Lights Books, San Francisco, 1963. Aileen Lee is credited on the copyright page. Thanks to her multiple carbon copies of *Queer*, the MS was able to be reassembled in 1972 from various caches of papers catalogued by this author.
23 The building was demolished by a fire in 1985.
24 *Palimpsest*, Andre Deutsch, London, 1995.
25 Aaron Latham interview, Allen Ginsberg Archives.
26 A letter to his publisher Mr H Brinchmann (sic) of JW Cappelens Forlag in Oslo, 1960, used as an introduction to the Norwegian translation by Colbjorn Helander. See item 304 in Bradford Morrow Bookseller's catalogue five: Jack Kerouac.
27 Interview with Ted Berrigan, op. cit.
28 'Written Address to the Italian Judge', 23 May 1963, *Evergreen Review*, 31 October 1963. An open letter in defence of *The Subterraneans*, which

had been published in Italy by Feltrinelli and had been banned since 1961.
29 Lerner and MacAdams, 'Kerouac', *Arena*, BBC Television, 1988.
30 Interview with Ted Berrigan, op. cit.
31 'Written Address to the Italian Judge', op. cit.
32 It was first published in translation in the USA in 1960 by Grove Press, New York. Of course, Kerouac may have read it in French.
33 John Clellon Holmes, *The Horn*, Random House, New York, 1958.

Chapter 9
1 JK interviewed by Alfred Aronowitz for 'The Year for Zen', *Escapade*, October 1960.
2 *Book of Blues*, Penguin, New York, 1995.
3 JK to Alfred Aronowitz in the *New York Post*, 10 March 1959.
4 Sigmund Freud to André Breton, 8 December 1937.
5 *Book of Dreams*, City Lights, San Francisco, 1960, p117.
6 JK to Alfred Aronowitz in the *New York Post*, 10 March 1959.
7 Interview with Ted Berrigan, 'The Art of Fiction XLI: Jack Kerouac', *Paris Review*, no. 43, 1968.
8 Ibid.
9 JK to Allen Ginsberg, 19 August 1955. See *Annotated Howl*.
10 It is still reported that Kerouac invented the title 'Howl' even though the original MS had that title on it before JK saw it. Only when Holmes returned it to Allen Ginsberg was it shown that 'Howl' was Allen Ginsberg's title all along.
11 Peter Orlovsky remembers this incident occurring at 1010 Montgomery Street, San Francisco, where he and Allen lived together, but Allen moved to Berkeley on 1 September 1955, more than a week before Jack even left Mexico City, so it must have been Milvia Street.
12 In conversation with the author.
13 Ibid.
14 DT Suzuki, *Zen Buddhism*, New York, 1956.
15 Many Tibetan *tankas* depict the Primordial Buddha Samantabhadra with his consort (Kuntuzangpo Yab-Yum).
16 *Sunday Times*, 25 October 1987.
17 JK to Carolyn Cassady, c18 January 1956. JK later gave twelve nights and ten nights as its composition time.
18 1963 press release from Farrar, Straus and Cudahy.
19 Ann Charters, *A Bibliography of Works by Jack Kerouac*, Phoenix, New York, 1967.
20 Charles Jarvis and James Curtis, WCAP Lowell, 8 October 1962.
21 Quoted in Carolyn Cassady, *Off the Road*, Black Springs, London, 1990.
22 Ann Charters, *A Bibliography of Works by Jack Kerouac*, op. cit.
23 John Antonelli, *Kerouac*, Mystic Fire Video, Amsterdam, 1986.
24 JK to John Clellon Holmes, 27 May 1956.
25 Faber and Faber, London, revised edition 1975.
26 Contained in *Stanzas in Meditation*, vol. 6 of the Yale edition of the unpublished writings of Gertrude Stein, 1956.

27 From 'Possessive Case' in *As Fine as Melanctha*, vol. 4 of the Yale edition of the unpublished writings of Gertrude Stein, 1954.
28 JK to Philip Whalen, 16 January 1956.
29 *Sunday Times*, 25 October 1987.
30 *Time Out*, 14 October 1987.
31 Interview with Ted Berrigan, op. cit.

Chapter 10
1 Allen Ginsberg, Brooklyn College lecture, 18 February 1987.
2 See Rupert Croft-Cook, *Smiling Damned Villain: The True Story of Paul Lund*, Secker and Warburg, 1959.
3 *Desolation Angels*, Granada, London, 1972.
4 Allen Ginsberg, 'Literary History of the Beat Generation', lecture 8, Naropa Institute. Unpublished.
5 See Gerald Nicosia, *Memory Babe*, Grove, New York, 1983, note 278. JK told Philip Whalen she was God in a letter of 30 April 1957, and his nephew Paul Blake mentioned it in Nicosia's interview.
6 Philip Whalen to Lew Welch, 13 May 1957.
7 *Village Voice*, 18 September 1957.
8 *New York Times*, 8 September 1957.
9 *Saturday Review*, 29 September 1957.
10 'Lamb, No Lion', *Pageant XIII*, no. 8, 1958.
11 *Detroit News*, 24 August 1958.
12 JK to John Clellon Holmes, 23 June 1957.
13 JK to Malcolm Cowley, 20 September 1955.
14 Barry Gifford and Lawrence Lee, *Jack's Book*, St Martin's Press, New York, 1978, p206.
15 Allen Ginsberg, 'Literary History of the Beat Generation', lecture 8, Naropa Institute. Unpublished.
16 Allen Ginsberg in his review of *The Dharma Bums* for the *Village Voice* of 12 November 1958. AG is contradicting JK here in saying that the published version is different from the original.
17 John Montgomery, *The Kerouac We Knew*, Fels and Fern, San Anselmo, 1986.
18 *New Directions*, no. 16, New York, 1957.
19 5 December 1957.
20 Lerner and MacAdams, 'Kerouac', *Arena*, BBC Television, 1988.
21 *Detroit News*, 24 August 1958.
22 Ann Charters, *A Bibliography of Works by Jack Kerouac*, Phoenix, New York, 1967 and 1975.
23 *Chicago Review*, summer 1958, published as a separate booklet by City Lights Books, San Francisco, 1960.
24 *New York Post*, 21 January 1958.
25 Henri Cru to Edie Parker, 1 August 1982.
26 Allen Ginsberg, 'Literary History of the Beat Generation', lecture 24, Naropa Institute, 14 May 1981. Unpublished.
27 Herbert Huncke talking to the Beat Generation class, Brooklyn College, date unknown.

Time Out, 14 October 1987.

29 Robert Frank, *The Americans*, Grove Press, New York, 1959. First published in Paris in 1958, without the JK intro.

30 Jesse Hamlin, 'How Herb Caen Named a Generation', *San Francisco Chronicle*, 26 November 1995.

31 At least according to the biographies. It is always possible he was there.

32 Gabrielle Kerouac to Allen Ginsberg, 13 July 1958.

33 William Seward Burroughs to Allen Ginsberg, no date (July 1958).

34 JK to Allen Ginsberg, 2 July 1958.

35 JK to Philip Whalen, 12 June 1958.

36 Later published in a revised, enlarged version in *Playboy* as 'The Origins of the Beat Generation'. It was his most complete and definitive statement on the subject.

37 To Alfred Aronowitz in the *New York Post*, 10 March 1959.

38 Quoted by Montgomery in his intro to *The Kerouac We Knew*.

39 Kingsley Amis, *Memoirs*, Century Hutchinson, London, 1991. *Harpers*, October 1959. Eric Jacobs, *Kingsley Amis: A Biography*, Hodder and Stoughton, London, 1995. Mark Schleifer, 'The Beat Debated: Is It or Is It Not?', *Village Voice*, November 1958.

40 *New York Herald Tribune*, 22 September 1958.

41 Hugh Sykes, *Rebels*, BBC Radio Four, 24 April 1987.

42 Allen Ginsberg conference, 1968.

43 JK to Gary Snyder, 5 May 1958.

44 Henri Cru to Edie Parker, 9 March 1982.

Chapter 11

1 Shields and Company, Weekly Market Letter, 21 April 1959.

2 *Third Rail* magazine, Los Angeles, 1984.

3 David Ossman, *The Sullen Art*, Corinth Books, New York, 1963.

4 Bremser's lecture to Allen Ginsberg's Beat Generation class at Brooklyn College, 1987. Unpublished.

5 Ibid.

6 Brad Gooch, *City Poet: The Life and Times of Frank O'Hara*, Alfred Knopf, New York, 1993.

7 Quoted in Gerald Nicosia, 'Catching Up With Kerouac', *Literary Denim: A Journal of Beat Literature*, Phoenix Az, 1984.

8 JK to Gary Snyder, 20 September 1960.

9 Anaïs Nin, *The Novel of the Future*, Macmillan, New York, 1968.

10 BH Friedman, 'Art World Details', *Grand Street*, no. 51.

11 *Guardian*, 5 June 1987.

12 Lew Welch, *I Remain: The Letters of Lew Welch and the Correspondence of His Friends, Volume One: 1949–1960*, Grey Fox, Bolinas, 1980.

13 Joe Smith, *Off the Record: An Oral History of Popular Music*, Warner Brothers, New York, 1988.

14 *New York Post*, 21 January 1958.

15 Allen Ginsberg, 'Literary History of the Beat Generation', lecture 1, Naropa Institute. Unpublished.

16 Henri Cru to Edie Parker, 30 June 1982.

17 Inspired by Kerouac's poem, Allen Ginsberg wrote 'Hum Bom!' during a 1971 visit to Bixby Canyon, using elements of Kerouac's rhythm:
  What do we do?
      You bomb! You bomb them!
18 JK interviewed by Charles E Jarvis and James Curtis on WCAP Lowell, 8 October 1962.
19 From the Allen Ginsberg conference, 1988.
20 *Big Sur*, Bantam, New York, 1963.
21 Tim Leary, *Flashbacks*, JP Tarcher, Los Angeles, 1983.

Chapter 12
1 To James Grauerholz. Tape transcript among Allen Ginsberg's papers, not dated.
2 Interview with Ted Berrigan, 'The Art of Fiction XLI: Jack Kerouac', *Paris Review*, no. 43, 1968.
3 John Antonelli, *Kerouac*, Mystic Fire Video, Amsterdam, 1986.
4 Hugh Sykes, *Rebels*, BBC Radio Four, 24 April 1987.
5 Paul Blake interviewed by Gerald Nicosia in *Memory Babe*, Grove, New York, 1983, p634.
6 *Newsday*, 18 July 1964.
7 Victor Bockris, *With William Burroughs*, Seaver, New York, 1981.
8 In an interview for WBAI-FM reprinted in Charles Raus, *Conversations With Amer-i-can Writ-ers*, Quartet, London, 1984.
9 Interview with Ted Berrigan, op. cit.
10 *Sunday Times*, 25 October 1987.
11 From the Allen Ginsberg conference, 1988.
12 Fernanda Pivano talking at the Kerouac conference, 30 July 1984.
13 Interview with Ted Berrigan, op. cit.
14 Ibid.
15 Ibid.
16 Allen Ginsberg to his Brooklyn College class, date unknown (c1986).
17 Ed Sanders was the lead singer with The Fugs.
18 Quote from the Buddha.
19 JK to Edie Parker, 8 September 1969.
20 Allen Ginsberg at a reading at Yale University, 23 October 1969.

Postscript
1 Allen Ginsberg, 'Literary History of the Beat Generation', lecture 2, Naropa Institute, February 1987. Unpublished.
2 *New York Post*, 6 January 1987.
3 *Washington Post*, 8 January 1987.
4 *Book of Dreams*, City Lights, San Francisco, 1960, p120.
5 Geordie Greig, 'Kerouac at Centre of £6m Will Feud', *Sunday Times*, 5 March 1995.
6 The two sides of the dispute are available at www.bookzen.com for the Nicosia view and many supporting documents and at http://members.aol.com/kerouacult/fraud.htm for an overview by journalist Diane De Roy.

7 William Seward Burroughs, 'Remembering Jack Kerouac', *The Adding Machine*, Seaver Books, New York, 1986.
8 Preface to *Big Sur*, Bantam, New York, 1963.
9 Jean-Paul Sartre, *Baudelaire*, Hamish Hamilton, London, 1949.
10 *Athanor* magazine, vol. 1.1–3, 1971–2.
11 *Independent on Sunday*, 25 February 1990.
12 Ian Fleming, short essay, source unknown, 1962.
13 Television interview on *Sel de la Semaine*, Radio Canada, Montreal, summer 1967.

Bibliography

Books by Jack Kerouac:
Big Sur, Bantam, New York, 1963.
Book of Blues, Penguin, New York, 1995.
Book of Dreams, City Lights, San Francisco, 1960.
Dear Carolyn: Letters to Carolyn Cassady, Unspeakable Visions of the
   Individual, California PA, 1983.
Desolation Angels, Granada, London, 1972.
Doctor Sax, Grove, New York, 1959.
Good Blonde and Others, Grey Fox, San Francisco, revised edition 1996.
Heaven and Other Poems, Grey Fox, San Francisco, 1977.
Home at Christmas, n.p., n.d.
Last Word and Other Writings, n.p., Zeta, 1985.
Lonesome Traveller, Andre Deutsch, London, 1962.
Maggie Cassidy, McGraw-Hill, New York, 1959.
Mexico City Blues, Grove, New York, 1959.
Old Angel Midnight, Grey Fox, San Francisco, 1993.
On the Road, Penguin, Harmondsworth, 1972.
Pic, Quartet, London, 1974.
Poems All Sizes, City Lights, San Francisco, 1992.
Pull My Daisy, Grove, New York, 1960.
Safe in Heaven Dead, Hanuman, Madras and New York, 1990.
San Francisco Blues, Pacific Red Car Press, Brighton, 1991.
Satori in Paris, Grove, New York, 1966.
Scattered Poems, City Lights, San Francisco, 1971.
Selected Letters 1940–1956, Ann Charters, ed., Viking, New York, 1995.
Some of the Dharma, Viking, New York, 1997.
The Dharma Bums, Granada, London, 1972.
The Mexican Girl, Pacific Red Car Press, Brighton, n.d.
The Portable Jack Kerouac, Charters, Ann, ed., Viking, New York, 1995.
The Scripture of the Golden Eternity, Totem/Corinth, New York, 1960.
The Subterraneans, Andre Deutsch, London, 1960.
The Town and the City, Grosset and Dunlap, New York, 1960.
Trip Trap, with Albert Saijo and Lew Welch, Grey Fox, Bolinas, 1973.
Tristessa, Avon, New York, 1960.

Jack Kerouac

Vanity of Duluoz, Paragon, New York, 1979.
Visions of Cody, McGraw-Hill, New York, 1973.
Visions of Gerard, Penguin, New York, 1958.

Books about Jack Kerouac:

Austin, James, *The Kerouac Collection*, CDs and booklet, Rhino Records, Santa Monica, 1990.

Beaulieu, Victor-Lévy, *Jack Kerouac: A Chicken Essay*, Coach House, Toronto, 1979.

Burroughs, William Seward, 'Remembering Jack Kerouac', *The Adding Machine*, Seaver Books, New York, 1986.

Cassady, Carolyn, *Heart Beat: My Life with Jack and Neal*, Creative Arts, Berkeley, 1976.

Cassady, Carolyn, *Off the Road: Twenty Years with Cassady, Kerouac and Ginsberg*, Black Spring, London, 1990.

Challis, Chris, *Quest for Kerouac*, Faber and Faber, London, 1984.

Charters, Ann, *A Bibliography of Works by Jack Kerouac*, Phoenix, New York, revised edition 1975.

Charters, Ann, *Kerouac*, Warner, New York, revised edition 1974.

Christian, Thomas, ed., *Kerouac: Chronicles of Disorder 2*, Schenectady, New York, 1996.

Clark, Tom, *Jack Kerouac*, Harcourt Brace Jovanovich, New York, 1984.

Clark, Tom, *Kerouac's Last Word: Jack Kerouac in Escapade*, Water Row, Sudbury MA, 1986.

Coolidge, Clark; Gizzi, Michael; Yau, John; Barrette, Bill and Coolidge, Celia, *Lowell Connector: Lines and Shots from Kerouac's Town*, Hard, West Stockbridge MA, 1993.

Dorfner, John J, *Kerouac: Visions of Lowell*, Cooper Street, Raleigh NC, 1993.

Eaton, VJ, ed., *Catching Up with Kerouac*, The Literary Denim, Nesa AZ, 1984.

Gifford, Barry and Lee, Lawrence, *Jack's Book*, St Martin's, New York, 1978.

Ginsberg, Allen, *The Visions of the Great Rememberer*, Mulch, Amherst, 1974.

Hipkiss, Robert A, *Jack Kerouac: Prophet of the New Romanticism*, Regents Press of Kansas, Lawrence, 1976.

Holmes, John C, *Gone in October*, Limberlost, Hailey IO, 1985.

Holmes, John C, *Visitor: Jack Kerouac in Old Saybrook*, Unspeakable Visions of the Individual, California PA, 1981.

Hunt, Tim, *Kerouac's Crooked Road*, Shoe String, Hamden CT, 1981.

Jarvis, Charles E, *Visions of Kerouac*, Ithica, Lowell Mass, 1973.

Knight, Arthur and Kit, eds, *Kerouac and the Beats*, Paragon, New York, 1988.

McDarrah, Fred, *Kerouac and Friends*, William Morrow, New York, 1985.

McNally, Dennis, *Desolate Angel: A Biography of Jack Kerouac*, Random House, New York, 1979.

Montgomery, John, ed., *Kerouac at the Wild Boar*, Fels and Firn, San Anselmo CA, 1986.

Montgomery, John, ed., *The Kerouac We Knew*, Fels and Firn, San Anselmo CA, 1987.

Moore, Dave, ed., *Kerouac Connection*, Bristol, various issues.

Morton, James, *The Distance Instead . . . is the Feeling*, n.p., Dream of Jazz, 1986.

Nicosia, Gerald, *Memory Babe: A Critical Biography of Jack Kerouac*, Grove, New York, 1983.

O'Brien, John, ed., 'Jack Kerouac: Robert Pinget Number', *Review of Contemporary Fiction*, vol. 3, no. 2, 1983.

Roark, Randy, ed., 'Documents from the Jack Kerouac Conference: Boulder, Colorado, July 1982', *Friction*, Boulder CO, vol.1, nos 2–3, 1982.

Turner, Steve, *Jack Kerouac: Angelheaded Hipster*, Bloomsbury, London, 1996.

Walsh, Joy, (and others), ed., *The Moody Street Irregulars: A Jack Kerouac Newsletter*, Clarence Center, New York, various issues.

Weinreich, Regina, *The Spontaneous Poetics of Jack Kerouac*, Southern Illinois University, Carbondale, 1987.

Other books consulted:

Alexander, Stuart, *Robert Frank: A Bibliography, Filmography, and Exhibition Chronology 1946–1985*, Centre for Creative Photography, University of Arizona, Tucson AZ, 1986.

Allen, Donald, ed., *The New American Poetry 1945–1960*, Grove, New York, 1960.

Allen, Donald and Butterick, George F, eds, *The Postmoderns*, Grove, New York, 1982.

Allen, Donald and Tallman, Warren, eds, *The Poetics of the New American Poetry*, Grove, New York, 1973.

Almon, Bert, *Gary Snyder*, Idaho State University, Boise, 1979.

Amram, David, *Vibrations*, Macmillan, New York, 1968.

Ansen, Alan, *William Burroughs*, Water Row, Sudbury, 1986.

Bartlett, Lee, *The Beats: Essays in Criticism*, McFarland, Jefferson NC, 1981.

Bockris, Victor, *With William Burroughs: A Report from the Bunker*, Seaver, New York, 1981.

Bremser, Bonnie, *Troia: Mexican Memoirs*, Croton, New York, 1969.

Burroughs, William Seward, *Junky*, Penguin, New York, 1977.

Burroughs, William Seward, *Letters to Allen Ginsberg*, Claude Givaudan, Geneva, 1978.

Burroughs, William Seward, *Queer*, Viking, New York, 1985.

Burroughs, William Seward, *The Adding Machine: Collected Essays*, John Calder, London, 1985.

Burroughs, William Seward, *The Burroughs File*, City Lights, San Francisco, 1984.

Burroughs, William Seward, *The Job*, Grove, New York, 1972, revised 1974.

Burroughs, William Seward, *The Letters of William S Burroughs 1945–1959*, Picador, London, 1993.

Burroughs, William Seward, *The Naked Lunch*, Olympia, Paris, 1959.
Burroughs, William Seward with Gysin, Brion, *The Third Mind*, Seaver, New York, 1978.
Cassady, Neal, *The First Third*, City Lights, San Francisco, 1971, expanded 1981.
Cassady, Neal, *Grace Beats Karma: Letters from Prison 1958–1960*, Blast, New York, 1993.
Charters, Ann, *Beats and Company*, Doubleday, Garden City NY, 1986.
Charters, Ann, *Scenes Along the Road*, Portents/Gotham Book Mart, New York, 1970.
Charters, Ann, 'The Beats: Literary Bohemians in Postwar America', *DLB 16*, Gale Research, Ann Arbor, Michigan, 1983.
Charters, Ann, ed., *The Portable Beat Reader*, Viking, New York, 1992.
Cherkovski, Neeli, *Whitman's Wild Children*, Lapis, Venice CA, 1988.
Clay, Mel, *Jazz, Jail and God: Bob Kaufman*, Androgyne, San Francisco, 1987.
Cook, Bruce, *The Beat Generation*, Charles Scribners's Sons, New York, 1971.
DiPrima, Diane, *Memoirs of a Beatnik*, Olympia, New York, 1969.
DiPrima, Diane and Jones, LeRoi, eds, *The Floating Bear: A Newsletter*, Laurence McGilvery, La Jolla CA, nos 1–37, 1973.
Fass, Ekbert, *Towards a New American Poetics: Essays and Interviews*, Black Sparrow, Santa Barbara, 1979.
Feldman, Gene and Gartenberg, Max, eds, *The Beat Generation and the Angry Young Men*, Citadel, New York, 1958.
Ferlinghetti, Lawrence and Peters, Nancy, *Literary San Francisco*, Harper and Row, New York, 1980.
Frank, Robert, *The Americans*, Aperture, New York, 1978.
Ginsberg, Allen, *Allen Verbatim: Lectures on Poetry, Politics, Consciousness*, Gordon Ball, ed., McGraw-Hill, New York, 1974.
Ginsberg, Allen, *Bixby Canyon Ocean Path Word Breeze*, Gotham Book Mart, New York, 1972.
Ginsberg, Allen, *Collected Poems 1947–1980*, Harper and Row, New York, 1985.
Ginsberg, Allen, *Gay Sunshine Interview with Allen Young*, Grey Fox, Bolinas, 1974.
Ginsberg, Allen, *Howl and Other Poems*, City Lights, San Francisco, 1956.
Ginsberg, Allen, *Howl: Original Draft Facsimile*, Harper and Row, New York, 1986.
Ginsberg, Allen, *Journals: Early Fifties, Early Sixties*, Grove, New York, 1977.
Ginsberg, Allen, *The Riverside Interviews 1: Allen Ginsberg*, Binnacle, London, 1980.
Ginsberg, Allen with Cassady, Neal, *As Ever: The Collected Correspondence*, Creative Arts, Berkeley, 1977.
Girodias, Maurice, ed., *The Olympia Reader*, Grove, New York, 1965.
Goddard, Dwight, ed., *A Buddhist Bible*, Beacon, Boston, 1994.
Gold, Herbert, *Bohemia: Where Art, Angst, Love and Strong Coffee Meet*, Simon and Schuster, New York, 1993.

Gooch, Brad, *City Poem: The Life and Times of Frank O'Hara*, Knopf, New York, 1993.

Gruen, John, *The Party's Over Now*, Viking, New York, 1972.

Gutman, Walter, *The Gutman Letter*, Something Else, New York, 1969.

Harrington, Alan, *The Secret Swinger*, Knopf, New York, 1966.

Hickey, Morgen, *The Bohemian Register*, Scarecrow, Metuchen NJ, 1990.

Holmes, John C, *Get Home Free*, Dutton, New York, 1964.

Holmes, John C, *Go*, New American Library, New York, 1980.

Holmes, John C, *Nothing More to Declare*, Dutton, New York, 1967.

Holmes, John C, *Displaced Person*, University of Arkansas, Fayetteville, 1987.

Honan, Park, ed., *The Beats: An Anthology of 'Beat' Writing*, JM Dent, London, 1987.

Horemans, Rudi, ed., *Beat Indeed!*, EXA, Antwerp, 1985.

Huncke, Herbert, *Guilty of Everything*, Paragon, New York, 1990.

Huncke, Herbert, *Herbert Huncke Special Issue*, Unspeakable Visions of the Individual, California PA, 1973.

Huncke, Herbert, *Huncke's Journal*, Poets Press, New York, 1965.

Huncke, Herbert, *The Evening Sun Turned Crimson*, Cherry Valley, Cherry Valley NY, 1980.

Johnson, Joyce, *Minor Characters*, Picador, London, 1983.

Jones, LeRoi, *The Autobiography of LeRoi Jones/Amiri Baraka*, Freundlich, New York, 1984.

Kelly, John, ed., *Beatitude Anthology*, City Lights, San Francisco, 1960.

Kerouac, Jan, *Baby Driver*, St Martin's, New York, 1981.

Kerouac, Jan, *Trainsongs*, Henry Holt, New York, 1988.

Kherdian, David, *Six San Francisco Poets*, Giligia, Fresno, 1969.

Knight, Arthur and Glee, eds, *The Beat Book*, Unspeakable Visions of the Individual, California PA, 1974.

Knight, Arthur and Kit, eds, *Beat Angels*, Unspeakable Visions of the Individual, California PA, 1982.

Knight, Arthur and Kit, eds, *The Beat Diary*, Unspeakable Visions of the Individual, California PA, 1977.

Knight, Arthur and Kit, eds, *The Beat Journey*, Unspeakable Visions of the Individual, California PA, 1978.

Knight, Arthur and Kit, eds. *The Beat Road*, Unspeakable Visions of the Individual, California PA, 1984.

Knight, Arthur and Kit, eds, *The Beat Vision*, Paragon House, New York, 1977.

Knight, Brenda, *Women of the Beat Generation*, Conari, Berkeley, 1996.

Krim, Seymour, *Views of a Nearsighted Cannoner*, Alan Ross, London, 1969.

Leary, Timothy, *Flashbacks*, JP Tarcher, Los Angeles, 1983.

Lee, Robert, ed., *The Beat Generation Writers*, Pluto, London, 1996.

Leyland, Winston, ed., *Gay Sunshine Interviews*, Gay Sunshine, San Francisco, vol. 1, 1978.

Lipton, Lawrence, *The Holy Barbarians*, WH Allen, London, 1960.

McClure, Michael, *Scratching the Beat Surface*, North Point, San Francisco, 1982.

McDarrah, Fred, *Kerouac and Friends: A Beat Generation Album*, William Morrow, New York, 1985.

McDarrah, Fred and McDarrah, Gloria, *Beat Generation: Glory Days in Greenwich Village*, Schirmer, New York, 1996.

Malina, Judith, *The Diaries of Judith Malina 1947–1957*, Grove, New York, 1984.

Miles, Barry, *William Burroughs: El Hombre Invisible*, Virgin Publishing, London, 1992.

Miles, Barry, *Ginsberg: A Biography*, Simon and Schuster, New York, 1989.

Morgan, Bill, *The Beat Generation in New York*, City Lights, San Francisco, 1997.

Morgan, Ted, *Literary Outlaw*, Henry Holt, New York, 1988.

Ossman, David, *The Sullen Art*, Corinth, New York, 1963.

Parkinson, Thomas, ed., *Casebook on the Beat*, Crowell, New York, 1961.

Parry, Alfred, *Garrets and Pretenders: A History of Bohemianism in America*, Dover, New York, revised edition 1960.

Perloff, Marjorie, *Frank O'Hara: Poet Among Painters*, University of Texas, Austin, 1977.

Phillips, Lisa et al, *Beat Culture and the New America 1950–1965*, Whitney Museum of American Art, New York, 1995.

Plimpton, George, ed., *Writers at Work: The Paris Review Interviews, Third Series*, Penguin, Harmondsworth, 1967.

Plimpton, George, ed., *Writers at Work: The Paris Review Interviews, Fourth Series*, Penguin, Harmondsworth, 1967.

Plummer, William, *The Holy Goof: A Biography of Neal Cassady*, Prentice-Hall, Englewood Cliffs NJ, 1981.

Podhoretz, Norman, *Making It*, Random House, New York, 1967.

Polsky, Ned, *Hustlers, Beats and Others*, Anchor, Garden City NY, 1969.

Rexroth, Kenneth, *An Autobiographical Novel*, Whittet, Weybridge, 1977.

Richards, Janet, *Common Soldiers*, Archer, San Francisco, 1979.

Rigney, Francis J and Smith, Douglas L, *The Real Bohemia*, Basic, New York, 1961.

Rodman, Selden, *Tongues of Fallen Angels: Conversations with Ginsberg et al*, New Directions, New York, 1974.

Rosset, Barney, ed., *The Evergreen Review Reader 1957–1961*, New York, Grove, 1979.

Ruas, Charles, *Conversations with Amer-i-can Writ-ers*, Quartet, London, 1984.

Sargeant, Jack, *Naked Lens: Beat Cinema*, Creation, London, 1997.

Saroyan, Aram, *Genesis Angels: The Saga of Lew Welch and the Beat Generation*, William Morrow, New York, 1979.

Sartre, Jean-Paul, *Baudelaire*, Hamish Hamilton, London, 1949.

Seaver, Richard; Southern, Terry and Trocchi, Alexander, eds, *Writers in Revolt: An Anthology*, Frederick Fell, New York, 1963.

Simpson, Louis, *A Revolution in Taste*, Macmillan, New York, 1978.

Snyder, Gary, *The Real Work: Interviews and Talks 1964–1979*, New Directions, New York, 1980.

Solomon, Carl, *Emergency Messages: An Autobiographical Miscellany*, Paragon, New York, 1989.

Solomon, Carl, *Mishaps Perhaps*, Beach Books, San Francisco, 1966.

Solomon, Carl, *More Mishaps*, Beach Books, San Francisco, 1968.

Stephenson, Gregory, *Friendly and Flowing Savage*, Textile Bridge, Clarence Center, New York, 1987.

Stephenson, Gregory, *The Daybreak Boys: Essays on the Literature of the Beat Generation*, Southern Illinois University, Carbondale, 1990.

Tytell, John, *Naked Angels*, McGraw-Hill, New York, 1976.

Vidal, Gore, *Palimpsest: A Memoir*, Andre Deutsch, London, 1995.

Wakefield, Dan, *New York in the 50s*, Houghton Mifflin, Boston, 1992.

Waldman, Anne, ed., *The Beat Book*, Shambala, Boston, 1996.

Watson, Steven, *The Birth of the Beat Generation*, Pantheon, New York, 1995.

Watts, Alan W, *Beat Zen Square Zen and Zen*, City Lights, San Francisco, 1959.

Watts, Alan W, *In My Own Way*, Cape, London, 1972.

Welch, Lew, *I Remain: The Letters of Lew Welch*, 2 volumes, Grey Fox, Bolinas, 1980.

Welldon, Estela V, *Mother, Madonna, Whore*, Guilford, London, 1988.

Whalen, Philip, *Off the Wall: Interviews with Philip Whalen*, Four Seasons, Bolinas, 1978.

Wilentz, Elias, ed., *The Beat Scene*, Corinth, New York, 1960.

Wolf, Daniel and Fancher, Ed, eds, *The Village Voice Reader*, Doubleday, Garden City NY, 1962.

Alfred G Aronowitz's *New York Post* articles:
Article 1: 'The Beat Generation', 9 March 1959.
Article 2: 'Jack Kerouac', 10 March 1959.
Article 3: 'Neal Cassady', 11 March 1959.
Article 4: 'A Certain Party', 12 March 1959.
Article 5: 'Allen Ginsberg, Prophet', 13 March 1959.
Article 6: 'The San Francisco Scene', 15 March 1959.
Article 7: 'On the Campus', 16 March 1959.
Article 8: 'More on the San Francisco Scene', 17 March 1959.
Article 9: 'Act of Violence', 18 March 1959.
Article 10: 'Now and Hereafter', 19 March 1959.
Article 11: 'The Mission', 20 March 1959.
Article 12: 'San Francisco Renaissance', 22 March 1959.

Index